Bureaucratic Archaeology

Bureaucratic Archaeology is a multi-faceted ethnography of quotidian practices of archaeology, bureaucracy, and science in postcolonial India, concentrating on the workings of the Archaeological Survey of India (ASI). This book uncovers an endemic link between the micro-practice of archaeology in the trenches of the ASI and the manufacture of archaeological knowledge, wielded in the making of political and religious identity and summoned as indelible evidence in the juridical adjudication in the highest courts of India. This book is a rare ethnography of the daily practice of a postcolonial bureaucracy from within rather than from the outside. It meticulously uncovers the social, cultural, political, and epistemological ecology of ASI archaeologists to show how the postcolonial state assembles and produces knowledge. This is the first book-length monograph on the workings of archaeology in a non-western world. It scrupulously shows how the theory of archaeological practice deviates, transforms, and generates knowledge outside the Euro-American epistemological tradition.

Ashish Avikunthak teaches at the University of Rhode Island and is a cultural anthropologist and filmmaker. He was named Future Greats 2014 by *ArtReview*. Subject of more than a dozen retrospectives and sixteen solo shows, his films have been shown in film festivals, galleries, and museums worldwide.

SOUTH ASIA IN THE SOCIAL SCIENCES

South Asia has become a laboratory for devising new institutions and practices of modern social life. Forms of capitalist enterprise, providing welfare and social services, the public role of religion, the management of ethnic conflict, popular culture and mass democracy in the countries of the region have shown a marked divergence from known patterns in other parts of the world. South Asia is now being studied for its relevance to the general theoretical understanding of modernity itself.

South Asia in the Social Sciences will feature books that offer innovative research on contemporary South Asia. It will focus on the place of the region in the various global disciplines of the social sciences and highlight research that uses unconventional sources of information and novel research methods. While recognising that most current research is focused on the larger countries, the series will attempt to showcase research on the smaller countries of the region.

General Editor
Partha Chatterjee
Columbia University

Editorial Board
Pranab Bardhan
University of California at Berkeley

Stuart Corbridge
Durham University

Satish Deshpande
University of Delhi

Christophe Jaffrelot
Centre d'etudes et de recherches internationales, Paris

Nivedita Menon
Jawaharlal Nehru University

Other books in the series:

Government as Practice: Democratic Left in a Transforming India
Dwaipayan Bhattacharyya
Courting the People: Public Interest Litigation in Post-Emergency India
Anuj Bhuwania

Development after Statism: Industrial Firms and the Political Economy of South Asia
Adnan Naseemullah

Politics of the Poor: Negotiating Democracy in Contemporary India
Indrajit Roy

South Asian Governmentalities: Michel Foucault and the Question of Postcolonial Orderings
Stephen Legg and Deana Heath (eds.)

Nationalism, Development and Ethnic Conflict in Sri Lanka
Rajesh Venugopal

Adivasis and the State: Subalternity and Citizenship in India's Bhil Heartland
Alf Gunvald Nilsen

Maoist People's War and the Revolution of Everyday Life in Nepal
Ina Zharkevich

New Perspectives on Pakistan's Political Economy: State, Class and Social Change
Matthew McCartney and S. Akbar Zaidi (eds.)

Crafty Oligarchs, Savvy Voters: Democracy under Inequality in Rural Pakistan
Shandana Khan Mohmand

Dynamics of Caste and Law: Dalits, Oppression and Constitutional Democracy in India
Dag-Erik Berg

Simultaneous Identities: Language, Education and the Nepali Nation
Uma Pradhan

Deceptive Majority: Dalits, Hinduism, and Underground Religion
Joel Lee

Colossus: The Anatomy of Delhi
Sanjoy Chakravorty and Neelanjan Sircar (eds.)

When Ideas Matter: Democracy and Corruption in India
Bilal A. Baloch

In Search of Home: Citizenship, Law and the Politics of the Poor
Kaveri Haritas

Bureaucratic Archaeology

State, Science, and Past in Postcolonial India

Ashish Avikunthak

CAMBRIDGE
UNIVERSITY PRESS

CAMBRIDGE
UNIVERSITY PRESS

Shaftesbury Road, Cambridge CB2 8EA, United Kingdom

One Liberty Plaza, 20th Floor, New York, NY 10006, USA

477 Williamstown Road, Port Melbourne, vic 3207, Australia

314 to 321, 3rd Floor, Plot No.3, Splendor Forum, Jasola District Centre, New Delhi 110025, India

103 Penang Road, #05–06/07, Visioncrest Commercial, Singapore 238467

Cambridge University Press is part of the University of Cambridge.

It furthers the University's mission by disseminating knowledge in the pursuit of education, learning and research at the highest international levels of excellence.

www.cambridge.org

Information on this title: www.cambridge.org/9781316512395

First published 2021
Reprint 2025

Printed in India by Repro India Ltd.

A catalogue record for this publication is available from the British Library

Library of Congress Cataloging-in-Publication Data

Names: Avikunthak, Ashish, 1972-author.
Title: Bureaucratic archaeology: state, science and past in postcolonial India / Ashish Avikunthak.
Other titles: State, science and past in postcolonial India
Description: Cambridge, United Kingdom ; New York, NY : Cambridge University Press, 2021. | Includes bibliographical references and index.
Identifiers: LCCN 2021029690 (print) | LCCN 2021029691 (ebook) | ISBN 9781316512395 (hardback) | ISBN 9781009067119 (ebook)
Subjects: LCSH: India--Antiquities. | Archæological Survey of India--History. | Archaeology--Political aspects--India. | Excavations (Archaeology)--India. | Sacred space--India. | BISAC: POLITICAL SCIENCE / World / General
Classification: LCC DS418 .A95 2021 (print) | LCC DS418 (ebook) | DDC 934/.01--dc23
LC record available at https://lccn.loc.gov/2021029690
LC ebook record available at https://lccn.loc.gov/2021029691

ISBN 978-1-316-51239-5 Hardback

For the unknown laborers in the archaeological
trenches of India

Contents

List of Figures   xi

Preface   xiii

Acknowledgments   xxvii

Note on Transliteration   xxxi

List of Abbreviations   xxxiii

1.   Anthropology of Archaeology   1

2.   The Making of the Indus–Saraswati Civilization   33

3.   Bureaucratic Hierarchy in the ASI   70

4.   Spatial Formation of the Archaeological Field   102

5.   Epistemological Formation of the Archaeological Site   128

6.   Theory of Archaeological Excavation   153

7.   Making of the Archaeological Artifact   178

8.   Performance of Archaeological Representations   205

9.   The Absent Excavation Reports   227

Conclusion   259

Bibliography   267

Index   314

Figures

3.1 End-of-the-day muster roll call at Dholavira, 2004   92

3.2 Working laborers at Dholavira, 2004   94

4.1 Dholavira campsite nestled in the wild countryside, 2004   107

4.2 The entrance to the Dholavira excavation camp, with its bamboo pole barrier, *chowkidar*, and the ASI plank, 2004   110

4.3 ASI campsites at Juni Kuran (*top*) in 2004, Dholavira (*middle*) in 2004, and Bhirrana (*bottom*) in 2005   113

4.4 The director's residence and the campsite office at Dholavira, 2004; at the top of the wall is a representation of the massive Harappan "sign-post" found at the site   114

5.1 Two 10 × 10 meter trenches divided into four quadrants each with Wheelerian balks at Dholavira, adjacent to the Eastern Reservoir, 2004   147

6.1 The floor of a mature Harappan room on a Dholavira citadel where carnelian beads were found, 2004   155

6.2 Examples of the ontological confinement by the Wheelerian square of the workers at the site of Dholavira, 2004 (top row) and Bhirrana, 2005 (*bottom row*)   159

6.3 An archaeologist marking the stratigraphy on the trench wall with his knife in Dholavira, 2004   169

6.4 Archaeological ways of holding the knife to mark the layer, 2004   173

6.5 Layer inspection and discussion in a Dholavira trench, 2004   174

6.6 A trench on the citadel at Dholavira with labeled stratigraphy, 2004   176

7.1 Tool-kits for digging, excavating, cleaning, and marking in a trench at a site in Bhirrana, 2005   185

7.2 Examples of pottery yards: *clockwise, from top left*—Dholavira yard with exposed pottery; Dholavira yard with pottery in bags from excavations from earlier seasons, 2004; Bhirrana and Hansi pottery yards, 2005   195

7.3 Marked ceramic fragments from Bhirrana, 2005   196

7.4 Examples of Harappan ceramic fragments found during my ethnography at Dholavira, 2004; *clockwise, from top left:* Black and Red ware; Red ware; Perforated ware; Reserve Slip ware — 197

8.1 Local schoolchildren peering into an archaeological trench at the site of Hansi, 2005 — 209

8.2 "Subject preparation" at the edge of the Lower Town in Dholavira, 2004 — 212

8.3 The photographer on the tower taking the photograph of a prepared subject in Bhirrana, 2005 — 214

8.4 A photography session in a trench on the citadel of Dholavira, 2004 — 215

8.5 An ASI photographer in Dholavira making images with human epistemic and ethnic markers, 2004 — 220

Preface

Sixth of December 1992 was an exuberantly bright day in Bombay. Winter had arrived calmly. Sultry, humid weather had given way to a pleasant, cool climate. I was working since dawn at Chaitya Bhoomi—the memorial of Dr Bhimrao Ramji Ambedkar located at the edge of the Arabian Sea, in the heart of Bombay. It was the 36th death anniversary of Ambedkar—the principal architect of the Indian constitution and, particularly, the revered leader of the Dalits, the lowest of the oppressive Hindu caste hierarchy. Like every year, a few hundred thousand devoted pilgrims gathered to pay their respects to the departed leader at the site where his last rites were conducted in 1956. The leafy, middle-class neighborhood of Dadar was bustling with multitudes that had journeyed overnight in trains, buses, and even by foot from neighboring districts in Maharashtra, Gujarat, and Andhra Pradesh. It was late afternoon; I was cautiously negotiating the massive crowd along with Dalit activists—assisting visitors, providing information about restrooms, food stalls, and train and bus stations. Unexpectedly, an associate of mine nervously rushed toward me through the teeming masses. He aggressively pushed through the crowd and scurried close to me. Gasping for breath, his face was contorted with fearful anxiety. He frantically announced: "Babri Masjid has been demolished! They tore it down! It happened a couple of hours ago." By the time all the activists regrouped, the enormous gathering was diminishing rapidly. The festive sprit that was stirring the energetic assembly had abruptly diffused. We sensed a palpable tension in the air. Those of us who were following the build-up of Hindu fundamentalists in the north Indian pilgrim town of Ayodhya over the past weeks were outraged. Not even in our wildest dream did we think that the government of India would allow the destruction of the disputed mosque.[1] By late evening, news of communal violence erupting in different parts of the country started pouring in. At midnight, rioting began. Muslim business establishment and shops on Lamington Road, in south-central Bombay where my hostel was located, were systematically targeted, ransacked, and looted. By the morning of December 7, riots had spread to different parts of the city. Bombay was burning.

In the next few days, the most widespread communal riots since the partition of India broke out throughout the country. Savage violence rocked Bombay in two cycles—the first, from December 6 to 12, 1992, and the second from January 6 to 20, 1993.[2] I saw the city scorched in front of my eyes. More than a thousand people were killed in these communal riots. Bombay changed. India changed. I changed. Forever. In the aftermath of the riots, I worked as a relief worker for six months. I assisted the victims of violence in some of the devastatingly affected Bombay suburbs (Bhandup, Ghatkopar, and Jogeshwari), procuring relief from the state government and aiding them in rehabilitation and restitution.[3] For the first time in my life, I viscerally experienced the stories that my parents narrated to me about the traumatic violence of partition. I belong to a refugee family. Both my parents' families were forced to abandon their homeland during the partition of India in 1947. My father's family moved from the Afghanistan–Pakistan border town of Hoti-Mardan in the North-Western Frontier Province (now called Khyber-Pakhtunkhwa) to towns in western Uttar Pradesh. My mother's family escaped from Lahore on the eve of partition in one of those blood-laced trains that have been immortalized in innumerable narratives of partition. They reached Delhi and lived in refugee settlements. Stories of death, terror, and trauma that were part of my imaginative universe unexpectedly became part of my daily reality. The genesis of this book began during my days in Bombay after the riots. My being was shaken with innumerable questions, as I worked in distressful relief camps, walked through charred slums, ravaged houses, and devastated neighborhoods. This book began as a journey in search of one question—what is the role of the past in the making of violence in India? This voyage took more than 26 years to unravel, taking me through the world of Indian politics, history, and, more importantly—archaeology, science, and bureaucracy.

A couple of years later, in the cold winter of 1994, during the third World Archaeological Congress (WAC 3) held at the Taj Mahal Hotel, New Delhi, I discovered the insinuating role archaeology played in the destruction of the Babri Masjid. As a young graduate student of archaeology, I was a delegate attending WAC 3—a gathering of international archaeologists held once in four years. The conference opened with disarray in organization, disordered logistics, and corruption allegations. Palpably, an unofficial gag order prohibiting any discussion on the demolition of the Babri Masjid was floating in the glittering corridors of the five-star hotel. I heard muted voices of dissent, and the simmering tension in the air threatened to disrupt the conference.[4] On the last day, during the plenary session held in the Taj Mahal Hotel's regal ballroom, fittingly called "Durbar Hall," tempers flared up; dreadfully.

An ugly fistfight broke out on the stage. The national and international delegates sat in stunned silence. Amid heated discussion and vociferous slogan shouting, a group of senior Indian archaeologists with graying hair and receding bald lines, wearing ill-fitted blazers, led by the diminutive Dr Braj Basi Lal and the belligerent Dr Swaraj Prakash Gupta, were seen rushing on to the stage. They snatched the microphone from the couple of Indian delegates who had come up the podium to read a petition for the WAC 3 to pass a resolution condemning the demolition of the Babri Masjid. The conference ended wretchedly, with the WAC Council boycotting the official closing ceremony in protest.[5] The demolition of the Babri Masjid was an ostracized topic for professional Indian archaeologists desperately seeking to preserve the discipline's credibility in front of international glare.[6] Sitting in that large ballroom of a five-star hotel in Delhi, with archaeologists from all across the world, the fraught relationship between archaeology and politics became acutely apparent to me. The question that I asked in Bombay took a sharper and concentrated focus. As a young archaeologist, I now deliberated what role archaeology played in the making of modern India. How is archaeology performed in postcolonial India? And this took me to the doorstep of one of the largest archaeological bureaucracies in the world—the Archaeological Survey of India (ASI).

The Babri Masjid was located in the early historic city of Ayodhya. The ASI excavated it in 1976–77 under the leadership of B. B. Lal as part of the contentious "Archaeology of the Ramayana Sites" (1970s), which had followed his controversial "Archaeology of Mahabharata Sites" (1950–52). Both these projects were precursors to the ideological formation of Hindutva archaeology, which attempted to archaeologically assert the veracity of the events that occurred in Hindu epic narratives. B. B. Lal's team undertook three seasons of excavations (1975–76, 1976–77, and 1979–80); however, no detailed report of the site was ever published. Only two minuscule reportages were published in the ASI's *Indian Archaeology: A Review* (*IAR*).[7] This excavation confirmed that Ayodhya was first occupied in seventh century BCE. Its most significant discovery was that of the earliest Jaina terracotta figurine (fourth century BCE) and Roman Rouletted Ware (first–second century CE). This showed that Ayodhya was not just part of the brisk ancient trade route, but it was a multicultural site (Shaw 2000). There was no mention of a Hindu temple at the site. The short excavation reportage ironically stated that the entire period after the eleventh century "was devoid of special interest" (*IAR 1976–77* 1980, 53).[8]

The archaeology of Ayodhya took the centerstage of Indian politics after 1986, when the doors of the Babri Masjid were unlocked and Hindu worshippers could enter after 37 years. By the late 1980s, the incendiary narrative that the first Mughal emperor, Babur (1483–1530), had destroyed an ancient temple marking the site of Ram's birthplace and constructed a mosque at the same spot became a political propaganda for the Hindu fundamentalist forces. The call for the demolition of the Babri Masjid became their war cry.[9] Other disputed structures such as the Gyanvapi Masjid in Varanasi and the Jama Masjid in Mathura were also being threatened. Both these mosques lie adjacent to venerable Hindu scared sites—the Kashi Vishwanath temple dedicated to Shiva in Varanasi and the Kesava Deo temple built at the birthplace of Krishna in Mathura respectively. Both these temple–mosque complexes, along with the Babri Masjid–Ram Janmabhoomi complex, were brought under the scanner of the political movement spearheaded by Hindu nationalist groups.

In 1990, over 10 years after B. B. Lal had excavated Ayodhya, in an influential article in a Hindu propaganda journal, *Manthan*, he announced that he had recovered Hindu temple pillar-bases during the excavation (Lal 1980). Lal asserted his authority as an eminent ASI archaeologist behind his egregious claim that remains of a Hindu temple existed under the Babri Masjid. He provided false archaeological justification of the claim the Hindu fundamentalists were making about the Babri Masjid (Lal 2008). Archaeology was irrevocably pushed into the greatest political debate of postcolonial India. Lal's assertion about the presences of temple debris under the mosque had erupted an acrimonious debate amongst archaeologists and historians in India. On the one hand, Lal led a group of historians and archaeologists along with his collaborator and self-proclaimed Hindu nationalist archaeologist, S. P. Gupta, who provided archaeological justification to the political project of Hindu fundamentalism (Gupta 1994). On the other hand, K. M. Shrimali, Irfan Habib, and others argued that empirical evidence in the archaeological and material cultural record was misinterpreted to produce a skewed account of the past (Ratnagar 2004). The debates were unambiguously rancorous. Ideological fault lines were drawn deep and the politics of the past in India became hostile. By the mid-1990s, Indian archaeology had become a tainted discipline—its discursive legitimacy compromised and undermined—burdened under cavernous epistemological duress, caught in political crossfires between nationalist appropriation and the empirics of a scientific discipline.

It came as an unpleasant surprise to the officers of the ASI, nine years later in 2003, when the Lucknow Bench of the Allahabad High Court ordered the ASI to excavate under the demolished debris of the Babri Masjid. Was there a temple under the mosque? The High Court demanded evidence (Khan, Agarwal, and Sharma 2010, xix–xxxii). Unexpectedly, the judiciary dragged the ASI into the epicenter of the greatest confrontation about the past in India. The 2003 archaeological excavation of Ayodhya by the ASI was the most unusual excavation in the history of the organization. The conditions were so abnormal that the ASI archaeologist heading the excavation wrote a special note in the introductory chapter of the Ayodhya excavation report in a section revealingly titled: "Constraints" (Manjhi and Mani 2003, 9–11). What would have taken any ASI Excavation Branch in an analogous medieval site in north India three to four season of work (around 400–500 days of digging) was excavated in less than 150 days from March to August 2003. It was agonizing to work uninterruptedly during the penetratingly hot summer months followed by the wet and humid monsoon season. Excavations were conducted under a thick canopy of plastic sheets, lighted by the sharp glare of high-power halogen lamps, cooled only by buzzing industrial fans. ASI archaeologists dug in 20-meter-deep dark trenches in sweltering conditions, which prevented them from making accurate observation.[10] This was aggravated by continuous surveillance and the daily intrusion of the numerous representatives of the feuding parties overseeing minute details of the excavation. The national media reported every potshard discovered, making this one of the most reported archaeological excavations in Indian history. The excavation site represented a military operation. Local police and paramilitary forces of Uttar Pradesh and the central government guarded the location zealously. Some ASI archaeologists abandoned the excavation midway because of unbearable stress levels. The ASI excavated a staggering 98 trenches, or close to 10,000 square meters, and recovered many thousand antiquities, ceramics of different periods, coins, architectural fragments, terracotta objects, figurines, and bones. The astonishing nature of public fascination with the excavation and, crucially, the judiciary's belief in archaeology's ability to unearth the truth about the past intrigued me. Juridical dependence on archaeology in disputes about property and cultural remains was not unusual. This was common in North America—laws such as the Native American Graves Protection and Repatriation Act (NAGPRA) juridically justified archaeological excavations (Fine-Dare 2002)—but this was the first time in India.

The Lucknow Bench of the Allahabad High Court in 2010, and subsequently the Supreme Court of India in 2019, instrumentally deployed the finding of the unpublished ASI Ayodhya excavation report to adjudicate that a monumental Hindu temple complex existed under the medieval mosque. The finding of the ASI—a staid but gargantuan bureaucracy of the Indian state—played a pivotal role in deciding the most important question of postcolonial Indian politics. The ASI was a slow-moving bureaucratic juggernaut, responsible not only for preserving the archaeological heritage in India, but, prominently, producing massive empirical knowledge about the Indian past. The ASI excavated large swaths of ancient sites. It uncovered monumental structures, generated millions of artifacts, and produced a large volume of scholarly literature. Although it was predominantly a heritage conservation bureaucracy, it gained enormous legitimacy and prestige through the production of scientific knowledge about the past—data, information, facts, evidence—disseminated through the publication of articles, reports, and surveys. It was the ASI's archaeological ability that "provides scientific factual data for reconstructing ancient historical material, culture, understanding" (Khan, Agarwal, and Sharma 2010, 2375) which qualified it to be summoned by the highest courts of India to provide evidence (Supreme Court 2019, 552). As a knowledge producing organization, civilizational questions rather than local or topical issues drove its epistemological inquiry. However, by being pushed into national limelight, the ASI's politics of practice unexpectedly received unprecedented scrutiny. The past was always a contested domain in India, but the practice of archaeology by the ASI with the Ayodhya dispute took an unparalleled center stage of political and nationalistic discourse in India.

The terrestrial location of this book's ethnographic inquiry is not the ASI excavations of Ayodhya, but the far-flung excavation sites belonging to the Indus civilization or the Harappan civilization that the ASI has been excavating since the 1920s. ASI excavations at Ayodhya were an anomaly; however, the excavations at Harappan sites were part of its routine archaeological work for nearly a century. The discovery of Mohenjo-Daro and Harappa radically altered India's civilizational history, pushing it back by as far as 2,000 years than previously known.[11] The scientific justification provided by archaeology gave this discovery an objective legitimization, whose profound impact continues to reverberate in the imagination of postcolonial South Asia. Through the Harappan civilization, archaeology bestowed colonial Indians with an unbroken cultural legacy of more than 5,000 years and provided a subjugated people with a history that was older than that of their colonial occupiers. This intersection of scientific archaeology and ideology transformed the discourse on Harappan culture into a contested location for multiple theories and myths— nationalistic, imperialistic, postcolonial, and, now, ultra-nationalist.

Between 2003 and 2005, I conducted ethnography at Harappan sites in Gujarat, Rajasthan, and Haryana, which formed the core of a short-lived but controversial project undertaken by the ASI—the Saraswati Heritage Project (SHP)—with the goal of searching for the lost civilization of the Vedic Aryans (the authors of ancient Vedic literature). By remapping archaeological evidence from the prehistoric Harappan civilization (c. 3800–2000 BCE) on to textual evidence from the oldest Vedic literature (c. 1500 BCE), this project attempted to both debunk the Aryan migration theory and push back the dates of the Vedic Aryans to an earlier period, creating an entirely new category of the indigenous "Vedic Harappans" (Singh 1995). Moreover, in scientifically linking archaeological evidence to religiosity, this project also attempted to validate the latter's historicity and, in the process, shifted the territorial locus of the Indus civilization (mainly located in Pakistan) to within Indian boundaries. This contentious history of Harappan archaeology forms the narrative web over which the anthropological account is described in this book.

The ASI's excavations at Ayodhya and the SHP are not incommensurable to the ethnographic narrative of my book; they instead complement each other. Both are products of the bureaucratic archaeology of the ASI; both mark a culmination of convoluted networks between archaeology as a scientific discipline and religious and national fundamentalism; both are exemplary examples of statist manufacture of archaeological knowledge in postcolonial India. The discovery of the Harappan civilization by the ASI in the 1920s and the subsequent consolidation of scientific archaeology by the colonial archaeologist-bureaucrat Mortimer Wheeler in the 1940s laid the foundation for this statist archaeological practice. After 1947, ASI archaeology was reinforced by the burgeoning postcolonial bureaucracy and eventually maneuvered by ASI archaeologists harboring Hindutva allegiance to pursue their ideological objectives. By the time I conducted my ethnographic investigation, these divergent currents were acutely intertwined in the making of the ASI's knowledge production apparatus. The SHP and Ayodhya are epistemological embodiments of this complex process. Furthermore, the ramifications of Ayodhya's excavation were felt during my ethnographic work in the SHP sites, not just ideologically but also socially, because most of my informants had worked at the Ayodhya excavation, and that experience had significantly impacted their professional life. It is in these complex political and historical conditions that the ethnographic narrative of the book unfolds.

Bureaucratic Archaeology is an ethnographic investigation of the ASI's micro-politics of epistemic practice. In this book, I show how empirical archaeological evidence produced by the ASI in Harappan sites—epistemologically homologous to those utilized by the highest courts of Indian judiciary to adjudicate the presence of a temple under a mosque as an empirical fact—is manufactured in the dusty and deep trenches of ASI excavations. The archaeological practices of the ASI have been questioned, debated, and disputed in the quagmire of the Indian public sphere. This book steps into this contested world and provides a critical, theoretically nuanced, empirically rich insight into the making of meaning about the past in contemporary India. It is an anthropological investigation of archaeology as a bureaucratic practice in the times of science, religion, and politics. I meticulously follow archaeological material culture discovered in ASI trenches to its transformation into empirical facts published in statist reports and employed as official evidence in courts. The journey from excavated materiality to published epistemology, as I show in this book, is mediated by the complex conjunction of scientific and bureaucratic practices of the postcolonial state, negotiating the institutional world of the ASI, fraught with troubled colonial legacy, turgid governmental machinery, and entrenched disenchantment amongst its rank and file. Through painstaking ethnographic observation, I lay open this social, cultural, and scientific universe of postcolonial archaeologists and demonstrate the impact of bureaucratic ontologies on epistemological practices.

The focal point of my ethnographic lens is the ASI excavation site. It is in this epistemic location that scientific practice and bureaucratic rationality conjoin to produce postcolonial archaeology. It is at the excavation site that the material artifacts of the past are discovered, excavated, organized, qualified, labeled, catalogued, represented, and produced as objects of scientific archaeology. Employing everyday micro-practices at the excavation sites as the modality of ethnographic investigation, I show that the epistemology of archaeology in India is a product of a postcolonial bureaucratic rationality where science, state, and religion are ingeniously contrived to manufacture a nation with a seemingly empirical past. This meaning-making of the past, I argue, is not only an embodiment of a practice carried out by an unyielding bureaucracy acutely entrenched in the culture of a hegemonic state, but is also the product of the disciplinarian discourse of archaeology that has an ambivalent relationship between materiality and epistemology. I answer a few fundamental questions in this book: How does the ASI do archaeology? How does the ASI manufacture data, evidence, and facts about the Indian past? What kind of techniques, methodologies, and practices does it employ? What are the sociological, political, and the ideological processes of its knowledge production mechanism? More scrupulously, this book investigates how the ASI conducts excavations. How does it discover artifacts in a trench? How are artifacts transformed into facts? Or succinctly, this book investigates how the ASI *acts* in the making of *artifacts* into *facts*.

Structure of the Book

In this book, I make theoretical and causality-based arguments between ideology and practice; therefore, it is critical to proceed step-by-step, gradually and systematically enabling the ethnographic evidence to speak for themselves. Chapters 1 and 2 outline the theoretical, historical, and political intersections of the book's epistemological landscape. Subsequently, my observations, arguments, and assertions are progressively uncovered ethnographically, from Chapters 3 to 9, in a meticulous sequence. Chapters 3 and 4 consist of thick descriptions of the ASI as a bureaucratic organization and probes into the social and the cultural ecology of ASI archaeologists, whereas the ethnography of Chapters 5 to 9 minutely examines the micro-practices of the ASI's bureaucratic archaeology. Finally, the narrative of the manuscript arrives at the Conclusion of the book, where I close with statements of my findings and their implications on the state of Indian archaeology today.

Chapter 1, "Anthropology of Archaeology," provides the theoretical and methodological framework of the book and elucidates the political impetus of my anthropological intervention. It situates the book at the intersection of science studies, archaeology, postcolonial studies, and the ethnography of the state. It locates the anthropological genealogy of the project envisaged as a post-Kuhnian, Latourian, postcolonial investigation of archaeology as a bureaucratic science. It also provides a historical overview of the state of Indian archaeology in the context of the ASI and charts the transformation of the colonial ASI into a postcolonial bureaucracy. This section gives a brief overview of the organizational history of the ASI, and its contemporary administrative structure. It delineates the transformation of a minor colonial organization of the late nineteenth century into a formidable bureaucratic institution of the early twenty-first century.

Chapter 2, "The Making of the Indus–Saraswati Civilization," locates the contested politics of Harappan archaeology by examining the epistemological emergence of the River Saraswati and interrogating its historical and ideological relationship to Harappans and Aryans. It argues that the epistemic trajectory of the Saraswati from a literary entity to an empirical category followed four phases.

First, it emerged as a mythical river of colonial Indology; second, as a civilizational river of colonial archaeology; third, as a hydrological body of postcolonial geology; and, fourth, as an empirical fact of postcolonial archaeology and history. Contrary to historians who attribute the resurrection of the Saraswati solely to the growing influence of Hindutva ideologies, this chapter argues that the Saraswati is also an epistemic product of the disciplinarian discourse of colonial Indology and postcolonial science. This chapter outlines the historical and political contours through which the subsequent ethnography navigates. At the end of this chapter, I describe the four SHP excavation sites where I did my ethnographic work—Dholavira, Hansi, Baror, and Bhirrana. I provide descriptions of each site, their significance within the archaeology of the Harappan civilization, the research plan of the ASI for each site, and the nature of the materiality discovered.

Chapter 3, "Bureaucratic Hierarchy in the ASI," is a critical examination of the organizational hierarchy of the ASI, and the impact of its authoritarian structure on the lives of archaeologists who spend their entire careers working for this organization. Assistant archaeologists, superintending archaeologists, and director generals, along with archaeological laborers, are some key characters of this chapter. Their professional careers, lives in the field and in the office, relationship with their colleagues—subordinates and superiors—their ambitions, scholarly and professionally, and their frustrations are evocatively employed to describe the domineering authority of postcolonial bureaucracy. I show how the bureaucratic hierarchy of the state shapes the professional subjectivity of archaeologists and produces disenchanted archaeologists, despondently struggling with the task of creating knowledge. This chapter reveals the social and cultural world of bureaucratic archaeologists and argues that the institutional apparatus of the postcolonial state does not differentiate between the subjects it employs and the subjects it governs. The oppressive impact of its institution was pervasive, and its influence was exerted on all the members that constituted its structural apparatus.

In Chapter 4, "Spatial Formation of the Archaeological Field," I show that the ASI's archaeological excavation is a *(post)colonial exploration project*—a genre of colonial science which emphasized that the *real* process of knowledge production is situated outside the domains of the metropole at the fringes of the nation. This chapter destabilizes the conception of archaeological fieldwork defined in epistemological terms and demonstrates that such fieldwork involves an ideological engagement with the landscape. I show how the spatial formation of the archaeological excavation, with its physical dialectics between the campsite and the excavation site, governs the epistemological framework of the archaeological project. Here, I destabilize the notion of the field and argue that, in the context of the archaeological field, non-epistemic locations like the campsite are equally, if not more, important than the excavation site. Because the field in archaeology has always been conceptualized as *(field)work*, the non-epistemic locations in the field have been ignored in the scholarship on fieldwork. Through a spatial analysis of the archaeological field, I argue that the archaeological project, from its inception, involves an ideological manipulation of the landscape, evident in the archaeologist's choice of excavation sites, acquisition of private land, erection of camps, and demarcation of excavation zones through tangible boundaries between archaeologists and the local people.

In Chapter 5, "Epistemological Formation of the Archaeological Site," I demonstrate how a "wild landscape" at the fringes of the nation is first discovered as a site and then domesticated by the institutional apparatus of postcolonial governmentality into a materialized epistemic space—an excavation site—an ideologically framed spatial regime of inscription. This process is brought about through the application of what in ASI parlance is called the "Wheeler method"—a practice through which an untamed landscape is rationalized and brought within the encompassing grasp of Cartesian perspectivalism. Introduced in Indian archaeology by Sir Mortimer Wheeler—the ebullient military-archaeologist who revolutionized the practice of colonial archaeology in India as a scientific enterprise during his tenure as the director general of the ASI between 1944 and 1948—the Wheeler method systematically converted the undomesticated landscape into a scientific laboratory, whereby the generated data could be confined, controlled, and codified. In this archaeological laboratory, facts and artifacts about pasts could be accurately documented and scientifically retrieved by keeping a detailed three-dimensional record of the finds. I argue that this transformation of a wild landscape into an excavation site not only controlled the archaeological epistemology but also controlled the ontology of the very subjects who produced knowledge.

In Chapter 6, "Theory of Archaeological Excavation," I localize my ethnographic narrative from the wider landscape of the excavation site into the narrow confines of the trench—the archaeological laboratory. I shift my focus from the epistemic landscape to the epistemic square. Through an ethnography of micro-practices, I describe the process by which material culture in the trench-laboratory is recognized, discovered, and transformed into archaeological evidence. The theoretical framework of this practice is the concept of stratigraphy—the geological principle through which archaeological materiality is chronologically dated. I argue that the systematic scientific process in the micro-context of the trench-laboratory that produces material evidence for the construction of the narrative of the past is a practice dependent on a non-objective idea of time and space.

In Chapter 7, "Making of the Archaeological Artifact," I minutely demonstrate how ASI archaeologists and workers in the trench-laboratory unearth material artifact as a controlled experiment and how they name the artifact, date it, and epistemologically fix it to a cultural context. Here, I discuss the terminological difference between artifact and "antiquity," structural remains and "monuments," and archaeological traces and "archaeological features," to distinguish between the disciplinary discourse of archaeology and the ASI's reconfiguration of the practice. It details the daily practice of ASI archaeology in the excavation site focusing on the process through which artifacts and structures are recognized, discovered, recorded, and measured at the site. I focus on the practice of how an artifact becomes a fact.

In Chapter 8, "Performance of Archaeological Representations," I argue that the ritual of the state and its fetish for superficial perfection subsumes daily practices of archaeology. ASI archaeologists engaged in the performative practice of presenting and (re)presenting the evidence they unearthed. At a minute level, this comprised of rituals of photography and drawing at the site—of the artifacts, trenches, stratigraphy, and the excavation site. At a spectacular scale, this consisted of site visits by visiting dignitaries and officials, from the local district magistrate to the chief minister of the state. These diverse performative strategies were simultaneously aimed at the epistemic articulation of the archaeological site as an ideological location of state performance and the representation of excavated material culture as scientific evidence. The excavated site was transformed into an arena of spectatorial performance where the precision of scientific archaeology along with the statist power was exalted in uncovering the ancient civilization that made up the nation. This spectatorial ritual was an essential post-excavation process of the ASI archaeological intervention and it deployed the performative aspect of the excavation site to further the ideological and epistemological goal of the statist organization.

In Chapter 9, "The Absent Excavation Reports," I synthesize the major arguments in this book by concentrating on the final epistemological artifact of ASI archaeology—the excavation report. I employ the unpublished and controversial ASI's Ayodhya excavation report of 2003 as an epistemological site to underscore the foremost argument of this book, that, in postcolonial India, ASI archaeology was a structural construct of bureaucratic governmentality rather than a knowledge-producing epistemological practice. I show how the logic of bureaucratic corruption outlines the contours of an excavation project in the ASI.

Finally, I have fashioned the narrative of this monograph by bookending the history and political genealogy of ASI archaeology (this Preface, Chapters 1–2, Chapter 9, and Conclusion), which envelops the ethnographic account of ASI archaeology (Chapters 3–9). The anthropological core of the book is the thick description of archaeological practice, ensconced within a bureaucratic ecology of the ASI. This postcolonial bureaucratic archaeology is politically engendered by the Hindutva ideology that is personified by the ASI's intervention in the SHP and Ayodhya.

Notes

1. According to the sequence of events listed in the Liberhan Ayodhya Commission of Inquiry, the earliest "assault" on the disputed structure occurred at 12:15 p.m. The first dome of the mosque was demolished by 1:55 p.m (Liberhan 2009, 254–55). By 2:30 p.m., the news of the demolition spread in Bombay. This report is the definite account of the Indian state's investigation into the causes that led to the destruction of the Babri Masjid, which took 17 years to write (1992–2009).

2. See the *Report of the Srikrishna Commission* (1998) for a detailed chronology of the riots as it raged in different parts of the city. This is one of the most comprehensive documentation of the Bombay riots. The Government of Maharashtra under the Congress regime instituted it in 1993. It indicted the Shiv Sena and Hindu fundamentalists for instigating, aggravating, and conducting riots. Also, see Engineer (1993) and Masselos (1994) about the key distinction between the first and the second phase of riots.

3. I was then a student of social work at the College of Social Work, Nirmala Niketan, Bombay University, which was designated by the Government of Maharashtra as the primary nodal agency to route non-governmental organization (NGO) intervention during the post-riot relief work. For a report of the intervention by the College of Social Work, see Joseph (2000).

4. See Lal (2001) and Sharma (2001) for two opposing views on the Ayodhya dispute; both these papers were presented at WAC 3.

5. For multiple perspectives and different voices on the events of WAC 3, see Muralidharan (1994); Rao (1994, 1999); Hassan (1995); Colley (1995); and Golson (1996).

6. The Indian organizational committee for WAC 3 consisted of S. P. Gupta, B. B. Lal, and Makkhan Lal along with ASI functionaries like J. P. Joshi and M. C Joshi, who were reported to be close to the Hindu right-wing Rashtriya Swayamsevak Sangh (RSS). This committee thwarted attempts to hold any session pertaining to the destruction of the mosque and the ethics of archaeology. For a comprehensive account of backdoor machinations pertaining to WAC 3, see Navlakha (1994).

7. *Indian Archaeology: A Review* is the official publication of the ASI, edited by the director general (DG) of the ASI. First published in 1954, it is the annual publication of the ASI, in which the account of the various archaeological works is reported.

8. See *IAR 1976–77* 1980, 52–53; *IAR 1979–80* 1983, 76–77 for specific reports on the Ayodhya excavations.

9. Here, I am not using "war cry" metaphorically, but categorically. Numerous slogans were heard during those years, which explicitly called for the destruction

of the mosque. Some of the most popular ones were: *Ram naam satya hai/Babri Masjid dhvasth hai* (Ram's name is truth/Babri Masjid is destroyed); *Ek dhakka aur do/Babri Masjid tod do* (Give another push/Break the Babri Masjid); *Mitti nahin khiskayenge/Dhancha tor kar jayange* (We will not move earth/We will break the structure).

10.   For instance, in a letter dated July 3, 2003, Gauri Chatterjee, the DG of the ASI, writes to Rajeev Kumar, District Commissioner of Faizabad:

> … you are requested to ensure that there is proper height of "Shamiyana" so that there is enough light and air for persons working in excavation trenches. You may in consultation with Shri Hari Manjhi, Director, ASI, Team Leader, Ayodhya Excavation, remove these from northern, western and eastern sides so that there is sufficient light in recognizing stratigraphical features and details on cuttings. (AACD, File No. 29/1/95-Pt IV)

11.   The Indus civilization is also known as the Harappan civilization, Indus Valley civilization, Indus–Saraswati civilization, and Sindhu–Saraswati civilization—each of these names has potent political and ideological genealogies. John Marshall, the DG of the ASI (1902–28) who excavated Mohenjo-Daro, had earlier used the term "Indo-Sumerian" to signal the cultural relationship between the Indus and the Sumerians. However, in 1931, he adopted the term "Indus civilization." Ernst Mackay, who had excavated both Mohenjo-Daro and Chanhudaro, called it "Harappa Culture," following the archaeological type-site convention of naming a culture/civilization by the site where it was discovered for the first time (Mackay 1943); this term was subsequently made popular by Stuart Piggott in his well-known book *Prehistoric India to 1000 B.C.* (Piggott 1950). Throughout this book, I also follow the type-site convention and use the term "Harappan."

Acknowledgments

This book is the end product of a 25-year long journey that oscillated between the disciplinary boundaries of archaeology, anthropology, science studies, and postcolonial studies, meandering though many enriching institutional homes that bestowed me with their munificence, accruing incalculable debt of inspiring teachers, affable colleagues, steadfast friends, and a supportive family.

First, I would like to thank my teachers at Deccan College Post Graduate and Research Institute, Pune (1994–96), who planted the kernel of studying the past as a conceptual entity—K. Paddayya for introducing the intellectually stimulating world of theoretical archaeology, V. N. Misra and Vasant Shinde for making archaeological excavation exciting, Ajay Dandekar for generous encouragement, mentorship, and friendship, and Vikas Harish and Y. S. Alone for guidance. I am thankful to the cherished companionship of my batch-mates, Abhinav Goswami, Milan Kumar Chauley, Swayam Panda, and Varada Khaladkar, the joyous comradeship of my hostel buddies, Rajan Chedambath, Shriram Joshi, Kaushik Gangopadhya, Abhijit Dandekar, Selvakumar Veerasamy, Shiva Aruni, and Ritu Mehrotra.

At Stanford University (1999–2007), I was extremely fortunate to work with two of the foremost thinkers of theoretical archaeology—Ian Hodder and Michael Shanks—both had arrived from England the same year I reached Stanford. Over the course of eight years, Ian was not just a sympathetic and astute adviser but also an intellectual benefactor of my theoretical eccentricities. Michael Shanks not only sharpened my critical faculties but was also a strong advocate of my cinematic works. He was a constant source of cerebral and theoretical insights at a number of forums, including the Stanford Humanities Center's workshops on Visual Anthropology and Critical New Media. Akhil Gupta's shrewd advice, both scholarly and practical, have been valuable for seeing this work through; Ewa Domanska's annual visitations to Stanford from Poland in the spring brought in fresh "theory" that has inevitably permeated into the conceptual substratum of this book; Shiv Visvanathan's brief visit in Spring 2003 and numerous engaging conversations with him in Stanford and subsequently in Ahmedabad are deeply treasured.

My career at Stanford was linked to the genesis of two academic experiments—the Cultural and Social Anthropology (CASA) department and the Stanford Archaeology Centre. I had the enviable privilege to be part of both these intellectually invigorating communities, which have shaped my thinking. The buzzing excitement of the newly evolving Archaeology Centre, with its constant stream of visitors from the world of archaeology, eclectic workshops, intense student conferences, with a slew of exciting course offerings, had a great impact on my academic life at Stanford. I would like to generously thank John Rick for allowing me to work at the exhilaratingly enchanting Andean site of Chavín de Huántar, Peru (first millennium BCE), and Ian Morris for providing me the opportunity to work at the pre-Hellenic site of Monte Polizzo, Italy (sixth century BCE). The erstwhile CASA with its close-knit community and theoretically stimulating environment has played an important role in shaping my anthropological practice. I would like to thank the late Hayden White, Tim Lenoir, Gregory Schopen, Renato Rosaldo, Paulla Ebron, Lynn Meskell, and Miyako Inoue for taking keen interest in my work. The years at Stanford would have been socially insular if not for the many friends who shared their life and times with me—Suraj Jacob, Pankaj Gupta, Madhav Ranganathan, Ijaz Syed, Shailini Gera, Ali Hasan Cemendtaur, Sabahat Ashraf, Maya Dodd, Manishita Dass, Mukta Sharangpani, Tim Webmoor, Chris Witmore, Shubhra Swarup, Heraz Marafatia, Tania Chattopadhya, Pushkin Chattopadhya, Manju Chattopadhya, Pawan and Meghna Kumar, Itamar Francez, Nama Rokem, Fernando Armstrong-Fumero, Dante Alejandro Angelo, Tiffany Romain, Katrinka Reinhart, Angad Singh Bhalla, and Neepa Acharya.

At Yale University (2007–10), I was the affiliated with Center of South Asian Studies. I am especially grateful to Dudley Andrew, Phyllis Granoff, and K. Sivaramakrishnan for giving me an opportunity to teach courses in South Asian Studies, Films Studies, and Anthropology, Dean William Whobrey for giving me a fabulous chance to teach in the Yale Summer Aboard Program in Bombay (2010–14), Charles Musser for being a lifelong friend, mentor, and indulgingly supportive colleague, Shivi and James C. Scott for closely reading the manuscript of this book, and Karsten Harries for letting me audit his cerebral seminars on Martin Heidegger. During those years, the friendships of Kasturi Gupta, Vikramaditya Thakur, Uday Chandra, Richard Suchenski, Charu Gupta, Sumati Sundaram, Annu Jalais, Aniket Aga, Shreeyash Palshikar, Kedar Kulkarni, Basuli Deb, Jaret Vadera, Pete Moran, Shafqat Hussain, Pankaj Rishi Kumar, Mokshay Madiman, Marylea Quintana, Domingo Medina, Maria Pinango, Maria-Threese Serana, Boris Greenshpun, and Diana Blank were very valuable.

The Film/Media Program at the Harrington School of Communication at the University of Rhode Island has been a perfect home (since 2010) to work on my cinematic career and simultaneously devote time to my critical scholarship. I would like to thank: Mary Healy, Justin Wyatt, Jean Walton, Ian Reyes, Robert Manteiga, Keith Brown for collegiality and friendship; program directors Sheri Wills and Rebecca Romanow for being enthusiastic advocates of my work; Ryan Trimm for being an invigorating intellectual comrade, judiciously reading the manuscript and generously commenting; and finally Tony Balko for sparkling my social life in

Providence, his unwavering friendship, and resolute companionship. Special thanks are also due to Ashwini Deo, Neepa Acharya, Cyril Ghosh, Paroma Maiti, Madhavi Tangella, and Michele Meek for painstakingly proofreading drafts of this manuscript at various stages. I would like to thank Michael Dodson, Simanti Dasgupta, Pushkar Sohoni, Uzma Rizvi, and Namita Sugandhi for being fellow compatriots in corridors of innumerable conferences and workshops.

Acknowledging informants whom one cannot name is a difficult task, but I must try. I am profoundly beholden to all members of the Archaeological Survey of India (ASI) who took the time and energy to speak to me and spend time with me in the field and in their offices. For their generous hospitality, I shall always be appreciative. This book would not have been written without their patience with my inquisitive questioning and openness to my work. I am also grateful to the innumerable local villagers working at these sites for letting me partake in their laboring life and sharing stories about their experiences. I would especially like to thank the office and staff members of the director general of the ASI, joint director general, and the director of Excavation and Exploration, R. S. Bisht, for giving me the necessary permission to work at the various archaeological sites. I am also deeply thankful to the director of the Dholavira Excavation and the superintending archaeologists of the Nagpur Excavation Branch, the Patna Excavation Branch, and the Delhi Excavation Branch for allowing me into their camps and treating me as their own with warmth and kindness. My heartfelt appreciation is due to the staff of the Monument Section of the ASI headquarters in New Delhi for helping me work at the ASI archives, along with the staff of the National Archives, New Delhi, Central Archaeological Library, New Delhi, Parliament Library, New Delhi, Indian Archaeological Society Library, New Delhi, and Deccan College Library, Pune. I am also grateful to the office and staff of the American Institute of Indian Studies, New Delhi—especially Pradeep Mehendiratta and Purnima Mehta for helping me procure innumerable official permissions.

This book would not have been completed without the Junior Research Fellowship from the American Institute of Indian Studies, the Stanford University's Graduate Research Opportunity Grant, and the Mellon Foundation Dissertation Fellowship. Sections of this book were presented at numerous locations: World Archaeology Conference (WAC), Washington DC, USA (2003), Theoretical Archaeology Group (TAG) Conference, Sheffield University (2005), Annual South Asian Studies Conference, Madison (2007), Annual American Anthropological Association Meeting, Washington (2007), Association for Asian Studies Meeting, Chicago (2009), along with invited talks at Yale University, Harvard University, Tufts University, Indiana University, and Syracuse University. Earlier versions of some chapters or parts of chapters, which I have updated and, in most cases, considerably developed and expanded, were originally published in the *Journal of Material Culture*

(2002) and *Contributions to Indian Sociology* (2011). I thank the editors and reviewers of these articles for their comments and observations.

I would like to thank my editor Qudsiya Ahmed at Cambridge University Press for believing in this project; Jinia Dasgupta and Aniruddha De of the editorial team for meticulously copyediting the manuscript; and the five anonymous peer reviewers for their comments and suggestion, which I have incorporated in this book. On a personal note, I want to thank my teenage daughter, Iravati, my parents, Lalit and Urmila Chadha, for being there unconditionally, my brother, Sachin, and his wife, Rohini, for their love and hospitality in Delhi and Bombay, Ashwini Deo and her parents, Sharad and Chhaya Deo, for unflinchingly supporting me, and finally, I want to thank my wife, Debleena Sen, for firmly believing in me and tenaciously holding my hands in this undulating journey.

Providence, 2020

Note on Transliteration

The conversations in this ethnography were conducted in English and Hindi. All translations from Hindi to English and vice versa are my own. I have employed a simple and contemporary transliteration system for Hindi words that do not use diacritics. I have tried to incorporate the sound-values of the letters and the acute and grave accents within the Romanization process. This system does not distinguish between long and short vowels or between dental and retroflex consonants.

Abbreviations

AA	assistant archaeologist
AACD	ASI Archive Collection, New Delhi
ADG	additional director general
AIIS	American Institute of Indian Studies
ASA	assistant superintending archaeologist
ASI	Archaeological Survey of India
BJP	Bharatiya Janata Party
CBI	Central Bureau of Investigation
CABA	Central Advisory Board of Archaeology
CAC	Central Antiquity Collection
CAG	Comptroller and Auditor General of India
Dy SA.	deputy superintending archaeologist
DG	director general
Ex. Br.	excavation branch
IAS	Indian Administrative Service
IAR	Indian Archaeology: A Review
Jt DG	joint director general
LDC	lower division clerk
MLA	member of the legislative assembly
MP	member of parliament
NAGPRA	Native American Graves Protection and Repatriation Act
OBC	Other Backward Classes
OSL	optically stimulated luminescence
PWD	Public Works Department
RSS	Rashtriya Swayamsevak Sangh
SA	superintending archaeologist

SSC	Staff Selection Commission
SHP	Saraswati Heritage Project
TA	technical assistant
UDC	upper division clerk
UGC	University Grants Commission

1 Anthropology of Archaeology

It was my first day at the archaeological site of Hansi, excavated by the Archaeological Survey of India (ASI). The excavation director—a middle-aged, burly north Indian man wearing a white bush-shirt and donning dark shades—took me on a site tour. Hansi was a monumental, multilayered site nestled in a medieval fortification adjacent to a bustling town in Haryana's Hissar district. It is known for its thriving agrarian marketplace. We strolled to the site from the campsite located on the cricket grounds of the local intermediate college. Walking slowly, we meandered through the town's congested streets, marketplace, and Dalit slums encroaching the edge of the site, and reached the citadel at the top of the mound. The excavation director, an upper-caste Brahmin from Uttar Pradesh, explained to me, in chaste Hindi, the archaeology of the site and the challenges of excavating a large multilayered site. We walked past a series of deep excavation trenches exposing late medieval Muslim layers and early medieval Rajput layers. Suddenly, during his narration, he paused, removed his dark shades, and peered at me; with pride, spiked with a firm sense of explicatory finality, he declared: "If you don't discover in archaeology, then it is pointless" (*archaeology main discovery nahi ki, toh kya kiya*). "But what about theory?" I asked. The excavation director of Hansi swiftly quipped: "It is you people who do theory. We in the ASI dig" (*Theory-weory aap karthe hain. Hum ASI main khudai karthe hai*). "If we do not produce data, what will you theorist do?" (*Agar hum ne data nahi nikaala toh, aap theorist kaya karenge?*).

The past has played a formidable role in the self-fashioning of the modern Indian nation state. Along with historical narratives, archaeological materiality has significantly contributed to the reimagination of India as a contiguous entity spanning over 5,000 years. The ASI has been the epistemological heart of the production of ancient materiality for more than 150 years. An institution of colonial genealogy, it is now an organization of postcolonial bureaucracy. In the colony, the ASI was an investigative apparatus of a state in search of the ancient at the fringes of the Empire; in the postcolony, the ASI is a custodian bureaucracy protecting the vast monumental heritage of India from disintegration, and a foremost producer of archaeological knowledge. Established by the British colonial state in 1861, it was the foundational statist apparatus for the production of archaeological data, facts, and information in colonial India in the form of sweeping surveys and excavations. It continued to play a pivotal role in the production of nationalist archaeological narratives after independence in 1947. Scholars have shown that the ASI's claims to factual legitimacy are associated with the disciplinarian discourse of archaeology as a science (see Chakrabarti 1989, 2003; Ramaswamy 2001; Chadha 2002; Guha-Thakurta 2005). Today, the ASI excavates large swaths of ancient sites. It uncovers monumental structures, generates millions of artifacts, and produces a large volume of scholarly literature. Since 1947, it has excavated more than 300 archaeological sites. Although the ASI is primarily a heritage protection and conservation bureaucracy, it gains enormous legitimacy and prestige through the production of authentic knowledge about the past.[1]

The book follows the archaeological material culture discovered in the ASI trenches to its transformation into empirical facts published in official reports. Through a "thick description" (Geertz 1973) of the "archaeological process" (Hodder 1999) in an outlying location of the "postcolony" (Mbembe 2000)— an idiosyncratic site compared to the relative stability of the Euro-American world—I establish the epistemological susceptibility of archaeology's "theory of practice" (Bourdieu 1977). The objective power of ASI archaeology emerges from both its role as an institutional formation of postcolonial bureaucracy and the fissured science of its archaeology. By concentrating on such a fractured location of knowledge production, I examine the epistemological enunciation of the discursive practice of archaeology as a science—signifying its ideological basis. Employing meticulous ethnographic examples, supported by historical data, this book argues that the bureaucratic ecology of the ASI's institutional apparatus is so pervasive that its social culture permeates the epistemic evidence it produces and represents as empirical facts. I anthropologically show that the bureaucratic archaeology of the ASI is an articulation of a colonial ideology performed in the postcolonial ecology that has a debilitating impact on the epistemology of the past in India.

The ASI is as an emblematic organization in this book imbricated in the institutional practices of the postcolonial state. There are many reasons that motivated me to conduct this ethnographic work at the ASI. The ASI is not just one of the oldest archaeological bureaucracies in the world, but also one of the largest of its kind and has enormous control over the archaeological heritage of India. Unlike other parts of the world, Indian laws did not allow private cultural resource management organizations to conduct archaeological excavations in India, thus making the ASI hegemonic compared to underfunded university departments and marginalized state archaeological departments.

Also, ASI bureaucrat-archaeologists are distinct from archaeologists working in a university setting in India because of the significant statist authority they wield. The ASI's dominance in archaeological knowledge production in India has legal validity and objective sanctity because it is part of the statist machinery. By a series of legislations dated to the late nineteenth century, the ASI was given the custodianship of archaeological heritage in India. It is illegal to excavate any site in India without a license issued by the director general (DG) of the ASI. Over the course of a century and half, it has created a huge archive of knowledge about the Indian past, far surpassing any other archaeological organization in South Asia. It also has the jurisdiction over a huge collection of artifacts and material culture, discovered and excavated since its inception. Thus, the ASI has an insurmountable hegemonic authority over the archaeological heritage of India. No other statist or non-statist actors could overrule its influence.[2] In these circumstances, the ASI becomes a potent site to study the intersection of archaeology, science, state, and bureaucracy.

There is indistinguishable ideological commensurability between bureaucracy and science—being archetypally rational, predominantly technocratic, historically modernistic, fetishizing efficacy, and emphasizing objectivity. The epistemic community of ASI archaeology is both scientists and bureaucrats at the same time. It is this aggregation of bureaucratic and scientific knowledge production apparatus that makes it a fertile site to investigate the nature of science and the state. This book, in particular, examines the everyday practices (De Certeau 1984) of the ASI bureaucracy at the archaeological site to focus on the theory of practice (Bourdieu 1977) of regulation, control, and management in micro-settings with an emphasis on investigating the technologies and assemblages of the postcolonial state, along with an interrogation of the operations of materials, agents, and techniques by the ASI to put these bureaucratic rationalities into practice. My aim is to examine the ontology of bureaucratic archaeology in all its specificity rather than providing a general theory of the state or archaeology.

At the ASI, the discursive authority of archaeology's disciplinary assertions do not derive from the scientific method of its practices, as claimed by the processual archaeologists. Nor does it derive from the interpretative nature of its knowledge construction processes, as argued by the post-processual archaeologists. Neither is archaeology a practice susceptible to subversion by political and nationalistic insinuation. Instead, I argue in *Bureaucratic Archaeology* that archaeology is itself an ideological and cultural knowledge production practice. The theoretical and methodological contrariness between construction of evidence and its interpretative creation of knowledge is not incommensurable. These dissimilarities present a retroactive perspective on the process of archaeological knowledge production.

It is the epistemic logic of archaeology and the social and cultural practice of its science that make it vulnerable to statist and nationalist appropriation in the ASI. In the vast, dusty, and desolate fringes of western India, I realized that the ASI's archaeology was a colonial epistemology (ideology) reinforced by science (process) and fortified by postcolonial bureaucracy (apparatus). Empiricism here is compromised three times—first, by an oppressive disciplinary apparatus (colonial archaeology); second, by an ideological discursive methodology of practice (science); and, finally, by an imperiously stratified hierarchy (postcolonial bureaucracy). I show in this book how bureaucracy (ontology) apprehends the discourse of archaeological practice (disciplinary apparatus) to construct a discourse about the Indian past (epistemology), and I argue that this past for the ASI is a bureaucratic *artifice* rather than a scientific *artifact*.

Ethnography of Archaeology as Science

Science in the non-western world has been historically positioned as a deferred trajectory of advances in the west, pushing, for instance, postcolonial science at the periphery of its epistemological deliberations (Chambers and Gillespie 2000). Correspondingly, the discourse of science and technology studies has been dominated by an obsession on "big" science, "real" science, and "techno" science—high-energy physics, biosciences, new media, and other dominant scientific enterprises. These areas provided high visibility and accountability to the sociological and historical workings of science—its contradictions, incongruity, and its epistemic dominance. Non-big sciences and scientific practices in the non-western world have been often relegated to scholarly margins (Collins and Pinch 1979; Collins and Evans 2002). Disciplines such as archaeology have mostly been consigned to the discursive margins of sociological, historical, and philosophical deliberation of science studies (Wylie 2002; Chapman and Wylie 2016). On the other hand, within the history of archaeology, the non-western trajectory of its disciplinary discourse has been relegated to the margins of its Euro-American-centric worldview. Likewise, the anthropological discourse on bureaucracy has primarily given importance to the preponderance of western ideological teleology, overlooking the idiosyncratic afflictions of postcolonial polity and its statist ideology. In this book, I engage with both these marginal forms of modernity—archaeology and the postcolonial bureaucracy—in order to examine the articulation of their ideological and conceptual contraption.[3] This I do by examining the practice of one formation, archaeology, as a marginal science, ensconced within the ideological grasp of another marginal configuration, the postcolonial bureaucracy. The theoretical emphasis of this book is to study both these marginal structures of modernity, intricately braided in a non-western setting—postcolonial India. *Bureaucratic Archaeology* is an anthropological investigation of a marginal science, articulated by a marginal state, at the margins of its boundaries. Theoretically, my multi-sited ethnographic intervention (Gupta and Ferguson 1997) is envisaged as a post-Kuhnian, Latourian, postcolonial investigation of archaeology as a bureaucratic science in India.

The discursive trajectory of archaeology as an epistemological practice has struggled with its disciplinarian subjectivity in the second half of the twentieth century.[4] The rise of the scientific imagination endowed with powerful cultural, social, and political authority—specifically, after its resurgence in the atomic age—relegated the social sciences to the periphery of the academy, where they were compelled to assert their scientific legitimacy (Barnes 1974). Historically, by the end of the nineteenth century, archaeology viewed itself as a science in terms of the empirical knowledge that it created (see Daniel 1950; Christenson 1989; Trigger 1989; Kehoe 1998; Schnapp 1996). Employing the received wisdom of the geological sciences—the systematic process of excavation and the use of a typological and classificatory analytical framework—culture-history archaeology gained scientific legitimacy (see Dunnell 1978; Lyman, O'Brien, and Dunnell 1997; Lyman and O'Brien 2003).

In the early 1960s, a concerted attempt to refurbish archaeology's objective authority was launched. The earlier variant of culture-history archaeology, considered closer to the subjective practices of historical and cultural approaches, was pugnaciously resuscitated as a positivist science. Predisposed to Carl Hempel's "logical positivism," archaeology, in the form of processual archaeology (Binford 1968, 17), cast off its subjective culture-history model of knowledge construction for a robust analytical emphasis, through the greater deployment of scientific methodologies into archaeological theory and practice. Processual archaeology, inclined as it was by cultural-evolution theories of change, now attempted to reinforce archaeology's objective claims to the past by applying scientific methods, creating data through observation and experimentation. They particularly insisted on the use of the Popperian hypothetico-deductive method in archaeology to make law-like claims about past human behavior. This gave rise to an environmental deterministic view of the past, lacking human agency, and delegitimizing cultural categories, along with overt proclamations of objectivity based on rigorous application of the scientific method.[5] Christened as "New Archaeology," this new turn in archaeology advanced a positivist view of the past. This had a widespread methodological impact throughout the world of archaeology, including India (Fuller and Boivin 2002).[6]

New Archaeology's scientific ascendancy was, however, short-lived. The upsurge of post-structuralism in the 1980s mounted a trenchant critique of positivist approaches in archaeology, indicting its claims to objectivity as deterministic and faulting its narrow theoretical morphology of being incompetent to comprehend the fluidity and flux of past cultural systems.[7] This theoretical onslaught led to acrimonious debates that profoundly exacerbated the predicament of archaeology's disciplinarian subjectivity wrestling alongside the earlier tussle between history and science (Hodder 1984; Shanks 1992; Hodder et al. 1995). The discordant theoretical squabbling was exacerbated by the widely heterogeneous discursive genealogy of archaeology within the Euro-American world. In America it was disciplinarily aligned to anthropology (Willey and Sabloff 1993; Reyman 1992; Kehoe 1998), whereas in Europe it was closely associated with history (Trigger 1989; Hodder 1991).

Furthermore, the tension in the twentieth-century trajectory of archaeology between science and nationalism also brought archaeology to the forefront of the politics of the modern nation state (Arnold 1990, 1992; Kohl, Fawcett, and Philip 1995; Díaz-Andreu and Champoin 1996; Meskell 1998). The appropriation of archaeology in constructing nationalist ideologies by European nations presents a vivid illustration of this deep-seated tension (Trigger 1984, 1989; Jones 1997), which after World War II played a prime role in the making of the newly decolonized nations (Kuklick 1991; El-Haj 2001, 2012; Shepherd 2002). By the early 1990s, archaeology was in the throes of a serious crisis regarding its disciplinary subjectivity. It had to reluctantly come to terms not just with the heterogeneity of theory and practice but also with the regional diversity of the methodological framework that it once considered homogenous. These factors were the subtext of the assertion of the World Archaeological Conference (WAC) in 1986 in solidarity with the anti-apartheid struggle (Ucko 1987). It was the most explicit symptom of the disciplinary discordance in archaeology (Ucko 1995; Shanks and McGuire 1996; Zimmerman 2006). The destruction of the Babri Mosque in 1992 brought into sharp focus the politics of ethics, the science of archaeology, and the state and nationalism not just in India, but also in the world of archaeology at large—faced with the destruction and deterioration of heritage monuments (Lowenthal 1998; Meskell 1998, 2002; Vitelli and Colwell-Chanthaphonh 2006); the commercialization of archaeological practice; the repatriation of antiquities (Mihesuah 2000; Thomas 2000; Bray 2001); the international trade in illegal antiquities (Brodie et al. 2001); the assertion of the rights of indigenous people (Layton 1989; Atalay 2006); and the excessive subversion of archaeology by politics (Gathercole and Lowenthal 1990; Hamilakis 1996; Jones 1997; Lamberg-Karlovsky 1997). These unrelenting concerns along with the quandaries about disciplinary subjectivity resulted in archaeology's need for reassessing the historical antecedents of its theory and practice—a process that has continued until now, and of which this book is also a part.[8]

Concurrently, during the last two decades of the twentieth century, the various tensions in the disciplinary subjectivity of archaeology were consistently explored and sorted in the meta-theoretical domain (Fleming and Johnson 1990). This fixation was born with excessive theory building in the discipline during the rise of processual archaeology (Binford 1962; Clarke 1968; Binford and Quimby 1972; Schiffer 1976, 1987; Binford 1977) and prospered during the rancorous struggle with post-processual archaeology.[9] The meta-theoretical approach gave rise to the need to write a history of archaeology, concentrating on the discipline as a cultural and political practice. A discourse evolved, attentively linked to the ascendancy of the nation state in Europe and the expansion of colonialism (Trigger 1984; 1989; Robertshaw 1990; Graves-Brown, Jones, and Gamble 1995; Ucko 1995). The excessive need to theorize the praxis of archaeology within larger meta-historical shifts often ignored the historical genealogy of its disciplinary trajectory in the context of the ideological genesis of its methodologies. In India, this was followed by the writing of a subcontinental history of archaeology, locating the evolution of the discipline in the colonial context (Chakrabarti 1988, 1997; Paddayya 1995).[10] These global and local historical projects were undertaking the documentation of the socio-political genealogies of the discipline. Projects encompassed the chronological accounts delineating the trajectory of archaeology in relation to larger meta-narratives of nationalism, colonialism, and imperialism. However, with post-processual approaches, the necessity to examine the micro-practices and micro-processes of archaeological fieldwork emerged. This gave rise to the historical and anthropological interrogation of archaeological methods (Hodder 1999; Lucas 2002, 2012; Chadwick 2003).

Ethnographic methods in archaeological research have been deployed since the days of processual archaeology, in the form of "ethnoarchaeology" (Watson 1979, 2009) grounded in analogical and homological rationality (David 1992). These approaches problematically mapped ethnographic evidence of contemporary societies inhabiting in the vicinity of the archaeological sites onto the past material culture (Wylie 1985). However, the theoretical genealogy of *Bureaucratic Archaeology* is not located in this discursive moment. Beginning with the dominance of post-processual archaeology in the 1990s, ethnography was deployed to study the disciplinary forms rather than the past (for example, Edgeworth 1990, 2003; Castañeda 1996; Handler and Gable 1997; Bartu 2000; El-Haj 2001; Breglia 2006). This was driven by a conscientious attempt to go beyond the meta-theoretical critique in archaeology in order to explore its own archives and to uncover the historical genealogy of its disciplinarian impulses—to delve at the edge of the trowel as it were—to examine the interpretative basis of its practice (Hodder 1997, 1999, 2000, 2003; Andrews, Barrett, and Lewis 2000; Berggren and Hodder 2003; Chadwick 2003). The focus was to study the genealogy of archaeological field methods rather than create meta-narratives of disciplinary discourse (Fotiadis 1993; Hodder 1999; Andrew, Barrett, and Lewis 2000; Lucas 2002). The feminist critique of archaeological fieldwork attempted to employ ethnographic intervention to provide a critique of archaeological methods (Gero 1985, 1994, 1996; Conkey and Tringham 1996; Politis 2001). Post-processual archaeologists, in their pursuit of self-reflexive knowledge production, introduced the ethnographer as an important actor to understand the impact of archaeological intervention on the local community, and to study the consequence of their own archaeological practices (Hodder 2000; Berggren 2001; Berggren and Hodder 2003). This has given birth to a distinct field of inquiry in archaeological discourse called "archaeological ethnography" (Meskell 2005, 2007; Castañeda and Matthews 2008; Hollowell and Nicholas 2008; Hamilakis and Anagnostopoulos 2009; Hollowell and Mortensen 2009; Hamilakis 2011) and "ethnographies of archaeology practice" (Edgeworth 2003, 2006, 2010). Here, ethnographic strategies are explicitly employed to interrogate methodologies of archaeological intervention—its diverse practices and technologies to create knowledge about the past. *Bureaucratic Archaeology* extends these initiatives of ethnographic investigation of the "ecology of practices" (Stengers 2005; Olsen et al. 2012, 56; Witmore and Shanks 2013, 380), informed by the potential to decolonize methodology, practice, interpretation (Atalay 2006; Smith 2012), and postcolonial theory (Liebmann and Rizvi 2008; Lydon and Rizvi 2016) by dexterously shifting the site of inquiry from meta-narratives of archaeological theory to the ontological location where material culture is discovered, analyzed, and shaped into epistemology.

Ethnography of Archaeology as Bureaucracy

It was late one night when I reached Dholavira after a long journey of over 26 hours. The director of the site, who was sitting in the courtyard of a mud hut, greeted me, dressed in a warm woolen sweater, monkey-cap (ski-cap), pajamas, and Hawaii *chappal*s (flip-flops). It was the end of November and winter was snugly settling into this arid and dry belt of western India, with the nights becoming bitterly cold. He was sitting in a yellow molded plastic chair, in the company of his staff members—the two assistant archaeologists (AAs) present at the site, and a storekeeper. The director introduced me to the members of his staff, who were crouched over a blue molded plastic table scattered with papers and notebooks, discussing the logistics of the next day's work. In the course of the introductions, he commented that it was a pity that I had reached the site late at night or I would have had my first glimpse of the archaeological site from at least a kilometer away. "Dholavira is the second largest Harappan site in India. It is mammoth [*ekdum vishal*]. You have never seen a Harappan site like this in your life," he energetically remarked. During my stay at Dholavira, almost all the archaeologists and the staff members talked about Dholavira as a site with a "stunning" (*dhaansu*) mound. Of all the stories that I heard about the monumental visuality of Dholavira, the most fascinating one was about an Indian Army general, who was on a scouting trip in this India–Pakistan border zone, flying above the site. He ordered his entourage of helicopters to land to take a whirlwind tour of the site. An AA, recounting this episode, noted that the army general had revealed that he had never seen such a large archaeological site in his life. When he glimpsed the site from "above" (*upar se*) he was tempted to land and tour the site on "foot" (*zameen par*).

ASI excavation sites, which come in many shapes and sizes—big (*bada*), small (*chota*), sunken (*daba*), and scattered (*bikhra*)—are the focal point of my ethnographic narrative. The excavation site is an epistemological terrestriality in which the materiality of the past is discovered, excavated, organized, qualified, labeled, catalogued, represented, and produced as objects of scientific archaeology. Through archaeological excavation, a landscape is carved out to produce an excavation site—scientific, performative, ideological, disciplinarian, and political in its display. The earth is divested of the unwanted and what remains is a spectacular *epistemic spatiality*. I focus my ethnographic intervention on this archetypal location of archaeology. Here, through sociological and epistemological micro-processes, archaeological materiality is transformed into an epistemic thing (Rheinberger 1997). Such an endeavor involves fathoming how a material culture comes into existence and how it is shaped as an artifact in the archaeological project. The ASI excavation site is not just another location of epistemic production; it is a scientifically symbolic, ideologically charged, hierarchical, and a bureaucratic embodiment of postcolonial archaeology. Here, the archaeological knowledge produced is simultaneously a product of the scientific trajectory of archaeological epistemology and the political genealogy of the postcolonial bureaucracy.

For the ASI archaeologist, the excavation site was conceived as an abstract macro-entity, whereas the trench was the micro-area, "where real [*asli*] archaeology happens." The director of the Dholavira site once underscored the ontological authenticity of the site: "Real archaeology is done in the trench. It is in the trench where you connect with ancient civilization. The site is about the big picture. The trench is where you dirty your hands" (*hum apne haath trench ki mitti mein gande karte hai*). The director explained, "*The trench is the whole and soul of archaeology* [English words used]. If you cannot dig the trench properly, then the whole site will get messy [*agar trench kharab tarike se khoda toh poore site ka satyanaash ho jayega*]." The ethnographic description of this book further dovetails into the sociological and the epistemological working at this micro-site—the archaeological trench. For archaeology this is the most profound epistemological location, akin to the laboratory of the "real" sciences—the ontological site for archaeology—mediated by technology (instruments, equipment, tools), social factors (interests, goals, structures), and conceptual frameworks (representations, models, theories) that come together to produce empirical evidence. Here evidence is discovered, knowledge is created, and objectivity is performed. In the unearthing of accumulated material culture, ASI archaeologists generate empirical evidence for the construction of narratives.[11] Through the ethnography of micro-practices, I describe the process by which material culture in the trench-laboratory was recognized, discovered, and transformed into archaeological evidence. In the analysis that follows, I meticulously demonstrate how ASI archaeologists and workers in the trench-laboratory unearth material artifact as a controlled experiment and how they name the artifact, date it, and epistemologically fix it to a cultural context.

My ethnographic intervention in the archaeological site is grounded in the understanding of the scientific construction of knowledge as a social process interrogated by the discursive framework of the sociology of science. In the 1970s, indebted to the works of Robert Merton, influenced by the paradigmatic *The Structure of Scientific Revolutions* by Thomas Kuhn (1965), and propelled into the forefront of science studies by the Edinburgh School's Strong Programme, the sociology of science and technology emerged as a significant disciplinary practice to comprehend the social structure of scientific knowledge production (Barnes 1974; Bloor 1976; Barnes and Shapin 1979). Scholars working in these traditions were concerned with apprehending how scientific knowledge is produced in laboratory, disciplinary, and broad social contexts, focusing on the method of scientific argumentations and negotiations. This inquiry has sought to demonstrate the inseparability between the social location and the manufacture of scientific knowledge. It established that scientific knowledge is constructed, maintained, determined, and shaped by cultural practices (Latour 1987; Haraway 1989, 1991; Pickering 1992; Fuller 1993, 1997).

In *Bureaucratic Archaeology*, I conceptualize the ASI archaeologists working in the archaeological sites as members of a specific "epistemic community"—

scientist-bureaucrats (Knorr-Cetina 1999). These communities of scientists have been called "epistemic cultures," analogous to the ideas of "knowledge societies" (Stehr 1994) or "information societies" (Webster 2006), which constitute knowledge through social, discursive, and material practices. It is a heterogeneous practice of knowledge production conducted in the *laboratory* or the *field*, mediated by technological elements (instruments, equipment, tools), social factors (interests, goals, structures), and conceptual frameworks (representations, models, theories) that are irreducible and mutually constitutive (Knorr-Cetina 1981; Latour and Woolgar 1986; Latour 1987). It interrogates ways in which members of a cultural system, through their theory of practices, produce the social structure of everyday activities. Its aim is to explicate these ways of meaning production, and attempts to describe those practices and show how they work (Lynch 1993). Its investigation is directed to uncover social processes underlying the construction of social phenomena ranging from factual knowledge, social organization, and attributes such as race and gender, to the acquisition of tacit skills (Polanyi and Sen 2009). The focus of this scholarship is to study how the scientific method works and creates knowledge, with an intense scrutiny on a single location of its performance. In the case of my research, it will be the archaeological site. Concurrently, the critique of science leveled by feminist critics illustrated that scientific discourse, embedded in the larger western epistemological system, is androcentric, Eurocentric, and not culturally transcendental. It is bound by specific cultural histories and relations, and that its claims to objectivity must be deconstructed (Haraway 1989; Harding 1991, 2006, 2008). These works have located the emergence of the disciplinarian formation of field sciences within the discursive framework of the Enlightenment, which they show strengthened the latter within the ideological context of colonial expansion.[12] In this book, I employ these theoretical persuasions to investigate the peculiarities of knowledge production in a non-western space. It locates archaeology in this rise of science by engaging with the growing literature on the development of science as a colonial knowledge production system[13] and its imbricative relation to the postcolonial nation state. The discursive insinuations of *Bureaucratic Archaeology* are in conversation with an analytical body of scholarship that in India has examined with provocative perspicacity the connection between the ambitions of the Indian postcolonial state and science.[14]

The theoretical genealogy of interrogation of the modern bureaucratic state can be located in numerous thinkers that have inspired the trajectory of anthropology—from Weber, to the Marxist Gramsci, and the post-Marxist Althusser. However, it is in the 1990s with the rise of Michel Foucault–inspired governmentality studies (Foucault 1991) that the state as an object of anthropological inquiry made an analytical resurgence in anthropology.[15] He conceptualizes the state as an operative network ensemble through which it articulates the "analytics of government" (Dean 1999). In order to comprehend the workings of such an operative system, Foucault argues for the adoption of a theoretical approach in which power is fragmented into political rationalities, technologies, and techniques of governance. The analytical focus is on the practices of regulation in micro-settings with an emphasis on investigating the technologies and assemblages of governance, along with interrogating the operations of materials, agents, and techniques by the state to put these governmental rationalities into practice. The aim was to examine the particularistic apparatus of government in all its specificity rather than providing a general theory of the state; the impetus was to comprehend the "how" of government (Dean 1999). By the early 1990s, anthropologists recognized the consequences of statist intervention in the material, and the subjective formation of the "local"— the normative center of anthropological examination (Mitchell 1991; Mbembe 1992; Taussig 1997; Scott 1998; Steinmetz 1999). This analytical approach to the state is informed by the view that the state is a formidable site of symbolic and cultural production and not just a means of bureaucratic apparatus for governance. It is not merely the nation that is an imagined entity but that the state is made up of assembled ideological formations that are conceptualized and made bureaucratically effectual through culturally potent symbolic systems (Hansen and Stepputat 2001; Ferguson and Gupta 2002; Das and Poole 2004; Sharma and Gupta 2006; Fuller and Benei 2009). Methodologically, this anthropology of the state calls for an approach that does not isolate the various functionalist personification of the state, but argues for an investigation of the modern state as a combination of its various embodiments—political economy, institutional apparatus, social structure, everyday practice, representation system, and its ideological formations. In South Asia, this theoretical attention on the state has given rise to piercing anthropological understandings into the workings of the postcolonial bureaucracy, by scrupulously studying discourses of corruption (Gupta 2012), hegemony of bureaucratic documents (Hull 2012), and quotidian instrumentality of the bureaucratic apparatus (Mathur 2016).

A Short History of the Postcolonial ASI

The ASI was established in 1861, soon after the revolt of 1857, when the East India Company was relieved of its control over India and the colony came under the direct jurisdiction of the British crown. This caused an administrative shift in colonial governmentality.[16] From a policy of military occupation of territory, the emphasis shifted to extracting of surplus through governance and bureaucratic methods. The birth of the ASI as a colonial knowledge production agency was framed as "an enlightened ruling power" (Cunningham 1871, ii).[17] Its ideological genealogy can be traced through two distinct forms of colonial engagement with the "other" and framed by the necessity to accumulate knowledge about the colonized: historical and travel writings, and the geographical mapping of physical territory for military expansion (see Pratt 1992; Raman 2001; Rubiés 2002). Even before the ASI came into being, the cartographical and chronological apprehension of colonial India was underway with the establishment of the Survey of India in 1767, as an unmistakable military reconnaissance organization, and the creation of the Asiatic Society of Bengal in 1784 to study Indian history and language. The Great Trigonometrical Survey of India represented a military project envisaged to encompass the entire subcontinent into the epistemological grasp of a Cartesian cartographical project (see Driver 2001; Barrow 2003). William Jones's identification of the linguistic resemblance between Sanskrit, ancient Iranian, and European languages laid the groundwork for a probing inquiry into ancient India.[18] The incipient mapping endeavor (Edney 1997) along with the historical bracketing of the colonial universe was instrumental in the rise of the Indological project and the birth of the ASI. By 1783, Colonel Colin MacKenzie, who eventually became the first surveyor general of India (1815–21), undertook one of the first systematic archaeological surveys in India (Blake 1991).[19]

The ASI was one of several colonial organizations that generated information for the colony's governance by producing scientific facts about India.[20] The colonial ASI's epistemological genesis was situated between what Bernard Cohn calls the "historical modality" and the "survey modality." Cohn lists these categories as the numerous "investigative modalities" of knowledge production mechanisms invented by the imperial ideology and perfected in the colonies. Facts were produced, categorized, and classified in order to control and govern subjects. Other such modalities include the "observational/travel modality," "enumerative modality," "museological modality," and "surveillance modality" (Cohn 1996, 5). For Cohn, "historical modality" is a means of knowledge production, instrumental in "the ideological construction of Indian civilizations," whereas "survey modality" is involved in "mapping and bounding to describe and classify the territory's zoology, geology, botany, ethnography, economic products, history and sociology" (Cohn 1996, 7). The ASI emerged out of the combination of these modalities. It was fundamentally a cartographic (temporal and terrestrial) bureaucracy that discovered, excavated, categorized, and classified

India's past, and provided concrete evidence for the construction of an ideological history of India's past through the analyses of architectural remains, epigraphical inscriptions, and archaeological excavations.

The archaeological surveys of Sir Alexander Cunningham marked the early years of the ASI in the second half of the nineteenth century. Cunningham was appointed as the first DG of the ASI in 1871. Employing observations written by seventh-century Chinese travelers, Cunningham combined this archival material with the "topographical approach" of a military cartographer.[21] Traversing the subcontinent, his work encompassed a vast amount of area, hitherto unknown under the purview of Indological archaeology.[22] He focused his energies on the discoveries of Buddhist monuments.[23] However, things slowed down with his successors, who were deemed so ineffective that the post of DG was finally abolished.[24] The ensuing years were a "bleak period" (Roy 1961: 73) dominated by philological concerns rather than archaeological.[25] In 1901, after Viceroy Lord Curzon appointed Sir John Marshall as the DG of the ASI, archaeological research was undertaken again and with renewed vigor.[26] Marshall reinvigorated the ASI and not just emphasized the need to excavate and explore new territories but also inaugurated a concerted policy of conservation based on his influential *Conservation Manual*, which is still in use today (Sengupta 2013; Niti Aayog 2020, 75).

Along with the discovery and excavation of Buddhist sites in central and eastern India, it is the association with the Harappan sites that the genesis of the colonial ASI is symbiotically linked to.[27] The discovery of the Harappan civilization in the 1920s marked a paradigm shift in the practice and imagination of an Indian past. No longer was the civilizational history of Indian antiquity materially originated with the Mauryan Empire (c. 322–185 BCE) or the subsequent spread of Buddhism. Neither was it located within the emergence of Aryans in India. The excavations of Harappa by Daya Ram Sahni, assistant superintendent of the ASI, in 1921–22 and of Mohenjo-Daro by Rakhaldas Banerji, superintendent of the Western Circle, in 1922–23, and Madho Sarup Vats, officiating assistant superintendent of the Western Circle, in 1923–24, along with the public announcement of the discovery of a new civilization in the *Illustrated London News* in 1924 by John Marshall, ushered in a new era of archaeological imagination in India. Prior to this discovery, Indian archaeology was obsessed with Buddhist material culture, medieval Hindu temple architecture, epigraphy, and numismatics. Other than a few colonial surveyors who had collected lithic tools, prehistoric material culture did not have a pre-eminent place in colonial Indian archaeology.[28] With the discovery of the Harappan civilization, proto-historic archaeology came to the forefront. This discovery was the catalyst in the formation of the Exploration Branch in the ASI with a deputy director general and three assistant superintendents.

Administratively, the ASI was an evolving bureaucracy since its inception. Like most colonial bureaucracies, it was a slothful institution, with scarce funding, lackluster leadership, and one that was resistant to change and transformation for most of its colonial career.[29] For example, in 1848, when Cunningham was a second lieutenant of the Bengal Engineers, he formulated a proposal for an Indian Archaeological Survey. However, it was only in 1861 that he could begin the work after being appointed as an archaeological surveyor. Historians of the ASI summarily divided the colonial trajectory of the ASI under the creative leadership of just three DGs—Cunningham, Marshall, and Wheeler.[30] During the first 50 years of its existence, the ASI saw numerous financial and administrative disheveling—with recommendations of the abolishment of the DG's post to a serious state of affairs in 1895 when the Government of India requested the Asiatic Society to bear its responsibility. By 1899, the ASI was divided into five Circles—Bombay with Sind and Berar; Madras and Coorg; Panjab, Baluchistan, and Ajmer; Northwestern Provinces with Oudh; and Bengal and Assam. With John Marshall becoming the DG due to the intervention of Lord Curzon (1899–1905), the focus of the ASI shifted to conservation and protection of the archaeological heritage with the enactment of the Ancient Monument Preservation Act of 1904.[31] In 1921, the ASI was declared a central governmental organization under the provisions of the 1919 Montagu-Chelmsford Reforms, thereby instituting a secure system of financial stability and a structured bureaucracy (Ghosh 1954, 36). However, by the 1930s administrative apathy had again set in. Leonard Woolley, the excavator of Ur in Mesopotamia, was appointed as a "foreign expert" to evaluate the state of the ASI. In 1939, Woolley submitted a controversial report, which was not published because of its critical and damaging analysis.[32] He recommended that external intervention was essential in reinvigorating the colonial bureaucracy. This led to the appointment of Sir Mortimer Wheeler as the DG of the ASI in 1944.[33]

Wheeler's role at the helm of the ASI in restructuring Indian archaeology and the enormity of his contribution toward disciplining Indian archaeology in four years (1944–48) have been described as a series of developments that would have taken the erstwhile bureaucracy 40 years (Paddaya 1995). The central aim of Wheeler's intervention was to rectify the ills of the ASI that were reported by Woolley. This goal had a disciplinarian impetus and was aimed at not just restructuring the institutional apparatus of the ASI, but also its epistemological efficacy. The most crucial event of this transformation was the holding of the Taxila School of Archaeology in 1944. Arguably the first organized school of field archaeology in the discipline's history, it was to play an influential role in the postcolonial trajectory of Indian archaeology in later years (Wheeler 1976, 32). Students from this training camp went on to head various archaeological departments throughout the country and run the ASI for the following few decades (Chakrabarti 1988, 176). It was at Taxila and the various excavations that Wheeler conducted during these years at the sites of Arikamedu, Brahmagiri, and Harappa that he inscribed on the ASI ideas about scientific excavation. Commentators and historians of Indian archaeology have underscored Wheeler's influence on Indian archaeology in no uncertain terms (see Clark 1979; Chakrabarti 1988; Paddayya 1995; Boast 2002; Chadha 2002; Guha 2003; Ray 2008). Wheeler's contribution toward the bureaucratic restructuring of the ASI was not just administrative, but also ideological. As the readers will observe, this influence reverberates throughout this ethnography—conducted more than half a century after Wheeler's tenure. Mortimer Wheeler is the *epistemic leitmotiv* of this book. During my ethnography, I observed that his epistemological shadow overwhelmingly informs the methodological and theoretical bulwark of archaeological practices of the contemporary ASI.[34]

The partition of South Asia in 1947 forced the ASI to reevaluate the archaeological heritage that came under its purview (Wheeler 1949; Chakravarti 1950; Vats 1951; Ghosh 1954). Wheeler's tenure was over in 1948. He was subsequently appointed as an adviser to the Department of Archaeology in Pakistan. The ASI had relinquished the jurisdiction of a substantial portion of the Old Frontier Circle, covering the entire region of the erstwhile West Pakistan and parts of its Eastern Circle, comprising the areas of East Pakistan. Some of the most prominent Buddhist archaeological sites such as Taxila and the northwestern Buddhist Gandhara complex were now in Pakistani territory (Ghosh 1953: 44). Furthermore, the loss of Harappa and Mohenjo-Daro embodied a crucial setback to the organizational subjectivity of the postcolonial ASI. These sites informed the professional subjectivity of the ASI in the last decades of its colonial avatar.[35] The partition of the subcontinent caused radical administrative reorganization. Along with artifacts, the personnel were also divided; soon the number of Circles went up to nine from seven.[36]

By the early 1950s, a systematic exploration of the western states of independent India started.[37] These explorations led to the large-scale excavation of the Harappan sites of Lothal (1955–63), Rangpur (1953–56), Kalibangan (1960–69), and Surkotada (1971–72).[38] These sites were epistemological precursors to the archaeological excavations that this ethnography is based on. With the adoption of the Constitution of India in 1950, "archaeology" was made a concurrent subject under the Seventh Schedule of the Constitution, and in

1953, the ASI undertook the additional responsibility of the upkeep of heritage sites of the 565 princely states that merged with India between 1948 and 1949. The ASI was now the central authority involved in all aspects of archaeological explorations and excavations.[39] It also undertook the maintenance, conservation, and preservation of protected monuments and archaeological sites, and remains of national importance; chemical preservation of monuments and antiquarian remains; architectural survey of monuments; epigraphical and numismatic studies; setting up and running of site museums; training of students in archaeology; archaeological publications; archaeological expeditions outside India; and horticulture operations in and around ancient monuments and sites. The ASI also saw the implementation and regulation of a wide-ranging arsenal of laws for the protection and preservation of archaeological heritage in India.[40]

The ASI is now a bureaucracy attached to the Department of Culture with its headquarters in New Delhi. It now has a three-tier bureaucratic structure: the ASI headquarters based in Delhi headed by a DG, who is assisted by an additional director general (ADG), two joint director generals (Jt DGs), and a group of directors. Each director heads one of the ten Directorates—Horticulture, Science, Epigraphy, Excavation, Museum, Publication, Monument, World Heritage Sites, Conservation, and Antiquity. Then there are Regional Directorates headed by regional directors, followed by twenty-nine Circles headed by superintending archaeologists (SAs) and three Mini Circles headed by deputy superintending archaeologists (Dy SAs). Each Circle is responsible for the maintenance of its monuments in its jurisdiction. Structural conservation is headed by SAs supported by engineers and conservators. The Circles are further divided into Sub Circles headed by conservation assistants who are responsible for the activities carried out at the monuments. There are six Excavation Branches (Ex. Br.), one Prehistory Branch, one Building Survey Project, two Temple Survey Projects, two Epigraphy Branches, and one Science Branch functioning in the ASI.[41] It also has a Horticulture Branch that has four Divisions in Agra, Delhi, Mysore, and Bhubaneswar. Of these numerous wings for conducting specialized archaeological research, the most prominent are the six Excavation Branches. Wheeler established the first Excavation Branch during his tenure, now in Nagpur. Any of the Circles, and the various state departments of archaeology along with the Institute of Archaeology can conduct archaeological excavations.

In 2020, the ASI employed thousands of workers throughout the country, who were in turn responsible for the protection of 3,691 monuments, including 38 UNSECO World Heritage Monuments and ran 45 site museums.[42] By 2005, the ASI had conducted 740 excavations in 300 sites, over the course of 52 seasons, consisting of varied types of archaeological sites—Paleolithic,

Neolithic, and Megalithic sites, burials, rock-cut caves, *stupas*, temples, mosques, churches, forts, water systems, pillars, inscriptions, relics, monolithic statues, and sculptures.[43] Its annual budget, when I undertook this ethnography in 2004–05, was INR 22.3 million, whereas for the year 2016–17 it was INR 76.9 million; and in 2020–21 it is estimated to be INR 124.75 million (Niti Aayog 2020, 127). The ASI's allocation is 30 percent of the total budget of the Ministry of Culture.

The bureaucratic evolution of the postcolonial ASI has been marked by a series of statist review committees to appraise it. This evaluative convention originated in 1939 with a report by Sir Leonard Woolley. Since 1947, there have been many such reviews of the postcolonial ASI. Members comprised politicians, parliamentarians, senior bureaucrats, ex-DGs of the ASI, independent specialists, and university scholars. These review reports have been episodic disciplinarian interventions of the state to regulate the ASI. Systemic criticisms of the workings of the ASI are leveled in these texts and explicit recommendations are put forth. These reports have had an emblematic status in the career of the ASI as a bureaucratic institution. They informed the organizational subjectivity of the ASI as a postcolonial bureaucracy as it evolved and transformed into a dominant statist organization. The Review Committee report (1965) was the first of such postcolonial reviews headed by Mortimer Wheeler, followed by the Expert Group on Archaeology, Mirdha Committee (1983–84), which was headed by Ram Niwas Mirdha, minister of the Water Resources Department. The B. B. Lal Review Committee report (2001), the reverberations of which I felt during my fieldwork, was a comprehensive review of the workings of the organization made by senior ASI archaeologists. This was followed by the Moily Committee (2010), set up by Prime Minister Manmohan Singh under the chairpersonship of former Union Law Minister Veerappa Moily. The statutory statist bodies have also played an important role in appraising the workings of the ASI—from the report of the Estimates Committee of the Lok Sabha (1973–74) to the most recent report of the comptroller and auditor general (CAG) of India (2013) and the Niti Aayog (2020). These review committees' reports acquired a quasi-legal status. They instituted major organizational changes, causing significant bureaucratic transformations in the ASI. However, the recommendations of these reports also had an ambiguous trajectory in the obdurate world of the upper echelons of Indian bureaucracy. They were tabled with authoritative solemnity but were often not heeded, and occasionally forgotten, while their implementation was exceedingly tardy.[44]

In 1984, the Mirdha Committee announced that based on the context and content of the work the ASI conducts, the organization should be declared a scientific organization: "The Archaeological Survey of India should not be considered merely an administrative organization, in view of its highly specialized functions, should be accorded the status of a scientific institution, enjoying autonomy in its functioning, like other comparable institutions under the Government" (Mirdha 1984: 64). It is this disciplinary comprehension of archaeology as a science that was employed by the Allahabad High Court to summon the ASI to conduct archaeological excavation at Ayodhya in 2003 (Khan, Agarwal, and Sharma 2010: 2375; Supreme Court 2019: 567). Many of my informants, who I have regularly spoken with for the past 15 years, have often expressed their frustrations with the Ministry of Culture under which the ASI was instituted. They believed the ASI, like the Survey of India, should be considered a scientific organization under the preview of the Department of Science and Technology.[45] Their concern also had professional ramifications—the most prominent of which was the possibility of acquiring a higher salary. The issue was both a matter of professional status and disciplinary subjectivity. In 1989, a group set up by the Department of Science and Technology further recommended that the ASI be declared a scientific and technological department. However, the shift has not yet occurred. The *91st Report of the Department-Related Parliamentary Standing Committee of Transport, Tourism and Culture*, devoted to the functioning of the ASI, and headed by the member of parliament Nilotpal Basu and tabled in the Rajya Sabha on November 25, 2005, pronounced:

> The Committee is constrained to note that even after a lapse of fifteen years from the date of issue of the notification in this regard no concrete action was taken by Ministry of Culture and Archaeological Survey of India for developing Archaeological Survey of India as a Scientific and Technical Department, which amply indicates the administrative apathy towards the whole issue.... The Committee observes that there has been deviation in the working of Archaeological Survey of India and that it has failed in terms of developing Archaeological Survey of India not merely as an administrative body but also as a spearhead for consolidating the scientific discipline of archaeology in the country. The Committee is of the view that the Archaeological Survey of India needs to reinvent itself, not merely as an administrative wing of the Government, but as an agency for protecting and safeguarding our national heritage, which involves a lot of scientific and technical work. Unless the Archaeological Survey of India converts itself fully into a scientific and technical organization, the basic role and function of the organization will be defeated. (Basu 2005, 10)

In 2013, the CAG report also notes the tardiness:

> The ASI was designated as "Science and Technology department" vide notification of October 1989 by the Ministry of Human Resource Development…. However, the ASI was unable to collect the data as of November 2012. As a result, the department could not be included within the framework of a Science and Technology Institution. (CAG 2013: 173)

The link between science, state, and bureaucracy within postcolonial archaeology is best exemplified by this struggle—between an unwilling Ministry of Culture, which does not want to transfer the ASI, its most prized organization, to the Department of Science and Technology, and the latter department, which, although willing to admit the ASI under its wing, is disciplinarily reluctant.[46] This tension—among governmentality and science, bureaucracy and archaeology—which is at the center of the ASI's postcolonial archaeology, has had a powerful impact on its epistemological production. This palpable anxiety lies at the heart of the epistemic tension explored in this ethnography.

It is important to note here that I only focus on one set of activities of the ASI in this book—archaeological excavations. Excavation is a small part of the massive organizational work that the ASI is involved in, most of which is not engaged with in this book—heritage conservation, preservation, protection of archaeological sites and monuments, running site museums, and horticulture. Archaeological excavations account for a mere 1 percent of the total annual budget of the ASI; however, it is the most crucial task in the making of the organizational imagination of its professional and epistemological subjectivity.[47] Archaeological excavation is the key to its aspiration to be considered as a scientific organization. By the time I began my fieldwork in 2003, the ASI had conducted 292 excavations since 1947 (AACD, File No. 24/2/2003-EENP). It included many archaeological sites in India—prehistoric, proto-historic, Harappan, early historic, Buddhist, Jain, Hindu, Islamic, and even British colonial sites. The ASI has amassed a vast archive of archaeological knowledge about the subcontinent and collected a huge amount of artifacts and material cultures, housed in various sites and museums across the country and in the Central Antiquity Collection of the ASI.[48] It has published a large volume of reports, pamphlets, and books. *Bureaucratic Archaeology* does not attempt to evaluate this enormous knowledge production activity about Indian antiquity by the ASI. This book only delves into the most crucial function of the ASI—archaeological excavations.

In 2013, the CAG produced one of the most momentous reports on the workings of the ASI. This was a "performance audit" carried out by a governmental audit institution on the occasion of 150 years of the ASI.

The audit was conducted between April 2012 and February 2013, based on a close inspection of files and documents related to multiple organizations that worked with the ASI.[49] The CAG's audit was to "assist the executive in identifying the reasons behind deficient performance of the organizations in the field of heritage preservation and conservation for enabling effective rectificatory steps" (CAG 2013, vi). This was a scathing report. It unequivocally stated that the ASI was in a state of disrepair and needed long-term interventions in numerous departments to function as a satisfactory governmental department.

> The most significant failure of ASI related to its core function of field archaeology that included excavation, survey and publication of excavation reports. Presently, ASI's expenditure on excavation is less than one per cent of its total budget. We noted that ASI has no policy governing the selection of excavation sites, timeframes for the completion of excavations and the publication of its findings. (CAG 2013, 221)

My ethnography undertaken nearly eight years earlier preempts this indictment by the CAG. This book is an anthropological study of this epistemological failure of the ASI—it ethnographically plunges into the minutiae of this breakdown.

Ethnographic Methodology

Once, while doing archival research at Cambridge University, I met a senior American archaeologist who had spent a lifetime working in India. On hearing about my project, he pronounced that I was committing career suicide: "ASI will never let you ever excavate in your lifetime," he asserted. "It has a deep memory. It does not forgive," he sonorously proclaimed in an ominous tone. The world of ASI archaeology that I describe in this book is familiar both to Indian and western archaeologists. Trenchant criticisms were often voiced discreetly, but were not articulated publicly. A tangible fear of reprisal by the ASI is an inevitable reality. For both Indian and western archaeologists, any voice of censure or denunciation against the ASI would mean revocation of their license to excavate in India, and an end to their career as archaeologist, in India at least. Many stories abound in the trenches of Indian archaeology of distinguished archaeologists with longstanding experience being denied licenses to excavate because of their public differences with the ASI.

Bureaucratic institutions in the Indian state are impregnable structures. Obtaining permissions and getting access to influential officials require intricate maneuvering through turgid structures. Complex machinations and convoluted intrigues are at work. Every transaction is met with stubborn resistance and often protracted antagonism. An elderly informant once grimly and laconically remarked, when I asked him about his life as a career archaeologist with the ASI: "Everyone gets crushed in ASI" (*ASI mein, sab pis jaathe hain*). In such a situation, it was not a simple task for an outsider like me to unassumingly enter the ASI and conduct ethnographic investigations. It was inexorably daunting, involving enormous amount of patience, laborious paperwork, inconsiderate officials, indifferent orderlies, and an obstinate bureaucracy that was corrupt, as well as intimidating. If I had exposed my true "ethnographic self" to this impervious organization, it would have been impossible to get official permission to work at the excavation sites. To embed myself in ASI archaeological sites and do immersive ethnography, I had to negotiate two forms of bureaucratic hurdles. The first involved getting official permission, "in writing" (*likhit mein*), from the DG headquarters in New Delhi to go to an archaeological site. Second, I had to explain my research objectives and the nature of ethnographic research to my informants at the ASI sites. Each required a different strategy.

In the official letters I submitted to the DG office of the ASI in New Delhi, I introduced my project as a "history of Indus archaeology."[50] This strategy was not always successful. In two cases, excavation directors denied me permission to stay at the site and work. As an Indian citizen, I had the right to visit archaeological excavation anywhere in the country. However, the permission I sought was to allow me to stay in the ASI camp—which was only possible through the generosity of the organization. For my ethnography, it was indispensable to embed myself in an ASI excavation camp. It was imperative not just to observe the happenings in the archaeological site but also to be part of the social and cultural life in the ASI camp. Although I visited all the sites mentioned in this book, I was only allowed permission to stay in four archaeological campsites. I spent two excavation seasons conducting ethnographic work in the ASI sites. In the first season of 2003–04, I lived and worked at the sites of Dholavira (Gujarat), Baror (Rajasthan), and Hansi (Haryana), and visited the sites of Juni Kuran (Gujarat), Chak 86 (Rajasthan), and Tarkhanewala Dera (Rajasthan). In the second season of 2004–05, I worked at the sites of Baror (Rajasthan), Bhirrana (Haryana), and Hansi (Haryana), and visited Rakhigarhi (Haryana). The time I spent at the sites ranged from three months to three weeks, depending on the generosity of my bureaucratic host.

To gain the confidence of the members of the ASI, I explained the objectives of my project to everyone I came in contact with—from senior officers to laborers. The levels of suspicion, anxieties, and misgivings were high. Due to the just concluded ASI excavations at Ayodhya, the winter of 2003 was a time of astonishing duress and pressure for the ASI archaeologists and staff. The apprehension was also exacerbated by the Central Bureau of Investigation

(CBI)—the national crime-investigating agency—scrutinizing corruption charges against several top ASI officials. In 2002, it had brought corruption charges against the ASI staff of the Rakhigarhi excavation—the largest Harappan site in the country. An informant once told me after a few weeks of my stay at Dholavira that some staff members thought I was an undercover CBI agent investigating corruption in the ASI. In a week of my interaction with the members of the ASI staff at a site, most knew that I was an Indian citizen working as a historian and anthropologist and was affiliated with an American university. However, due to a heightened sense of suspicion, no one was willing to be interviewed on tape. If I was seen in the field with a notepad and pen, my informants felt uncomfortable. The quotes I use in this book were consigned to memory and written between a few minutes to two hours after the interactions with my informants. The ethnographic evidence used in this book is based on detailed field notes I wrote multiple times a day. The ASI is a central government bureaucracy with a multilingual cadre; however, most of my informants spoke to me in Hindi, with English words and phrases liberally employed, especially for technical terms. I have cautiously and judiciously embedded these Hindi inter-texts in my ethnographic narrative to accentuate the cultural ecology of my interaction with my informants in order to provide a semantic texture to the orality of my ethnography. I have taken all the photographs that appear in this book with official permission from the directors of the respective excavation sites.

At the ASI, like all statist apparatuses, bureaucratic discourse is articulated through inscriptive texts—memos, plans, budgets, note-sheets, letters, official orders, permissions, and files (Hull 2012). Along with these, I observed that the most overwhelming form through which the bureaucratic discourse circulated and enacted was through physical, corporeal interaction in the offices and the excavation sites. As an ethnographer who was embedded in the ASI camp and excavation sites, I had become a participant-observer. I was privy to intimate interactions between officers, archaeologists, staff, and laborers. Through minute observations, close conversations, and informal dialogue with my informants and participation in group activities, I accumulated ethnographic evidence for this book. Long narratives, stories, anecdotes, tales, complaints, criticisms, grumblings, gossips, jokes, puns, hearsay, rumors, murmurs, and even fables were related to me. These were shared in the close confines of tattered tents in the middle of bitterly cold nights; in the vast open expanse of sunny winter afternoons atop ancient archaeological mounds; under the shade of rainbow-colored umbrellas crouched over wooden tables stacked with drawings of site stratigraphy; and even in the claustrophobic enclosures of dusty, suffocating offices.

Within organizational studies, this kind of discursive ecology has been defined as "instances of talk, text, and conversations that take place within organizational 'boundaries'" (Bergström and Knights 2006, 355), which become indispensable to comprehend the subjectivity of individuals while working in an institution (Chia 2000, 514; Fairclough 2005). I observed that the organizational discourse circulated as an ontological affect—evolving, changing, transmuting, breathing alive (Hardt and Negri 2009, 379)—like a living subject rather than the sterile, fixated discursive universe of inscriptive texts. Over the two years of expansive fieldwork, through regular interaction, and more than a decade of friendship, I have become a confidant of sorts to my informants. Many spoke freely about their personal anxieties and professional tribulations. I have liberally inserted into this book this affective evidence; sauntering ephemerally throughout the narrative of this book, it forms the bulk of my ethnographic account.

For readers who are looking for stable paper-based evidence, I have appended my assertions in this book with evidence and citations from the ASI archives. *Bureaucratic Archaeology* is an ethnography of practice; this is not a textual study, and, therefore, I use textual archive as secondary data, subsidiary to my observation. My primary data is ethnographic observations. This is not a historical study or an organizational study, although both these scholarly fields deeply inform my ethnographic narrative. The innumerable official documents I have cited in this book emerge from the extensive archival research I conducted at the ASI headquarters. I was given permission by the DG to work in the Records Room of the ASI at its headquarters in Delhi. It was a tiny, dingy, dilapidated, dusty, and despairing niche of colonial architecture. A single padlock guarded this weary room full of old and new files stacked on tired wooden racks, lit by a single incandescent bulb. However, here I could access a large number of documents from the colonial and postcolonial period, which are cited throughout this book (as AACD). The Right to Information (RTI) Act of 2005 opened up for the common public access to the workings of the Indian state like never before. I gained access to many of the documents that I have cited in the book with the availability of these texts in the public arena courtesy of the RTI Act. The CAG report (2013) and the most recent Niti Aayog report (2020) are deployed throughout the book as corroborative documents (of statist bureaucracy) that retrospectively provide evidential reinforcement to the ethnographic claims I make.

Finally, it is important to underscore that the long lag between the ethnography and its eventual publication is my attempt at safeguarding the professional well-being of my informants. Most of my informants belonged to the lower levels of the organizational hierarchy of the ASI. During my work, I became viscerally conscious of the punitive consequences on my informants if they were identified. "ASI has the memory of an elephant" (*haathi ki yaadash hai*, ASI *ki*). "It rarely forgets" (*kabhi nahi bhooltha*), an upper division clerk (UDC) reminded me during an extensive exchange with him. Another time, an AA who I had become close to during my days at the ASI cautioned me: "Carefully publish your book Ashish *ji*. ASI has to change, but not at the cost of our jobs" (Ashish *ji, dhyan se chappana apni kitabh ko*. ASI *ko badlna jaruri hai, per koshish karna ki haamari naukari na chin jayae*.). Sometimes this kind of warning would be articulated indiscreetly, other times it was suggested prudently. The fear was palpable, and the trepidation tangible. I was cognizant of the fact that if the ASI bureaucracy turns vindictive because of the critical nature of the disclosures in this book, it will be able to identify my informants and threaten their careers. However, today nearly 16 years after my ethnography, most of my informants have either retired from the ASI or have risen to powerful positions within its institutional hierarchy. Identification does not pose a risk to their careers now. An AA whom I met 10 years after my ethnography was surprised that I had not published my book. "There is nothing to fear now" (*Ab darne ki koi baath nahi hai*). He assured me that my anxieties were unfounded.[51] Needless to say, in such apprehensive circumstances, it becomes imperative for me to continue to protect the identity of my informants. Therefore, I disaggregate their voices; dislocate their spatiality; and only use official designations to maintain a coherence of my ethnographic narrative—lower division clerk (LDC), UDC, AA, assistant superintending archaeologist (ASA), Dy SA, SA, Jt DG, and the DG.

Notes

1. By 2002, the ASI had conducted 292 excavations (Basu 2005, 14).
2. My ethnographic intervention is bounded by archaeological work conducted by the ASI; this book is not a work of comparative anthropology. My choice was driven by the fact that university-led archaeological excavations in India do not command the epistemological valence or political legitimacy and statist authority that an ASI excavation exerts. I believe that it is important to study how university archaeological departments produce archaeological knowledge in India, exclusively or in collaboration with international universities and partners, along with various provincial statist archaeological institutions. I hope that the work I have done will provide a theoretical framework for others to do historical and anthropological interrogation of non-ASI excavations in India.
3. Here I am very specifically differentiating between Appadurai's "alternative modernities," Lisa Rofel's "other modernities," Marilyn Strathern's "new

modernities," Marshal Sahlins's "indigenous modernities," or Sivaramakrishnan and Agrawal's "regional modernities" (Appadurai 1991; Rofel 1999; Strathern 1999; Sahlins 1999; Sivaramakrishnan and Agrawal 2003 respectively).

4. There is a large literature on this self-reflexive disciplinary struggle (especially see Flannery 1967; Clarke 1973; Hodder 1991; Preucel 1995; Van Pool and Van Pool 1999; Joffe 2003; Rathje, Shanks, and Witmore 2013).

5. Some of the canonical texts that forthrightly informed and formulated the theoretical world of processual archaeology are Binford (1962, 1965); Clarke (1968); Watson, LeBlanc, and Redman (1971); Binford and Quimby (1972); Schiffer (1976, 1987, 1988); Salmon (1978); and Dunnell (1980).

6. The excavations conducted by K. Paddayya in the Paleolithic and Neolithic sites in Hunsgi Valley (Shorapur Doab), peninsular India, are some of the foremost examples of procesual archaeological methods in India (Paddayya 1974, 1978, 1987, 1990, 2016).

7. Some of the most combative texts that constructed the theoretical universe of post-processual archaeology are Hodder (1982, 1986, 1991, 1992, 1995); Shanks and Tilley (1987, 1992); Bapty and Yates (1990); and Tilley (1993).

8. During my years at Stanford University as a graduate student, I witnessed the de-escalation of some of these bitter debates during a series of talks and discussion by the proponents of both processual and post-processual archaeology under the aegis of the Stanford Archaeology Centre (between 2002 and 2011). A resulting reconciliatory approach forms the book *Archaeology in the Making: Conversations through a Discipline* that brings into dialogue some of the foremost thinkers and theoreticians of multiple schools of archaeology. The importance of this book with 21 interlocutors formidably suggested that the battle lines between processualists and post-processualists had mellowed down and a holistic approach toward archaeological practice had to be pursued. At the center of this resuscitated archaeological practice was an undiluted emphasis on an empirical evidential paradigm irrespective of theoretical orientation (Rathje, Shanks, and Witmore 2013).

9. For a recent appraisal see Lucas (2019, 42–57).

10. Dilip Chakrabarti's *A History of Indian Archaeology from the Beginning to 1947* published in 1988 is arguably the first disciplinarian history of India archaeology. Written as an evolutionary chronology of Indian archaeology, it emphasized the teleological move of archaeology from the literary confines of Indological studies in the eighteenth century with the establishment of the Asiatic Society in 1784 and ended with the transformation of the ASI into a scientific organization by Mortimer Wheeler in 1948. In his book, the dramatic interventions of individuals were framed within the disciplinary discourse of archaeology and its evolution from an antiquarian fixation of the colonial elite

to a scientific exploration of the Indian material past. The individual's agency was subsumed under a broader evolutionary account of archaeology. However, this book fails to take into account the hegemonic structure of the colony. Although the colonial apparatus was given agency for the development of the discipline, Chakrabarti did not analyze its ideological impetus.

11. The relationship between archaeologists and excavation is similar to the metaphor that is invoked by Peter Galison about the goals of the experimentalist in high energy physics: "They are like the relationship of Michelangelo's *David* to the block of marble from which it was hewn: the statue is in stone, but the background has to be carved away in order to see it" (quoted in Lenoir 1997, 38).

12. Similar works of historically locating the scientific genealogy of other field disciplines such as geology (Rudwick 1985; Secord 1986; Laudan 1987), paleontology (Rudwick 2008), and geography (Edney 1997) frame the critical framework of my discussions in the book.

13. Along with the rise of subaltern studies (Chatterjee 2012), historians of the colony in India also began an investigation of the impact of science in the making of the colony (for example, see Kumar 1995; Barber 1996; Praksh 1999; Chakrabarti 2004; Raina and Habib 2006), including medicine (Arnold 2000; Chakrabarti 2010) and indigo plantation (Kumar 2013).

14. This includes laboratory science and technology (Visvanathan 1985, 1997), physics (Abraham 1998; Phalkey 2013; Chowdhury 2016; Banerjee 2020), space program (Raj 2000), digital technology (Aneesh 2006), biotechnology (Rajan 2006; Prasad 2014; Copeman and Banerjee 2020), information technology (Dasgupta 2015; Amrute 2016), and development (Nandy 1988; Alvares 1992), to name some influential and invigorating book-length studies.

15. Some examples of early works were Rose and Miller (1992); Barry, Osborn, and Rose (1996); Braun (2000); Ferguson and Gupta (2002); Bratich, Packer, and McCarthy (2003); Agrawal (2005); Walters and Haahr (2005).

16. The term "colonial governmentality" was first deployed by the anthropologist David Scott's rather persuasive essay that delineates the topography of colonial power of state governance by creating distinctively new forms of subjectivity and society in colonial Sri Lanka. Scott concentrates on a particularly precise moment of Sri Lankan history where he argues that modernity emerges following the Colebrooke-Cameron constitutional reforms in the early 1830s (Scott 1995). A more elaborate exposition of "colonial governmentality" is conducted by Gyan Prakash, who investigates the colonial state's civilizing mission in the context of the scientific project in India. Prakash argues that the advancement of the native population through the inculcation of a

scientific temperament with brute force lays bare the political forms of colonial oppression. Prakash provocatively argues that European governmentality was distinctly dissimilar to the one deployed in the colony because the purpose here was to dominate in order to liberate (Prakash 1999). The theoretical fecundity of "colonial governmentality" has given rise to numerous works that have vigilantly investigated the distributed strategies and effects of colonial power and its relationships to political modernity; for instance, see Li (2007).

17. On January 22, 1862, Lord Canning noted:

> It will not be to our credit, as an enlightened ruling power, if we continue to allow such fields of investigation, as the remains of the old Buddhist capital in Behar, the vast ruins of Kanouj, the plains around Delhi, studded with ruins more thickly than even the Campagna of Rome, and many others, to remain without examination that they have hitherto revived. Everything that has hitherto been done in this way has been done by private persons, imperfectly and without system. (Quoted in Cunningham 1871, ii)

18. On the impact of William Jones on the history of Indology see Mukherjee (1968); Kejariwal (1988); Chakrabarti (1988, 1997); Paddyya (1995); Trautmann (1997); and Murray (1998). The Lucknow Bench of the Allahabad High Court also traced the origin of the ASI to William Jones's work (Khan, Agarwal, and Sharma 2010, 2177–79).

19. See Chakrabarti (1988, 1997); Paddayya (1995); Dirks (1994); Cohn (1996); and Guha-Thakurta (2005) for a discerning narrative of the historical teleology of colonial archaeology in India.

20. Other organizations were the Survey of India (1767), the Geological Survey of India (1851), the Botanical Survey of India (1890), and the Anthropological Survey of India (1945). The Zoological Survey of India (1969) and the Forest Survey of India (1981) were established by the postcolonial state.

21. Cunningham was able to locate the sites of Taxila, Sangala, Srughna, Ahichchhatra, Bairat, Sankisa, Shravasti, Kaushambi, Padmavati, Vaishali, and Nalanda mentioned by the Chinese traveler Hsüan-tsang. Some of these sites saw extensive archaeological excavation under the ASI in the twentieth century. See Paddayya (1995, 130); Chakrabarti (1988, 115); Singh (2008, 265); Ray (2019).

22. On a comprehensive history of the archaeological exploits of Alexander Cunningham, see Imam (1966).

23. For an extensive history of Buddhist archaeology in India with specific reference to Cunningham, see Leoshko (2003). She argues that the direction of subsequent archaeological research of Buddhism in India has been acutely hindered by Cunningham's fetish for geographically locating sites connected with the life of the historical Buddha.

24. James Burgess succeeded Cunningham as the DG of the ASI (1886–89). He was an architect who joined the ASI as the surveyor for western India and along with James Fergusson was instrumental in extensively mapping the Buddhist rock cut caves of western India. From 1889 to 1902, the ASI was bereft of a DG. Also see Paddaya (1995, 133).

25. J. B. Kieth, a senior officer of the ASI, who had headed the North Western Circle, wrote to Lord Curzon in 1900, while the search for a new DG was on: "For years the necessities of Indian Archaeology have fallen into the hands of philologist who have made a preserve in pressing home the exploded theories of professor Max Muller, largely responsible for the exaggerations of Western civilization" (quoted in Lahiri 2005, 45).

26. For an engrossing history on the Marshall period of the ASI, see Lahiri (2005, 2012).

27. It is vital to note the rather overbearing relationship of Buddhism over Harappan sites in the scholarship of colonial archaeology. Archaeologists and explorers who visited the sites of Harappa and Mohenjo-Daro before these were official declared sites of the "Indus civilization" in 1924 viewed them through the hypothetical scaffolding of Buddhist archaeology. From Alexander Cunningham to R. D. Bhandarkar, none was able to comprehend their pre-Buddhist significance because they were obsessively searching for Buddhist remains. It was a series of chance discoveries and the "brilliance" of two colonial native archaeologists—Rakhal Das Banerji and Daya Ram Sahni—under the leadership of John Marshall that caused the discovery of the civilization (AACD, File No. 839/1925). See Lahiri (2005) for an engaging account along with Trautmann and Sinopoli (2002), and more recently Ray (2008).

28. Philip Meadows Taylor, who discovered the Megalithic sites in the Deccan during his service with the Hyderabad state (1824–58), and Robert Bruce Foote of the Geological Survey of India, who discovered close to 450 Paleolithic sites in southern India and Gujarat, were pioneers of pre-historic Indian archaeology. See Taylor (1929) and Foote (1866, 1916); also see Paddayya (1995) and Chakrabarti (1979) for a historical account.

29. See Lees (2019) and Dodson (2020) for recent accounts on the nature of colonial bureaucracy in India.

30. The history of Indian archaeology (and especially the ASI) has been overwhelmed by the fixation on individual figures rather than the political genealogies that determined the discursive trajectory of the discipline. Extraordinary agency was attributed to individual character but the ideological structures in which they worked were ignored if not undermined. While colonial temporality was acknowledged, its ideological implications were treated as a historical inevitability without an adequate theorization of its contingent nature. In these historical narratives, spectacular individuals

mediated archaeology's march of uncovering the Indian past. Examples range from William Jones and his discovery of the resemblance between Sanskrit, ancient Greek, and Latin, to James Princep and his decipherment of Brahmi and opening up the world of Ashoka; Alexander Cunningham and his exposure of Buddhist monumentality; and finally Sir Mortimer Wheeler and his transformation of the ASI into a scientific organization. These were not disciplinary histories of archaeology in India but predominantly chronological accounts of individual figures and their contributions. In these narratives, prominent individuals were made the center of the historical trajectory of the discipline while the ideological and structural mediation of the colony was taken for granted. For example, see Singh (2004); Lahiri (2005); Ray (2008).

31.   The earliest colonial legislation for heritage protection in colonial India was the Bengal Charitable Endowments, Public Buildings and Escheats Regulation, of 1810, followed by the Madras Endowments and Escheats Regulation of 1817. However, it was the Indian Treasure Trove Act of 1878 that was the first legislation explicitly enacted to regulate archaeological material culture. See Trivedi (2018).

32.   See AACD, File No. 1013/1939 and File No. 1195/1940 for letters, articles, and notes criticizing the Wooloey report by ASI officials and influential explorers such as Aurel Stein. Also see Possehl (1993b, 1); Paddayya (1995, 134).

33.   Gregory Possehl in his detailed assessment of the report rather unforgivably and probably accurately notes:

> When an experienced man offers "proofs" that are not "proofs" but only opinion based on shaky observations and interviews, causing a sensation may bring ill notice to him. It was after all, a hasty trip to a huge country, reviewing a very substantial institution with hundreds employees and a tradition that goes back to mid-nineteenth century. In the end one has the impression that Sir Leonard Wooly was a man of strong opinions, not all of which have survived the test of time. (Possehl 1993b, 14)

34.   Before I began this ethnography, I had conducted archival research on the impact of Wheeler's tenure on the colonial ASI (Chadha 2002).

35.   B. B. Lal in his 2001 review of the ASI called this a "stunning blow to its cultural heritage" (Lal 2001, 26).

36.   The composition of the Central Department of the ASI in 1949 consisted of: (*a*) the supervisory staff, comprising director general, joint director general, deputy director general for administration and deputy director general for explorations; (*b*) the technical staff consisting of archaeological engineer and assistant engineer, archaeological chemist and assistant archaeological

chemist at the headquarters; (*c*) the specialized staff comprising epigraphical superintendent, assistant superintendent and assistant superintendent for Arabic and Persian inscriptions in the Epigraphy Branch. Superintending and assistant superintending archaeologists were appointed in the nine Circles to organize and supervise the work in each Circle (Thakran 2000, 48).

37. A. Ghosh explored the dry bed of the Ghaggar whereas B. B. Lal concentrated on the upper Ganga basin. Ghosh discovered 150 Harappan, Painted Grey Ware and successive cultural sites (Thakran 2000, 48).

38. Sites of Banawali, Kuntasi, Daimambad, Rojdi, Padri, Bhagwanpura, and Kunal were some of the other prominent Harappan excavations until the 1980s.

39. Each state in India has its local state department of archaeology; by 1982, there were 23 such departments, which also conducted excavations and conservation work.

40. Some of the most important of these laws are the Indian Treasure Trove Act (1878), the Ancient Monuments Preservation Act (1904), the Ancient and Historical Monuments and Archaeological Sites and Remains Act (1951, 1958, and 2010), and the Antiquities and Art Treasures (AAT) Act (1972).

41. The Science Branch of the ASI was established in 1917. It is mainly focused on the science of conservation and preservation of monuments and artifacts. It is rarely involved with the science of archaeological excavation.

42. According to the Niti Aayog's 2020 "Working Report of Improving Heritage Management in India," there are more than 400,000 heritage structures in India including the centrally protected monuments, state protected monuments (4,538), heritage buildings under various religious trusts, 50 historic cities, and more than 1,800 archaeological sites (Niti Aayog 2020, 27).

43. From 1953–54 to 2004–05, a total of 1,851 excavations were conducted by the ASI, various state departments of archaeology, and university departments. These have been reported in the ASI's annual bulletin—*Indian Archaeology: A Review* (hereafter, *IAR*).

44. For details on the non-implementation of the recommendations on these reports see CAG (2013, 209–14).

45. The Survey of India was the cartographic and mapping organization of the Indian state. The Anthropological Survey of India was also under the Ministry of Culture, whereas the Geological Survey of India was under the Ministry of Mines.

46. The Basu report noted: "The nature of functions and activities of Archaeological Survey of India were of such nature that it could not be so far made into a wholly scientific and technical institution. However, efforts have been made

to take advantage of technical and scientific expertise in various disciplines of archaeology" (Basu 2005, 9).

47. The CAG report states that between 2007 and 2012 only 1 percent of the total ASI budget was spent on excavation projects. During this time period, 41 percent was used for conservation work and 2 percent for running site museums; the rest of the 56 percent of the budget was for establishment costs (CAG 2013, 158). However, in 1984, the Mirdha Committee reported that 7 percent of the total budget was used for excavation and exploration work (Mirdha 1984, 15).

48. The Central Antiquity Collection was established in 1954 and is housed in Purana Quilla in New Delhi.

49. This included the Ministry of Culture, National Monument Authority, National Museum, Delhi, National Culture Fund, Indian Museum, Kolkata, Salar Jung Museum, Hyderabad, Allahabad Museum, Allahabad, Victoria Memorial Hall, Kolkata, Asiatic Society, Kolkata, Asiatic Society, Mumbai, and the Chhatrapati Shivaji Maharaj Vastu Sangrahalaya, Mumbai.

50. Latour and Woolgar in their introduction to *Laboratory Life* underscore that the scholarly "label" of a historian or a philosopher is more successful in subduing the participant's sense of suspicion than the disciplinary grasp of anthropology or sociology, which have more intrusive emphases (Latour and Woolger 1986, 20).

51. There is a vast literature in the ethics of anthropology that delves into the significance of protecting informants; however, my decision was informed by my own personal ethics that I acquired during my days as a trained social worker and a political activist working in the tribal areas of Maharashtra and Gujarat in the 1990s. Subsequently, as a student anthropologist at Stanford, the ethics of the discipline were put into a very sharp relief with the publication of Patrick Tierney's *Darkness in El Dorado* that documented the unethical exploitation of the Yanomami, an indigenous people of Venezuela and northern Brazil, by scientific researchers and anthropologists (Tierney 2002). For recent debates and conversations in anthropological ethics, see Plemmons and Barker (2017).

2 The Making of the Indus–Saraswati Civilization

It was early morning at the Archaeological Survey of India (ASI) excavation site at Bhirrana. The mechanized roar of passing tractors along with the sound of chirping birds broke my sleep. It was my first day at the site. I had arrived the previous evening from Baror, another ASI site in Sri Ganganagar district in Rajasthan, around 20 kilometers away from the Pakistan border.[1] Bhirrana was in the Fatehabad district of Haryana, located next to a bustling village of the same name.[2] After breakfast at the campsite canteen, I was soon walking on the excavation mound. The 30,000 square meter site was less than 50 meters away from the ASI camp. It was separated by a nondescript district road on which plied the occasional state transport buses and local tractors (*IAR 2003–04* 2011, 43). The excavation mound, rising 5 meters above the road, was neatly divided into many dozen squares.[3] Around 100 workers were busy in the various activities typical of an excavation site—digging, cleaning, and hauling the excavated soil to a dump at the edge of the mound. At one corner of the site, I located the site director—the superintending archaeologist (SA) of the ASI Excavation Branch (Ex. Br.) 1, Nagpur. He was a man in his mid-fifties, donning a white, cotton, wide-brim cricket hat. The SA was engrossed in overseeing a group of women workers, giving instructions as they meticulously cleaned a trench with brushes of varying sizes. He was reputed to be one of the best field archaeologists of the ASI, who had spent a large part of his earlier career in the 1980s and 1990s working at the Harappan sites of Banawali (Haryana) and Dholavira (Gujarat). According to my informants, he was an "old Harappan hand" and now headed the best excavation branch of the ASI—the Nagpur Ex. Br.

Bhirrana was discovered in 1982. Ineffective protection by the Haryana Department of Archaeology and Museums meant that a football field, an abandoned Muslim cemetery, and the mud huts of Dalit encroachers now crowded the site (Rao et al. 2004; *IAR 2003–04* 2011, 42–56). The excavation began 20 years after the site's discovery, in 2003–04, under the ideological aegis of the Saraswati Heritage Project (SHP), and continued for three seasons until the spring of 2006. My ethnographic work was conducted in its second season of excavation in 2004–05. An article discussing the first season's excavation described the site as a Harappan mound, "located in the northern outskirts of the village [Bhirrana], overlooking the left bank of the Saraswati" and defined the excavation objectives as: "[D]etermining the regional identity of the Harappans in the Saraswati river valley; understanding the cultural sequence and chronology of the site; and settlement pattern of the early Harappans in the Saraswati valley" (Rao et al. 2004, 20).

The SA began the site tour by taking me to the western corner of the mound, next to the Muslim burial ground, to show the circular pit dwelling discovered the previous season. The earliest settlers of Bhirrana had lived in subterranean pit dwellings, circular in structure with an average diameter of 2.3 meters, occasionally lined with mud bricks (*IAR 2003–04* 2011, 43). As we stood talking, a draughtsman under the shade of a multicolored field umbrella made drawings of the unearthed structure. He was assisted by a couple of workmen who crouched in the 2-meter-deep trench meticulously taking measurements of features unearthed in the trench. During the course of our conversation, the SA proudly remarked that the carbon-14 dates that they had obtained from these pit dwellings had temporally dated the site to as early as Kot Diji (in Sindh, Pakistan), one of the earliest of the Early Harappan sites dated to 3200–2600 BCE (*IAR 2004–05* 2014, 57).[4] These dates, he explained, were obtained from about half a dozen charcoal samples given to the Radio Carbon Dating Laboratory of the Birbal Sahni Institute of Paleobotany in Lucknow.[5] "This area that you see," he gesticulated with his outstretched hand, pointing to the verdant greenery that surrounded the site,

> was the fertile bed of the river Saraswati. Right in its centre is this site inhabited for three millennia. And here we are getting dates analogous to the Kot Diji phase of the Harappans. And we know that the *Rig Veda* was composed in this area. This proves beyond doubt that the Harappans in the Saraswati basin were not only as early as those found in the western part of the Indus civilization, but that these were Aryans—the Vedic Harappans.[6]

This "scientific" association between the Vedas, the Harappans, and the River Saraswati and its synthesis into a narrative whole at an archaeological site of the ASI in 2005 in the dusty countryside of northern India was not without history or politics, and continued to reverberate even in 2020.

Archaeology of the Harappan civilization was not without politics in South Asia. Since its discovery nearly a century ago, controversies and contestation have followed its epistemological trajectory. We know a great deal about the Harappan civilization's vast terrestrial expanse, distinct material cultural assemblages, highly evolved settlement pattern, efficacious subsistence system, complex architectural planning, proficient resource extraction, and widespread trading connections.

However, meaning-making in Harappan archaeology has been a turgid process. Multiple opposing theories and contrasting interpretations of its birth to its demise, its language and script, its society, social organization and religion, and its ethnicity and genetic identity have densely populated the discursive ecology of Harappan archaeology. At its birth, this immense knowledge production activity was closely linked to colonialism and imperialism—its institutional apparatus and its civilizing mission. Subsequently, with a rising nationalist movement in pre-partition India, followed by the construction of a statist identity in the ensuing postcolonial decades, Harappan archaeology played a formidable role in providing India with a hoary past—intimately tied to the idea of the nation state.

This congested intersectional field of contesting narratives, mythological tales, scientific data, interpretative fictions, religious dogmas, and nationalist ideologies has produced an "epistemic murk" (Taussig 1987). In this murkiness, facts are clouded, data is undermined, narratives are invented, myths are naturalized, and science is subverted—not dissimilar to the archaeology of Ayodhya. If Lord Rama was the divine center of the property dispute at Ayodhya, then Goddess Saraswati was the celestial pivot of the reconfiguration of the Harappan civilization. By 2004, she had been summoned as a riverine divinity by Hindu fundamentalist forces by appropriating the disciplinary discourse of archaeology, geology, and geography to dislodge the River Indus as the territorial center of the ancient civilization. The 100 years of Harappan archaeology was not merely an epistemological topography, it was a fraught political terrain—the backdrop of my ethnography.

Saraswati in the Aryan–Harappan debate

By the late twentieth century, Indo-European linguistics had established a formidable evidential consensus on the linguistic homogeneity of the Aryan people or race.[7] However, other aspects of the Aryans remain a matter of conjecture and controversy. There is consensus neither on the claims of an original Aryan homeland and an original proto-Indo-European mother language (Bronkhorst and Deshpande 1999; Bryant 2001; Bryant and Patton 2005) nor on theories about the dispersal (Anthony et al. 1986; Anthony 1991, 1995, 2007; Lamberg-Karlovsky 2002) and movement of the Aryan people.[8] This uncertainty has fostered Hindutva scholarship that challenges the idea of Aryan migration into India, and argues that the Aryans are indigenous to India.[9] On the other hand, in the case of the Harappans, there is a sizeable archaeological record that provides rich evidence about their material existence, but no undisputed empirical evidence about the language they spoke and their religious and social life.[10] Only circumstantial evidence is available, which has led to a large scholarship based on assumptions and conjectures.[11] The weak empirical nature of archaeological evidence has provided easy fodder for Hindutva narratives about Harappan archaeology, facilitating the creation of a new archaeo-ethnic category—the Vedic Harappans—that combines the literary description of the Vedic texts with the vast material culture of the Harappan civilization.[12] The Vedic Harappans are considered to be authors of the "Out of India theory"—a speculative premise in which the Harappan civilization becomes the birthplace of the indigenous Aryans who spoke the proto-Indo-European language and spread throughout the Eurasian world (Frawley 1994; Elst 1999).

Accounts of ancient India produced in the nineteenth and early twentieth centuries centered on the Indo-European Aryans. Colonial Indologists had created a historical narrative attributing to Aryans the birth of the Indian civilization (Trautmann 1997, 2008; Chakrabarti 1997). From William Jones's influential work in 1807, which proposed the notion of the "Aryan race" and "Indo-European linguistics," until the discovery of the Harappan civilization (Jones 1807), it was widely believed that the Aryans entered India from the west and inhabited the subcontinent for the first time. By the 1920s, the Aryan theory of racial intrusion had been buttressed by more than a century of comparative philology and ethnology. The fundamental assertion of this theory was that the Aryans were a superior racial group that occupied the river valleys of northwestern India and the Gangetic plains by vanquishing the weaker indigenous tribes and creating colonies (Leach 1990; Chakrabarti 1997; Trautmann 1997, 2008; Bryant 2001; Thapar 2001). However, the date of the arrival of the Aryans is a conjectural area of scholarship principally based on the philological analysis of the internal structure of the *Rig Veda*.[13] We do not have any absolute dates; only relative dates are postulated, and these fluctuate between 1700 BCE and 1100 BCE.[14] It is widely assumed that around this time the authors of the *Rig Veda* were in the geographical area of the Sapta-Sindhu—the land of seven rivers geographically located in northwestern India in the Punjab. Therefore, the period between 1700 BCE and 1100 BCE becomes significant, because it is only within this small time slot that the Harappans and the Aryans could have overlapped.[15]

It was Mortimer Wheeler who attempted to fix this contact, albeit envisioning it as a violent confrontation. This revived Gordon Childe's 1926 theory that the "Aryans were just the destroyers of the newly discovered [Harappan] culture" (Childe 1926, 34).[16] Wheeler's conclusions were based upon the analysis of skeletons found in Cemetery "H" in Harappa.[17] His claims seemed objective and definitive, for he was able to not only marshal archaeological evidence but also successfully employ anthropometric criteria to reinforce his propositions. The argument for anthropometric similarities between the skeletal remains in

Mohenjo-Daro and the southern Indian Dravidian "race" gained legitimacy, giving rise to the theory of the Dravidian origin of the Harappans.[18] Both theories attempted to provide a scientific bulwark to the narrative of the invading Aryans in their horses and chariots who decimated the Dravidians and pushed them southward. Wheeler's flawed theory was subsequently discredited (Dales 1964; Kennedy 1994), and the narrative of Aryan invasion was toned down into the idea of Aryan mobility—a diffusion model of migrating Aryans interacting with indigenous settlers (Thapar 1984; Allchin and Allchin 1997; Jha 1998; Sharma 1999).

In addition to debates about the exact moment of interaction and its sociopolitical character, the question of the physical location of contact has been at the center of the Aryan–Harappan debate. It is here that the River Saraswati comes into play. Until 1947, major archaeological sites of the Harappan civilization had been chiefly located on the banks of the River Indus;[19] however, following extensive exploratory work in Haryana, Rajasthan, and Gujarat, more than 1,400 sites were discovered in India by the 1990s (Thakran 2000). All these sites were at a considerable distance from the catchment area of the Indus (200 to 500 kilometers away) and were located in the arid zones of Saurashtra and Kutch in Gujarat and the semi-arid region of northern Rajasthan and Haryana in India, and Bahawalpur in Pakistan. Large clusters of these sites were situated on the dry paleo-channels of the Ghaggar–Hakra Rivers in India and Pakistan. It is this monsoon-fed Ghaggar–Hakra that has been suggested as the terra-firma manifestation of the Saraswati. The endeavor has been to force-fit the literary, social, and religious imagination of the Vedic Aryans with the monumental material manifestations of the Harappans, giving birth to the category of the Vedic Harappans (as indigenous Aryan) living on the fertile plains of the Indus and the Saraswati.[20] These discoveries and subsequent archaeological excavations were responsible for the birth of the idea of the Vedic Harappans, so the Indus civilization was renamed as the Indus–Saraswati civilization, or the more Sanskritised "Sindhu Saraswati Sabhyata."[21]

The ramification of this move is profound. If successful, Vedic Harappans of the Indus–Saraswati civilization would manifest as an archaeological fact by potentially challenging one of the most fundamental theories of linguistic, archaeological, and Indological scholarship in the last 200 years, namely the origin of the Indo-European languages. It has been claimed that the Aryans who spoke the various Indo-European languages spread from a Central Asian homeland to the rest of the Old World (Africa, Asia, and Europe). However, if the Vedic Harappans or indigenous Aryans are indeed a fact, then this would undermine the Central Asian homeland theory and make India the original

Aryan homeland and Vedic Sanskrit the original proto-Indo-European mother language. This is the "Out of India theory." The historical, political, social, and religious implications of such a possibility are immense. However, this postulation was challenged by numerous scholars and has led to fierce and publicized debates (Erdosy 1995; Trautman 1997, 2008; Bryant and Patton 2005), with now its most acerbic confrontation palpable on the social media ecology.

The SHP was a statist product of such an epistemological framework to force-fit the varying pieces of *two* jigsaw puzzles in an attempt to make *one* conceptual whole. However, this was not the first time that there had been an attempt to archaeologically identify the Aryans with a specific material culture. Aryans had been earlier associated with the Gandharan Grave culture, Cemetery 'H' culture, Banas culture, Malwa culture, Chalcolithic culture of western and northern Deccan, Copper-hoard culture, and Painted Grey Ware culture (Thapar 1970, 147). The SHP project was the ASI's attempt to participate in this "Aryan debate" and was explicitly intended to generate archaeological data to propagate the "Out of India theory" (see Nath 2015, 9–14; Bisht 2015, 870–89).

Colonial Indology and the Birth of the Saraswati

For the seers of the *Rig Veda*, the River Saraswati was *ambitame, naditame, devitame*—"the best of mothers, the best of rivers, and the best of goddesses" (*Rig Veda: mandala* 2, hymn 41, verse 16 in Griffith 1889, 402). The term "Saraswati" epitomized both a riverine body and a magnanimous feminine divinity—a polysemic characterization that, in the complex etymological universe of Vedic Sanskrit, has multiple meanings and connotations depending on the context of the usage. One frequent analysis showed that the term "Saraswati" occurs around 68 times in the *Rig Veda*, 15 times more than the frequency of the term "Sindhu" (Singh 1998). Eloquently and evocatively described in the *Rig Veda* as a majestic river, the Saraswati is often referred to as that waterbody which rushed from the mountains to the ocean (Gupta 2001, 30). The later Vedic texts attest to the disappearance of the mighty river. For instance, in texts like the *Satapatha Brahmana*, *Aitareya Brahmana*, and the *Jaiminiya Brahmana*, the magnificent Saraswati of the *Rig Veda* is described as a vanishing river, which had shrunk in size and virtually disappeared. In the Mahabharata, the river is described as drying up in a desert. In later Puranic lore, the Saraswati is referred to as a subterranean river that eventually resurfaces at the *triveni sangam* (tri-river confluence) in present-day Allahabad, where two of the most sacred rivers of Hinduism merge—the Ganga and the Yamuna. Within the multivalent Hindu religiosity, Saraswati was an iterative divinity—more multifaceted than a mere river. In the *Rig Veda*, in association with Indra she killed Vritraasura (*Rig Veda*:

mandala 6, hymn 61 in Griffith 1890, 409–11), who is said to have hoarded the earth's waters, and was often seen as an equivalent to other Vedic goddesses such as Vak, Savitri, and Gayatri. In Puranic lore, she is the wife of Brahma and is the heavenly representation of intelligence, consciousness, cosmic knowledge, creativity, education, enlightenment, music, the arts, and power. Within the heterogeneous universe of pre-modern Hinduism (from the Vedic to the Tantric), Saraswati, like most figures of the celestial pantheon, was a polysemic divinity having manifold manifestations and not existing exclusively as a vanishing riverine body.[22] However, the genealogy of her essentialization as a hydrological entity can be traced to the epistemologies of nineteenth–century Indology and colonial cartography within the "inscription field" of colonial modernity.

The study of language and the making of maps have pre-modern roots. However, in colonial India they emerged almost simultaneously in the late eighteenth century as ideological embodiments of European Enlightenment. Introduced into the subcontinent by colonial administrators in the eighteenth century, they had become formidable modalities of colonial governmentality. Their ideological genealogy was situated in two distinct forms of colonial engagement with the "other", framed by the necessity to accumulate knowledge about the colonized—historical and travel writings (Pratt 1992; Raman 2001; Rubiés 2002; Travers 2008)—and the geographical mapping of physical territory for military exploits (Edney 1997; Barrow 2003). For instance, William Jones established the Asiatic Society in 1784 (Kejariwal 1988; Franklin 2011), just a year before James Rennell, the first surveyor-general of India, published the earliest accurate cartographic representation of India, *Map of Hindoostan* (Chattopadhyay 2016). Both moments were ideological products of European modernity in the colony. Jones and Rennell were pioneer administrator-scholars who were part of the discursive field of colonial epistemology, a field that evolved from a complex interpolation of European Enlightenment, modernity, science, and colonial governmentality.[23] Matthew Edney, in his edifying book on modern map-making in colonial India, demonstrates persuasively that through cartographic intervention the British reduced India into "a rigidly coherent, geometrically accurate, and uniformly precise imperial space, a rational space within which a systematic archive of knowledge about the Indian landscapes and people might be constructed" (Edney 1997, 319).

On the other hand, it was the disciplinary discourse of Indology initiated by the institutional apparatus of the Asiatic Society that led the mystical, religious, cultural, and linguistic space of India to be mapped and codified within the bounds of European and imperial consciousness. The Great Trigonometrical Survey of India represented a military project envisaged to bring the entire subcontinent into the epistemological grasp of a cartographical framework (Edney 1997; Barrow 2003), whereas William Jones's identification of the linguistic resemblance between Sanskrit, ancient Iranian, and European languages laid the foundation for the inquiry into ancient India.[24] Both cartographical and textual framings of the colonial universe were instrumental in the rise of the Indological project, and, subsequently, the birth of the ASI. Thus, the disciplinary framework of colonial Indology subsumed within the Orientalist discourse of European Enlightenment and colonial governmentality was an epistemic project of producing knowledge about the colony, whereas colonial cartography was distinctly a military project of enclosing captured territory within an objective representation system. The ideological agency to survey and map a conquered terrain in order to claim territorial sovereignty and to map the cultural field of the dominated subjects emerged from the same discursive epistemology that epitomized colonial modernity. If colonial cartography was the East India Company's attempt to scientifically rationalize the subjugated territory, then colonial Indology was the product of the same ideological provenance to essentialize a subjugated culture.

For Bruno Latour, inscription "refers to all the types of transformations through which an entity becomes materialised into a sign, an archive, a document, a piece of paper, a trace" (Latour 1999, 306). Latour persuasively shows that scientific knowledge is produced through a "cascade of inscriptions" in the laboratory and/or in the field to be eventually ossified as empirical evidence in the pages of journals and books. He argues that it is at this discursive location that rhetoric stripped of its various modalities is reified into a fact, which is "nothing but a statement with no modality … and no trace of authorship" (Latour and Woolgar 1986, 82).[25] Throughout the nineteenth century, the inscription field of colonial epistemology consisted of a small group of journals along with books about India being published in Calcutta, Bombay, Madras, and London. Almost all administrator-scholars of early colonial India in the late eighteenth and early nineteenth centuries published in the *Asiatick Researches*—the prestigious journal of the Asiatic Society, first issued in 1788 and widely circulated in Europe soon after (Trautmann 1997, 29). *Asiatick Researches* was modeled as a journal of a learned society of colonial gentlemen, and published papers of extraordinary diversity.

For instance, a cursory look at the titles published in Volume XI of the *Asiatick Researches*, issued in 1812, shows astonishing variety and range: "An account of the Petrifactions near the village of Treevikera in the Carnatic" (Warren 1812b, 1–10) and "An Account of experiments made at the Observatory near Fort St. George, for determining the length of the simple Pendulum beating seconds of time at that place, &c." (Warren 1812a, 294–308), are situated next to "A catalogue of Indian Medicinal Plants and Drugs, with their names in the Hindustani and Sanscrit languages" (Fleming 1812, 153–96) and "On the Sources of the Ganges, in the Himadri or Emodus" (Colebrooke 1812, 429–45) as well as "Narrative of a Survey for the purpose of discovering the Sources of the Ganges" (Raper 1812, 446–564). In other words, cartographers, linguists, archaeologists, surveyors, doctors, biologists, botanists, physicists, travelers, numismaticians, ethnologists, and philologists came together in the *Asiatick Researches* to contribute to the larger sphere of colonial epistemology. It is in this scholarly eclecticism that India emerges as an epistemological category that had to be studied scientifically. By the middle of the nineteenth century, journals such as the *Asiatick Researches* attached to scholarly societies abounded in the inscription field of colonial epistemology both in the colony and in the metropole. Here are some early examples: *Journal of the Royal Asiatic Society of Great Britain and Ireland* (1824), *Calcutta Review* (1844), *The Journal of the Asiatic Society of Bengal* (1832), *Gleanings in Science* (1831), and *Journal of the Bombay Branch of the Royal Asiatic Society* (1841). This, along with the books and treatises written since the late eighteenth century describing all aspect of the colony, comprised a wide epistemological field. It is in this inscription field of colonial epistemology that the Saraswati as a geographic incongruity surfaced.

The search for this "lost river" began with the interpretation of the much-celebrated "Nadistuti-sukta" or the hymn of praise of rivers (*Rig Veda*: *mandala* 10, hymn 75 in Griffith 1897, 490–91) by a French Indologist, M. Viven de Saint-Martin, who in 1860 suggested that this hymn "must have been composed, or technically *seen* (revealed), after the arrival of the Vedic Aryans on the banks of the Saraswati" (Thomas 1883, 363).[26] The notion of the river as a physical geological body occurred as a literary insight within the disciplinarian discourse of colonial epistemology. The topographic interpretation of Vedic literature in order to construct a sacred geography of ancient India was of considerable interest to colonial Indologists in the early nineteenth century as, one after another, Vedic and Puranic texts were being translated into European languages.[27] The co-relationship of the physical landscape with the extant literary description was well under way, and attempts to map the Aryan homeland became markedly important. Saraswati presented a challenge as it had glorious descriptions in the *Rig Veda* but there was no evidence of such a hydrological body in the cartographic realm of colonial territoriality.

By the late nineteenth century, articles about the "lost river of the Indian desert" made appearances in the inscription universe of colonial scholarship. Hypotheses about various dry riverbeds in western India being the Rig Vedic Saraswati were being postulated (Nearchus 1875; MacLagan 1885;

Oldham 1886, 1893; Raverty 1892). These early works were products of the cartographic modality of the colonial project, which attempted to locate the sacred geography of ancient India in the geology of colonial territoriality. These articles were the consequence of robust Indological scholarship that dexterously invoked eclectic sources from ancient Greek, Turkish, and Persian travel records, along with local medieval and Sanskrit texts to bolster their arguments. For instance, Minhaj-i-Siraj's *Tabaqat-i-Nasiri* (c. 1259) and travel writing by Ibn Battuta were often cited along with numerous European travel literatures. The discussions in these articles were frequently centered on the paleo-channels of the Rivers Ghaggar, Hakra, Sotra, and Nara and their hydrological relationship to the Indus, Yamuna, and Sutlej rivers in the present regions of Sindh, the Punjab, Haryana, and Rajasthan. For instance, C. F. Oldham in his 1874 article "Notes on the Lost River of the Indian Desert" argues that it is the Sutlej and not the Ghaggar or the Saraswati that is the lost river of the desert (Oldham 1874, 27), whereas in a later article he put forward the Ghaggar as the Rig Vedic Saraswati (Oldham 1893, 76).

On the other hand, Nearchus, in his "The Lost River of the Indian Desert," talks of a mythic river called Marut Bredha (Nearchus 1875, 351) and suggests that this river did not reach the sea but ended its course in the Indus (Nearchus 1875, 323). These rivers had been the objects of surveys and travels by various colonial officials in the early nineteenth century.[28] Their emergence as empirical hydrological categories was brought about through the discursive interaction between colonial cartography and geology. However, resurgent interest in revisiting the dry riverbeds of the Hakra and the Nara was also caused by burgeoning interest in mapping the geography of ancient India, influenced by the works of Alexander Cunningham from the latter half of the nineteenth century (Cunningham 1871). While most of these articles provided incompatible views, a general consensus seemed to be that the Ghaggar–Hakra riverbed system must have been a formidable hydrological body when the Aryans arrived; however, the association with the Rig Vedic Saraswati was, at best, speculative in these articles.

Archaeology and the Reconfiguration of the Saraswati

The decade of the 1920s saw spectacular discoveries in Egypt and West Asia with the opening of Tutankhamen's tomb in 1922, the library of cuneiform tablets and a palace from Kish in 1924, and royal cemeteries in the Ur of Chaldees in 1926. These discoveries were sensationally announced in the *Illustrated London News*, London. Not surprisingly, this location was also chosen by John Marshall, the director general (DG) of the ASI (1902–28), to announce the discovery of the Harappan civilization in 1924.[29] By announcing the official news of its discovery not only in the metropole but also in an extravagant inscription location such as the *Illustrated London News*,[30] Marshall located the Harappan civilization as the product of a larger imperial scientific intervention of the metropole in the colony to discover an ancient past for its subjects: "Not often has it been given to archaeologists, as it was given to Schliemann at Tiryns and Mycenae, or to Stein in the deserts of Turkestan, to light upon the remains of a long forgotten civilization" (Marshall 1924, 428).[31] Thus, the unearthing of the Harappan civilization by the ASI was both a continuation of the civilizing mission—the patronizing outcome of European Enlightenment—and the productive possibility of colonial science as manifested in its geographical imagination.[32]

This discovery marginalized scholarly interest in the Aryans and the Vedic period as colonial archaeologists focused on correlating Harappan material culture with other western Bronze Age civilizations. Instead of the Aryans, the Harappans became the new ethnic link between India and the west. For example, Rakhaldas Banerji, the discoverer of Mohenjo-Daro, was comparing artifacts found in Mohenjo-Daro with Minoan artefacts in 1923 (AACD, File No. 839/1925). Within weeks of the publication of Marshall's discovery, it seemed certain that the Harappans were in contact with the Mesopotamian civilization (Marshall 1924, 1931). The Aryans, whom colonial Indologists had politically subsumed within their racial ideology (Trautmann 1997, 2008), were further eclipsed because—in the public imagination of a nation resisting colonial domination—the Harappan civilization provided India with a chronology that predated the Aryans by at least a millennium. Evidentially, the historicity of narratives in Sanskrit literature had always seemed questionable. More often than not, Greek and Chinese sources—literary and numismatic—were used to delineate the chronology of ancient India (for instance, Cunningham 1871). Thus, the discovery of formidable archaeological sites of the Harappan civilization eclipsed the already suspect historicity of Sanskrit literature and consequently diminished the scholarly obsession with the Aryans without altogether obliterating it.

However, the Saraswati had not completely disappeared from the world of Indological scholarship. In 1927, a German scholar of Indo-Iranian languages argued that the term "Saraswati" was a cognate of old Iranian "Harahuvati" and referred to a cosmological water divinity, Aredvi Sura Anahita, in the *Avesta* (Lommel 1927, 1954). This led to the identification of Harahuvati with the River Helmand in Afghanistan, and by default to the Saraswati. This hypothesis did not find many takers, for the Helmand does not enter the sea, but drains into a marshy area—nonetheless it is still a theory that is ardently pursued by some (Kochhar 1999). In 1942, Sir Aurel Stein, a British political agent, explorer, philologist, and archaeologist, who had been associated with the ASI since the late nineteenth century and had conducted extensive archaeological explorations in western India and Afghanistan, declared that the Ghaggar–Hakra paleo-channel was indeed the Saraswati. He laboriously justifies:

> It would be hazardous to correlate the archaeologically attested changes of conditions along the Ghaggar-Hakra bed with the reference found in Vedic texts to the Sarasvati river: but the evidence shows that down to historical times the Ghaggar carried water for irrigation under existing climatic conditions much farther than it does now. This makes it intelligible how the Sarasvati has come in hymns of the Rigveda to be praised as a great river. (Stein 1942, 182)

With this assertion began the next phase of correlations of dry riverbeds with the Saraswati.[33] If the Saraswati was the riverine center of the Vedic civilization, then the Indus was the riverine center of the Harappan civilization. With Stein's proclamation, followed by the partition of the Indian subcontinent in 1947, the co-relationship of both the rivers seemed inevitable.

In the 1920s, when Marshall came across the first archaeological evidence of material culture at Harappa and Mohenjo-Daro, he located these two sites within the hydrological realm of the Indus, thereby positing the river as the center of this civilization. Like his fellow archaeologists at the time in Mesopotamia and Egypt, he interpreted the archaeological finds at Harappa and Mohenjo-Daro as a civilization within the fluvial confines of a riverbed. The Indus was to the Harappan civilization what the Nile and the Euphrates were to Egyptian and Mesopotamian civilizations respectively. The river was central to this modern civilizational imagination along with writing, monumental architecture, urbanism, fortifications, long-distance trade, craft specialization, and social stratification. But the unquestioned domination of the Indus as the center of the Harappan civilization was challenged by the discovery between the 1950s and the 1970s of sites that lay far beyond the Indus basin both in India and Pakistan. Until 1947, less than 40 Harappan sites were known (Wheeler 1953, 95–96), of which only 2 were in India—Kotla Nihang Khan in the Punjab and Rangpur in Gujarat (which were excavated by the ASI in 1929–30 and 1934–35 respectively), but this was soon to change.[34]

The partition of South Asia forced the ASI to re-evaluate the archaeological heritage that came under its purview. By 1948, the ASI had relinquished the jurisdiction of a substantial portion of the Old Frontier Circle, covering the entire region of erstwhile West Pakistan, and parts of its Eastern Circle, comprising areas in East Pakistan. Furthermore, the loss of Harappa and Mohenjo-Daro represented the biggest blow to the organizational morale of the postcolonial ASI, since these sites had constituted the professional core of the ASI in the last decades of its colonial legacy. However, by the early 1950s, the ASI began a systematic exploration of the western states of independent India (Ghosh 1952, 1956, 1959; Thakran 2000, 48). This exploration was a follow-up to Stein's work and was meant to compensate for the loss of nearly all the Harappan sites to Pakistan and to re-establish the pre-eminence of post-independence India as an ancient civilization. Significantly, Rafique Mughal's exploration in eastern Pakistan adjoining the Thar Desert on the bed of the Hakra along with the discovery of Harappan sites in Baluchistan and western Pakistan was also responsible for this shift (Mughal 1992, 1997). These discoveries, along with the excavations of the Harappan sites of Lothal, Kalibangan, Surkotada, Bhagwanpura, and Banawali over the decades by the ASI as well as the excavations of Harappa, Kot Diji, Mehrgarh, Nausharo, and Sutkagan Dor in Pakistan, further undermined the thesis of the Indus as the hydrological center of the Harappan civilization.

By 1984, 1,400 Harappan sites were discovered due to the extensive exploration efforts of the ASI, the Departments of Ancient Indian History, Culture and Archaeology at the Universities of Kurukshetra and Baroda, Deccan College (Pune), and the State Department of Archaeology in Gujarat (Misra 1994, 511–12) along with the efforts of independent scholars (Ram 1972; Bhan 1973). These discoveries, while restoring the losses of Partition, also shifted the locus of the Harappan civilization away from the Indus valley to a larger geographic area as far as the Gangetic plains in the east to Saurashtra in the south (Possehl 2002; McIntosh 2008). The Indus lost its pre-eminence as the riverine center of the Harappan civilization. Soon, the Ghaggar–Hakra paleo-channels as a geological River Saraswati was being promoted as the coeval hydrological center of the Harappan civilization. This occurred with the discursive intervention of another postcolonial science—geology.

Postcolonial Geology and the Birth of the Hydrological Saraswati

The work of postcolonial geologists—some attached to the Geological Survey of India, others to university departments in India—in analyzing remote-sensing satellite data and in paleo-climatic and paleo-seismic research led to scientific claims establishing the correlation between the Ghaggar–Hakra and the Saraswati as empirical facts. In the 1970s and the 1980s, invoking the "Nadistuti-sukta" hymn and earlier hypotheses from Oldham to Stein, a group of geologists interpreted remote-sensing images taken during 1972–77 (Ghose Kar, and Hussain 1979; Yashpal, Sood, and Agrawal 1980; Bakliwal and Grover 1988). These were "Landsat" satellite images that provide synoptic multi-spectral and multi-temporal data and have powerful scientific legitimacy. These were composite images, which showed paleo-channels in western South Asia from the Siwaliks to the Rann of Kutch. Paleo-channels are ancient streams and rivulets that are monsoon-fed and on the surface are usually disconnected from contemporary water bodies. These channels have been traced by satellite and the resultant digital images processed to categorize paleo-channels in northwest India and adjoining parts of Pakistan.[35] They vigorously attempted to validate the century-old speculation that the Ghaggar–Hakra had indeed been a large river, and argued that the paleo-channels of the Rig Vedic Saraswati coincided with the bed of the present-day Ghaggar. They postulated that the Sutlej and the Yamuna were the main tributaries of the Ghaggar and that subsequent tectonic movements might have forced the Sutlej westwards and the Yamuna eastwards, causing the Ghaggar to dry up.

However, on closer reading of the papers published by this community of scholars, it seems that there were contradictory claims circulating, not just about the origin of the river, but also its nature. The most exaggerated of these studies painted a picture of the river as dynamic and powerful, similar to that described exuberantly in the *Rig Veda*. Like its mythical incarnation, the geological entity flowed from the Siwalik Hills at the edge of the Himalayas and through the Punjab, Haryana, northern Rajasthan, through the Thar Desert in Pakistan, and finally entered the sea at the Rann of Kutch in western India. Some argued that the Ghaggar–Hakra was a perennial river (Puri 2001); others said that it was fed by the Yamuna (Wilhelmy 1999) and the Sutlej (Kar and Ghose 1984; Bakliwal and Grover 1988); while yet others stated that the river was monsoon-fed (Radhakrishna and Merh 1999). Theories about its demise also abound—attributing it to the changing course of the Sutlej and the Yamuna (Bakliwal and Sharma 1980), to seismic activity in the region which made it subterranean (Snelgrove 1979; Kar 1998, 1999), to its disappearance in the Kutch (Valdiya 2002; Ramasamy 2005). The only consensus seems to have been that the Ghaggar–Hakra had indeed once been a powerful paleo-hydrological body; and an empirical spurious attempt to amalgamate the Ghaggar–Hakra as the Saraswati (Gupta Sharma, and Sreenivasan 2011, 5214). Significantly, in these studies no conclusive evidence was presented to pinpoint when the river dried up or, importantly, if the paleo-channel finally drained into the sea or the Thar Desert.

Recent robust paleo-climatic research has shown that the Thar had started to become arid by 4800 BCE (Staubwasser et al. 2003; Durcan et al. 2019), more than a millennium before the Early Harappan phase (3300–2600 BCE). This suggests that Harappan culture must have risen and fallen in semi-arid climatic conditions similar to the present day (Sarkar et al. 2016; Orengo and Petrie 2017). A study of the isotopic content of the alluvium of the

Ghaggar–Hakra (Tripathi et al. 2004) argues that its waters did not originate in the Himalayas, thus contesting the very idea of a perennial Saraswati. A recent study that reports five quartz optically stimulated luminescence (OSL) dating from the Chautang paleo-channel argues that the conjectural links between the Ghaggar–Hakra and Harappan settlements in the area were incorrect: "Our results disprove the proposed link between ancient settlements and large rivers from the Himalayas and indicate that the major palaeo-fluvial system traversing through this region ceased long before the establishment of the Harappan civilization" (Dave et al. 2019, 230).

In addition, other studies that have employed luminescence-dating of sand grains (Singh et al. 2017), uranium–lead dating of zircon grains (Clift et al. 2012), and sedimentological analyses supported by OSL chronology (Singh and Sinha 2019) have unambiguously shown than the Ghaggar–Hakra dried up because the Sutlej and Yamuna rivers that fed this paleo-channel shifted course around c. eighth to sixth millennium BCE. Radiocarbon and OSL dating of the potteries from the Mature Harappan period (2600 to 1900 BCE) at Kalibangan suggests that "the sediments in the Ghaggar as used by the potters did not have a higher Himalayan provenance and hence, were not derived from glaciated Himalayas. These findings imply that during the time of the Mature Harappans the Ghaggar had already become a foothill-fed river" (Chatterjee and Ray 2018, 1203). These findings unambiguously demonstrate that the Ghaggar–Hakra may have been a powerful hydrological body before aridity set in in the Thar Desert (that is, before c. 4800 BCE), therefore preceding the emergence of the Harappan civilization (c. 3300 BCE). Archaeological and geological research has shown beyond doubt that a significant portion of the Harappan civilization was situated in the Ghaggar–Hakra region, but this riverbed was already dry by this time and not a mighty river, as the proponents of the Saraswati argue.

It is with the intervention of the disciplinary discourse of postcolonial geology that the Saraswati emerges as a *boundary object* (Star and Griesemer 1989) with a seemingly powerful empirical value and ability to move between the domains of different epistemic communities. Within information and science studies, boundary objects have been defined as epistemological entities that both inhabit several communities of practice and satisfy the informational requirements of each of them. Boundary objects are, thus, plastic enough to adapt to local needs and constraints of the several parties employing them, yet robust enough to maintain a common identity across sites (Fujimara 1992; Bowker and Star 1999, 297). With the intervention of postcolonial geologists and archaeologists, the Saraswati slowly emerged as a boundary object with an intricate internal structure that allowed multivariant agents to project complex interpretations onto it. Thus, with the rise of Hindu fundamentalism in the early 1990s, and its ascendancy to power at the national level in 1998, politicians, Indologists, archaeologists, and geologists who were politically invested in the idea of the Saraswati civilization were instrumental in transforming the Saraswati from a marginal boundary object into a "visionary" one (Briers and Chua 2001).[36]

The Harappan Archaeogenetics

The politicization of Harappan archaeology was not merely limited to the geological origin of a mythological entity or the Saraswati's hydrological existence in arid paleo-climate ecology. With the rise of genetics and archaeogenetics, big science ventured into the contested world of ancient India. By the last decade of the twentieth century, studies based on polymorphisms in mitochondrial DNA (mtDNA) indicated extensive genetic diversity in the Indian population (Mountain et al. 1995) and significantly showed that caste-based social stratification corresponded with genetic stratification (Bamshad et al. 1996; Bamshad et al. 1998). These insights corroborated linguistic and anthropological understanding of variation in contemporary India. Soon, series of papers deploying genetic data argued for the non-occurrence of the Aryan invasion theory dubbed as "massive Indo-Aryan invasion" (Kivisild et al. 1999; Roychoudhury et al. 2000) and further noted that the "Indian tribal and caste populations derive largely from the same genetic heritage of Pleistocene southern and western Asians and have received limited gene flow from external regions since the Holocene" (Kivisild et al. 2003). By the early years of the twenty-first century, mtDNA studies using a larger sample size proliferated—showing concurrently the indigeneity of the Indian gene pool (Thangaraj et al. 2006) and its widespread diversification (Basu et al. 2003).

In 2009, an influential mtDNA study using a bigger dataset introduced two conceptual genetic epistemic categories into this scientific ecosystem—"Ancestral South Indians" and "Ancestral North Indians"—the former having a close relationship to pre-Holocene Asian hunter-gatherer groups, whereas the latter having genetic affinities to Middle Easterners, Central Asians, and Europeans (Reich et al. 2009).[37] This study provocatively asserted that the majority of the contemporary populations of India are a result of admixture between these two ancestral populations.[38] A subsequent analysis contended that this admixture occurred between c. 2200 BCE to c. 50 CE (Moorjani et al. 2013). These dates are temporally synchronous with the collapse of the Harappan civilization and the rise and consolidation of the Vedic civilization in the Indo-Gangetic plains of north India (Reich 2018, 140). However, this study was careful not to imply migration from West Asia but indicated that "strict endogamy" took roots in the Indian society around that time period when the *Manusmriti* (second–third century CE) was written (Moorjani et al. 2013, 430). Both these studies showed that "West Eurasian-related mixture in India ranges from as low as 20 percent to as high as 80 percent" (Reich 2018, 136). Their analysis was conducted using data sets of contemporary population that was stored at the Centre for Cellular and Molecular Biology in Hyderabad. These mtDNA studies captured the imagination of archaeologists and soon genetic materials sourced from archaeological excavations was being used to construct a genome map of the ancient world.

Although ancient DNA (aDNA) research developed with the invention of the polymerase chain reaction (PCR) in 1983, the contamination of DNA samples, especially in tropical ecologies such as India, did not make it an area of significant investigation. But with the advance sequencing technology developing, it did not take long for a new body of genetic data to brazenly enter into the debates of the mobility of population not just of ancient South Asia, but all across the world. At the forefront was the David Reich Lab, established at Harvard University in 2010, which persuasively penetrated the world of archaeology by making aDNA "industrial" (Reich 2018, xix)—amassing a library of whole genome aDNA data of close to 5,000 individuals (by the end of 2020) sourced from all across the globe. The Lab commenced an aggressive publishing record with a flurry of multi-authored articles in prestigious scientific journals (*Science, Nature, Cell*) to provide genetic evidence on a wide spectrum of knotty archaeological debates—origin and spread of Indo-European languages (Haak et al. 2015; Tassi et al. 2017); origin of farming in the ancient Near East (Lazaridis et al. 2016); origins of the Minoans and Mycenaeans (Lazaridis et al. 2016); history of the pre-contact Caribbean (Fernandes et al. 2021); human population shifts in northern and southern China (Yang et al. 2020); and population histories of the Andes (Nakatsuka 2020), among others.

This precipitous production of new epistemological data in the world of archaeology was met with anxiety and censures (Heyd 2017; Callaway 2018) which was given a derisive rebuttal by Reich, underscoring the pioneering nature of evidence that his lab was producing, and most importantly the scientific clout this category of data wielded:

> We geneticists may be the barbarians coming late to the study of the human past, but it is always a bad idea to ignore barbarians. We have access to a type of data that no one has had before, and we are wielding these data to address previously unapproachable questions about who ancient peoples were. (Reich 2018, 128)

Now, archaeogenetics is swiftly expanding its epistemological coverage; archaeologists are cautioning for curtailing the "grand narratives" it is making (Veeramah 2018, 83), by often grossly simplifying historical, cultural complexities found in the archaeological record (Gokcumen and Frachetti 2020).

The first archaeologist to be attentive to the scientific leverage of genetic data in the thorny deliberations of the Indian past was Vasant Shinde from Deccan College, who was excavating a small Harappan settlement of Farmana (Haryana) between 2006 and 2008 with a team of Japanese archaeologists. The team found 56 burials of the Mature Harappan phase at the site (Shinde Osada, and Kumar 2011), but they failed to extract the aDNA because of extensive contamination due to poor retrieval methods adopted, further exacerbated by the degraded nature of the samples that is typical of the tropical ecology of the north Indian plains. Armed with experience and a fresh ASI excavation license, Shinde decided to excavate the necropolis of Rakhigarhi, which had been discovered during an earlier excavation between 1997 and 2000 by the ASI (Nath 2015, 127–67). Shinde in collaboration with Seoul National University used extensive precautions to prevent the contamination of skeletal remains at Rakhigarhi (Shinde et al. 2018, 5). After screening more than 60 skeletal samples, for the first time in history of Harappan archaeology, genetic data was extracted from one individual—an adult woman identified as 16113 (Shinde et al. 2019). It is with this data of a single individual that the politics of archaeogenetics infiltrated into the relatively sedate world of Harappan archaeology courageously attempting to provide decisive answers about both its origin and demise.

The genetic data from 16113 was used in two scientific articles that were published simultaneously in September 2019, in *Science* (Narasimhan et al. 2019) and *Cell* (Shinde et al. 2019). These were multi-authored articles with the unmistakable stamp of David Reich's Lab. The *Science* paper had more far-reaching research objectives as it used a DNA of 523 ancient human spanning the last 8,000 years, across Central Asia and South Asia, and described mobility patterns from the Eurasia Steppe into both South Asia and Europe. Eleven genome data sets—3 individuals from the Gonur Depe, in Turkmenistan, from the Bactria–Margiana Archaeological Complex (2500 and 2000 BCE) and 8 individuals from the Bronze Age site of Shahr-i-Sokhta, in Baluchistan, Pakistan (3300 and 2000 BCE)—became central to the story of mobility in Harappan civilization. The genetic data from 16113 matched with these 11 individuals, and all 12 had a distinct admixture of ancestry of Southeast Asian hunter-gatherers and an Iranian-related lineage specific to South Asia. Both the papers showed that, first, none of the 12 individuals had evidence of ancestry from Steppe pastoralists, consistent with our archaeological knowledge that the original authors of the

Harappan civilization were native to South Asia (Shinde et al. 2019); second, that the origin of farming in South Asia (7000–3000 BCE) was not due to the movement of people from the earlier farming cultures of the west; instead, local foragers adopted it; and third, the *Science* paper produced corroborative evidence that between 2000 and 1000 BCE people of largely Middle to Late Bronze Age Steppe ancestry moved toward South Asia, mixing with people of the Harappan civilization, providing compelling new evidence in favor of a Steppe origin for Indo-European languages in South Asia (Narasimhan et al. 2019).

In the same week that these two papers were published, Vasant Shinde discredited the idea of migration from the Steppes and argued in contrary to both the papers that evidence of the 11 individuals found in Gonur Depe and Shahr-i-Sokhta along with 16113 suggests that Aryan and Sanskrit were native to the Harrapans—projecting the indigenous Aryan theory (Mishra 2019; Rajendran 2019). During the 2020 Covid-19 lockdown in India, in a series of lectures, talks, podcasts, and interviews which were uploaded on YouTube on channels of the National Council of Science Museums, Indian Institute of Science Education, Pune, and Swadeshi Indology of Rajiv Malhotra's Infinity Foundation, and many others, Shinde has interpreted the archaeogenetic data, craniofacial reconstruction of Rakhigarhi skeletal remains, along with traditional material culture, asserting that the Harappans moved westward—propagating the "Out of India theory"—a return to the Hindutva claim of the Vedic Aryan, now invoking aDNA data as arsenal.

Hindutva Politics and the Making of the Indus–Saraswati Civilization

For Hindutva ideologues, the idea of India as a definite territorial center of Hindu civilization was the crux of the exclusionary politics that they espoused.[39] The genealogy of this idea of a Hindu India was historically defined by its description in the Sanskritic literary traditions from the Vedic enunciations to the later Puranic reconfigurations. It is this conflation between geographic territoriality, linguistic identity, and nationalism that gave birth to the ideological extremism of Hindutva. Although the appropriation of history to construct a specific narrative of the past has been a hallmark of any nationalistic politics, the use of archaeology has never been far behind. The correlation to material manifestation of the past by nation states to legitimize their authenticity has been a significant cause for the transformation of archaeology from an antiquarian enterprise to a disciplinary formation in the nineteenth century. This genealogy of the emergence of scientific archaeology has been symbiotically linked to the growth of nationalism in Europe (Trigger 1984, 1989). In the twentieth century, the trajectory of the disciplinary discourse of archaeology as one representing the coupling of science and nationalism also brought archaeology into the forefront of the politics of the modern nation state (Arnold 1990, 1992; Kohl and Fawcett 1995; Díaz-Andreu and Champion 1996; Meskell 1998). The appropriation of archaeology in constructing nationalist ideologies by European nations presents a vivid illustration of this deep-seated tension (Trigger 1984, 1989; Ucko 1995; Jones 1997). After World War II, this link between archaeology and nationalism has been central to the making of newly decolonized nations such as India, Israel, and others (Kuklick 1991; El-Haj 2001; Shepard 2002).

In the early decades of postcolonial India, the relationship of Hindutva ideologues with Hindu nationalism was broadly tied to history; archaeology, although part of their discursive arsenal, was still marginal. It was with the ASI's "Archaeology of the Mahabharata Sites" project in 1950–52 that the earliest link between Hindutva ideology and archaeology can be dated. B. B. Lal, one of the most distinguished archaeologists of the ASI, who began his career at Mortimer Wheeler's famous archaeology field school at Taxila in 1944, and who eventually became the DG of the ASI (1968–72), headed this project. Unlike nineteenth-century excavations of sites mentioned in Chinese travel literature by Alexander Cunningham[40] which had unambiguous historical origins, Lal explicitly attempted to correlate events and sites mentioned in the epic to archaeological excavations at Hastinapura and explorations of Mathura, Kurukshetra, Banawa, Panipat, Ahichchhatra, and other places (Lal 1954, 2002a).[41] This led him to the controversial assertion that the pre-Buddhist Painted Grey Ware (PGW) found at these sites was associated with the Mahabharata (Lal 1978; Bhan 1997; Habib 1997). PGW was identified in Ahichchhatra in 1946, and it was during the Hastinapur excavation that it was culturally interpreted. Lal emphatically correlated the PGW with Period II in Hastinapur, thereby controversially pushing the date of the events in the Mahabharata to 1000 BCE. However, in his conclusion to the excavation report of the Hastinapur excavation published in *Ancient India*, he notes with caution "that the evidence is entirely circumstantial and until and unless positive ethnographic and epigraphic proofs are obtained to substantiate the conclusions they cannot but be considered provisional" (Lal 1954, 151). Lal's project was driven by the faulty logic of correlating material culture (PGW) with ethnicity (Aryan) (Bhan 1997; Habib 1997).

In keeping with the practice of cultural-history archaeologists, Lal's effort was mimetic of Wheeler's equally problematic correlation between the material culture of Cemetery 'H' at Harappa and the notion of invading hordes of Aryans. Again, headed by Lal and motivated by the same concerns, a joint project of the ASI and the Indian Institute of Advanced Studies, Shimla, on the "Archaeology of the Ramayana Sites" followed the Mahabharata project between 1975 and 1980, with excavations at Ayodhya, Sringaverapur, and Nandigrama (Lal 1975; *IAR 1976–77* 1980, 52; *IAR 1979–80* 1983, 76). The epistemic logic for both of these projects was to employ the objective authority of scientific archaeology to legitimize the historicity of the epic traditions, and to establish the Sanskritic past as empirical fact. The possibility of transforming a mythological Sanskritic literary universe into an empirical reality, materially located in the geographic territoriality of India, justified archaeology's role among Hindutva ideologues. Although these two projects were not framed within Hindutva logic, they were appropriated in the 1980s by the rise of Hindutva politics, especially in the case of the Ram Janmabhoomi–Babri Masjid controversy. The reinvention of the Bharatiya Jana Sangh as the Bharatiya Janata Party (BJP) and its coming to power as part of the Janata Party coalition was contemporaneous with the excavations at Ayodhya by Lal between 1976–77 and 1979–80. The Sangh Parivar–led Ram Janmabhoomi movement in the 1980s successfully employed Lal's fabricated claim of a destroyed temple under the Babri Masjid. With it, the project of Hindutva's epistemological appropriation of archaeology's discursive legitimacy to pursue its divisive politics reached its logical conclusion on December 6, 1992, when the Babri Masjid was destroyed.[42]

Around the late 1980s, with the rise of political Hindutva, historians and archaeologists closely associated with the Hindutva ideology initiated the project of the "Aryanization of the Indus Civilization" (Bhan 1997, 13, 2000; Thakran 2000, 62; Guha 2005). A symposium was organized by the Deen Dayal Research Institute and Voice of India (active arms of the RSS) in New Delhi in 1993 to take the project firmly into the public sphere of Indian polity.[43] This project argued against the migration of the Aryans from the west and asserted that the Harappans were Vedic Aryans (Rajaram 1995; Singh 1995; Gupta 1996; Elst 1999; Talageri 2000; Lal 2002b). The hydrological center of this process of "Aryanization"—the practice of reading Aryan elements into Harappan material culture—was the River Saraswati which, by this time, as I have shown earlier, had moved from the mythological to the archaeological realm, its epistemic valence made more powerful by the assertions of postcolonial geological sciences.

At this stage, the Saraswati was transformed from a *boundary object* to a *visionary object* (Briers and Chua 2001, 242). This occurred through Hindutva's appropriation of archaeology to push its ideological agenda. Overwhelmed by the hydrological validation of the Saraswati, as well as the high concentration of Harappan sites in the Ghaggar–Hakra region, archaeologists sympathetic to the Hindutva cause provocatively argued that it was the Saraswati rather than the Indus that was the center of the Harappan civilization (Gupta 1995, 1996, 2001;

Joshi 1984; Misra 1994; Lal 1997, 1998, 2002a; Bisht 1999; Kalyanraman 1999). These discoveries, along with the archaeological excavations of the Harappan sites at Rupar (1954–55), Lothal (1954–63), Kalibangan (1960–69), Surkotada (1964–68), Bhagwanpura (1975–76), Banawali (1974–77), Kunal (1985–86, 1991–95), Rakhigarhi (1997–2000), and Dholavira (1990–2004), exacerbated the debate about the existence of the Vedic Harappans. The presence of horse bones in Surkotada (Sharma 1990);[44] the interpretation of the Harappan fire hearth as the Vedic fire-altar at Kalibangan (Lal 1984; Lal et al. 2003),[45] Lothal (Rao 1985),[46] and Banawali (Lal 2002a); the representation of spoke wheels on terracotta toys in Kalibangan and Banawali (Lal 2002a; Rao 2006); along with several alleged decipherments of the Harappan script as proto-Sanskrit (Shendge 1977; Rao 1982; Jha and Rajaram 2000) were covertly introduced as archaeological evidence.

This theory of the Vedic Harappans, coupled with the rejection of the theory of an Aryan invasion and the discoveries of Harappan sites in the Ghaggar–Hakra region, all contributed to the gradual emergence of the Indus–Saraswati civilization as an unquestionable factual reality. This can be seen in its most manifested form in the unpublished report of Rakhigarhi (Nath 2015, 9–14) and Dholavira (Bisht 2015, 870–89). Alongside this, the absence of a credible and unifying explanation for the collapse of the Harappan civilization (c. 1600–1300 BCE) provided a fertile gap into which the possibility of Vedic and Harappan overlap was shrewdly inserted. Incestuous citing practices on the part of geologists and archaeologists supportive of the Hindutva cause created a perception that the Ghaggar–Hakra was indeed the Saraswati river, and that it could be treated as an objective scientific fact.[47] Soon, even archaeologists who were not part of the Hindutva ideological formation were convinced by these rhetorical moves and began calling the Harappan civilization the Indus–Saraswati civilization (Kenoyer 1997, 57; Possehl 2002, 36), a trend that still continues unabated even in ostensibly scientific scholarly journals (for instance, Sarkar et al. 2016; Shinde et al. 2018). The archaeogenetics data that has recently emerged to thwart the indigenous Aryan narrative has also been challenged (Danino 2019), making the field politically charged.

By the time I commenced my ethnography in the autumn of 2003, the Saraswati river was already an undisputed fact and the SHP was a project through which the statist machinery of the ASI was activated to procure empirical evidence to reinforce the evidence for Indus–Saraswati civilization, as is evident in the Rakhigarhi and Dholavira reports. To accomplish this project, the ASI planned to set up a two-tier bureaucratic structure: one at the Secretarial Office level in New Delhi, and another at sites as 15 Hub Offices. While the Secretariat would centralize, monitor, direct, and participate in all efforts of the fieldwork and research analysis, the Hub Offices would carry out extensive and intensive fieldwork in the defined areas. To realize the objectives of the SHP, a time frame of four years was set with a proposed creation of 27 posts in various cadres at the Secretariat, and 45 at 15 Hub Offices.[48]

The Saraswati Heritage Project (SHP)

The Saraswati Heritage Project (SHP) originated in 2002 through a Government of India gazette notification leading to the constitution of the Advisory Committee for the Multidisciplinary Study of the River Saraswati,[49] under the chairmanship of the then minister of tourism and culture, Jagmohan. The project was aimed at

> conducting a multidisciplinary study of River Saraswati and its basin stretching in India from the Sivaliks to the Arabian Sea, falling in the Indian states of Haryana, Rajasthan, and Gujarat, and formulating and implementing integrated development programmes [*sic*] in the area by creating 15 hub sites as centers of culture, tourism, and good civic life. (Basu 2005, 11)

Headed by the joint director general (Jt DG) of the ASI, the project not only included archaeological investigations but also geomorphological, geotechnological, hydrological, ethnological, paleo-botanical, paleontological, and pedological studies, and a detailed analysis of historical literature and oral traditions.[50] The objective of the proposal was

> [to] define the River Saraswati and its tributaries in the basin by adopting a multidisciplinary approach: to identify special items of geotechnical studies; to promote multidisciplinary archaeological research by way of exploration, excavation and specialized studies such as ceramic, metallurgical, mineralogical, botanical, zoological, geotechnical, petrological, sedimentological; to carry out structural and chemical conservation of sites, monuments, and excavated structures as well as moveable objects; to accomplish environmental upgradation of the sites; realize all these objectives in an integrated, concerted and planned manner under a special drive during a period of three years, to begin with. (Basu 2005, 11)

In September 2002, the Advisory Committee prepared a project proposal for the SHP with a budget of INR 360 million, but this was eventually reduced to INR 49.8 million for a period of three years. For excavation and exploration, the SHP was largely planning to harness the existing resources of the ASI. Initially, the excavation was proposed at the prospective sites for a period of three years with a total budget outlay of INR 17.6 million.[51]

The SHP was the product of the ASI's intervention to legitimize the objectivity of the Indus–Saraswati civilization. The SHP was conceived as not only an academic project, but also as a political project couched as tourism development. To justify funding from the Ministry of Tourism and Culture, the project supplemented its research program with a proposed transformation of 15 archaeological sites into tourist attractions under the plan of "Integrated Development of the Tourism Circuit from Adi Badri to Dholavira." Of these, some of the hub sites such as Thaneswar, Rakhigarhi, Banawali, Adi Badri, Aghora, Dholavira, Rangmahal, and Kalibangan had been excavated; Sirsa, Kalyat, Hanumangarh, and Narayan Sarovar were local historic sites; whereas fresh large-scale excavations were planned at the sites of Chak 86, Tarkhanewala Dera, Baror, Hansi, Bhirrana, and Juni Kuran.[52] Jagmohan, the then minister for tourism and culture, under whose tenure the SHP was initiated, had inserted the SHP under his INR 3,000 million "Regeneration India" project, aimed at boosting "cultural and spiritual tourism" in India to exploit the domestic market.[53] The SHP was designed not only to celebrate the Indian cultural landscape, but also to establish the empirical basis of the Saraswati's terrestrial manifestation in the Harappan material culture record. The central aim of the project was to produce credible data of indigeneity in order to scientifically show that the Rig Vedic Aryans were the authors of the Harappan civilization. For the first time, a state-sponsored project was instrumental in trying to investigate the relationship between the Ghaggar–Hakra Harappan culture and Rig Vedic literature, under the hydrological rubric of the Saraswati river. Senior archaeologists of the ASI, some retired and some still serving, who had earlier articulated the idea of the Vedic Harappans, were at the forefront of the conceptualization of the SHP. They were also members of the ASI-instituted Advisory Committee for the Multidisciplinary Study of River Saraswati. Some of these members had intimate connections with the Hindutva movement.[54]

Since its inception, the SHP was embroiled in controversies about its ideological impetus. This role of the ASI and the government turned the SHP into a politically potent project, and this was the reason for its premature end. An assistant superintending archaeologist (ASA) at the Baror site, who had worked in the DG office in New Delhi for several years, explained the birth of the SHP and its connection with the Hindu right-wing political project:

> All senior archaeologists in the ASI have right wing sympathies. They might not be RSS propagandists [*pracharak*s], but they are openly with the BJP. It is no secret that Bisht was always close to Guptaji (S. P. Gupta), and B. B. Lal, who, as we all know, are saffron [*bhagwa*] archaeologists. The Saraswati project has always been

on the back of the minds of the RSS people [*RSS wale*]. It was perhaps secondary to the Ram Janmabhoomi issue, but it was always important. So when the NDA came to power, Gupta*ji* began lobbying with the government to get money for the Saraswati project. But there was no political will [*rajnitik dabab*]. It was only with Jagmohan that the money came. Bisht was successful in selling the project on its scientific and archaeological merit. And Jagmohan could convince the cabinet of its heritage and tourist value.

I heard this narrative from several informants, and all attributed the funding of the SHP to Jagmohan's clout in the cabinet, Bisht's argument for its scientific merit, and Gupta and Lal's RSS connections.

The excavations under the SHP lasted only for one season (2003–04) when the National Democratic Alliance (NDA), under the leadership of the Hindu nationalist BJP, was in power. In the national election during the summer of 2004, the NDA was defeated and the United Progressive Alliance (UPA), under the leadership of the centrist Congress and with the support of the Left parties, came to power. During the BJP's tenure, archaeologists and scholars who were not sympathetic to its political subtext had criticized the SHP; among these were prominent scholars close to the Left parties (Basu 2005). Jaipal Reddy, the first minister of tourism and culture under the UPA government, scrapped the SHP by the end of 2004 and its funding was cut. A "high powered" parliamentary committee was set up with the explicit aim of investigating the workings of the ASI. This committee, formed at the behest of the Left parties who were a significant partner of the UPA government, had the implicit aim of investigating the SHP. The *91st Report of the Department-Related Parliamentary Standing Committee of Transport, Tourism and Culture*, devoted to the functioning of the ASI, indicted the organization:

> After going through the replies furnished by the Ministry of Culture, the Committee is of the firm view that Saraswati Heritage Project did not conform to the criterion fixed for excavation of archaeological sites since no academic body or university had recommended the project.... The Committee further notes that the Ministry is not clear as to which research agency/scientific survey actually pointed out that the dry beds of River Ghaggar and River Chautang (River Drishadvati) are the beds of River Saraswati. The Committee understands that the existence of River Saraswati is purely a mythological one and a scientific institution like Archaeological Survey of India has not correctly proceeded in the matter.... The Committee would like to advise the Archaeological Survey of India that it should prevent itself from taking up exercises without a scientific basis which have all potentiality for subjective interpretation of historical facts thereby, leading to controversies. (Basu 2005, 13)

Thus, for the season 2004–05, excavations ceased at the sites of Chak 86, Tarkhanewala Dera (Trivedi 2009; *IAR 2003–04* 2011, 205–12), and Juni Kuran (Pramanik 2004a; *IAR 2003–04* 2011, 22–31)—sites that were being excavated by the ASI's Bhubaneshwar Ex. Br. and Vadodara Ex. Br. respectively. However, the Nagpur Ex. Br., the Delhi Ex. Br., and the Patna Ex. Br. continued excavations at Bhirrana (*IAR 2004–05* 2014, 40–59), Hansi, and Baror (*IAR 2004–05* 2014, 111–35) respectively for the season 2004–05.[55]

The SHP as a political project of the ASI met with an untimely end, but its historical and ideological foundations have not withered; they still continue to occupy a significant epistemological space in the archaeological imagination of ancient India. I have collected the bulk of the accounts in this book during my ethnography at the SHP excavation sites and camps between 2003 and 2005, and subsequently conversations and multiple updates given by my informants in the past few years. I conducted the ethnography of the ASI sites during both its excavation under the ideological and financial auspices of the SHP in 2003–04 and subsequently after the SHP was terminated in 2004–05. The ideological overview of the Aryan debate, the possibility of the Vedic Harappans, and the Ghaggar–Hakra as Vedic Saraswati were regular points of discussion in conversation with my informants. ASI archaeologists that I spoke to knew of the political valence of the SHP but it did not have any influence on the daily practice of their archaeology, which, as I show in this book, was framed by far more dexterous ideologies and organizational formations. The sites at which I did ethnography between 2003 and 2005 were Dholavira and Juni Kuran in Gujarat; Bhirrana and Hansi in Haryana; and Tarkhanewala Dera, Chak 86, and Baror in Rajasthan. The sites of Juni Kuran, Hasi, Baror, Bhirranna, Tarkhanewala Dera, and Chak 86 were chosen for fresh excavation, whereas Dholavira had been excavated for more than a decade in the past (1984–85, 1989–90 through 2004–05).

The Archaeological Sites of This Ethnography

In search of possible land routes connecting the Harappan epicenter in Sind with the outlying province in Gujarat, Jagat Pati Joshi in 1967–68, then a superintending archaeologist (SA) in the ASI, discovered, among others, the enormous Harappan site of Dholavira in the district of Kutch (*IAR 1967–68* 1968, 13–17). Preliminary exploration work at the site was done in 1984–85 (*IAR 1984–85* 1987, 14); however, excavations only commenced in the year 1989–90, undertaken by R. S. Bisht, the then SA of the Vadodara Ex. Br. (*IAR 1989–90* 1994, 15–20) for 13 seasons until 2004–05 (Bisht 2015, 27). During these years, Bisht rose in rank from the SA of the Vadodara Ex. Br. to the director of the Institute of Archaeology. He was transferred as the director of the Exploration and Excavation Department in the DG headquarters in Delhi, and eventually became the Jt DG of the ASI.[56] As a result of the ASI excavations, Dholavira has emerged as the fourth largest Harappan city, remarkable for its exquisite planning, monumental structures, aesthetic architecture, and an elaborate water-management system.[57] The center of the huge 100-hectare site is a fortified township comprising of the citadel, the Middle Town, and the Lower Town—so named by archaeologists based on their relative location, layout, and architecture. The citadel and the Middle Town are fortified with elaborate defense walls while the Lower Town has no such fortification, although it is encapsulated by the larger fortification of the town. The citadel is in the south, and it is said to have two conjoined subdivisions—the castle on the east and the bailey on the west (Bisht 2015, 107–30). Surrounding this main fortification is a series of reservoirs, part of the elaborate water-harvesting system in Dholavira fed by seasonal streams. Dholavira also yielded an inscription of 10 large-sized signs of the Harappan script, which the excavators argue was the oldest signboard in the world. Through the enormous accumulation caused by successive settlements of over a millennium, the archaeological excavations have revealed eight significant cultural stages (numbered from Stage I to VIII) of the rise, culmination, and fall of the Harappan urban system.[58] Other than the archetypal mature Harappan architectural characteristics of planned township and drainage systems, one of the most important discoveries of Dholavira has been an elaborate water conservation system consisting of 16 reservoirs of varying sizes. During my ethnography at the site (2003–04), the excavation work at Dholavira involved exposing the fourth corner of the Eastern Reservoir; features of Southern Reservoirs; settlement deposits in the Castle where a well-plastered mud wall of Stage III was exposed; and "Tumulus 2," where new characteristics of funerary structures were awaiting excavation (Bisht 2015, 647–63).

Bhirrana was in the district of Fathebad in Haryana, discovered in 1982. It was a Muslim burial ground in use before the partition of the Indian subcontinent at the time of decolonization in 1947. The archaeological site, at the edge of the village of Bhirrana, was supposed to be "overlooking the left bank of the now dried up river Saraswati" (Rao et al. 2004, 20), or the Ghaggar. The first season of excavation suggested that the site consisted of three distinct periods—early Harappan, transitional, and mature Harappan. The characteristic feature of the early Harappan settlement that the excavators found was circular pit dwellings, which had also been reported at the sites of Mithathal and Kunal in the adjoining region. The Period II, which has been designated as a transitional period, was identified with the fortification of the site. These periods were followed by a mature Harappan phase with distinctive town-planning and material cultural assemblages (*IAR 2003–04* 2011, 42–56). The objectives of the excavation during the season I was working (2004–05) were elaborated as:

> 1) a detailed study of the town planning of the mature Harappan phase; 2) to identify the dividing line between citadel and the lower town; 3) to locate the extent of fortification wall towards north, south, and east; 4) to study the real nature and purpose of the circular structures found within habitation; 5) an intensive study of the early Harappans in view of a considerable deposit of 1.70 meters, and to know the nature of the pit dwellings found in this region. (Rao et al. 2004, 20)

The excavation at Bhirrana continued until the season of 2005–06. The Carbon-14 dating of the site has made it one of the earliest Harappan settlements in India (Dikshit 2013; *IAR 2004–05* 2014, 57).

In Rajasthan, I worked at the site of Baror, Anupgad *tehsil*, of Sri Ganganagar district (29° 10' 07" N, 73° 18' 49" E).[59] It is about 100 kilometers southwest of the important Harappan site of Kalibangan that was excavated by the ASI in the 1960s. The archaeological mound of Baror was 183 meters in diameter and had 11-meter-high cultural deposits. Excavations have unearthed the remains of the pre-Harappan and mature Harappan cultures. The Patna Ex. Br. had undertaken excavation at this site; I worked at the site for two seasons: 2003–04 and 2004–05. This site had both early Harappan and mature Harappan layers (Sant et al. 2004; *IAR 2003–04* 2011, 225–43; *IAR 2004–05* 2014, 111–35). Near Baror in the same district were the sites of Tarkhanewala Dera and Chak 86 that were excavated for only a single season, of 2003–04, by the Bhubaneshwar Ex. Br. Tarkhanewala Dera (29° 14' 17" N; 73° 13' 27" E) was not a prominent mound, being heavily destroyed by a contemporary brick-kiln. This site was discovered and first excavated by A. K. Ghosh. The archaeological site measured approximately 50 meters N–S × 100 meters E–W. The assistant archaeologist (AA) working at the site informed that before the excavation, the surface was strewn with a large quantity of typical mature Harrapan ceramic type. The site of Chak 86 (29° 14' 12" N; 73° 13' 45" E) was located adjacent to Tarkhanewala Dera. Both the sites were on the road to Anupgarh—Tarkhanewala Dera was on the left of the district highway and Chak 86 was on the right. According to my informants, they were apparently the same mound that was torn apart by a contemporary road. This site was also partly destroyed by contemporary brick-kiln work. The mound was approximately 2 meters high from the surrounding plain (Trivedi 2009; *IAR 2003–04* 2011, 205–12).

Finally, I also spent two seasons at the multicultural mound of Hansi in Haryana (Hissar district) excavated by the Delhi Ex. Br. This site, near the dry bed of the River Drishdavati, was a medieval fortification—occupied by the Rajputs, the Mughals, and the British. Unlike other SHP sites, this was not known to be a Harappan site, although the explicit aim of the excavations was to locate the Harappan layers. During the two seasons I was present, a few vertical trenches were excavated but no Harappan layers were found. A trench laid on the southern end of the fortification had reported Iron Age culture horizons, while the intervening cuttings within the fortification have reported Kushana and Gupta levels at an average depth of 15 meters to 13 meters. The upper levels reported extensive remains of structures of medieval and British periods.

Notes

1. Along with Bhirranna (Lat. 29°33'N; 75°33'E), Fatehabad district has a number of Harappan sites, most notable being the site of Banawali (Lat. 29°37"5'N; 75°23"6'E) excavated by R. S. Bisht in 1983–84 under the aegis of the Department of Archaeology, Haryana (Bisht 1978, 87; Bisht and Asthana 1979; *IAR 1983–84* 1986, 24–28).

2. My informants told me that the choice of the excavation was driven by a chance discovery of a horde of lapis lazuli beads from the site.

3. Its excavators described Bhirrana as a site with a mound that

   > measures 150 m North–South and 190 m East–West and rises to the height of about 5.50 m from the surrounding area of flat alluvial-sottar plain. The eastern part of the mound is slightly higher than the western part as the latter was flattened for agricultural purposes in the recent past. (Rao et al. 2004, 20)

4. Archaeological levels at Bhirrana based on relative dating of the material culture along with Carbon-14 dates are: Pre-Harappan Hakra phase (7500–6000 BCE), Early Harappan (6000–4500 BCE), Early Mature Harappan (4500–3000 BCE), and Mature Harappan (3000–1800 BCE). See Rao et al. (2005); Rao (2006); Dikshit (2013).

5. Radiocarbon dating in India can only be done at the Physical Research Laboratory, Ahmedabad, Biren Roy Research Laboratory for Archaeological Dating, Jadavpur University, and Birbal Sahni Institute of Palaeobotany, Lucknow. India's first radiocarbon laboratory was set up at the Tata Institute of Fundamental Research, Bombay, under D. P. Agarwal, and later moved to the Physical Research Laboratory. It produced the earliest radiocarbon dates; however, for the last 10–15 years, the ASI has been using the Birbal Sahni

Institute of Palaeobotany as its preferred lab for getting dates. However, these dates would often take a long time to arrive. The CAG report noted:

> We observed cases of inordinate delay in getting the results of the dating samples taken from Banawali and Dholavira which were sent to Birbal Sahni Institute and Physical Research Laboratory and copper samples sent to IIT Kanpur. In Vadodara Circle, six samples from Junikaran excavation were sent for testing to Institute of Physics, Bhubaneswar in June 2005, and July 2006 but results were still awaited. (CAG 2013, 121)

6.   G. L. Possehl is cautious about temporal assertions made on the basis of radiocarbon dates: "There are inherent problems in the archaeological record in terms of an archaeologist's control over the precise relationship between charcoal samples used for dating and their association with the history we are attempting to date" (Possehl 1993a, 244–45).

7.   Prominent texts amongst the vast literature are Deshpande and Hook (1979); Renfrew (1987); Parpola (1988); Mallory (1989); Erdosy (1995); Gamkrelidze and Ivanov (1995); Trautmann (1997); Bryant (2001); Witzel (2001); and Parpola (2015).

8.   Pit Grave culture(s) of the Pontic-Caspian steppe at 4000–2800 BC, its descendant the Catacomb Grave culture(s) of 2800–2000 BCE, its successors the Timber Grave (Srubnaja) culture(s) of 2000–1000 BCE and the related Andronovo cultures of 2000–900 BCE are some of the prominent cultures that archaeologists claim to be material evidence of the Indo-Aryan people. However, there is no consensus on their relationship to each other (Lamberg-Karlovsky 2002).

9.   There is a vast body of literature that has emerged from Hindutva commentators on the making of the Aryan ethnicity. However, some of the most astonishingly outlandish are Deo and Kamath (1993); Talageri (1993); Frawley (1994); Danino and Nahar (1996); Rajaram and Frawley (1997); Elst (1999); and Danino (2010). In the last two decades with the rise of social media, these ideas have been regurgitated, exaggerated, and propagated by innumerable Hindutva sites, Facebook groups, and Twitter handles.

10.   The history of the discovery of the Harappan civilization has been fraught with claims, assertions, and disputes about evidence since its discovery in 1924, which has made this sub-discipline of Indian archaeology an epistemological conundrum. See Pande (1982); Possehl (1982); Thakran (2000); Bhan (2001); Ramaswamy (2001, 2004); Singh (2004); Guha (2005); and Lahiri (2005) for some examples of the convoluted nature of the field.

11.   The nature of society, forms of religious belief, complexities of cultural systems, linguistics family, and the kind of script are areas of scholarship

where interpretative and speculative narratives based on insufficient empirical evidence have been widespread. For instance, see Rao (1982), Jacobson (1986); Atre (1987); Parpola (1994, 2015).

12. For literature on the making of Vedic Harappans' subjectivity as archaeological ethnicity, see S. P. Gupta (1995, 1996); Singh (1995); Lal (1998, 2002b); Kalyanaraman (1999); and Bisht (1999).

13. For a polemical yet rigorous scholarship based on minute philological analysis of early and later Vedic linguistics, see the works of Michael Witzel (1987, 1995, 1997, 1999).

14. Philological arguments do not provide solid empirical evidence for the 1200 BCE date for the compilation of the *Rig Veda*. However, that is the generally accepted date by the Indological community (Bryant 2001, 266).

15. Harappan chronology and categorization is not fixed. However, there is consensus that there were three major periods or phases. The first was the Early Harappans (3300–2600 BCE), followed by the most discernible Mature Harappans (2600–1900 BCE) and, finally, the Late Harappans (1900–1300 BCE). The period of overlap between the Aryans and the Harappans is supposedly the Late Harappans. See Kenoyer (1998); Possehl (2002); Madella and Fuller (2006); Wright (2009).

16. During the excavations at Harappa, Wheeler maintained regular correspondences with Childe on his discoveries and interpretation of the site. See AACD File No. 19/15/44. Also see Coningham and Manuel (2009).

17. In his report on the excavation in Harappa, Wheeler notoriously adjudicates:

> Climatic, economic, political deterioration may have weakened it [Harappan civilization], but its ultimate extinction is more likely to have been completed by deliberate and large-scale destruction. It may be no mere chance that at a late period of Mohenjodaro men, women, and children appear to have been massacred there. On circumstantial evidence, Indra stands accused. (Wheeler 1947b, 82)

18. For an extended argument on the racial category of the Dravidian race, see Heras (1953); Zide (1970); and Zvelebil (1985). For a critique of the idea of Dravidian origins of the Harappans, see Ramaswamy (2001) and Guha (2005).

19. Following the discoveries of Mohenjo-Daro and Harappa, extensive explorations were undertaken in Sindh and Baluchistan by N. G. Majumdar, who discovered mounds at Chanhudaro and Amri, along with more than 60 sites in that region. He was a close associate of Rakhaldas Banerjee and was killed by bandits in Sindh during an archaeological survey in 1938. See Majumdar (1934).

20. The literature is very large; however, some of the earliest texts which make these assertions are Shendge (1977); Singh (1995); Gupta (1996); Bisht (1999, 2006); and Lal (2002b).

21. I use the term "Harappan civilization" throughout the book, although my informants mostly used the term "Indus civilization" or "Sindhu sabhyata" when we spoke in Hindi.

22. Although most of the rivers mentioned in the *Rig Veda*—Indus, Sutlej, Yamuna, and Ganga—have their terra-firma manifestations, it is the Saraswati whose terrestrial evidence is absent.

23. For a critical account of the ideology of the colonial knowledge production enterprise in the eighteenth and nineteenth centuries, see Bayly (1988); Scott (1995); Cohn (1996); Metcalf (1997); K. Raj (2000); and Dirks (2001).

24. See Mukherjee (1968); Chakrabarti (1988, 1997); Kejariwal (1988); Cannon (1994); Paddayya (1995); Trautmann (1997); Murray (1998); and Franklin (2011).

25. For more details, see Latour and Woolgar (1986); also see Latour (1987, 1999).

26. Thomas cites this work as *Etude sur la géographie et les populations primitives du Nord-Ouest de l'Inde, d'aprés les hymnes Vediques*, which appeared in *Mémoire couronné, en 1855, par I' Académie des inscriptions et belleslettres*, Paris, Imp. Impériale, 1860 (Thomas 1883, 357). M. Viven de Saint-Martin's work was based on a French translation of the *Rig Veda* by S. A. Langlois published in 1848 about which Max Müller in the preface of his own translation notes with contempt as "thoroughly uncritical, guess-work of a man of taste" (Müller 1869, xv).

27. On the politics of translation in colonial Indology, see Dirks (2001) and Dodson (2007).

28. By the 1830s and 1840s, the areas around the Indus in Sindh (annexed in 1843) and Punjab (annexed in 1849) had become increasingly important for the British because of its turbulent geopolitics fuelled also by the humiliating defeat in Afghanistan in 1838–42. Thus, this part of India had become a fertile ground for travel writings mostly by military personnel on reconnaissance missions. Also see Burnes (1834a); MacMurdo (1834, 1839); Baker (1840).

29. John Marshall in the "breaking news" article underscores the importance of the discovery:

> Up to the present, our knowledge of Indian antiquities has carried us back hardly further than the third century before Christ ... now, however, there has unexpectedly been unearthed, in the south of the Panjab and in Sind, an entirely new class of objects which have nothing in common with those previously known to us, and which are unaccompanied by any data that might have helped to establish their age and origin. (Marshall 1924, 528)

30. The *Illustrated London News* was established in 1842, in London, with an emphasis on the pictorial commentary on domestic and imperial affairs. By 1887, it pioneered the printing of photographs and, by 1897, it had a circulation of 400,000 copies, making it one of the largest weeklies in Europe.

31. The discovery of the Harappan civilization was not a result of heroic brilliance of John Marshall as Nayanjot Lahiri's account suggests (Lahiri 2005, 2012, 2017), but the epistemological outcome of "investigative modalities" of knowledge production mechanisms of colonial modernity—to survey, discover, name, and, eventually, control an occupied territory.

32. Charles Masson of the Bengal Artillery records the earliest mention of the Harappan material culture in 1826 when he traveled in the Punjab after deserting the army (Masson 1844), along with Alexander Burns in his accounts in Bokhara (Burnes 1834b). James Tod during his time as a political agent in western Rajputana noted the presence of Kalibangan in Bikaner state (Tod 1832, 215).

33. Almost all archaeologists who have surveyed the Ghaggar–Hakra valley in India and Pakistan (Ghosh 1952, 1956, 1959; Ram 1972; Bhan 1973; Singh 1981; Mughal 1992, 1997) and even contemporary archaeologists invoke Stein as an inspiration (Gupta 1995, 1996; Bisht 1999; 2015, 22; Nath 2015, 50).

34. Alexander Cunningham was one of the earliest to survey the Harappan countryside (Cunningham 1875). Other prominent explorers include Luigi Tessitori, R. D. Banerjee, and Daya Ram Sahni, followed by Aurel Stein (Stein 1988 [1943], 1942) in the last years of pre-partition India. A. H. Dani (Dani 1981) and A. K. Ghosh (Ghosh 1956, 1959) conducted exploration work in Pakistan and India respectively after the division of the sub-continent. For a historical narrative about the prehistory of the discovery of the Harappan civilization, see Lahiri (2005).

35. This moment has been greatly celebrated and argued as the watershed moment in the history of Indian archaeology. See Ghose, Kar, and Hussain (1979, 1980); Snelgrove (1979); Bakliwal and Sharma (1980); Yashpal, Sood, and Agrawal (1980); Kar (1983, 1989, 1994, 1998 1999); Sood and Sahai (1983); Kar and Ghose (1984); Bakliwal and Grover (1988); Raghav and Grover (1991); Sahai et al. (1993); Sharma, Srinivasan, and Dhabriya (1992); Radhakrishna and Merh (1999); Rajawat, Sastry, and Narain (1999); Ramasamy, Bakliwal, and Verma (1991); Puri (2001); Roy and Jakhar (2001); and Ramasamy (2005).

36. A type of epistemic entity, visionary objects are defined as "conceptual objects that have high levels of legitimacy within a particular community. They can evoke similar emotive and affective responses from a wide spectrum of people, possessing a sacred quality that makes it difficult for a 'rational' person to be against them" (Briers and Chua 2001, 242).

37. For a captivating narrative about the genesis and the political undercurrents of these peculiar coinage, see Reich (2018, 134–35).

38. Two more terms were later introduced in this mapping process: "Ancestral Austro-Asiatic" for the tribal population of central India and "Ancestral Tibeto-Burman" for the population in Northeast India. It was argued: "The genomic structure of mainland Indian populations is best explained by contributions from four ancestral components" (Basu, Sarkar-Roy, and Majumder 2016, 1594).

39. Early Hindutva ideologues such as V. D. Savarkar and M. S. Golwalkar had an ambivalent relationship to Aryans and their homeland. Savarkar did not challenge the Aryan invasion theory and skirted the issue by arguing for Hindu indigeneity on the basis of religion and not geography (Savarkar 1923). While Golwalkar agreed with Tilak's theory of Aryans in the Artic, he, however, suggested that the North Pole was not stationary but was once in northern India (Golwalkar 1939).

40. The publication of Fa Xian's *Foe Koue Ki ou Relation des Royaumes Bouddhiques* in 1836, and Stanislas Julien's translation of Xuan Zang's *Mémoires sur les contrées occidentals* in 1857–58 was used by Cunningham to physically locate places and monuments related to Buddhism in India.

41. Also see AACD File No. 19/11/55; 1955—"Regarding Report on Hastinapur and Bhopal Excavations required by the Prime Minister of India." The last paragraph of the report says: "… archaeology seems to shed light on the ethnic fixation of the people that succeeded the Harappans in the upper Indo-Gangetic basin. May not these be the Aryans as the consensus of evidence tends to suggest?"

42. For more on the relationship between B. B. Lal's archaeological narrative of the ASI, the Hindutva movement, and the Ayodhaya crisis, see Chakrabarti (2003); Mandal (2004); Ratnagar (2004); and Roy (2004).

43. A statement emanating from the conference was reflected in the editorial of the RSS magazine *Manthan* (15 [2–3], April–September 1994), which unequivocally stated:

> The Aryan Race and Invasion Theory is not a subject of academic interest only; rather it conditions our perceptions of India's historical evolution, the sources of our culture and socio-economic political institutions. Consequently, it has a strong bearing on the contemporary Indian politics as well as the future of Indian nationalism … almost all the current disintegrative and separatist movements—whether regional or casteist in character-have their intellectual root in this Aryan Race and Invasion Theory.… [T]he issue assumes importance because it is a question relating to the origins of our culture. In fact our identity depends on it.… [N]

ow with the discovery of the lost track of the Rigvedic river Saraswati, the excavation of a chain of Harappan sites from Ropar in the Punjab to Lothal and Dholavira in Gujarat all along this lost track, the discovery of the archaeological remains of Vedic Yupas connected with Vedic Yajnas at Harappan sites like Kalibangan, decipherment of the Harappan script by many scholars as a language of the Sanskrit family ... the discovery of the lost Dwarka city beneath the sea water near Gujarat coast and its similarity with Harappan civilization, all these new discoveries establishing full identity of the Harappan civilization with Vedic civilization, demand a re-examination of Aryan Race and Invasion Theory. (Quoted in Bhan 1997, 13–14)

44. The occurrence of the horse has a conjectural association with the arrival of Aryans in India. Thus, Sharma's claim of the presence of their faunal remains in Surkotada has been regarded as evidence for the Vedic Harappans. However, this claim has been challenged by Richard Meadow who has argued that prevailing evidence in India does not suggest the presence of the domesticated horse before 1000–700 BCE (Meadow 1996).

45. B. B. Lal interpreted fire-hearths in Kalibangan as Vedic fire altars, and specifically that of *dhisnya* hearths of the Vedic *soma* sacrifice, where the priests sit west of the altar, facing east (Lal 1984, 57).

46. At Lothal, Rao is careful and interpreted fire-hearths as ritualistic; however, he took that as evidence of Indo-Aryan presence (Rao 1993, 175).

47. See Radhakrishna and Merh (1999), along with issues of journals like *Man and Environment* and *Puratattva* from the late 1980s to the early 2000s where scholars, geologists, archaeologists, and unambiguous Hindutva ideologues (David Frawley, Koenraad Elst, Navaratna S. Rajaram, Bhagwan Singh, Michel Danino, and others) through incestuous citations were involved with the making of the Saraswati river an unquestionable fact.

48. See AACD File No. 9/10/2003-SH. The academic justification of the project is given as:

> The "lost" Sarasvati of the "Rigvedic" fame has been identified ever since the 19th century onwards by the geographers, geologists, cartographers, historians and archaeologists with the palaeochannel that originates from Siwaliks and runs through parts of Haryana, Rajasthan, Cholistan in Paksitani Punjab, Sind and Kachchha in Gujarat then it meets the Arabian Sea through the Kori creek. The different segments of its channel are variously known as Sarasvati from the Siwaliks to Bahar in Haryana, as Jioia Nalah from Tohana to Chandu Khera—Kunal, as Rangoi from Kunal through Fatehabad to Sirsa, as Ghaggar from Sirsa-Otu to Binjor; as Hakra in Cholistan in Pakistan, and as Eastern Nara in Sindh, Pakistan,

and from there it runs through the Rann and passes through the Kori creek to the sea. Archaeologically, its entire flood plain is dotted with numerous sites ranging from pre-urban/proto-urban/mature urban and late/decadent urban phases of the Indus Valley Civilization of Copper-Bronze Age, cultures of early Iron Age, early historical through different historical phases down to late medieval times—all ranging from 4th millennium B. C. onwards. However, there is observed a perceptible dwindling both quantitatively and qualitatively in the settlement pattern which must be due to the changing water regime in the river which remained variable which is even vouched for in the ancient literature itself. While the "Rigveda" clearly describes the Sarasvati as a mighty river from the mountains to the ocean: ekachetat Sarasvati nadinam suchir yati giribhya a samudrat, (the Sarasvati moves on from the mountains to the ocean) by the time of the later Vedic period, it was already on the path of desiccation as is found in the Satapatha Brahmana, Panchvimsa Brahmana and the Mahabharata. Environmentally, it coincides with the onset of the global aridity around c. 2000 B.C. The Sarasvati, along with the Indus, supported a large number of Harappan settlements including the urban centres at Banawali, Kalibangan, Ganweriwala Ther, Mohenjodaro, Kot Diji and Amri, Rakhigarhi, besides numerous other sites of later period. A study of satellite imageries has vividly shown floodplain of the Sarasvati. Still, a set of modern historians and scholars have questioned the identification. Hence an imperative need for settling the issues of different school of thoughts.

49.   This committee was instituted with a gazette notification S.O. 1329 (E), dated December 18, 2002. Its members were: J. P. Joshi, S. P. Gupta, D. K. Chadha, M. S. Nagaraja Rao, M. C. Joshi, V. M. K. Puri, Baldev Sahai, S. Kalyanaraman, V. N. Misra, D. S. Chauhan, D. L. Jain, and T. R. Anatharaman, along with the director general of the ASI and secretaries of the Culture and Tourism Ministry (AACD, File No. 9/10/2002-EE).

50.   The ASI requested the Department of Expenditure, Ministry of Finance, to create new positions for 56 staff members for a period of four years for the Sarasvati Heritage Project (AACD, File No. 9/10/2003-SH).

51.   The budget includes money for the "construction of archaeological complexes at 15 sites; exploration and excavation; conservation; horticulture and ecological up gradation; equipment; operational vehicles; library and related material; staff at the secretarial and hub Offices; consultancy and research activities; publication of reports; conducting seminars/workshops" (AACD, File No. 9/10/2003-SH).

52.   Each of the sites termed as a "Hub" was proposed to have an archaeological complex consisting of

an orientation centre; a documentation centre; a thematic library; a pavilion containing a model of the Saraswati basin in its cultural and topographical perspectives; dormitories for a short stay of research scholars, students as well as interested tourists. All above to be set in a garden setting with a pool of water symbolically representing the river(s). (AACD, File No. 9/10/2003-SH)

53. In a national newspaper, Jagmohan explained his justification as:

> Last year [2002] alone, domestic traffic increased by three crores. I have multiple objectives—to bring to life culturally significant monuments, towns, and sacred spots, improve the surrounding area and infuse keen civic sense to make it a pleasant experience. I also want to encourage visitors to come in contact with the profound minds which created all these wonders. (Gopinath 2003)

54. Some of the members such as S. P. Gupta and S. Kalyanaraman were openly part of Hindu fundamentalist organizations like the RSS. Others such as J. P. Joshi, M. C. Joshi, V. M. K. Puri, Baldev Sahai, and V. N. Misra were considered close to the BJP. See Thakran (2000); Habib (2001); Mukherjee (2001); Guha (2005); and Johnson-Roehr (2008) for more discussions of the relationship between Hindutva ideology and the ASI.

55. Excavations at Hansi were not reported in the *IAR 2003–04* (2011) or *IAR 2004–05* (2014).

56. R. S. Bisht was awarded the Padma Shri (the fourth highest civilian award of the Government of India) for his contribution to the field of archaeology in 2013.

57. The Dholavira excavation budget for the year 2003–04 was estimated to be INR 43.30 lakhs. This was the 12th season of excavation at Dholavira that began on November 14, 2003, and continued until March 4, 2004 (AACD, File No. F.15/30/2003-EE).

58. Stages I and II (c. 7500–4500 BCE) have been identified with early farming village, whereas Stages V–VI (c. 3200–1900 BCE) are considered Harappan urbanism, and Stages VII–VIII (c. 1900–700) are when the collapse of the metropolis occurs (Bisht 2015, 10).

59. This was a known site and had been surveyed by L. P. Tessitore (1916–17), Aurel Stein (1940–41), and A. Ghosh (1953).

3   Bureaucratic Hierarchy in the ASI

It was around 8.30 in the morning at the site of Baror in western Rajasthan, at the sprawling edge of the India–Pakistan border. The sun was shining gingerly, and the early morning mist was slowly clearing away. It was a short walk from the camp to the site—from a barricaded spatiality to another. As I climbed the excavated mound, I observed that the floor of the trenches was still damp. The outline of the famous mud-brick walls of Harappan architecture, common in this part of the Indus civilization, was visible. An assistant archaeologist (AA) cautiously accompanied me. We were prudently walking across the excavated areas, balancing ourselves on the balks of the Wheelerian Grid, careful not to let dirt fall into the trenches. He was a stout, middle-aged man with a coarse beard, sporting a white baseball cap. A black woolen muffler protected his neck. He was wearing a full-sleeved blue check shirt, dark blue rugged jeans, and white Nike sport shoes (a knock-off bought from Delhi's Palika Bazaar). He tucked a fake steel-rimmed black Ray-Ban sunglasses in his shirt's breast pocket. The trenches were 2 or 3 meters deep—empty, devoid of structural features. Five laborers were working in each of the trenches, huddled together in a circle, crouched with brushes and knives, methodically removing dirt from the floor of the trench. There was winter chill in the air but the bright sunlight's warmth embraced us gently. The AA was sharing details, cheerfully, about his career trajectory in the ASI. In the course of the conversation, he narrated a mesmerizing analogy—a "theory" he had "inherited" (*viraasat mein mili hai*) from a senior, retired ASI archaeologist, who, after spending a career in the ASI, merely (*kewal-matr*) retired as a deputy superintending archaeologist (Dy SA).

The AA elaborated that the Dy SA had often compared the hierarchy in the ASI to the divisions proposed in the "Purusha Sukta" in the tenth *mandala* of the *Rig Veda*, Book 10, hymn 90 (Griffith 1897: 517–20).[1] These hymns describe the ritual sacrifice of the primordial man. The "Purusha Sukta" has become the quintessential fragment from the *Rig Veda*, often invoked in popular culture in contemporary India to illuminate the mythological foundation of the caste hierarchy in India: "The Brahman was his mouth, of both his arms was the Rajanya made. His thighs became the Vaisya, from his feet the Shudra was produced" (Griffith 1897: 519). During the ritual sacrifice of the primordial man, the highest caste—Brahman—emerged from the mouth of the primordial man; the Kshatriya, or the warrior caste, emerged from the arms; the Vasiya, the trading caste, from the thighs; the Shudra, the lowest caste, emerged from the feet. The "Purusha Sukta" is categorically a sociologically diagnostic hymn of the *Rig Veda*—Indologists and colonial officials have deployed it since the early nineteenth century to vindicate caste hierarchy in Indian society.[2] This cosmogenic metaphor has since been incorporated in the popular culture of middle-class Indians after caste-based affirmative action was institutionalized in the Indian Constitution for the lowest castes (Scheduled Castes and the Scheduled Tribes) in 1950.

In 1989, there was a 23 percent increase in caste-based "reservations," based on the Mandal Commission report, which recommended that not just the Scheduled Castes and the Scheduled Tribes but also the Other Backward Classes (OBCs) be provided with reservations in government jobs and in jobs at academic institutions. This led to widespread violence in urban India (Roy Burman 1992; Maheshwari 1995). Extensive media coverage and heated public debates brought hymns such as the "Purusha Sukta" and other Sanskrit texts such as the *Manusmriti*, which sanctified the caste system, into sharp focus (Rao 2009). It was not a surprise to see an upper-caste Brahmin archaeologist using the "Purusha Sukta" analogy.[3] He had been "hit [*maar*] by the reservation system" in the ASI. This was an emotional topic of discussion in the ASI, in the context of recruitments and promotions. Like thousands of students, he had protested against the Mandal Commission report in Patna—his hometown—during the student unrest in the autumn of 1990 (Rao 1990; Engineer 1991). As we slowly walked at the edge of the trenches, he continued:

> Like in the Rigveda, in the ASI a strong hierarchy exists. The Brahmins are those bureaucrats [*babus*] who sit [*baithiye rahte hai*] in the D.G. office. These are the senior officers, who chart out major plans, sit in planning meetings, and give general directions to the ASI. The Kshatriyas are the archaeologists who work in the Excavation Branches (Ex. Brs.). These are the SAs and the Dy SAs, who work in the field—*the battlefield* [English word used]. Whenever outsiders challenge the ASI's contribution to the world, it is the work of the archaeologists in the field that is showcased. They are the front-line soldiers of the ASI. The Vaisyas are those officers who work in the Circle Offices, the Conservation Assistants, who make a lot of money. They are the real traders and businessmen [*baniya*]. The Shudras are workers [*mazdoor*] like us, the AAs, the technical staff, the lowest in the hierarchy, the draughtsman, the surveyors, and the artists. We are the ones who toil the hardest [*hum sabse jyada khatathe hai*].

The ASI employees, in their daily practice, engaged with the bureaucratic structure of the organization mediated by three levels of power structure, defined by official spatiality—the Director General (DG) Headquarters Office, the Circle Offices, and the Ex. Brs. With the right "luck, caste, and connections" (*kismet, caste aur connection*), a student, after obtaining a diploma from the Institute of Archaeology, joins the ASI as a junior officer—AA—through a written exam and an interview conducted by the Staff Selection Commission Board (SSCB).[4] With the "luck, caste and connections configuration remaining constant," in the words of another informant, the AA would be promoted to an assistant superintending archaeologist (ASA), then to the post of a Dy SA, and then a superintending archaeologist (SA), before retiring from the "service." The second rung of the hierarchy comprised the SA, who heads the Circle Offices and the Branches. Depending on the seniority and cadre, a Dy SA could be promoted to the post of an SA, and to the post of a director.[5] But there were only about a dozen directors in the ASI, and the promotion from an SA to a director was solely based on meritocracy.[6] "Merit means a lot of politics and networking," insinuated one of my informants. The director's post fell under the highest posts in the ASI hierarchy, along with two joint directors general (Jt DG), an additional director general (ADG), and the director general (DG). However, for many years in the history of postcolonial ASI, these topmost posts had been outside the reach of the junior ASI officers. Each of these promotions could take as little as 2 years or as much as 10 years to materialize—depending on how the "promotion files moved in the DG office." I heard multiple stories about AAs, ASAs, and Dy SAs who, because of several reasons, had been "stuck" (*atak*) in their positions for as long as 10 years. One of these "horror stories" (*bhayanak qissa*) appears in a letter written by B. B. Lal as the chairman of the Lal Committee to the minister of human resource development in March 2001:

> The Committee visited Kalibangan to determine the conservation measures to be taken to preserve for posterity this unique site of the Harappan Civilization. During the visit the Committee met Shri Sant Lal, Deputy Superintending Archaeological Engineer, Jaipur Circle. The committee was shocked to learn that this officer, recruited through UPSC in 1978, has not got even a single promotion in all these 23 years, even though higher vacancies were available and Shri Lal's record has been good. The same has been the fate of the other officers recruited after him. What a picture of utter indifference!! (Lal 2001, 22)

This was not an isolated case. During my fieldwork, I often heard such narratives and met a few officers who were frustrated and disheartened about their stagnant career growth. They viewed their entire career as passing "in front of their eyes" (*hamari aankhon ke samne*) without promotions, credit, or recognition.[7] This problem, the Lal Committee argued, caused the decline in the ASI:

> In the absence of any prospects of promotion in the foreseeable future, it would be too much to expect that they would continue to give their best to the ASI. Such a moribund situation has resulted in rapid deterioration in the quality as well as the quantum of the output. (Lal 2001, 30)

As an ASA who had joined the ASI more than 25 years ago, and who had been promoted only once, he dismissed a young AA's enthusiasm during a conversation we were having about career prospects in the ASI: "We just want to pass out our time in the ASI [*Hume toh ASI mein abhi time katana hai*]. Now you all should work [*Ab aap log kam kijiye*]. Let's see how much you can do."

The problem was so stark that the organizational structure of the junior officer cadre in the ASI reflected an hourglass. At the base were a large number of AAs and at the top were a large number of Dy SAs whereas in the middle there were a few ASAs. Many AAs I spoke to were anxious about this state of affairs. They disclosed that this caused perpetual "tension" in their lives and work, as bleak career prospects were "staring in our face." Commenting on this organizational structure, the Lal Committee notes: "Because of the faulty cadre structure there has been acute frustration or stifling stagnation sapping the cadre of all energy" (Lal 2001, 37). The committee argued that the crux of the problem has been the absence of the mandatory cadre review once in five years: "Not a single cadre-review has so far been done for the ASI. But, most other departments of the Government of India have benefited, repeatedly, because the Administration there had conscience and some accountability and organized cadre reviews" (Lal 2001, 39).[8] It placed the blame on the topmost in the hierarchy of the ASI (the DGs), who were not archaeologists but bureaucrats from the Indian Administrative Service (IAS) on deputation in the ASI. The committee accused these deputed IAS DGs for the organizational chaos:

> Such agony may not be seen anywhere else in the Government of India. Still, this state of affairs has not pricked the conscience of any of the deputationist Administrators entrusted with the Cadre management of the ASI for the last two decades. Their achievements have not been just zero, but stunningly negative, destroying the careers of about three generations of officers and staff when we reckon that unless the person climbed the ladder, step by step, during the first ten years of service, in unison, they are stumped or stampeded out. The deputationist had no stakes in the ASI and no accountability to anybody in the ASI. Their careers were secure in their present cadres without vicissitudes which could strike them

had they been there. They got promotions, even accelerated promotions, in their cadres. The ASI had been a "rest-house for them." (Lal 2001, 40)

The committee also noted: "The top posts at the top three levels in the Department have been kept vacant or filled by deputationists choking the breath of the cadre.... It appears, in the ASI, the fence has been eating the crop to be guarded" (Lal 2001, 55).

The bureaucratic structure of the ASI exacerbated the institutional oppression that was endemic to it. Each rank member blamed the higher officers in the hierarchy for systemic oppression in the form of arbitrary transfers, delayed promotions, exasperating work conditions, or inadequate infrastructure to produce "quality work." This was a cause for high stress (*bahut tension*) levels among all cadres of officers. However, each cadre expunged its own complicity in this systemic oppression of the statist bureaucratic apparatus. I conducted my fieldwork in the background of utter resignation and discontent that prevailed through the rank and file of the ASI staff, which still continues. I have been told by my informants with whom I have been in touch over the past decade that "nothing much has changed" (*vyesa ka vyesa hi hai, kuch nahi badla*) since my ethnography. This is also evidenced by the various recommendations that are suggested by the CAG report (2013: 169–76) and the Niti Aayog report (2020: 145–53).

Director General Headquarters

At the top of the ASI hierarchy was the DG, whose office is in New Delhi—referred to as just "Headquarters." For nearly 60 years, it was situated in a temporary location—a large colonial bungalow in Lutyens' Delhi, tucked in an alleyway between the National Museum, housing the treasures of Indian art and antiquities, and the Vigyan Bhavan, a premier conference hall of the Government of India, the venue for some of the most important national and international conventions and conferences held in the capital. In 2018, this office was shifted to a new location within the national bureaucratic district, not far away from its previous location. The old DG office had a quaint aura of Indian bureaucracy; it was overcrowded, congested, overflowing, and cramped. Workplaces were erstwhile oversized colonial bedrooms and living rooms converted into partitioned office spaces. Wooden tables with large desktop computers, electronic typewriters, and modular steel chairs jostled with each other for space. The quotidian material culture of government officialdom overflowed from weary cabinets, feeble steel racks, and exhausted wooden cupboards. Men and women could be seen crouching over their tables doing paperwork, hidden behind stacks of files, or peering into archaic desktop computers. The quivering sound of ceiling fans or the deep drone of air coolers would penetrate the dry heat of Delhi when I visited the DG office.

This prime location gives the ASI its status as one of the most significant survey organizations of the Indian state. The employees claimed this central location in New Delhi made it the most prestigious of all the survey organizations in India and bestowed on it a unique status. None of the other Government of India survey organizations—the Geological Survey of India, the Survey of India, and the Anthropological Survey of India—had their headquarters in New Delhi.[9] Thus, because of having its headquarters in New Delhi, the ASI got a special place in the bureaucratic structure of the Government of India. It had the privilege of a "truly central government organization." This prominence was significant for all the informants. An AA in Dholavira, explaining the importance of being a *Dilliwale* (an inhabitant of Delhi), at the faraway fringes of the nation in Kutch, remarked: "We do not get as much respect as military officials. But even the military respects us when they come to know we are from Delhi" (*Hame military jaisi ijjat toh nahi milti hai per Dilliwale hone ke kaaran military wale bhi ijjat karte hai*). Even temporary laborers who worked at the excavation site, far away from New Delhi, asserted it was prestigious to be working for a central government agency with its headquarters in the capital city (*rajdhani*). This politics of location was important in the self-imagination of ASI employees. It instilled in them a sense of self-importance, which was essential to their daily work as bureaucratic officials, far away from the center of governance.

The headquarters housed the offices of the topmost officers of the ASI. Along with the office of the DG, the offices of the ADG, 2 Jt DGs, and 11 directors of various departments were also located there. These 11 departments spanned all the work of the ASI: Administration, Expeditions Abroad, Conservation, Mission and Project Planning, Publication, Monument (2), Antiquities, Exploration and Excavation, Central Archaeological Library, and Museum. These officers were supported by a number of SAs, Dy SAs, ASAs, and AAs. A retinue of technical staff, clerks, peons, and temporary workers formed the bulk of the bureaucratic community at the headquarters. The DG office was at the top of the ASI "chain of command" and "strictly controlled" (*sakthi se kaboob mein rakha hai*) the daily workings of every aspect of the ASI. Both the terms "Headquarters" and "Director General" were vestiges of the colonial military genealogy of the ASI. It personified an authoritative relationship between the DG office in New Delhi and the rest of the regional offices in various parts of the country. I observed that even in temporary excavation sites of the ASI, far away from the physical reaches of the headquarters, small and minute daily decisions were subjected to the DG office's authority.

The post of the DG of the ASI was a contentious one. Since the early 1990s, this post has been mired in controversies, which had a significant impact on the character of the ASI and the self-image of archaeologists working there. The ASI was considered by its archaeologists to be a national organization (*raashtriya sangathan*) whose sole purpose was to produce the "glorious heritage [*viraasat*] of ancient India [*praacheen bhaarat*] and bring it to the attention of the nation." ASI archaeologists believe that they are involved in a national task: "We work for the Indian nation" (*Hum bhartiyata ke liye kaam karte hain*). They believe the knowledge produced by the ASI is indispensable (*anivariya*) because it allows "a third-world nation like India to be proud of its heritage and past [*virasaat aur itihas*]." Central to their pride is the belief that the ASI is not a mere bureaucratic organization, like a department in the Ministry of Irrigation and Water, for example. "We are different [*hum alag hai*] because we are scholars involved with producing knowledge for the nation [*desh ke liye itihas banate hai*], housed in a bureaucracy," clarified an AA. "But things have changed since the post of the DG and other top levels of ASI have been captured by the IAS mafia."[10] He continued:

> Since the inception of the ASI in 1861, it has been led by an archaeologist, a practice that continued for more than a century. But in 1993, for the first time, a non-technical IAS officer was made the DG of the ASI. This has affected the morale and the workings of the ASI a great deal.[11]

The AA further explained,

> IAS DGs know nothing [*kuch nahi maloom*] about archaeology. They cannot make out the difference between a Harappan and an early historic site. They don't understand that archaeology is a field science and that ASI is not a standard [*saadhaaran*] governmental organization. Besides, the post of the DG of the ASI is not considered to be prestigious with the IAS officers. The only incentives that the DG gets are government-sponsored trips abroad showcasing Indian heritage. So, they don't care [*faraq nahi padatha*] about the real worth [*asli ahamiyat*] of the ASI.

This was not an unusual sentiment. All the archaeologists I spoke to allege that there had been a "serious degradation" (*geheri giraavat*) in the workings of the ASI since the post of the DG had been taken over by IAS officers. One excavation director even went to the extent of telling me that "the death knell [*barbad kar diya*] of the ASI was struck the day an IAS officer took over as the DG of the ASI."

I first came to know about this controversy in December 1994, when I attended the infamous plenary session of the World Archaeology Conference (WAC 3) in New Delhi. The restitution of the post of the DG from the IAS was one of the many motions that were presented. It was argued that the ASI was a "scientific and a technical" organization and from "the day it was established, the DG was always an archaeologist"; therefore, it was necessary that the post be restored to a "technical person." This motion was presented by the ex-DGs of the ASI, along with some senior archaeologists of the ASI. It was met with resounding approval from the Indian delegates present in the conference hall. Almost all the informants I spoke to contended that the deteriorated state of the ASI was related to the absence of appropriate leadership. "We are without a true leader. There is no inspiring archaeologist like Wheeler or even like Dr B. B. Lal leading us," explained a draughtsman at Bhirrana. "Things were different when the DG was an archaeologist. He would come to the excavation site and jump into the trench, scratch the trench floor with his knife or draw the stratigraphy lines on the trench wall. They knew what archaeology was all about. They were archaeologists," lamented the senior draughtsman who had experience of more than 20 years in the ASI. He further continued:

> They lived like us in the tents. Ate the food we cooked. Since they were archaeologists, they were sensitive to our concerns. They understood [*samajthe*] the daily needs of an archaeological camp. They were sympathetic [*sahanubhuti*] to issues related to postings, promotions, and transfers of officers. But that is not the case now [*abhi vaysi baath nahi*].

By 2003, it was not just the post of the DG of the ASI that had been taken over by the IAS cadre but also other top posts, including that of the ADG and the two Jt DGs. This choking of senior posts had caused a considerable amount of frustration for ASI officers who had joined the ASI as AAs and had spent their entire careers hoping to reach the top of the organization before they retired.

In 2002, the first recommendation that the Lal Committee submitted to the Government of India was the restoration of the DG post to the departmental archaeologist officer, as the committee believed this to be the crux of the problem that the ASI was facing (Lal 2001, 8). The report is very critical of the fact that a non-archaeologist DG had been the head of an archaeological organization. It voiced a similar concern that the archaeologists I spoke to did. In a stringent and severe condemnation of the policy, the committee notes:

First and foremost: For nearly a decade now the successive occupants of the chair of the Director General of this great archaeological organization have been bureaucrats who, to say the least, were far removed from archaeology. These persons, being non-technical, have clearly been utter failures in providing any leadership in matters of excavation, conservation, research, and other technical matters. Some of the members of this Committee, during visits abroad, have in fact been questioned by senior fellow archaeologists in various countries: "Is your country bereft of archaeologists that you have one bureaucrat or another as the Director General?" What a shameful situation to face, merely on account of the continued indifference of the Government to such vital a matter. Even the British rulers, who were known for their despotic ways, never dared to appoint a non-technocrat as the Director General of Archaeology. (Lal 2001: 30)

In 2009, the then prime minister Manmohan Singh took a special interest in the workings of the ASI. This was not extraordinary. This intervention was at the behest of his daughter Dr Upinder Singh, who is a historian of ancient and medieval India. The prime minister's intervention initiated substantial policy shifts in the ASI, elaborated in his address to the 34th meeting of the Central Advisory Board of Archaeology. He announced:

I recognize that ASI cannot function in the manner that we expect without a drastic overhaul of its rules and procedures.... Professionalism and work culture that require that attracts talents and creates a sense of pride and motivation are vital and I agree with one of the scholars who said that the ASI must be given maximum professional freedom. I assure you that will be the direction in which I would like the Ministry to be supportive of the maximum possible functional freedom being given to ASI for its work. I agree that professionalism and work culture attracts talent and creates a sense of pride and motivation are vital if we are to revitalize this great institution that the ASI is.[12]

This policy shift led to the recruitment of the first archaeologist DG of the ASI after more than two decades—Dr Gautam Sengupta (2010–13). Before taking over as the DG of the ASI, Sengupta worked as director of Archaeology and Museums, West Bengal, and was a member-secretary, Centre for Archaeological Studies and Training, Eastern India. Rakesh Tewari (2014–17), who headed the Uttar Pradesh Archaeological Department for 24 years, succeeded Sengupta.[13] Although the presence of archaeologist DGs did effect certain "superficial" (*bahari*) changes in the workings of the ASI, most of my informants whom I have been in touch with over the years have confided to me that at the ground level things have not changed. "The tattered tents have not changed. The hierarchies have not become less entrenched. The rules about transfer still remain the same.

The excavations still continue to be underfunded. And the laborers are still treated like dirt [*kachara*]," complained an AA who had now become an SA. A draughtsman, who has now retired, explained: "How will things change Sirji? We are ASI; here things move slowly, very slowly. It is only when things become dead like antiquity [*antiquity ki tarha mar na jaye*] that the ASI wakes up. The archaeologist DGs have done nothing for us." The disenchantment was bitter. Another informant who is no longer with the ASI disparagingly clarified that the "system had become so rotten [*system itna sard gaya hai*] that even archaeologist DGs like Gautam Sengupta and Rakesh Tewari could not make any changes." In 2017, an IAS officer again took over as the DG of the ASI, replaced with another IAS officer in 2020.

Excavation Branch

"We form a direct lineage from Wheeler. He trained B. B. Lal, B. K. Thapar (ex DGs of ASI). They trained almost all the senior archaeologists who have worked in the ASI, along with Dr. Bisht. We have been trained by Dr. Bisht, who is our guru; in effect Wheeler is our guru," explained the director of Dholavira one late evening after the excavation for the day was over. We were relaxing on plastic chairs, drinking warm milky tea served by a turban-clad, trouser-wearing laborer in the campsite. Reverence for the teacher was not unusual in the ASI. I had often seen students and senior archaeologists touch B. B. Lal's and R. S. Bisht's feet as a mark of respect. ASI archaeologists considered themselves to be "direct descendants" (*vanshaj*) of the work ethic, the academic excellence, and the scientific rigor that Mortimer Wheeler epitomized. "He gave a new life to the ASI, and made it a truly [*ekdum*] scientific organization," clarified the co-director.

For the ASI archaeologists, to be part of an Ex. Br. rather than any other department of the ASI was prestigious because it was an indicator of their academic acumen. An ASA explained,

> Earlier, all those archaeologists who had an *academic bent-of-mind* [English phrase used] were sent to the Excavation Branch. But since the IAS has taken over the reins of the ASI, things have gone to dogs [*khak ho gaya*]. Now they send anyone [*kisi bhi aire-gaire-nathu-gaire*] to the Excavation Branch. That's why things are in such a bad state [*dayaniya sthiti*].

For archaeologists in the ASI, it was the Ex. Br. that distinguished the ASI from other departments of the central government. "If it was not for the archaeological knowledge we produce, we could have been any other central government organization, like the irrigation department or

PWD [Public Works Department].[14] We are different because we do science [*hum science karte hai*]," clarified an AA at Dholavira. This ability to "do science" was important for the ASI archaeologists because it created a distinctive identity, which to them was "more than governing a district or making roads and dams."

In the ASI, conducting archaeological excavations was the exclusive prerogative of the six Ex. Brs. in the different parts of the country—Nagpur (Ex. Br. I), Delhi (Ex. Br. II), Patna (Ex. Br. III), Bhubaneswar (Ex. Br. IV), Vadodara (Ex. Br. V), and Mysore (Ex. Br. VI). The Ex. Br. was abolished during the financial restructuring of the ASI in 1932 but was restarted by Wheeler in 1944 (Staff Memorandum No. 1, AACD, File No. 33/24/44, 1944; Wheeler 1946a, 2). After 1947, the vigor to explore, discover, and excavate archaeological sites in the independent country led to an unprecedented amount of archaeological work. The Nagpur Branch was established in 1958,[15] New Delhi and Patna in 1971, Bhubaneswar and Vadodara in 1984, and Mysore in 2001.

The task of the Ex. Brs. was exclusively epistemic: "Carrying out problem-oriented survey including exploration and excavation of ancient sites and mounds; Research on the ensuing exploration and excavation work; Preparation of reports based on the fieldwork; Interaction with various universities and research institutions."[16] The administrative hierarchy of the Ex. Br. was structured to optimize the efficiency of the bureaucratic knowledge production mechanism. The Ex. Br. was conceived as a scientific organization that is singularly involved with the discovery of new archaeological sites, and their classification and categorization within the body of academic literature on Indian archaeology and history. It was not responsible for conservation, heritage management, and other administrative activities. ASI archaeologists asserted that the Ex. Br. was considered as that section in the ASI where the most "brilliant" archaeologists with an "academic bent" would be posted. An archaeologist's brilliance in the ASI was judged more by his ability to manage staff and labor in the field than his proclivity toward things epistemic; Wheeler had termed this ability of administrating staff and labor in an excavation site as "man-management" (Wheeler 1954, 173). Although the Ex. Br. was imagined as an academic oasis in a bureaucratic ecology, its organizational structure was no different than other departments of the ASI, and it mirrored Wheeler's recommendations in *Archaeology from the Earth* (Wheeler 1954, 153).

The SA was at the helm of the Ex. Br., who was assisted by two Dy SAs, three or four ASAs, and AAs. These were the "officer" rank staff members, followed by technical staff—photographers, artists, draughtsmen, and surveyors. The non-technical administrative staff of the Ex. Br. consisted of a storekeeper, who was involved in the procurement and maintenance of excavation tools and equipment, a lower division clerk (LDC), and an upper division clerk (UDC), who maintained accounts and managed general administrative work in the Ex. Br. office, along with a stenographer. The last stratum in the bureaucratic hierarchy was called the Class IV staff—office assistants, drivers, and janitors. The lowest were the contractual daily wagers (*dahari*), who did the unskilled work. They were often relatives or close family members of the other staff members. I was told that some had worked for decades on this provisional status, and others would be later hired when a retirement occurred. During the excavation season, the alumni of the Institute of Archaeology would often be employed on a contractual basis as excavation supervisors in the field. They were paid daily wages (*dahari*)—albeit at the pay scale for technical staff.

The Ex. Brs. were spread throughout India and each Branch had developed an area of expertise. Some specialized in historical archaeology of medieval India, others in Buddhist archaeology, and some in Harappan archaeology and prehistoric archaeology. These specializations were related to the geographic territory that an Ex. Br. handled. For example, the Patna and the Bhubaneswar Ex. Brs. were specialists at excavating Buddhist sites. They were in eastern India where numerous Buddhist sites were located. The Delhi Ex. Br. had proficiency in excavating historical sites related to medieval Muslim and pre-Muslim habitation in the Gangetic valley in north India. The Vadodara Ex. Br. specialized in the excavation of the Harappan sites since it was in western India close to most Harappan sites. This idea of specialization was built upon the perception that Indian archaeological heritage was complex and diverse, and each geographical and topical area required years of expertise to be understood. Specialization was also centered on reputation. For example, the Nagpur Ex. Br. was considered to be "the best" Ex. Br. It had a reputation for excavating Harappan sites even though the Harrapan sites it dug were far away from its territorial bounds. It was associated with large-scale Harappan excavations conducted in post-independence India at Ropar (1952–55), Lothal (1959–61), Surkotada (1970–73), and Kalibangan (1961–69). The decision to excavate at a particular site was not only directed by academic curiosity and "problem-oriented" research questions, but also dictated by logistical issues, ideas of academic territoriality, and the specialization and reputation of each Ex. Br.

The Saraswati Heritage Project (SHP) was an exception. For the first time in the history of the ASI, all the Ex. Brs. were ordered to abandon the projects they were involved in and to dig the sites that the office of the DG had allocated them. The SHP was the political project of R. S. Bisht, who was the chief architect of the project.[17] In 2003, he was the excavation director of Dholavira, the director of the Excavation and Exploration Department, the director of the SHP, and the

Jt DG of the ASI. According to my informants, Bisht was close to the cabinet minister of tourism—Jagmohan—and exercised tremendous clout in the ASI during his tenure as a Jt DG. By October 2003, orders had been sent to all the Ex. Brs. to discontinue earlier work in order to take part in the SHP (AACD File No. 9/10/2003-SH). Within the bureaucratic structure of the ASI, it was impossible for any of the Ex. Brs. to ignore the order. Many informants I spoke to were unhappy. They maintained that the order violated the freedom of the SA of the Ex. Br. to determine its own research agenda. For instance, several ASI staff members of the Patna and Bhubaneswar Ex. Brs. were unhappy that they were ordered to excavate sites that lay at "the other end of the country" (*desh ka doosere chhor*)—more than 1,500 kilometers away from their Branch headquarters. Both the Ex. Brs. had no experience in excavating Harappan sites. "We are experts on the archaeology of Buddhism, we have no clue [*maloom nahi*] about black and red ware or perforated pottery. How are we supposed to excavate Harappan sites?"

In 2003, when I questioned the SA of the Vadodara Ex. Br. who was appointed to direct the excavations at the SHP site of Juni Kuran about this issue, she replied: "I will go wherever my DG orders me to." This was an official response. However, when I queried members of her staff, they told me that the Jt DG had compelled her to abandon the excavation at the early historic site of Hathab (second–sixth century CE) on the coast of Saurashtra that the Vadodara Ex. Br. was scheduled to do that season (Pramanik 2004b). The BJP-led NDA government lost the general election in October 2004, which led to the minister of tourism, Jagmohan, relinquishing his position and the Jt DG R. S. Bisht retiring. During this season (2004–05), both the Ex. Brs. of Vadodara and Bhubaneswar discontinued excavating at Juni Kuran and Tarkhanewala Dera/Chak 86 respectively. The original plan was to excavate each of these sites for a period of three to five years. I was told that the SAs of both of these branches were uninterested in excavating SHP sites.

My informants in the Bhubaneswar Ex. Br. confided that they had been "miserable" (*dukhi*) working so far away from home, whereas the excavation director of Tarkhanewala Dera/Chak 86 excavations stayed on the site only for a few days a month. He supervised the excavation through telephone conversations, and he was "happy [*kush*] to not return." In Baror, during the first season (2003–04), the excavation was conducted in the absence of the excavation director. While talking to an ASA, who was bitter about this forced excavation, more than 1,000 kilometers away from his home, I was told that

there was no need for Bisht to order the Bhubaneswar, Patna, and Nagpur Ex. Brs. to leave their home areas to excavate in SHP sites. He could have requested the Archaeological Departments of Haryana, Rajasthan, and Gujarat to excavate these sites. He could have just constituted a new SHP excavation department, and deputed archaeologists and staff from various Circle and Branch offices.

This disenchantment was not unusual; it was a product of the structural hierarchy of the ASI, which had a debilitating impact on the epistemic objectives of the archaeological excavation. Disconsolate archaeologists and dispirited staff members were often forced to undertake work because of bureaucratic compulsion. The excavation at Ayodhya in 2003, I was told by many in the ASI, was also undertaken due to the coercive power of the bureaucracy, pressured by the judiciary.

Superintending Archaeologists

The SA was the "boss" or the *kartha-dharta* (head) of the Ex. Br.; he or she was designated as the director of the excavation. The SAs that I met fulfilled the qualities of the model director of the excavation that Wheeler describes:

> It would be easy to be trite in describing the qualities of the director. It goes without saying that he must have the combined virtues of the scholar and the man of action … the director sets standard of achievement and must know enough to impose his standards without questions on his experts. (Wheeler 1954, 154)[18]

This was not different from what Flinders Petrie wrote in his seminal book on archaeological field methods, *Methods and Aims in Archaeology*, more than half a century ago:

> Scheming how to extract all that is possible from a given site, how to make use of all conditions, how to avoid difficulties; and training laborers, keeping them all firmly in hand, making them all friends without allowing familiarity, getting their full confidence and their goodwill;—these requirements certainly rank high in an excavator's outfit. (Petrie 1904, 4)

From the above description of the ASI structure, it might appear that each Ex. Br. would be associated with one archaeological site, from the beginning to the publication of the report. But this, paradoxically, was not the case. The excavation site was not associated with an Ex. Br., but rather with the excavation director. For example, the Vadodara Ex. Br. undertook the Dholavira excavation, which began in 1991, because the excavation director of Dholavira was R. S. Bisht, who was then the SA of the Vadodara Ex. Br. In 1994, he was transferred as the director of the Institute of Archaeology, which continued the excavations at Dholavira. He subsequently became the director of the Excavation and the Exploration

Department of the ASI. During that period, the Dholavira excavation team consisted of members from the DG's office in New Delhi where the Excavation and the Exploration Department was located. In 2003, R. S. Bisht became the Jt DG of the ASI and then the members of the Dholavira excavation were drawn from various Branches and Circles. When I reached Dholavira in the season of 2003–04, the director of the Dholavira excavation was a Dy SA from the DG office, whereas the AAs and the technical staff were drawn from various departments, Branches, and Circles.

Sites such as Rakhigarhi and Surkotada were also intrinsically linked to the individual excavator. One of my informants, an ASA, informed me that this had led to a "cult of proprietorship [*zamindari*]," where the individual excavation director controlled access to the excavation site and "had nearly dictatorial control over the material excavated [*excavation director ki dictatorship chalti hai*]. He was the lord of the site [*pura control rahta hai, site ki zamindari hoti hai unke pass*]." In the ASI, excavation was driven by the scholarly predisposition of the excavation director; other members of the Ex. Br. were merely "technical help." Although this "cult of proprietorship" was not articulated as an official policy, the bureaucratic system of the ASI perpetuated this association between the individual excavator and the archaeological site. Historically, the proprietary relation between the excavation site and the individual excavator has a distinct colonial genealogy, with the first DG of the ASI—Sir Alexander Cunningham, who began his career in India as an army engineer. The excavation was carried out in an established colonial military hierarchy in which the director was the officer-in-charge, whereas the rest of the excavation team were subordinates, with the subaltern laborers at the bottom. Mortimer Wheeler further strengthened this system. He consolidated the military discipline with professional ethic, tightening the unequal relationship between the excavation director and the rest of the excavation community.

My informants often disclosed that the post of the SA of an Ex. Br. was considered to be a "punishment posting" in the ASI. It referred to the posting of government employees to posts which were not desirable because they were in remote areas, or because they were not prestigious or lucrative positions. To be posted as the director of a remote Site Museum such as Lothal (Gujarat), Kalibangan (Rajasthan), or Aihole (Karnataka) was often cited as an example of a punishment posting, since they were very far from metropolitan centers. "These are great [*badiya*] postings for a bachelor," explained a Dy SA, "but for a married man with children, these are most unsuitable [*ghatiya*]. There are no good schools, houses, or even proper bathrooms." On the other hand, a posting as an SA of the Monument Section in the DG's office or as an SA in the ASI

Central Library, both of which were in New Delhi, were also considered to be punishment postings. Despite being well located, these positions did not have enough responsibility and were not considered "powerful." The most lucrative postings were those that had the potential for "making money" (*paisa banaana*). Similarly, the posting of an SA of an Ex. Br. was considered to be a punishment posting because it was "non-lucrative" (*koi fayada nahi hai*). This was emphasized by a number of informants whenever the issue of corruption cropped up in conversations. Unlike an Ex. Br., which had an annual financial outlay of less than INR 10 million, the Circle offices had a financial outlay of more than INR 500 million (in the early 2000s).[19] "Corruption happens in both places, but the potential for corruption is unlimited [*aseem*] in a Circle, where there is big money [*mota paisa*]," explained an AA.

> That's when you make the most money [*sab se jayada paisa*] in your career in the ASI. There are many SAs who were notorious [*badnaam*] for their corrupt practices. They even have CBI cases slapped against them. As a matter of fact, more than half of the Directors who sit in the DG office have CBI enquires being conducted, on various charges of corruption.

While giving me a detailed description about how corruption has become a "regular habit" of an ASI officer, he suggested: "They make money off every small thing [*har choti cheeze main paisa banate hai*]. Given a chance, I will also not let go of any opportunity of making money," he remarked unapologetically.

"The SA of a Circle," an informant explicated, "in the old days was more powerful than the Chief Secretary of the State, as the Circle consisted of not just one federal state but at least two to three states. He had power and prestige. But things have changed." The power and prestige, I was told, was not limited to the privileges that equaled those of the topmost bureaucrat of the central government; it lay in the power of jurisdiction over a huge geographical area and the funds allocated to each Circle. The informant, who was an AA, elaborated, "The SA of a Circle was so prestigious that when he went on a tour, the District Collector and the District Magistrate would accompany him. But those days are now gone and the things have changed." When I asked him what he meant by things having changed, he said: "Now each state has a Circle because protected monuments have increased, and also because our pay scale has decreased."

There was a crisis of staff members and officers in the ASI and that the Ex. Br. was the most neglected division of the ASI and most of the Branches were understaffed. For example, the Delhi Ex. Br. had only two AAs along with the SA. During the 2003–05 season, the Patna Ex. Br. was digging in the field without an SA; the excavation director was a Dy SA. In these circumstances, the

Ex. Br. would employ the alumni of the Institute of Archaeology to supervise most of the excavations in the field. Along with these ex-students, the continuing students of the Institute would form the lowest layer of the ASI's institutional hierarchy in the excavation site. Student archaeologists were a constant fixture in ASI excavation sites since 1944 (Wheeler 1976, 32). For Wheeler, the student archaeologists were not just extra assistance; they fulfilled an intellectual purpose at the site:

> They impose a constant need for clear exposition and therefore clear thinking. They ask simple, awkward questions, which have to be answered convincingly or with frank and wholesome admission of ignorance. You can't fool them. They are the friendliest and most stimulating of critics, and the best of them rapidly become the most co-operative of colleagues. (Wheeler 1954, 153)

Assistant Archaeologists

At the bottom of the ASI officer-cadre was the AA. These were the youngest officers in the ASI—students who had recently graduated from the Institute of Archaeology in Delhi. They were floor managers of the archaeological excavation, unlike the senior officers who played the role of supervisors. Along with the technical staff members of the excavation team, the AAs considered themselves to be the ones who "sweated in the field" (*hum field main pasina bahate hai*). When I first reached the site of Baror in 2004, I had met an AA who had applied for the intra-ASI promotion interview for the post of a Dy SA. While talking to him then, it had appeared to me that he was sure to get it. He had the requisite qualifications—experience, academic degree, and also the necessary "connections" among the "higher ups." The "interview went well," he informed me as he was giving me a tour of the excavated area a year later in 2005, "but luck was not with me" (*kismet ne saath nahi diya*), he said, showing me the newest discovery of the season and explaining the objectives of the current season's excavation. He believed he should have gotten the job, but internal "favoritism and politics," along with "reservations" for the lower castes, had negated his chance. For the last 13 years, he has been waiting for a promotion. The prospect of being an AA for the next five to seven years was daunting to him. He remarked, disheartened, "I am staring at a stagnant future [*bhaddha bhavishya*], and more than half my career will be over." He was shocked to discover that the colleagues who had been promoted were younger than him. He and other AAs had filed a writ petition in the Delhi High Court against the promotions, which they argued were rigged. They had been successful in getting a stay order on the promotions, but the final hearing was due in the next few weeks. The AA had joined the

ASI in the early 1990s, and had been an AA for 12 years. He was the last of the AAs from his cohort awaiting promotion. He had been fascinated with archaeology in high school and had done an MA in Ancient Indian History and then obtained a diploma from the Institute of Archaeology. After the diploma, he had been unemployed for two years, but worked as a "daily wage" archaeologist in two ASI excavations of historical sites in north India. Then in 1993, he had been recruited as an AA. He had applied for several internal promotions but had been unsuccessful, and so his depression and frustration had grown manifold. He said he was "resigned to his fate, but not without a fight."

The professional discontent among AAs also emerged from one of the thorniest issues in the career of an AA—salary: "Until two decades ago, the salary of the AA was more than that of a university lecturer. Then it became same as a university lecturer, and now it has become less than that of a university lecturer," explained an AA. This disparity in salaries has also been noted in the Lal Committee report, which states: .

> The entry grade to technical posts in the Archaeological Survey of India is Assistant Archaeologists (Rs. 1640–2900).... A demand for a higher pay scale at this level has been made. The Archaeological Survey of India, in their official memorandum, have stated that keeping in view the educational qualifications, nature of duties and responsibilities attached to the post of Assistant Archaeologist and the all India Transfer liability, the present pay scale of Rs. 1640–2900 for the post is not commensurate with job requirements. Further, the initial entry in other sister organizations like Geological Survey of India is in the pay scale of Rs. 2000–3500. The ASI is experiencing difficulty in appointing qualified persons. They have, so, recommended upward revision in the pay scale of Assistant Archaeologist. (Lal 2001, 43) [20]

Until the late 1970s, the post of the AA, then called the technical assistant (TA), was filled through internal recruitment practices. Other than the AA, all other senior ranks of the ASI were recruited through the central government recruitment agency—the Union Public Service Commission (UPSC).[21] But in the 1970s, the recruitment at the AA level was taken over by another central government recruitment agency called the Staff Selection Commission Board (SSB).[22] An ASA explained to me that before the SSB took over the recruitment regime of the ASI, the AAs were recruited through informal channels known as the "Bhatinda Line." This informant was one of the first cohorts of AAs to be recruited by the SSB, and was proud of this achievement. He explained that the "*Bhatinda Line* was the backdoor channel of getting a job in the ASI before the SSB recruitment kicked in." The backdoor channel worked in a casual way and "most senior officers who have risen to high ranks from the post of the TA entered through the *Bhatinda Line*. Even today, all the technical staff—photographer, draughtsman, surveyor—enter the ASI through the *Bhatinda Line*."

The phrase "Bhatinda Line" was a condescending idiomatic phrase used for a commuter train-line between Delhi and Bhatinda—an industrial town in Punjab, northwest of Delhi. On this line run daily intercity express, ferrying blue-collar workers from the hinterland to Delhi. During peak office hours, these trains are often very crowded, and it is difficult to get even a "standing place." In the ASI context, the term "Bhatinda Line" did not refer to this intercity train, but instead signified many such overcrowded feeder commuter trains. These ran during office hours and fed into Delhi, carrying rural, working-class population from the neighboring states of Rajasthan, Punjab, Uttar Pradesh, and Haryana. From the middle-class subjectivity (Joshi 2010; Dickey 2012; Donner 2012) inhabited by my informant, this migrant workforce was viewed as "rustic" (*dehati*), "uncouth" (*ganvaar*), "uncivilized" (*badtameez*), and incongruous with the elite bureaucratic culture of Delhi. By using the term "Bhatinda Line" for those officers who had been recruited informally into the ASI, this ASA emphasized distinct class delineation (Fernandes and Heller 2006). He underscored that his recruitment was based on merit and not through the exploitation of informal networks or corruption (Das 2000). This was also an important distinction made by many AAs to distinguish themselves from other technical and non-technical staff of the Ex. Brs. These employees were not recruited through the SSB and were considered to be at a lower, non-officer grade in the ASI hierarchy.

The "Bhatinda Line" had both its advantage and disadvantage. The advantage was that senior and experienced officers could handpick site supervisors who they thought had a "knack for archaeology." But it also opened avenues for recruitment malpractices. Referring to the intervention of the SSB, a senior SA noted that this was a "good thing" because "corruption was rampant and all sorts of people without adequate training came into the ASI. You know how coveted [*kimti*] a government job is. Anyone was willing to pay to get a permanent job in a central government service." My conversations about recruitment practices among technical and non-technical staff members of the Ex. Brs. and the Circle offices also produced narratives of corruption. I came to know through my conversations with the technical staff and the lower staff of the Ex. Brs. that, at their grade, "backdoor entry" into the ASI was widespread and that "each post had a price [*har post bikau hai*], from that of a peon to a photographer." A photographer at Baror narrated how for the past three years his son had been working as a daily-wage laborer in the Ex. Br., "helping with all the tasks of the excavation—photography, site supervision and everything." He remarked that "my son has even done a diploma in photography from a reputed institute, but he had not been taken into the ASI." When I asked him why that was so, even though he himself had been in the ASI for more than 20 years, my informant replied:

> There are three problems. First, I was not in the good books of the SA. Second, I don't have enough money to pay the bribe for the post. Thirdly, the SA has his own favorite candidate who obviously paid him the bribe [*sala, khoob paisa khaya SA ne*]. He took two lakhs [INR 200,000] to give the post to this favorite candidate.

Although it is impossible to get documentary evidence to substantiate these narratives about corrupt practices, yet every informant I spoke to narrated tales of corruption—the ubiquity was staggering. I was told that several SAs took bribes during the recruitment of lower-grade staff. It was this "standard procedure" that made the SA post lucrative (*faydemand*). However, I was always reminded that not all SAs were corrupt: "There are a few SAs who are incorruptible [*imandari ki kamai khate hai*]." Some SAs, I was told, would even bring their own food during field visits. They did not allow their family members to use official vehicles for personal use, a common practice throughout the bureaucratic community in India.

Alumni Student Workers

"It was not easy to get a job [*aasan nahi tha*] as an AA in the ASI," explained an alumnus of the Institute of Archaeology who worked as a site supervisor in Dholavira. He was one of many alumni or ex-students who had graduated with a diploma in Archaeology from the Institute of Archaeology and worked as "technical daily wagers" (*dahari karmachaari*). The custom of hiring ex-students as site supervisors was old. It fulfilled two functions: "First, it gave an opportunity to work in the field until we can get permanent job in the ASI. Second, we play an important role in substituting for AAs in large-scale excavations," explained an ex-student at Baror with whom I shared my tent. There was a serious shortage of AAs in the ASI. In 2016, there were just 87 AAs instead of the allotted strength of 178.[23] In the organizational hierarchy of the excavation team, these ex-students had an ambivalent place.

The Institute of Archaeology is the official training school for ASI archaeologists. It was modeled after the Institute of Archaeology in London and was established by one of Wheeler's illustrious students, Amalananda Ghosh, in 1959 (Ghosh 1960, 2) and its first director was B. B. Lal.[24] The Institute was not an independent educational institute, but was a part of the ASI bureaucratic structure. The Mirdha Committee of 1984 recommended that the diploma course should be extended to two years from one year, so that students could receive more intensive field training (Mirdha 1984, 46). Since then, it has become mandatory that any archaeologist who applies for the job of an AA has to have a diploma from the Institute along with at least a master's degree in a discipline related to archaeology, history, or epigraphy. This insistence on a diploma from the Institute was an attempt by the ASI to distinguish its technique and method of archaeological excavation from other university departments, and aimed at inscribing the "Wheelerian method" on the students. The Institute did not have its own faculty. Courses were taught by visiting faculty members who were invited from the various Ex. Brs. and university departments in the country. The most significant part of the two-year-long course is the two field seasons (90–100 days each) of archaeological excavation under various Ex. Brs. During these two years, the students not only learn how to dig the "ASI way" (*tareeka*) but are also socialized into the bureaucratic practice of the ASI.

The symbiotic link between the Institute's diploma and the ASI has become so essential that almost all AAs who join the ASI are trained at this Institute. Students from other universities who even had PhDs in Archaeology were not inducted in the ASI, as they did not have the mandatory diploma from the Institute. This "in-breeding," as an AA called it, was the main cause of the inability of the "ASI to learn new methods of digging and new technologies of excavation. This makes people in the ASI insecure about new theories in archaeology— processual or post-processual. They are closed and uninterested in learning [*bandh budhi hai aur seekne ki iccha nahi hai*]." In the trenches of the ASI, I observed that this was true—the theoretical and methodological influence of both processual and post-processual archaeology was minimal, if not completely non-existent. Most trained archaeologists in the ASI were barely aware of these theoretical approaches in archaeology, even when some of the methods used in processual archaeology were more than 30 years old in 2003–04. The Lal Committee noted: "Though it has the high-sounding title of an 'Institute', it is in no way a seat of higher learning or research." It recommended a total restructuring of the Institute and suggested that the Institute be an independent university which "follow[s] the structural pattern and working system of a central university, in order to emerge as the premier archaeological and art history institution of the country comparable to similar institutions abroad" (Lal 2001, 139). In 2019, the Institute was renamed as the Pandit Deendayal Upadhyaya Institute of Archaeology and was shifted from New Delhi to a new campus in Noida, in the neighboring state of Uttar Pradesh; however, it has yet to become an independent educational center.[25]

Once the students graduated from the Institute, the ASI did not directly absorb them "automatically" (*apne aap*). They had to wait for the ASI to issue the "job advertisement" in *Employment News*.[26] This "waiting period" could range from two years to five years. In 1996, ex-students of the Institute who had been waiting for six years for the job announcement formed a students' union and organized a relay hunger strike followed by picketing (*gherao*) at the DG's office to demand the issuing of AA posts. They undertook this as a last-ditch effort after numerous petitions through official channels had failed. An AA at Baror who was the chief organizer of the protest justified it by saying:

> The *gherao* was the last resort [*aakhri rasta*]. It had to be done for the livelihood [*rozi-roti*] of unemployed students. We had lobbied with everybody from the officers in the Ministry to the MPs [Member of the Parliament]. We even got questions raised in the Parliament. But nothing happened. We then had to *gherao* the DG and court-arrest ourselves. This gave us a lot of press coverage. The next day I was given an audience with the Home Minister [L. K. Advani]. Soon they released more than thirty posts. But it took more than a year from the posts being advertised to the jobs being awarded. But most of those students who took part in the strike got the job.

It had become standard practice for students to wait for a considerable period before they could apply for a job at the ASI. When I started my fieldwork, I could sense an excitement, as there was a rumor that the ASI would soon be advertising for 55 posts of AA. By the time I completed my fieldwork, half the number of jobs had been announced and some of the ex-students I had known had become AAs. I was told that these posts were released because Jagmohan, who was then the minister, had pushed through the upper echelons of the decision-making body at the Cabinet level. "Or we would have had to also do some kind of an agitation," remarked an ex-student who would scan the copy of *Employment News* every week. He would take a bus from Dholavira to Rapar—100 kilometers away—to get the *Employment News*.

Laborers

The workday at the Dholavira site started with an enumerative ritual of the postcolonial state—the "muster-roll call." Every morning, hundreds of local laborers who worked at the site would appear from the pleasant mist, as the rising sun would cast its golden light on the spectacular archaeological mound. At the edge of the site, these men and women would squat on the dry earth. Men in brown and black cotton trousers and polyester shirts, along with women in colorful *ghagra* (long-pleated skirt) and *choli* (short-sleeved bodice), with their faces covered, would sit in two separate gender-segregated clusters. Each cluster would consist of a series of rows. Each laborer would sit in a pre-assigned spot in a single file. At the head of the congregation on a rusted and aged metal folding chair would sit an LDC. He was a Haryanvi, an upper caste Jat, who was a stout and overweight man with a naturally harsh voice—always freshly bathed, with neatly combed oiled hair, he would sit in a stern pose. In his hand was a ballpoint pen, and a worn-out, hardbound, cardboard register. The LDC in a deep Haryanvi-accented Hindi would yell the name of each laborer. On hearing their name, the laborer would shout back, "Present, sir!" (*Hazir, sir!*), and unhurriedly walk toward the excavation site. One-by-one all the laborers would disappear into the trenches, and the LDC would put a tick mark (check) with his ballpoint pen in the register. This ritual would be repeated again, every day, at the end of the day. The only difference was that, this time, after their name was called, the laborers would scream *Hazir, sir!* and zealously sprint toward their village. In the process, a mild dust storm would form in the horizon. Men and women would be seen running like children after school into the slanting rays of the setting sun. The "muster-roll call" occurred in every site that I worked at. At some sites, there would be only 50–70 laborers, but at Dholavira, there were 250 laborers (Figure 3.1).[27]

Figure 3.1 End-of-the-day muster roll call at Dholavira, 2004

Source: Photograph by the author.

I want to return to the moment I began this chapter with—the short walk I was taking with the AA, as he narrated the Rig Vedic analogy to explicate the hierarchy in the ASI. As he completed his analogy, the AA jumped off the balk we were walking on, and into the trench, about a meter deep. He steadily moved toward a middle-aged laborer, with an uneven grey moustache, sporting a week-long stubble on his rugged face, bronzed with years of working in intense heat. The laborer was wearing a printed cotton bush shirt and a pair of brown terry-cot trousers, a white turban covering his head. He was kneeling barefoot in the trench. The laborer had a section-cutter (a wood and iron axe contraption with a very thin blade) in his hand. He was concentrating on straightening the wall of the trench—the stratigraphic section—by scraping the uneven portion of soil jutting out. "What kind of section-cutter are you? You have been working at the site for two years and you still cannot do a simple task of cutting a section straight?" yelled the AA. The laborer jumped up and looked at the AA awkwardly. The AA ordered him to come up on to the top of the balk and reprimanded him. He vigorously gestured to the laborer to look cautiously from the top of the trench balk, and see how he was scraping into the trench wall rather than cutting the section perpendicular to the trench floor. After a few brusque instructions, which seemed more like admonishments, the AA was back up on the trench balk where I was standing. We continued the site tour as if nothing had happened. He then looked at me and remarked: "One has to reprimand the laborers or it is impossible to get work out of them" (*Laborer ko hardkana jaroori hai, nahi toh en se kaam nikalna mushkil hai*).

Hardkana is a Hindi slang that refers to the act of forcefully shaking or vibrating. This was a pejorative term, commonly used in chastising a subordinate working-class subject—household servants, farmhands, or daily laborers. At the ASI, I observed that it was always uttered in the context of the laborers and the acts of disciplining them. I had also heard the word being used by AAs and Dy SAs in the context of castigating their students and staff members. Likewise, it was also used by the SAs when talking about disciplining their juniors. *Hardkana* was an operational expression—its verbalization illustrated the oppressive instrumentalization of the relationship that the upper echelons of the bureaucratic hierarchy had with the lower, irrespective of rank or status.

The AA's Vedic analogy was ideological. Similar to the Rig Vedic hymn, his description of the ASI hierarchy did not mention the Ati-Shudras or the Dalits. He had unconsciously erased their presence in his narrative. In the "Purusha Sukta," the lowest in the caste hierarchy were the Shudras who emerged from the feet of the primordial man. This lowest group was still subsumed under the dominant caste hierarchy. The "Purusha Sukta" does not mention, and thus erases, a large group of people whom the Vedic Aryans were antagonistic toward.

These were the *dasyu* (servant), who in later Vedic and post-Vedic texts were described as the Ati-Shudras.[28] They were the untouchables, who were outside the caste system of the Rig Vedic community. They were the perpetual outsiders, always subjugated in the mythic battles of the Aryans.[29] Likewise, the AA did not mention those that were outside the ASI hierarchy—the laborers—the largest category of workers at an ASI site. They were temporary, contractual workers numbering from more than 100 at small sites like Tarkenwala Dera to around 500 at monumental sites such as Dholavira. Laborers were outsiders in the ASI hierarchy—hired on minimum daily wages—who did the most labor-intensive work at the sites. They were a non-unionized workforce that worked in the ASI trenches, excavated the soil, and removed it. Some, who were more fortunate, worked as watchmen (*chowkidar*) and servants in the excavation camp, cooking, washing clothes, shaving and cutting hair, and even massaging the legs of the ASI officers and staff members.[30] The irony of the AA's analogy was that he believed that he was structuring a narrative of self-pity. He had framed his subjectivity as the lowest in the ASI hierarchy, which was not entirely untrue, but in this narrative of self-victimization, he neglected to mention the workers who were at the bottom of the ASI hierarchy. The laborers I observed in my ethnography were the most consequential members of a postcolonial archaeological excavation, and its most oppressed subject (Figure 3.2).

Figure 3.2 Working laborers at Dholavira, 2004

Source: Photograph by the author.

A large majority were landless Dalits who worked as daily-wage agrarian workers throughout the year. At Dholavira, most of them belonged to tribal and lower caste populations, and many of them were women workers, whereas at Hansi, Baror, and Bhirrana, I observed that a few poverty-stricken, landless, upper caste and Muslim laborers would also work at the site. These ASI sites were located in dry and arid climates where agrarian activity was monsoon-fed and occurred only once a year. The rest of the year, Dalit and landless laborers would migrate to urban areas or work in highly exploitative brick-kilns that dotted the rural landscape adjacent to dry river beds, especially in northwestern India (Singh 2005; John 2014). Working at the ASI site as a daily-wage laborer was lucrative because they "at least" (*kum-se-kum*) received the stipulated legal daily wages, whereas as agrarian or brick-kiln laborers they had to do "back breaking" (*kamar-tod*) work and were often given half the legal daily wages or even less—"it is question of our stomach" (*papi pet ka sawal hai*)—mouthing an oft-repeated Hindi film dialogue. Not all laborers lived in neighboring villages; many would walk or bicycle more than 10 kilometers to work at the ASI sites every day. "We like doing this work because it is easy [*asan*], slow [*sust*], and governmental [*sarkari*] project," explained a laborer in Baror. However, even within the laborers, hierarchy existed—upper class landless would resist Dalit trench leaders; drinking water receptacles were separated by caste and religion. At the lowest of the laborer hierarchy were women workers, who were never given a position of leadership (in the trench) and were consigned to doing the most menial and unskilled work.

The ASI staff, with its officers, represented a metropolitan subjectivity governed by class and the professional ethics and practices subsumed within the cultural politics of the bureaucratic state. On the other hand, the laborers represented a non-metropolitan and subaltern subjectivity, governed by caste, religious, and cultural-social formations, as well as local village politics and the existential imperative of surviving grueling rural poverty. Each of these groups of subjects was, however, involved in various tasks within a tightly governed regimentation of a bureaucratic project. The archaeological site thus became an intersectional location of interaction between these two disparate groups of subjects who reluctantly worked together cooperatively. Their roles were rigidly defined within the hierarchy of the archaeological project. Each individual was given a specific and unambiguous task to perform. The archaeologists and the laborers both viewed and engaged with the archaeological site using opposite perspectives. These contradictory modes of engagement with the same physical spatiality and epistemological practice are important to comprehend the nature of knowledge production activity conducted at an archaeological site. The archaeologists of the ASI imagined the archaeological site as an epistemological space, whereas the laborers working at the site viewed it as a means of livelihood, similar to agricultural work. The laborers conceived archaeological work as "work" (*kaam*), which gave them "bread and butter" (*rozi-roti*). However, this *rozi-roti* was transient even for those workers who spent their lives as custodians of the archaeological site. For instance, at Dholavira there were several laborers working at the site since the days when R. S. Bisht first started exploration work in 1989. By the time I began my ethnography, in 2003, five laborers who had worked at the site had petitioned the ASI to be made permanent staff. A senior laborer at the site, Dharmesh *bhai*, explained that they had been working at the site for more than 10 years, and now it was the duty (*kartavya*) of the ASI to make them permanent: "We have worked even before the excavation started and have given our entire lives [*saari zindagi*] for the site. At least the ASI should do this much for us." But nothing had yet happened. "Bisht *shaeb* has promised that he will do everything for us. Now he is the Jt DG, he will make it possible."

Thirteen years later, in January of 2017, I again visited Dholavira. Excavations at the site had ended more than a decade ago. Now, Dholavira was an attractive tourist destination in Gujarat. Dharmesh *bhai* along with other senior full-time *chowkidar*s continued to work as contractual daily-wage laborers. They made extra cash as tourist guides. I went to Dharmesh *bhai*'s house for lunch. He bitterly complained that even after working with the ASI for more than two decades they had not been made permanent employees. "Everyone failed us. No one in the ASI cares for us. We work because we are the custodians of Dholavira. But we are not given any credit. They have made us wait [*intazaar*] a lifetime [*zindagi bhar*]." This form of "chronic waiting" (Jeffrey 2008; Pardy 2009; Bailey 2019) was not unusual in the ASI. The treatment of casual, contractual laborers had reached such a discouraging state in the ASI that *The 233rd Report, Demands for Grants (2016–17) of Ministry of Culture Department-Related Parliamentary Standing Committee on Transport, Tourism and Culture*, making observations about the status of contractual employees in the ASI, notes:

> It was brought to the notice of the Committee that ASI employs a large number of people as security guards, watchmen and last grade employees for decades together, but without making them regular or permanent employees. They are being paid meagre wages and without any social security or health coverage. The Committee feels that this is total injustice and violation of all norms and practices laid down by various legislations. The Committee is disheartened to note that this anti-labor practice is being perpetuated by ASI, one of the premier Government institutions of the country. This Committee, therefore, recommends that the ASI and Ministry

of Culture should take all possible steps to ensure that its contractual employees are paid decent wages along with adequate social security schemes and health coverage, until they are given permanent status. (Singh 2017, 18)

It is important to note that these were not seasonal employees who worked at the excavation site for a year or two, but were dedicated individuals who had each spent a lifetime as custodians of the archaeological heritage of India, oppressed by a debilitating and chronic waiting for a stable future. As I sat and ate a freshly made millet chapatti (*bajra rotla*) along with curried vegetable (*sabzi*) and butter milk in Dharmesh *bhai*'s modest house in the village of Dholavira, Dharmesh *bhai*, who was now in his late fifties, solemnly affirmed:

> It would have been graceful on the part of Bisht sir to make us permanent, but he did not keep his promise [*wada nahi rakha*]. Now, I don't care [*koi farq nahi padatha*] if ASI makes me permanent or not, I have dedicated my life to the site. It is not an archaeological site for me, it is a living God [*jeeta-jagta bhagwan hai*].

Early twentieth-century archaeologists such as Flinder Petrie, Leonard Wooley, and Mortimer Wheeler who worked throughout their careers in colonial settings were very well aware of the relationship between the organizational structure and the production of archaeological knowledge (see Petrie 1904; Woolley 1930; Wheeler 1954). For them, this relationship between "man-management" (Wheeler 1954, 173) and archaeological knowledge was crucial. This awareness was a product of their need to streamline the excavation as a hierarchical process, which relied on hundreds of people to produce archaeological knowledge, as Petrie notes with candor:

> Organization, both of the plan of work, and of the laborers, in very necessary. Scheming how to extract all that is possible from a given site, how to make use of all the conditions, how to avoid difficulties; and training laborers, keeping them firmly in hand, making them all familiar without allowing familiarity. (Petrie 1904, 5)

I observed during my ethnography that the "ecology of practices" (Stengers 2005) of the bureaucrat-archaeologist of the ASI was identical to the lines that Petrie had written more than 100 years ago. The ASI excavation was not a mere epistemological performance of the postcolonial state—it was a profoundly ideological practice mediated, framed, and formed by a hierarchical ecology that had a debilitating impact on the subjectivity of each member of its organization. The bureaucratic hierarchy laid down the modes of engagement within which epistemology was manufactured. Here, knowledge was not a standardized outcome of deployment of the scientific methods and techniques, but was instead a product of an ideologically constructed social and cultural ecology.

Notes

1. The hymn is repeated in the *Atharvaveda* (Book 19, hymn 6), the *Shukla Yajurveda* (Book 31, verses 1–6), the *Taittiriya Aranyaka* (chapter 3, hymn 12, verses 1–18) and the *Manusmriti* (chapter 1, verse 31).

2. See Dumont (1980); Srinivas (1987); Quigley (1994); Smith (1994); and Olivelle (1999) for diverse interpretation, relevance, and sociological implications of this hymn in the context of the caste system in contemporary India.

3. The AA was a Bhumihar Brahmin from Bihar, who was narrating a theory that was explicated by a Kayastha senior of his. The Bhumihars are a political, powerful, land-owning upper caste of eastern India, who control large *zamindari* (landholding estates) in this region (Nandan and Santhosh 2019). On the other hand, the Kayasthas were a caste of scribes and accountants and ministers who gained prominence in the crumbling polity of post-Mughal India, and occupied important positions in the fledging bureaucracy of colonial India and continue be an important member of the postcolonial bureaucracy (Leonard 1978; Joshi 2010).

4. The ASI's officers were recruited in four technical cadres: Archaeological cadre, Conservation cadre, Science cadre, and Epigraphy cadre, along with the Horticulture cadre (non-technical).

5. In the "Draft Seniority List of Superintending Archaeologist as 31.05.2012" there were 40 SAs throughout India of the total sanctioned strength of 44 (File No. 5-2/2010-Adm.I, accessed on the ASI website, http:// www.asi.nic.in/, on November 2, 2017), whereas in January 2020, the number had alarmingly dropped to a mere 17 SAs (File No. 5-2/2020-Adm.I, accessed on the ASI website, http://www.asi.nic.in/, on August 25, 2020).

6. The 5 Regional Directorates headed by directors did not exist while I was doing my ethnography; they were formed in April 2009. Subsequently, 4 posts of Additional Director General Archaeology and 18 posts of Joint Director General were created in 2011, but they have been lying vacant since their creation (CAG 2013, 169).

7. In the "Draft Seniority List of Assistant Archaeologist as 31.12.2016," an AA who joined the ASI in 1987 was yet to be promoted. Unsurprisingly, he was a Muslim OBC candidate who was in the same post for 29 years (F. No. 15-4/2014-Adm. I, accessed on the ASI website, http:// www.asi.nic.in/, on November 2, 2017).

8. The Fifth Central Pay Commission (1997), for the first time, recommended the constitution of a Central Archaeological Service comprising cadres of archaeologists, scientists, epigraphists, and conservationists in the ASI (CAG 2013, 172).

9. The Geological Survey of India and the Anthropological Survey of India had their head offices in Kolkata, whereas the Survey of India had its head office in Dehra Dun, a plains town at the edge of the Himalayas in north India.

10. Formed in 1946, the Indian Administrative Service (IAS) was a successor to the colonial Indian Civil Service (ICS) and has been described as "the largest cadre of generalist managers anywhere in the world ... intended to be a continuation of the 'steel frame' that had kept India united under a single (colonial) administration" (Krishna 2010, 435). The IAS is considered to be the premier civil service of India, along with the Indian Police Service and the Indian Forest Service, which comprise the three arms of the All India Services. See Potter (1986) and Bagchi (2007) for an engaging history of the IAS.

11. Achala Moulik (IAS) was the first non-archaeologist DG of the ASI. She was appointed in 1993, after the preceding DG, M. C. Joshi, resigned in the wake of the demolition of the Babri Masjid.

12. See http://www.archivepmo.nic.in/drmanmohansingh/speech-details.php? nodeid=829, accessed on November 26, 2017.

13. His appointment was not without controversy. A case was filed with the Central Administrative Tribunal, Delhi, challenging the selection process, in 2013, which was dismissed by the court. Twenty-eight applications were submitted and finally five members were selected for final interviews. Of these Rakesh Tewari and B. R. Mani were bureaucrat-archaeologists and the rest—Ravindra Korisettar, Vasant Shinde, and Kishor K. Basa—were academic-archaeologists. For more details, see the lawsuit: *Vishnu Bhat vs The Union of India* on April 3, 2014.

14. For ASI archaeologists, PWD work was a pejorative. Often archaeologists would describe bad archaeology in the ASI as "PWD work" that consisted of merely digging earth.

15. The Ex. Br. I was established by Wheeler in 1944; it initially functioned from New Delhi. The Branch was shifted to Nagpur in 1958.

16. The text is from the ASI website, http://www.asi.nic.in/asi_excavations_ branches.asp, accessed on November 11, 2017.

17. See, for instance, AACD, File No. 1/3/2003-SP/EE; AACD, File No. 1/4/2003-SP; AACD, File No. 1/4/2003-SP; AACD File No. 9/6/2003-EE.

18. In UPSC recruitment advertisement (quoted from *Sanjay Kumar Manjul v. Chairman, UPSC and Others*, Civil Appeals No. 4098 of 2006 with No. 4099 of 2006 decided on September 2006, Supreme Court of India), the requisite essential qualifications for recruitment to the post of an SA was described as:

(i) At least a second class Master's Degree of a recognized University or equivalent in Indian History/Archaeology/Anthropology with knowledge of Stone Age Archaeology Geology with knowledge of Pleistocene Geology; (ii) Diploma in Archaeology from the Archaeological Survey of India with three years field experience; Or Field experience of at least five years in Archaeology and knowledge of Monuments and Antiquities; (iii) Doctorate Degree in any of the above subjects or equivalent published research work (evidence to be furnished). Desirable Qualifications: Knowledge of Sanskrit, Pali, Prakrit, Persian or Arabic upto degree level. Age prescribed for the post not exceeding 40 years on normal closing date relaxable for other Backward Classes candidates upto 3 years in respect of the vacancies reserved for them. Relaxable for Employees of Government of India and Union Territories upto 5 years.

19. For example, the planned budgetary allocation for the ASI for the year 2008–09 was INR 1.13 billion, of which INR 754 million was used for the preservation and conservation of heritage monuments and only INR 25 million was used for archaeology exploration and excavation, which is a mere 2.21 percent of the total budget of the ASI (accessed on the ASI website, http://www.asi.nic.in/asi_rti.asp, on May 2, 2011).

20. For an elaborate justification on the restructuring of the pay scale of the ASI archaeologist, and to make it equivalent to the University Grants Commission (UGC) pay scale, see Niti Aayog (2020, 149–53).

21. The Union Public Service Commission (UPSC) had been established under Article 315 of the Constitution of India. It is instrumental in selecting persons to man the various Central civil services and posts and the services common to the Union and states called the "all-India Services."

22. Earlier known as the Subordinate Services Commission, it was established in 1975. This Commission was subsequently renamed as the Staff Selection Commission in 1977.

23. "Draft Seniority List of Assistant Archaeologist as 31.12.2016 (AACD, File No. 15-4/2014-Adm. I, accessed on the ASI website, http://www.asi.nic.in/, on November 2, 2017).

24. The director of the Institute of Archaeology in New Delhi has often been drawn from some of the most influential archaeologists in the ASI, including R. S. Bisht (excavator of Dholavira), Amarendra Nath (excavator of Rakhigrahi), and B. R. Mani (excavator of Ayodhya).

25. For the latest proposal of restructuring the Institute of Archaeology, see the recommendations of the Niti Aayog (2020, 147, 205–07).

26. The educational qualification for the post of an AA reads as follows:

> Essential: Candidates other than SC/ST category should have secured at least 55% marks (without grace marks) in Master's Degree (or) equivalent in Ancient Indian History/Archaeology/Sanskrit/Persian/Prakit/Pali/Arabic/Anthropology/Geology of any recognized university or equivalent. SC/ST category candidates should have secured at least 50% marks (without grace marks) in Master's Degree in these subjects. Desirable: Knowledge of Stone Age Archaeology/Art and Architecture. (Lal 2001, 126)

27. For an invigorating ethnography of the bureaucratic politics of "muster roll" and its endemic bond with corruption in India, see Mathur (2016).

28. The historical understanding of the word *dasyus* is not without contestation; for diverse interpretations on the status of *dasyus* in Rig Vedic society, see Witzel (1995) and Parpola (1997, 2015).

29. On the history of Dalit criticism of the Vedic representation of caste since the late nineteenth century in the writings of Jotirao Phule, B. R. Ambedkar, and the later Dalit writers of western India, see Constable (1997); Omvedt (2006); and Kumar (2018).

30. Although the Hindi word is *naukar* for servants, it was never used to describe these laborers who worked on the campsite rather than the excavation site. This term was considered derogatory. They were also called *chowkidar*s, even though the tasks they did were primarily domestic chores.

4   Spatial Formation of the Archaeological Field

The ritual of *bhoomi pujan*, or earth worship, often preceded the inauguration of an ASI excavation. This is a Hindu ground-purification ritual usually observed at the start of an architectural construction, which involved the breaking of a coconut, the lighting of incense, and the uttering of Sanskrit mantras. At Juni Kuran, the chief guest conducted this ceremony—R. S. Bisht, who was then the additional director general (ADG), director of the Excavation and Exploration Department, and the director of the Saraswati Heritage Project (SHP).[1] Bisht had recently been on a whirlwind tour of the various SHP sites in western India. The director of the Juni Kuran excavation had invited him to inaugurate the excavation at this site. On a bright sunny winter morning, when the chill of the desert air was yet to be soaked by the warmth of the sun, all the members of the excavation unit gathered at the center of the campsite. On a newly made mud floor, still smelling of the cow dung with which it had been freshly plastered, stood a brown molded plastic table and three green molded plastic chairs. On these sat the ADG, the director of Juni Kuran excavation, and the director of the Dholavira excavation. In the company of staff and students, the excavation director of Juni Kuran gave the ADG a bouquet of flowers. After obligatory words of thanks and some perfunctory remarks on the significance of Juni Kuran in the context of the SHP, the ADG unwaveringly smashed a coconut on a flat slab of weathered limestone. Then, with a few quick swings of a new pickaxe, he dug the earth to symbolically inaugurate the Juni Kuran excavation. This rather simple ceremony was both an allegorical act of domesticating the wild and a resolute reiteration of the official hierarchies that govern the daily practice of the ASI. Through the symbolic sacrifice of the coconut, which was a substitute for the human head in Hindu rituals (Doniger and Smith 1989, 214), the wild was placated. The act was performed as a secular statist ritual devoid of its sacred context but still keeping its religiosity intact. The ceremonial excavation by the ADG with a pickaxe suggested that even in the wild field, official hierarchies had to be iterated. The gesture served to reinscribe the ADG's authority and rights over the knowledge produced at the site. It was ironic that this statement of authority could only be made explicit by appropriating the most unskilled task of an ASI archaeological excavation, the exclusive domain of the lowest-paid member of the archaeological excavation—the daily-wage laborer.

It was from the director of the Dholavira excavation that I heard, "We have transformed this place from a jungle into a civilized place" (*hum ne toh yahan jungle mein mangal kar diya hai*). It was uttered during the tour I was given of the Dholavira campsite by the director on the first day of my visit. He informed me that I would not have any "problem" (*dikkath*) at the site as "we in the ASI are experts [*maahir*] at transforming wild inhospitable terrain into livable space." He admitted that the ASI could not provide the luxuries and "amenities" (*suvidha*) that I must be used to in America, but emphasized that the campsite of Dholavira was the "finest" (*sabse badiya*) ASI camp I would ever visit during my fieldwork. He boasted that this was the only camp that had taps with running water in the tent, besides other amenities such as a constant hot water supply and a permanent toilet (*pucca latrine*). I heard this phrase, "from wilderness to a civilized place" (*jungle mein mangal*), at other sites too. It was used often in the camp's context when contrasting its organized and planned contours with the recalcitrant landscape in which the site was located. The camps, like the excavation sites, personified the organizational ability of the ASI excavation team to domesticate the wild field. It epitomized a redoubtable state control over the wilderness. The meaning of the Sanskrit word *mangal* is auspicious. This word not only rhymes well with jungle(*i*) but also presents the contrastive before-and-after picture. It suggests that the intervention of the ASI bureaucracy has transformed the wild and hostile terrain of the excavation site into an auspicious location. This phrase connotes the trope of domestication, the taming of the wild (*jangli*).

All the Harappan sites were in arid or semi-arid terrain, between 2 and 5 kilometers from contemporary settlements. The middle-class ASI archaeologists and staff described these sites as remote or *jangli*. This rather visceral adjective was deployed to describe the terrain where archaeological sites were located, underscoring a disjuncture from civilization. The category of *jangli* was also subsumed within the rubric of a developmental idiom—backward. In most cases, they used the English word. The Hindi term *pichada* was also used to refer to the underdeveloped economic and social culture in the area. Both these terms were used interchangeably to describe the surroundings that the ASI staff inhabited during the excavation. It was the ideological incorporation of these two terms—*jangli* and *pichada*—that defined the interaction of ASI bureaucracy with the spatiality they occupied. For the ASI, the wild is not only domesticated, but the landscape is also sanitized of negative elements and made favorable for hospitable habitation. The usage of the term *mangal* is significant because the ASI's act of taming the landscape, although essentially a colonial preoccupation, is justified within the logic of Hindu religiosity and acquits the act of domestication of its intrinsic violence and illegitimacy; as a result, domestication was not viewed as a violent act by ASI archaeologists—it was a patronizing bureaucratic intervention. Underlying this narrative is the subtext of the dread of the uncultivated, an anxiety made apparent in the spatial architecture of the archaeological site.

The *field* and the practice of *fieldwork* are vital to the self-imagination of the archaeologist as a scientist (for example, Daniel 1976, 5; Clarke 1989, 66). It is central in archaeology's claim to its epistemological status as a scientific discipline (Edgeworth 2003, 2010; Yarrow 2003; Carver 2011). The field is conceived of as an epistemic—a discursive location of knowledge production, analogous to a laboratory for the physical scientist—where data is discovered and generated (Lucas 2002; Olsen et al. 2012). The archaeological field is a terrestrial spatiality that is outside of, and demarcated from, the domain of the domestic space inhabited by the archaeologist in an academic or professional setting. The field is the place where an archaeologist ventures into the "outdoors" (Moser 2007, 255). It is a corporeal landscape on which disciplined intervention produces knowledge about the past. Leonard Woolley, in one of the earliest textbooks on archaeological methods and fieldwork, *Digging up the Past*, states: "Field Archaeology is the application of scientific method to the excavation of ancient objects, and based on the theory that the historical value of an object depends not so much on the object itself as on its associations, which only scientific excavation can detect" (Woolley 1930, 15–16). For Woolley, who spent a lifetime digging in the "Orient," field archaeology was a practice that involved transforming an archaeologically potent landscape into an epistemological space with the aim "to discover and to illustrate the course of human history" (Woolley 1930, 31). Philip Barker, writing in the *Techniques of Archaeological Excavation*, conceives the archaeological field as a landscape "which is a vast historical document. On its surface has accumulated a continuous accretion of hundreds of thousands of small acts of change, both natural and human" (Barker 2005, 1). The archaeological field is a spatial entity charged with epistemological meaning, anticipating discovery by the archaeologist willing to leave the confines of his armchair and venture into this potent landscape to "acquire" (Carver 1990, 77) and "create" (Frankel 1993, 875) data.

The field as a geo-epistemological category has its genesis in late nineteenth-century archaeology alongside other field sciences such as botany, zoology, geology, and anthropology (Lucas 2002, 3–6). Venturing into the field to amass knowledge was a well-known practice in the antiquarian traditions of seventeenth-and eighteenth-century European scholars (Schnapp 1996, 182–219).

In the colony, the field was genealogically tied to the emergence of intrepid explorers and travelers, whose exploits into unknown territories were aimed at producing knowledge of the other (Pratt 1992; Fabian 2000; Fuller 2017). It is this practice in the field that gives birth to fieldwork—the instrumental engagement with the terrestrial—an indispensable intervention into an unknown landscape for procuring knowledge. The significant distinction between antiquarian fieldwork and archaeological fieldwork was that the former focused on the collection of material culture whereas the latter involved a transformation of the landscape to produce scientific data. Antiquarian fieldwork was an observational engagement with the landscape whereas archaeological fieldwork was an interventionist engagement with the landscape.

Central to this interventionist practice was the theory of excavation, originating from the belief that uncovering the landscape would lead to the production of scientific knowledge about the past. As a result, the archaeological field was conceptualized as an epistemological practice, this conception being underscored and reiterated through more than a century of writing on archaeological theory and practice.[2] But in this chapter, I destabilize the meaning of the archaeological field defined as an epistemological sphere by theoreticians and fieldworkers alike (for example, Petrie 1904; Wheeler 1954; Woolley 1930; Clark 1968; Hodder 1999; Lucas 2002; Olsen et al. 2012). The archaeological field is a social and ideological engagement with the landscape. It is a manipulation of a landscape's spatiality to assemble an epistemic domain conducive for the production of archaeological knowledge. The field is both the epistemological field and the socio-ideological field (Gero 1985, 1994; Holtorf 2002; Moser 2007). Archaeological knowledge is not the product of an unmediated practice of knowledge production, but emerges from multifaceted cultural and political engagements with the landscape, materiality, people, and social networks. In this chapter, I show that the archaeological field in the bureaucratic archaeology of the ASI not only evokes the epistemological notion of the landscape (Ghosh 1960, 2), but is also a political and social engagement with the landscape. It is not only a "place" (*jagah*) where archaeologists situate themselves to perform science but also a discursive "space" (*sthan*) bound within the confines of a specific cultural sphere and social system. The ASI archaeological excavation is a (post)colonial exploration project—a genre of colonial science that emphasizes that the "real" (*asli*) process of knowledge production is situated outside the domains of the metropole at the fringes of the empire (nation). The ASI's conceptualization of the archaeological project is ordered by a predatory theory of land and landscape, constituted within the colonial framework of territory, and structured by invasive notions of discovery, occupation, and colonization.

Bureaucracy in the Camp

The day-to-day routine of the ASI archaeologists in the field revolves around two distinct categories of spatiality—the excavation site and the campsite. The reciprocity between these involves the movement of human and material culture, ideas, and power. Each of these distinct entities is defined by a definite set of social activities and mores, and is limited by its spatial boundaries that harbor multiple zones of activity, each dedicated to producing specific outcomes. The excavation site is the terrestriality where the primary knowledge production process is executed, whereas the campsite is the site of rest and the setting for secondary knowledge production processes. In the institutional functioning of the ASI, it is in the campsite that the quotidian performance of the bureaucratic state is executed. Unlike the excavation site where the epistemic dominance is enacted over the landscape, the camp is the bureaucratic office in the field. It was the mimesis of the office that the archaeologist-bureaucrat occupied in the urban centers—the head office—the center of authority that affected and transformed the field. If the office in the postcolonial metropole was the central unit through which administrative power and regulatory control flowed in the postcolony, the camp was its mimetic manifestation in the field.

The ASI camp had its origin in eighteenth-century military explorations of the colony.[3] In its early years, the ASI campsite was a fortified temporary settlement that was accompanied by powerful paraphernalia of colonial authority—officers on horseback, survey instruments, and even armed soldiers (Dirk 1994). In later years, it was transformed into an administrative outpost of the bureaucratic state in the field—a frontier location at the fringes of the nation. The camp, as a manifestation of the official machinery, was not just the product of the field practice of the ASI, but rather was an outcome of temporary bureaucratic intervention in the country. The campsite was dissimilar from other permanent governmental edifices found in the rural countryside—primary schools, healthcare centers, and local government offices (*panchayat*). Unlike these permanent statist edifices, the camp was a transient spatial formation; it accompanied any form of temporary intervention of the state in the rural countryside, particularly during the construction of roads, bridges, dams, factories, mines, and industrial centers.

The ASI campsites were always distant from the local village settlements (see Thapar 1957: Plate III, for a photograph of a camp at Maski in Raichur district, Karnataka)—sometimes, a short walk from the village, at other times requiring a jeep ride. ASI archaeologists preferred "at the most" (*jyada se jyada*) a 10-minute walk to the excavation site from the camp.[4] The proximity of the campsite and excavation permitted the staff to oversee the excavation even while they did administrative work at the camp. ASI archaeologists underscored that it was important to have the campsite away (*door*) or separated (*alag*) from the village settlement to maintain the social distance between the state and the locals (*dehati*). They argued that to keep the social hierarchy intact, it was important to not "mix with them" (*mel-jol nahi kare*)—it was necessary to maintain a distance from the "squalid" (*gandh*) local politics and its "convoluted" (*pecheeda*) intrigues. As a governmental agency, it was imperative, my informants insisted, to be "independent, neutral, and non-interfering" (English words were used). Each of these three terms can be framed within the detached subjectivity of the bureaucratic ideology, which emphasized the impartial management of its subjects. Yet embedded within this ideology was the bureaucracy's aspiration to create an identity singular from that of its subjects. This drawing of distinctions was not dissimilar to the militaristic pattern of maintaining a distance between the state and its civilians. The extraordinary nature of the activity, which the ASI engaged at that location, accentuated that only the state apparatus, and not ordinary local subjects, could create this form of special knowledge. This ideological subtext of physical, social, and intellectual distance was iterative and persistently reproduced and reflected in all aspects of the ASI's functioning in the field. The geographic relationship of the campsite to the local habitation was modeled after the colonial military cantonments spread throughout India (Figure 4.1).

Figure 4.1 Dholavira campsite nestled in the wild countryside, 2004

Source: Photograph by the author.

A military cantonment is defined as "a condition in which personnel is housed in temporary structures especially erected for the shelter of troops, a collection of these structures, specially in India, a permanent military station or town, often connected with a native town or city" (Jacob 1994, 2). Cantonments were a temporary military habitation that emerged with the expansion of British power in the late eighteenth century. They established the earliest such cantonments between 1765 and the 1800s (Jacob 1994, 20). By 1857, cantonments were a formidable feature of the imperial military in British India. A crucial feature of these cantonment settlements was that they maintained an explicit spatial distance between themselves and the native habitation (Legg 2007; Wald 2014). Oldenburg, describing the new Lucknow cantonment established after 1857, notes, "The spatial arrangements in the cantonment were the antithesis of those in the old city and typical of the genre of colonial building" (Oldenburg 1989, 52). The primary motive of these cantonments was to

> create a small European cosmos at the edge of the city not only to compensate the officers for the hardship of serving their country in an alien land but also to provide European soldiers with adequate recreational facilities so that they would be less tempted to taste the pleasures the city had to offer. (Oldenburg 1989, 53)

These were established outside of the native settlements, determined by the characteristic militaristic need to maintain a distance between the military and the civilians and to emphasize the exclusivity of the military enterprise (Forth 2017). The ASI camp in postcolonial India used similar iterative semiotics of colonial difference to emphasize the distinction between the representatives of statist machinery and the subaltern villagers. This distinction was further accentuated in the architectural design of the camp. The camp was not only constructed outside the space of the local village, but also the design of the camp prevented free interaction between the ASI team and the local people.

There were other reasons for situating the camp away from the village, as one of my informants noted: that the possibility of "making money" (*paise banana*) was low if the camp was in the village and used the local infrastructure. The opportunity for laundering money was higher if a new infrastructure were to be set up for a campsite instead of renting space in the local village. For example, some of my informants told me that if the archaeological camp were to be set up in the village, the local infrastructure, like a school or the local government office (*panchayat* office), had to be used for accommodation. This did not allow the ASI team to make large purchases of the paraphernalia required to set up the campsite. Making money was done through inflated or false invoices while acquiring equipment and supplies for the camp. For example, only

10 bed sheets would be bought, and the local merchant would be asked to prepare a bogus receipt for 20 items. In another instance, receipts for bed sheets were prepared at the rate of INR 500 each, whereas the ASI team paid the merchants only INR 300 per bed sheet. I heard such "corruption talk" (Lazar 2008, 88) in innumerable exchanges throughout my fieldwork. Setting up camp for every excavation required a significant amount of purchases, which included tents, iron cots, blankets, pillows, bed sheets, coir carpets, fans, generators, kitchen equipment, tables, chairs, ladders, excavation equipment, tools, and many other things. Many of these would have been unnecessary if the camp was relying on local resources in the village, but this would diminish the prospect of making money. Thus, within this logic of (economic) corruption, it was rational to establish a new infrastructure for the camp at every excavation.

Architecture of the Camp

The architecture of the camp was designed to further accentuate the incommensurability between the bureaucratic state and the local citizens, produced by a physical separation between the inner and the outer domains of the camp—delineated by a bamboo and rope fence that encompassed the camp, covering an area between 2 and 5 acres. The fences were weak and porous, and did not provide a dependable barrier against any form of human or animal intrusion. Its erection had only a symbolic valence.[5] It demarcated the statist (*sarkari*) area and inscribed its power on the landscape. Each camp had a main entrance, which was manned 24 hours a day by a watchman/sentry (*chowkidar*), armed with a bamboo baton (*lathi*). The watchman in most cases was a young, well-built man whose demeanor represented that of a bouncer in a city club. He earned the same wages as the laborers at the excavation site, but he enjoyed a special status. The gate performed a symbolic function rather than a preventive one. It was frail and constructed out of a single bamboo pole. The task of the sentry was to remove the bamboo pole to allow vehicles to enter the camp and to prohibit unemployed laborers from entering the premises to plead for work. Adjacent to the bamboo pole gate was a plank, which announced the name of the camp. At Hansi, Baror, and Bhirrana, the plank also stated in Hindi and English that entry into the camp without permission was not allowed. The signboard, the gate, the barbed-wire fence, and the sentries guarding the gate undoubtedly provided an explicit, official appearance to the ASI camp. However, the most distinct architectural feature that corroborated this authoritative impression was the white tents pitched throughout the camp landscape. These were large, waterproof, canvas tents of varying sizes, erected in an orderly fashion. The ASI had used such tents, according to my informants, for more than a century.

The tents, along with other architectural paraphernalia of the ASI camp, did not resemble a typical statist building. Its architectural materiality bore a close resemblance to the military camp. In postcolonial India, the colonial bureaucratic archaeological campsite had transformed into a gated community, which not only prevented the disadvantaged from entering but also controlled the advantaged that inhabited it (Graham and Marvin 2001; Diken 2004) (Figure 4.2).

The Harappan sites were located in the border zone between India and Pakistan.[6] A ubiquitous feature dotting these landscapes of western India consisted of the Indian Army and the Border Security Force (BSF) camps.[7] Similar to the ASI camps, these were closed spatial establishments, fortified with multiple layers of barbed wire rising to a height of 8–10 feet, guarded by armed sentries. Along with other pieces of military equipment, these camps were characterized by canvas tents comparable to those found in the ASI camps. At Dholavira, the presence of a helipad strengthened the impact of the camp as a dominating site wielding state power. The army had constructed it when a general of the Indian Army and his archaeologically inclined wife took a tour of the site in the late 1990s. It had since become an important fixture of the camp. Its utility was limited to rare VIP visits, but its symbolic power added to the military-statist aura of the Dholavira ASI camp.[8] The spatiality of the ASI camp

Figure 4.2 The entrance to the Dholavira excavation camp, with its bamboo pole barrier, *chowkidar*, and the ASI plank, 2004

Source: Photograph by the author.

was more impressive than the common statist architecture in the countryside. Its semiotics was aligned with the daunting architectural manifestation of the military camp (Netz 2009; Forth 2017). This material similarity between the ASI and military camps produced the unmistakable effect of a powerful commanding presence. The ASI camp's materiality, its architectural and spatial formation, resonated with the authoritative aura of the state in the *(war)field*. Here the "topologies of power" (Allen 2016) were exerted to contain, control, and regulate its inhabitants.

The physical architecture of the gated-community-like camp was a corporeal reflection of the terms of engagement between the bureaucracy and the people. The architecture of the camp reflected the aspiration of the ASI to distance itself from the local community. Through its physical apparatus, it laid the ground rules of contact. By controlling the entry and exit of the local people into the camp, the ASI determined those to whom it bestowed its privileges and those that it deemed fit to reject. While the physical boundaries of the camp were flimsy and could not protect the camp from any outside offensive, its symbolic power defined the local inhabitant's interaction with the ASI.[9] Having its genesis in the colonial military camp, the ASI camp was rooted in the oppressive and dominating logic of such a structural apparatus (Gilroy 2000; Diken and Laustsen 2005). The ASI's intervention in the countryside was temporary. So, it was imperative for the ASI to produce an imposing impression in a short time, and the model of the colonial military camp was the ideal choice. This was the underlying subtext of the ASI's choice to construct an imposing spatial formation rather than to underplay its identity by using the infrastructure of the local village. The camp was the architectural representation of the state's power at the fringes of the nation. Its genealogy was embedded in the military expansion of the colonial empire. Thus, I observed that the campsite played the role of a spatial conduit of immense authority over the local people's engagement with the archaeological project.

Hierarchy in the Camp

The ASI camp as a socio-spatial, gated formation was the site where official bureaucratic hierarchy was produced; here, the elites of the ASI excavation were regulated and the state exercised control over its employees. The camp was simultaneously the official and the residential quarters of the archaeological unit in the field. The social and the official relationships within the ASI were recreated and iterated through this spatialized hierarchy. While a distinctive set of social negotiations governed official relationships in the field, the essential structure was similar. The camp recreated the hierarchy of the *head office* in several ways apparent in the daily practice of the ASI staff. Although these hierarchies and disciplinarian structures were constantly negotiated and subverted by all members of the staff, its impact on the daily life of the excavation members was ubiquitous. Each ASI camp comprised more than a dozen tents of varying sizes. The sizes and the quality of the tents reflected the status of the members of the camp. The director and the officers occupied larger tents, compared to the tents occupied by the other members of the staff and the students—often old and sometimes even in tatters. Two to six occupants shared a single tent. The director of the excavation, in contrast, had a tent to himself. In certain cases, as in Dholavira, the ASI officers lived in semi-permanent *boonga*s—a traditional habitation unit of Kutch, circular, made of stone and mud, and with a thatched roof. The rest of the staff and students lived in tents. In this hierarchical spatiality, the director's tent was unique. Most noticeably, the size of the director's tent was large.

In Baror and Dholavira, the director did not live in the tent but in a mud house. The habitational semiotics of the mud house and the *boonga*s as luxurious living space is noteworthy, especially in the climatic context of the Harappan sites. The *boonga*s and the mud houses were both semi-permanent structures. They could withstand the extreme temperatures in these arid parts of India, where temperatures would rise to more than 45 degrees centigrade in the day (in summers) and dip to around 2 degrees centigrade at night (in winters). Under these conditions, the canvas tents failed as adequate shelters, whereas the *boonga*s and the mud huts were impeccable housing. The tents were pitched in such a way that almost all members of the camp could see each other's tents, which had a rudimentary panoptical effect. Segregating the tents that belonged to the students, the staff, the officers, and the director in different sections of the camp allowed the director a privileged view. It was said of the excavation director at Dholavira that every day, early in the morning, at the start of the excavation, he surveyed from his tent the members of the excavation team who were late. Several informants disclosed that excavation directors from the days of Wheeler had adopted this surveillance practice as a way of disciplining the staff and the students living in the archaeological camp (Figure 4.3).

The interior of these habitation spaces entrenched the hierarchy of the bureaucratic convention, reflected in two primary forms of private spaces— the bathroom and the toilet. In the ASI camps, they were conspicuous sites of hierarchy. The temporary nature of the camps does not allow for luxurious zones to carry out intimate acts of body-care, but in all the camps, a rudimentary form of such spaces existed. Their place within the larger domain of an archaeological project was banal and minor, but ASI officers often asserted that their proper construction and regular maintenance was a vital part of the daily

Figure 4.3 ASI campsites at Juni Kuran (*top*) in 2004, Dholavira (*middle*) in 2004, and
Bhirrana (*bottom*) in 2005

Source: Photographs by the author.

practice of camp life. The interior of the tents was divided into two spaces—the
larger living cum bedroom consisting of two iron cots and two tables for personal
effects. The smaller space was a bathroom, enclosed behind each tent where the
laborers working in the camp would dutifully leave two buckets of hot water
every morning and evening. At Dholavira, "running tap-water" in this portion
of the tent, along with cement flooring, made it a "VIP camp." The toilets in
other camps were temporary dugouts (*kaccha latrine*), at the edge of the camp's
boundary, which was moved once the dugout filled up. Here, hierarchy was
inscribed in the form of exclusive dugouts for the directors and senior officers of
the camp. Toilets in Dholavira were permanent structures (*pucca latrine*) made of
cement and brick with modern ceramic commodes. All members of the Dholavira
camp except for the directors and senior officers who lived in the *boonga*s or the

mud houses, which had attached toilet and bathroom, used these. In the wild environs of the ASI gated-community-like camps, the prevalence of permanent (*pucca*) structures for the upper strata of the ASI bureaucracy and temporary (*kaccha*) structures for the lower strata exemplified the spatialized hierarchy whose genealogy was located in colonial cantonments (Cowell 2016) (Figure 4.4).

The director's residence, either in the form of a canvas tent or a mud house, had a special place in the camp. It was the "official area" (*sarkari daftar*) of bureaucratic power in the field. Besides its strategic location and the special building material it was made of, the interior of this space contrasted with other tents in its extravagance. I had the privilege to enter these habitations occupied by the director and noticed a marked difference in the interior of these spaces. They were larger than the usual tents (12-by-12 feet or 10-by-10 feet), and often contained sofas and large wooden beds, compared to the iron cots in the tents. An obvious luxury item was the television set. In two camps, the TV was kept in a common tent where any member of the camp could watch it, but in Bhirrana and Baror, the TV was not meant for public viewing and was in the director's tent. It was only brought out during special occasions, such as the cricket matches between India and Pakistan that were being played during the days when I was doing my fieldwork (2004–05 series).

Figure 4.4 The director's residence and the campsite office at Dholavira, 2004; at the top of the wall is a representation of the massive Harappan "sign-post" found at the site

Source: Photograph by the author.

Within this disciplinary regime, depending on the disposition of the excavation director, various other disciplining symbols were deployed to reinscribe the hierarchy among the ASI staff. At Juni Kuran, for example, I observed that in front of each tent a small wooden plank, fixed on an iron rod, had been planted into the ground announcing the official position of the occupant, rather than the person's name. Painted in white on a black background (customary ASI bureaucratic iconography), the designated position of the tent's occupant was mentioned both in English (Roman script) and Hindi (Devanagari script): driver (*vahan chalak*), chief-photographer (*pramukh chhaya-chitrakaar*), chief artist (*pramukh chitrakaar*), camp director (*utkhanan sanchalak*), cook (*bawarchi*), guest (*athiti*), and others. This form of official declarative nomenclature in Hindi was typically found throughout the bureaucratic offices in postcolonial India, where the nomenclatural emphasis was on the position of the person rather than on one's name. The disciplinarian ideology of such a nomenclatural signposting at Juni Kuran was taken to absurd levels where even spaces such as the kitchen (*rasoi*), dining room (*bhojanalaya*), and toilets (*shauchalaya*) were marked in such a fashion.

The Hindi terminology deployed was not commonplace. These words were statist Hindi (*sarkari Hindi*)—neologism that drew their etymology from Sanskrit (Rai 2001). Another manifestation of the ASI disciplinarian ideology was uniforms. At Juni Kuran, the excavation director ordered that each member of the ASI staff wear a blue *khadi* (hand-spun, hand-woven cotton) jacket to distinguish them from the laborers. This insistence on a dress code was uncommon even by ASI standards, as the director of Dholavira revealed. However, its prevalence appeared to be a vestige of the military disciplinarian subtext that lingered in the archaeological project. The ideological impetus of *sarkari* Hindi and *khadi* dress code were iterative mechanisms to entrench bureaucratic discipline on the members of the archaeological project.

The temporality of the camp was dictated by the disciplinary regime of factory time (Thompson 1967; Clark 1994; Ogle 2015). A bell made up of an iron bar was struck by the chowkidar with an iron hammer 24 times a day, like a human clock tower, with the number of strikes signifying the hour. However, this rule was broken four times a day—announcing the start of the morning shift, the midday break, the afternoon shift, and the end of the afternoon shift. At these times, a flurry of piercing strikes announced the prominence of that hour. Like the factory siren, the bell was a means of controlling both the laborers and the ASI staff who inhabited the camp. It governed their daily life after the day's work and even in the dead of the night when they were sleeping. Most ASI staff members as well as several laborers (including many women) owned and routinely wore wristwatches; thus, the valence of the bell was not in its utilitarian value but to institute a disciplinary regime. The sound of the bell was a relentless reminder that even though the ASI excavation camp was located on the fringes of the nation, the disciplinarian mechanism of the bureaucratic regime still governed their lives. An AA poignantly told me that the ubiquitous sound of the bell was so "penetrating" (*prakopi*) that it even infiltrated into their most pleasant dreams: "Even in our dreams the ASI bell does not leave us" (*Sapne mein bhi hume ASI ki ghanti chorthi nahi hai*).

The campsite, unlike the head office in the metropole, was a 24-hour engagement with the disciplinarian structure of the postcolonial bureaucratic apparatus. All the members of the excavation unit, from the director to the student laborer, knew that the excavation camp was a distinctive form of official engagement governed by a unique set of norms and mores, albeit framed within the disciplinarian logic of the "office" (*dafater*). At the excavation site, the laborer was the site for the enactment of the disciplinarian apparatus of archaeology and bureaucracy, whereas at the campsite, it was the ASI employees who were at the receiving end.

The gated camp of the ASI was not just a spatial formation that articulated the distinction between the state and the people it governed. It was also a disciplinary formation, which institutionalized bureaucratic difference and hierarchy through the spatial and temporal organization of camp life. The camp was not the office, but the disciplinarian regime of the office that controlled its daily life. It was an ideological mimesis of the office. The state in the field had no prototype other than the bureaucratic office of the metropole to impose its social formation, to domesticate the wild landscape, and to control not just the laborers used but also to regulate its own inmates in the field's wilderness. This mode of engagement had pervasive ontological reverberations on the epistemological project. ASI archaeologists saw themselves as scientists who penetrated the *heart of darkness*, because survival in the wilderness was paramount; thus, the middle-class, urban ASI bureaucrats had to domesticate its hostility. The usage of the colonial *heart-of-darkness* trope is conscious because I would like to emphasize the colonial impetus of this contemporary postcolonial bureaucratic intervention. The act of the excavation and the setting of the camp by the statist bureaucracy was an act of intrusion into a landscape that was imagined as *wild* (*jangli*).

Acquisition of the Excavation Site

The notion of the "protected monument" is central to legal control over any archaeological site by the ASI throughout India, defined by the Ancient Monuments and Archaeological Sites and Remains Act of 1958 as "an ancient

monument, which is declared to be of national importance by or under this Act"
(Tripathi 2007, 5). An ancient monument is defined as:

> Any structure, erection, or monument, or any tumulus or place of interment, or any
> cave, rock-sculpture, inscription or monolith, which is of historical, archaeological,
> or artistic interest, or any remains thereof, and includes—the site of an ancient
> monument; such portion of land adjoining the site of an ancient monument as
> may be required for fencing or covering in or otherwise preserving such monument;
> and the means of access to and convenient inspection of an ancient monument.[10]
> (Tripathi 2007, 3)

This Act gives unlimited power to the ASI to declare any piece of land in India
that it considers archaeologically valuable to be declared protected. The
ASI, through the Ministry of Culture, arranged the possession by issuing a
notification in the official gazette which declares the ancient monument to be a
"protected" site. Once the site has been declared protected, the lengthy process
of land acquisition (or eminent domain) begins.[11] One of the most disconcerting
realities of the ASI excavation sites I studied was that after it acquired the land for
excavation, the ASI did not pay the requisite compensation or the payment was
delayed by several years. Coercive acquisition of land for developmental work is a
norm in postcolonial India, and bureaucratic hurdles often result in the failure to
compensate.[12] The ASI, as a national organization, is no different from any other
bureaucratic apparatus of the postcolonial state. All the sites I worked in were
involved in legal disputes relating to land acquisition and compensation.

The SHP sites were "protected monuments." Dholavira and Juni Kuran were
declared protected in the 1970s soon after J. P. Joshi discovered them. Baror,
Bhirrana, Chak 86, Tarkhanewala Dera, and other SHP sites were discovered
by Dr A. K. Ghosh in the 1950s, but were only declared to be protected sites in
2003. The process of land acquisition of these SHP sites started in the middle of
2003. Letters were sent to the superintending archaeologists (SAs) of the Rajasthan,
Haryana, and Gujarat Circles to begin the paperwork necessary to acquire
land for archaeological excavations. In the meantime, advance teams from the
Excavation Branches (Ex. Brs.) were sent to the sites to conduct reconnaissance
trips to determine the nature of the mounds and to coordinate with the local
district level officials to acquire land to conduct excavations at the sites (see,
for example, AACD, File No. 1/3/2003-SP/EE; AACD, File No. 1/4/2003-SP).
However, the tension and contestation regarding proprietary rights over the
land in which the excavation was being conducted was a uniform feature of all
the sites. The primary cause of this tension was the (fair) compensation being
demanded by the owner(s) of the land and the ASI's inability to fulfill those

demands in a favorable way. The ASI's track record in giving compensation to the people who owned the land after acquisition was extremely poor. During a visit to the Kalibangan excavation site, I was informed that the landowners on whose land the Kalibangan Site Museum had been built in the 1980s had yet to be given compensation. Although it has been difficult to get statistics about the number of litigation cases over issues of land acquisition and compensation in which the ASI was involved, I was told by several ASI archaeologists that much of their time in the office was spent in preparing for litigations and court appearances regarding a number of land acquisition dispute cases.[13]

The process of land acquisition at Dholavira had begun in 1989, more than 15 years before I came to Dholavira to conduct this ethnography, but it was still not completed.[14] A large chunk of 120 acres of this land was uncultivable, and it belonged to Gujarat Forest Department; 14 private landowners owned the rest. Out of these, only two owners lost all their land; the others lost a fraction of their land. This was cultivable land, where only single millet crop (*jowar* or *bajra*) could be grown yearly, fed by the sparse monsoons in this arid region. Even in 2003, none of the 14 landowners had been compensated by the local district administration. I was informed that it was not in the jurisdiction of the ASI to compensate landowners. It was the responsibility of the Gujarat state's Revenue Department to pay the affected landowners. However, I came to know from the laborers that the officials responsible for acquiring the land had not even initiated the process of the valuation of the land and that the question of compensation was not even in the picture. The landowners belonged to the lower castes and had little political or social clout in Dholavira. The ASI archaeologists had defused the situation by employing two members of each of the landowners' families as daily-wage laborers at the site. These laborers were compensated with the minimum wage of INR 92 per day throughout the excavation season, which lasted nearly 100 to 120 days every year. This amount was a princely sum of money in 2003. It temporarily placated the landowners. However, it is important to point out that this was not a form of legal compensation for the acquired land. It was rather the result of an informal negotiation process to mitigate any form of protest from the landowners, which would interrupt the ASI's excavation.

Of these 14 owners, one member was not satisfied with the informal compensation that the ASI archaeologists had doled out—three members of his family were employed as daily-wage laborers on the excavation site. Mohan *bhai* (Gujarati suffix for respect) was one of the two owners who had lost all their land. Unlike the others, he was an upper caste Brahmin who had several times attempted to raise the banner of revolt against the temporary compensation offered by the ASI. Mohan *bhai* had considerable clout in the village, and it was no wonder he was the only one in the village willing to challenge the ASI. It was possible for him to raise his voice because he was an upper caste Brahmin— the only one in the village of Dholavira, which mainly comprised lower caste and tribal communities. I heard several stories about how he had shown his displeasure by destroying trenches on the site by digging through the quadrant walls and the balks in the middle of the night. One day, he had even accosted the director of the site in a drunken stupor, brandishing a sword. In my conversations with him, he told me he had lost 7 acres of land. He was not willing to accept the "paltry" (*chota*) compensation that the ASI was "throwing as crumbs" (*tukade phake rahe hain*) at him. He explained that now he was planning to go to court against the ASI and would not rest until he "stopped the excavation project." He explained that this was the last resort for him.

Five years ago, the director had promised him that the ASI would pay him INR 2,000 every season as compensation for the dirt they excavated from his land, along with the daily-wage employment of three members of his family. Although the ASI had kept their word as far as the employment of his family members was concerned, they had not paid him the promised INR 2,000 for the dirt that had been excavated in the past three years. He told me he had also approached the director several times to expedite the process of compensation, but nothing had been done (*kuch nahi kiya*). He claimed he had visited the Revenue Department office in Bhuj (district headquarters of Kutch) many times but no action had been taken. During our conversation, Mohan *bhai* pulled out a grimy plastic folder which contained a paper clipping from a local Gujarati newspaper, *Kutch Mitra*. He had written a letter to the editor explicating his grievance against the ASI. Mohan *bhai* was illiterate but he had enlisted the help of a college student to write this letter for him. The letter read,

> I was lucky that an archaeological site was discovered by the ASI in Dholavira, but this luck of mine has become a burden as the Government of India had not yet paid me compensation for the land I lost (6 acres and 26 guntas).[15] I have worked at this site for many years as a watchman [*chowkidar*] and this site is the pride [*gaurav*] of Kutch and of India, but this pride is weighing me down.

Mohan *bhai*, toward the end of the conversation, said he now did not really want any monetary compensation for the land he had lost because of the excavation: "this is my gift [*upahaar*] to the nation." However, he hoped that at least his son would be given a permanent job by the ASI—as a caretaker of the site. Mohan *bhai* had realized that his land had been permanently taken away from him and that the compensation would only provide temporary respite; by demanding a permanent job for his son he wanted to strike a more stable and long-term bargain. He had realized that Dholavira would become an important tourist attraction, and a salaried income would be a more viable than a one-time monetary recompense.

Twelve years later in 2017, when I went to Dholavira, a local informant told me that Mohan *bhai* was yet to receive compensation from the Government of India. The examples here were not isolated instances of the complications—logistical and otherwise—involved in the process of land acquisition by the ASI, but a broader illustration of how the ASI, as a statist institution, perceived its relationship to the landscape. For the bureaucratic ASI, land was property. It gained its access through the transference of legal proprietary rights. The ASI's conception of land did not differ from other statist organizations that acquired land for development—as territory that was procured for a national/nation-building task. The land had an instrumental value, deriving from the belief that archaeological work constituted service for the nation and that proprietary rights over land were securable through the legal infrastructure.

At Bhirrana and Baror, the situation was different. Both were small archaeological mounds with habitation deposits of around 6 to 8 meters. They had been declared protected monuments in the 1960s, soon after A. K. Ghosh reported them in the 1950s. Unlike other sites, a serious problem persisted in these mounds. They were regularly used as Muslim burial grounds. During the pre-partition years, there was a substantial Muslim population in this part of India. After independence, the proprietary rights of these mounds were given to the regional Wakf Board—Islamic endowment bodies. These are statutory bodies established by the Government of India administered by the Wakf Act, 1995, which managed Islamic religious and community property throughout India.[16] Until 2004, the local Muslim community members buried their dead on these mounds, though the frequency of such burials was low. I was told that the number of such burials was less than a dozen a year.

At Baror, the site had been declared a protected monument in 1962, but the Wakf Board continued to have proprietary control over the land and used the mound as a burial ground. The edges of the mound were also used as a cremation ground for the local Hindu and Sikh population. On the topmost portion of the mound was a brick-and-mortar shrine dedicated to a local Muslim saint who was buried there. According to the local informants, this was a very recent phenomenon. The Muslim shrine was not more than 20 to 30 years old, and its presence proved to be a logistical problem for the ASI. Soon after the Patna Ex. Br. had pitched their camp at the site, the local Wakf Board members, along with community leaders, lodged a formal protest against the ASI. They requested that the excavation be stopped because it violated their sacred space.

They even threatened the laborers at the site with dire consequences if they worked for the ASI. The Board simultaneously demarcated the mound with barbed wire to prevent the ASI from conducting the excavation. The ASI immediately informed the sub-divisional magistrate (SDM) of the Anupgarh block of the Sri Ganganagar district under whose jurisdiction the site was located. The SDM came with a police posse. The situation was tense. There was a likelihood that the confrontation would escalate into a communal altercation.

The SDM advised both the Muslim community leaders and the ASI to come to a compromise rather than escalate the confrontation. He informed the Wakf Board members that the ASI had the legal right to take over the mound as they had the "*Act* in their favor." He counseled the ASI archaeologists that although they could legally continue with excavation, "it was important to work with *tact*." He advised that in "this delicate situation" (*is nazuk waqt*), it is sagacious "to use *tact* rather than the *Act* and come to a *pact*" (English words used). It was decided that the ASI archaeologists would leave the area at the top of the mound, where the shrine was located, untouched, and also not dig in the western part of the mound where the most recent burials had taken place. This compromise was acceptable to both sides, and the excavation began soon after. However, later, an assistant archaeologist (AA) who had been involved in the negotiation told me that this "pact" had been just a temporary solution. In the next season (2004–05), the area that was considered out-of-bounds for the ASI was also excavated; however, the shrine and the surrounding area were left untouched (also see AACD, File No. 28/6/2003-EE).

Contested Politics of Discovery

The primacy given to discovery reflected the ASI's comprehension and engagement with the landscape. For the ASI, discovery was the most significant part of archaeological intervention. The semiotics of discovery did not pertain to uncovering a structure or an artifact in the trench or the quadrant, but notably to also identifying new archaeological sites. Here, the discovery was analogous to the sighting of a new land, framed within the colonial logic of the occupation of a terrain.[17] In the archaeological case, the discovery was not just a colonization of a landscape, but was also a spatial occupation of its temporality. An AA at Baror explicated, with mild conceit: "For us, archaeology is not work, but worship. We are digging the nation" (*Hamare liye archaeology kaam nahi, puja hai. Hum bharatiyata ko khod rahe hai*). The ancient landscape of the nation was expecting to be discovered by the ASI. This discovery was a matter of both personal prestige and national fame.

As professionals, all of the young AAs I spoke to desired to discover a site of their own and to report it to the archaeological community in the *Annual Report* of the ASI (*IAR*). The prestige of an archaeologist in the ASI was assessed not only by his/her analytical or theoretical contribution to Indian archaeology, but also on the number of sites discovered by him/her. The discovery of new sites was institutionalized in the ASI in the form of the "village-to-village survey for antiquarian remains" (AACD, File No. 24/2/2003-EE). After joining the ASI, archaeologists would conduct this survey, which involved: "... surveying all the villages in India district-wise for bringing to light archaeological remains" (AACD, File No. 24/2/2003-EE).[18] This was carried out through the posting of young AAs in the sub-circles. They were instructed to select districts and start the exploration systematically. During this operation, each discovery, however minute, had to be catalogued in an official format called the "Form – D." If a significant site was discovered, a senior ASI officer would further inspect it, and then this site might be declared a protected monument.[19] It was assumed that the older the site, the more prestigious it was to discover and dig it. Since the discovery of a site was a "matter of prestige," I learnt that it was not without political contestation.

Dr Jagat Pati Joshi "officially" discovered Dholavira along with 120 sites dating from the prehistoric to the historical periods in the 1960s. These discoveries were part of the "systematic and planned exploration" work in Kutch carried out by Joshi during 1964–65 and the winters of 1965 and 1968 (Joshi 1990, 3). The ASI archaeologists at Dholavira invoked this discovery of Dholavira in hagiographic terms. Joshi, according to the "legend," reached Dholavira after a three-day journey on camel-back while he was excavating the site of Surkotada.[20] However, the local villagers of Dholavira contested this official narrative. And there were two narratives.

In the dominant contesting narrative, Dholavira's discovery was attributed to Shambhudan Gadhvi, the upper caste ex-headman of the village.[21] In the 1960s, Gadhvi had recovered numerous Indus seals from the site-mound while he was a foreman at a drought relief project. While supervising the digging of a small dam (*bandh kaam*) to collect the monsoon waters, he discovered numerous artifacts; prominent among them were fragments of Indus seals. He recognized that the seals belonged to the Harappan civilization (*Harappan sabhyata*) by comparing it to the pictures that he found in his son's history textbook issued by the Gujarat government. He subsequently searched for more seals and collected numerous artifacts—decorative ceramics, fragments of carnelian beads, and metal objects. He took these artifacts to the district museum in Bhuj and showed it to the curator there.[22] During my interview with Shambhudan Gadhvi, he emphasized that he did not believe J. P. Joshi had ever come to Dholavira. He reasoned that being the headman of the village, he would have known about it. He suggested that Joshi must have seen the artifacts that he, Gadhvi, had submitted at the Bhuj Museum and reported the site to the ASI. According to him, it was R. S. Bisht who had been the first ASI official to visit the site in the mid-1980s. By that time, the backyard of his house was laden with artifacts, ceramics, and structural members from the site. Gadhvi had been an important collaborator of R. S. Bisht while large-scale exploration work was being carried out in the region in the late 1980s to create a settlement map of the island of Khadir where Dholavira was located (*IAR 1984–85* 1987, 14–17; *IAR 1987–88* 1993, 15–16). He claimed it was due to his contacts with people in other villages that the ASI discovered more sites. Once the excavation work began in 1990, Gadhvi helped the ASI to set up the camp and recruit laborers from the village of Dholavira for the first season of excavation.

On a sunny day soon after, while accompanying the site director on an inspection tour of the site, I questioned him about Shambhudan Gadhvi's claim. He admitted that Gadhvi had known of the site before the ASI's discovery and that he had been very helpful during the earlier years of excavation by providing important local logistical support, "but to give him the credit for the discovery of the site would undermine our role as archaeologists. It was one thing to be aware of the site and another to know the archaeological value of the site. *Discovery is not about awareness but about recognition* [English phrase used]," he explained. "Gadhvi is growing old. He does not remember Dr J. P. Joshi's visit to Dholavira," the site director dismissively continued and firmly added: "Remember the state has a better memory [*behatar yaaddaash*] than a village headman."

Shambhudan Gadhvi's claim was not the only subaltern narrative (Coronil 1994) of Dholavira's discovery; another contesting narrative undermined Gadhvi's assertions. This narrative attributed the discovery of the site to a young Dalit goat herder. While grazing his goats and sheep, he had found fragments of Indus seals and had shown it to Gadhvi, who, recognizing the importance of the seal, had taken it to the museum in Bhuj. When I questioned Gadhvi, he admitted this to be true. However, Gadhvi claimed he still should be given the credit for the discovery because he had recognized the importance of the seal and had reported the site to the Bhuj Museum. This narrative also reflected the caste tension between the various groups in the village. It should not come as a surprise that the boy, who is now a grown-up man, was from a lower caste than Gadhvi, and also wanted to be credited. For Shambhudan Gadhvi, the Dalit shepherd boy did not deserve the credit for discovering the site because he could not recognize its antiquity. For the ASI archaeologists, Shambhudan Gadhvi was not worthy of being credited as the discoverer of Dholavira because he could not recognize the epistemic valence of Dholavira as an archaeological site. These multiple contesting claims did not make a dent in the official hagiography of the ASI. The official ASI marker—the painted iron board erected at the entrance of the Dholavira site—erased the local narrative of discovery and officially announced: "The Harappan site at Dholavira (Lat. 23°53' 10" N and Long. 70°13' 00" E) has been discovered by Shri Jagat Pati Joshi in 1967–1968. The Archaeological Survey of India has started excavation for the first time in 1990, under the direction of Dr. R. S. Bisht."

Discovery in the ASI did not depend on the claim to initial sighting, but rather on the idea of recognition. Discovery did not signify the ability to locate new sites, but rather the ability to recognize the archaeological "potential" (Joshi 1990, 14) in an unknown landscape. In epistemological terms, recognition refers to the professional ability of the archaeologist to invoke the knowledge armature of archaeology to categorize the site as epistemologically valuable (Edgeworth 2003). The discovery of an archaeological site in the ASI constitutes both a discursive act of recognizing the landscape as archaeologically valuable and a process through which the landscape must be colonized for epistemological exploitation. This ability to recognize is operative to the bureaucratic practice of ASI archaeology, which mediates the daily practice of archaeology as discovery and determines the value of each archaeologist. We will see more of this unambiguously as we now enter the excavation site.

Notes

1. The director of the excavation, usually the SA of the Excavation Branch (Ex. Br.), conducted this ritual in most cases; however, sometimes a higher officer, like the DG of the ASI, might officiate as the "chief guest" of such a ceremony. At times, such an event would also be accompanied by the "opening ceremony" of the excavation season.

2. Since the early twentieth century, archaeological manuals as textbook have been in proliferation to socialize the uninitiated into the disciplinary discourse of its practice. Some of the influential texts used in India are Petrie (1904); Woolley (1930); Wheeler (1954); Hole and Heizer (1969); and Barker (2005). In the context of the ASI, the textbooks commonly used were Raman (1991) and Rajan (2002).

3. There is a formidable scholarship about the ideology and the bio-politics of the camp (see, for instance, Diken and Laustsen 2005; Hailey 2009), following Giorgio Agamben, who locates the origin of the concentration camp to Spanish colonization in Cuba at the end of the nineteenth century and the English in South Africa in the beginning of the twentieth century (Agamben 1998, 166–67).

4. This proximity also allowed the ASI staff to take more frequent breaks during the day and gave them sufficient time to rest in the afternoons. This last-mentioned benefit was so crucial that my informants at Juni Kuran complained about having to take their afternoon nap under the sparse shade of desert vegetation as their movement to and from the site depended on the mercy of the jeep drivers. When the jeep was not at the site, the ASI staff would have to walk 14 kilometers back and forth between the camp and the site. This was a key source of resentment for some members of the ASI staff at Juni Kuran, because they felt they were losing their free time, and were forced to stay at the excavation site throughout the day.

5. However, at times, the fences did have a utilitarian value, as in the case of Baror, where a barbed-wire fence replaced the bamboo and rope contraption after stray dogs entered the camp and attacked a student and an ASI jeep driver.

6. For example, Baror was just 8 kilometers away from the Pakistan border. Dholavira and Juni Kuran were about 50 to 60 kilometers away.

7. The huge army build-up in early 2002, during the India–Pakistan confrontation, also largely contributed to the ubiquity of the military camps in this area, some of which continued to remain while I was doing my fieldwork.

8. My informants noted that, during the India–Pakistan military build-up in 2001–02, the Indian army had regularly used the helipad.

9. By "local people" I primarily mean the subaltern labor force and other villagers who had direct interaction with the ASI and whose daily lives were impacted by the excavation's political economy.

10. In 1878, 20 years after the establishment of the ASI, the colonial government formulated the first in a series of numerous Acts and Regulations concerning the protection, governance, and acquisition of ancient remains. The first of these Acts was the Treasure Trove Act of 1878, followed by the Ancient Monuments Preservation Act in 1904 and the Ancient Monuments Preservation Rules in 1937. After 1947, the postcolonial government, taking the 1904 Ancient Monuments Preservation Act as their framework, formulated other Acts. These included: The Ancient and Historical Monuments and Archaeological Sites and Remains (Declaration of National Importance) Act of 1951; followed by the Ancient Monuments and Archaeological Sites and Remains Act of 1958; the Ancient Monuments and Archaeological Sites and Remains Rules of 1959; the Antiquities and Art Treasures Act of 1972; and the Antiquities and Art Treasures Rules of 1973. These, along with the Export Control Act of 1947 and the Public Premises (Eviction of Unauthorized Occupants) Act of 1971, constitute the legal armature through which the ASI protects all forms of archaeological heritage.

11. Elucidating the process of land acquisition, the ASI's *Archaeological Works Code* states:

> When land is required for public purposes by the Survey, the head of the Office, should, in the first instance consult the Collector/Revenue Officer of the District and obtain from him, all possible information as to the probable cost of the land, together with the value of the building, etc., situated on the property, for which compensation will have to be paid. Upon the information thus obtained an estimate should be framed by the head of the Office and submitted to the Director general for his sanction. When sanction to such an estimate has been obtained, the head of Office should communicate the matter to the Revenue Officer, who will take the necessary action for acquisition of the land, under the Land Acquisition Act, or its acquisition by private negotiation. (*Archaeological Works Code* 2017, 46)

12. During the time of my fieldwork, the colonial era Land Acquisition Act of 1894 governed land acquisition by the state in India, amended twice, in 1962 and 1984—both amendments expanded the state's appropriative powers. This Act has been responsible for the dispossession of nearly 60 million people between 1947 and 2004 of which 40 percent were Adivasis and 20 percent Dalits (Fernandes 2004). In 2013, the Indian Parliament enacted an updated Right to Fair Compensation and Transparency in Land Acquisition, Rehabilitation and Resettlement Act, but it was also not without problems (see Ghatak and Ghosh 2011; Chakravorty 2016).

13. For a lengthy paper trail of the land acquisition process of the SHP sites, see AACD, File No. 1/4/2003-SP; AACD, File No. 1/3/2003-SP/EE.

14. In a letter dated October 10, 2003, Minister Jagmohan writes to the then chief minister of Gujarat Narendra Modi: "... may I request your intervention for initiating the following for catalyzing the developmental works further: (a) The speedy transfer of land under private ownership at Dholavira to ASI for which the land owners are not averse. The land under Forest Department can be taken up after that" (AACD, File No. 1/4/2003-SP).

15. 1 *gunta* = 101.1714 square meters; 40 *guntas* = 1 acre.

16. There is a long history of Waqf legislations since 1810, taking a modern shape in the Mussalman Waqf Validating Act, 1913; followed by the Waqf Act, 1954, which was amended in 1959, 1964, 1969, and 1984. Now Islamic endowments in India are governed by the Waqf Act, 1995, which was amended by the Waqf (Amendment) Act, 2013 (see Obaidullah 2016; Tabasum 2017).

17. In the context of South Asian archaeology, surface exploration was considered an important way of identifying a physical location within a landscape as an

archaeologically potent site. It was deemed to play a "vital role in bringing to light the nature and the distribution of artifacts or cultures not only in a site but also over a wider region" (Raman 1991, 56).

18. Archaeologists such as A. K. Ghosh, B. K. Thapar, K. N. Dikshit, and J. P. Joshi were considered to be expert foot-surveyors. To understand their methodology and the sites they discovered, see, for instance, Ghosh (1953); *IAR 1954–55* (1954, 58–62); *IAR 1978–79* (1980, 1–34).

19. In the early years of the twenty-first century, village-to-village surveys had been discontinued, but a revival was being planned in 2003 (AACD, File No. 24/2/2003-EE). However, as late as 2018, my informants told me that this policy has been discontinued for good.

20. J. P. Joshi joined the ASI in 1956 and belonged to the first cohort of students of the ASI's Institute of Archaeology and subsequently became the DG of ASI from 1987 to 1990. For more details about the Surkotada excavations, see Joshi (1990).

21. Gadhvi is an honorific title for a bardic caste of Gujarat called the Charans—a non-mendicant upper caste (not, however, Brahmins or Kshatriya) who have exerted considerable influence on the local polity since medieval times (Shah and Shroff 1958).

22. Maharao Khengarji III, king of the princely state of Cutch, in 1877 established the Kutch Museum, formerly known as the Fergusson Museum after the colonial Indologist Sir James Fergusson. It is located in the city of Bhuj—the district headquarters of Kutch—in the medieval walled city.

5 Epistemological Formation of the Archaeological Site

My daily routine at Dholavira began with a quick early morning breakfast. Soon after, I joined the staff and students as they scurried to the excavation site. I usually accompanied one of the assistant archaeologists (AAs) and sometimes the director of the site during their daily "inspection round." There were between two and four AAs at Dholavira at all times. Some of them were from the New Delhi headquarters; others were on deputation from other Excavation Branches (Ex. Brs.) or Circles. By the time we arrived at the excavation trenches, all the students and ex-students in charge of the quadrants were at their respective locations, planning the day's work. The laborers were always the first to reach the site. They began the day by dusting the trench floor or clearing the dirt, preparing for the next "dig." Dholavira was a monumental site, so the inspection took up the entire day as we meandered from one trench to another. We would start by climbing the fortification wall into the citadel, trotting through the Middle Town into the Lower Town, descending into the various reservoirs, and reaching the burial grounds at the perimeter of this expansive Harappan metropolis.[1] As a ritual, we would return to the citadel and sit atop the highest point of the site—at the edge of the colossal fortification wall. Perched atop the fortification wall, sitting on ancient limestone blocks carved more than three millennia ago, we could see the entire ancient cityscape, across the Rann—its surreal snow-white salt-water marsh disappearing into the edge of the earth. The paleness of the still water was transformed into a golden expanse in the glimmering rays of the setting sun.

Sharp at 5 p.m., the *chowkidar* struck the makeshift bell made of a cast-iron cylinder, signaling the end of the day's work. He was an elderly, weary man with a luxurious salt-and-pepper moustache, who wore a colorful turban, and typically donned a terry-cot bush-shirt and a pale white *dhoti*. Supporting his frail gait with a wooden shaft, he walked every day from the campsite to the citadel, from where everyone could see and hear him. Soon, a small army of fatigued laborers arose rapidly from the trenches. Men and women, emerging from the sunken squares in the earth, treading toward the camp, their clothes covered in dust and soil. The men bent over with the heavy weight of the tools of their trade on their weary shoulders—spades, pickaxes, brushes, trowels, and knives.

The women carrying wicker baskets on their heads crammed with the pottery-shards and bone-fragments excavated that day. Alongside sauntered exhausted site supervisors and students bearing polyester backpacks stuffed with precious artifacts. It looked like a pre-industrial agrarian ritual. Farmers and pastoralists returning home after a hard day's work. "In Hindi this time [*waqt*] of the day is often called *godhuli*," mused an AA, who had grown up in a small village in north India. "The name comes from the cloud of dust [*dhuli*] raised by cattle or cows [*gau*] when they return home at dusk." During such nostalgia-evoking moments, my informants often asserted, with an air of affectionate finality and steadfast certitude: "This is what ASI archaeology is!" Once the director had gestured, exuding some gentle pride: "The ability to dig such huge areas, teeming with hundreds of laborers working in precision, is ASI archaeology. We produce perfect knowledge about the past." He uttered the phrase "perfect knowledge" in English.

Cardinal to the practice of archaeological fieldwork is the excavation site. This is a precisely defined knowledge production location where scientific archaeology is employed and performed (Leighton 2015). Here, the act of excavating the earth to reveal the material cultural deposits buried underneath was accomplished every day. Ever since the days of the Danish archaeologist J. A. Worsaae in the middle of the nineteenth century, the excavation site was conceived as a categorical spatiality where it was possible to harvest scientific knowledge through the physical removal of the earth (Trigger 1981, 140–41; Lucas 2002, 38). It is at this location that archaeological artifacts are first discovered, recognized, produced, categorized, and fixed in a defined spatiotemporal matrix. This makes the excavation site a privileged epistemological place within the discursive apparatus of archaeology (Cherry 2011; Edgeworth 2011). Post-processual archaeological theory has argued that the significance of the knowledge produced at the excavation site is interpretative (see Hodder 1982, 1986, 1992, 1995, 1999; Shanks and Tilley 1987, 1992; Shanks and McGuire 1996). However, the theory of excavation has not been destabilized from its central role as the producer of archaeological knowledge (Buccellati 2017). The process through which a spatialized location on a landscape, identified to have potential for archaeological intervention and designated as an archaeological site, is transformed into an excavation site involves a codified mechanism of inscribing on the landscape an *ideo-epistemological* formation.

Wheelerian Grid and the Disciplining Colonial ASI

The visual impact of an ASI archaeological site under excavation is intimidating. These Harappan sites are nestled in the dry and flat riverbeds hidden behind the dusty countryside of western India. Some lie in the rugged, deserted landscape of Kutch surrounded by low-lying salt-water marshes, where large colonies of *babool* (*Acacia tortilis*) scrub forests threaten to overrun any human occupation (Dholavira). Other sites are tucked away in the sprawling agrarian countryside between small farmsteads surrounded by expansive sugarcane plantations (Bhirrana, Baror), or constricted by congested villages, jostling for space, encroaching and intruding into the territory of an ASI protected monument (Hansi). At each of these locations, when I walked from the camp into the excavation site, I encountered the distinguishing archaeological mound shaped by the archaeological intervention typical to this part of the world; earth meticulously divided into an orderly alignment of squares laid out in a geometrical grid. Long slender pathways crisscrossing each other at right angles, clutching the earth under their persuasive grip, would inspire awe. Between these slender pathways were carefully and painstakingly dug gaping square pits of varying depths, proliferating the expanse of the mound. This Cartesian network known amongst archaeologists in India as the "Wheelerian Grid" was inscribed on the landscape devoid of any foliage.[2]

Since the excavation of Mohenjo-Daro in the 1920s, mature Harappan sites excavated by the ASI have seen large-scale horizontal excavation—Kalibangan (Lal et al. 2003), Lothal (Rao 1985), Bhagwanpura (Joshi 1993), Surkotada (Joshi 1990), Dholavira (Bisht 2015), and Rakhigarhi (Nath 2015), to name a few. This extensive unearthing of sites represented the epitome of conventional archaeological intervention of the ASI. The grid network was the embodiment of both the scientific innovation and the disciplinarian regime that Mortimer Wheeler introduced to stabilize the wavering ASI between 1944 and 1948. Methodologically, the Wheelerian Grid epitomized the scientific practice through which the ASI orchestrated archaeological excavations. This technology of converting ancient sites into locations for the production of scientific knowledge gained popular currency as the "Wheeler Method," and became standard practice in the trenches of India.

Wheeler's most important contribution to this technique was dividing the archaeological site into square grids and inscribing it with Cartesian coordinates in the form of freestanding walls of earth, called balks. This divided the earlier disorderly enterprise of knowledge production into a scientific laboratory held together by balks, whereby the generated information (physical artifacts, architectural elements, soil layers, geological features, and so on) is confined, controlled, and codified. In this archaeological laboratory, material facts about the pasts are systematically documented and accurately retrieved by keeping a detailed three-dimensional record of the finds. The carved-out laboratory space in the earth provides stratigraphical indices whereby the retrieved evidence about the past is further categorized according to Cartesian coordinates (Jones 2001, 49). This technology of archaeology excavation is known as the Wheeler–Kenyon method (Lucas 2002, 36). Wheeler first used this method between 1930 and 1935 during the excavation of the Roman site of Verulamium in Roman Britain (Wheeler and Wheeler 1936). Kathleen Kenyon, who assisted Wheeler at Verulamium, later improved this method at the Neolithic site at Jericho (1952–58) by introducing accurate observations and comprehensive recording of stratigraphy.[3]

The aura of Wheeler permeated every stratum of the ASI bureaucracy—from the students at the Institute where Wheeler's iconic persona is iterated in the classroom, to the many senior archaeologists, including the director generals (DGs) of the ASI (see Joshi 1990, iii). Wheeler and his influence foregrounded my archival research (Chadha 2002), but it was only during my fieldwork that I realized the prodigious authority that Wheeler had on the bureaucratic archaeology of the ASI. Postcolonial archaeology of the ASI in the early twenty-first century was a scrupulous mimesis of the disciplinarian regime that Wheeler brought in more than 60 years ago. The ASI used identical strategies and technological procedures to excavate, discover, and produce archaeological knowledge.[4] The ethnographic descriptions of postcolonial archaeological practices in these pages are epistemological and ontological simulacra of Wheeler's methods.

For Mortimer Wheeler, the news of his appointment as the DG of archaeology in India was a "complete bombshell," an apt metaphor used by a brigadier in the 42nd Light Anti-Aircraft Regiment of the British army. Wheeler was summoned to head "the largest and the most complex archaeological machine in the world" (Wheeler 1956, 179) which had "notoriously at that time fallen into complete disrepute" (Wheeler 1976, 10). This disrepute stemmed from the disorganized state of the ASI, perpetuated by the inability of weak successors (after the retirement of Sir John Marshall in 1926) to keep the disintegrating colonial agency cohesive. This led to the appointment of Sir Leonard Woolley to investigate the nature of the decay. Woolley, in his report of 1939, damningly notes that "the Department is altogether lacking in men trained for the work which they have to do" (Woolley 1993 [1939], 20). When this report was made public, it was not without controversy; it was suppressed and never published.[5] Officers of the ASI and members of the Indian archaeological community protested against the critique that Woolley leveled against the ASI. Most critics of Woolley's report were downright offended by his remarks and attacked him for his superficial understanding of Indian archaeology (AACD, File No. 1195/1940).

However, the recommendations of the report were resurrected in a few years, especially in the context of the "outside intervention" that Woolley had argued was necessary to transform the ailing state of the colonial ASI:

> In the matter of excavation, I have, on most sites which I have visited, found that the methods employed were bad, trained observation conspicuous by its absence, and the results in consequence, incomplete and untrustworthy.... If the present efforts of the Department can be so characterized, it is manifest that the staff, before it can train others, must itself be trained; I therefore recommend the employment of a temporary Adviser on Archaeology who could deal with all the points at issue. (Woolley 1993 [1939], 21)

In February 1944, when he arrived, Wheeler knew that his tenure was short and that he had a monumental task of transforming the ASI ahead of him, so he took up the task of disciplining the ASI. Recalling one of his first incidents of disciplining his staff, Wheeler in his professional autobiographical account, *Still Digging*, candidly notes:

> Had Jemdar Bagh Singh known the Revelation of St. John he might aptly have recalled the prophetic words: "The Devil is come down amongst you having great wrath, because he knoweth that he hath but a short time." The devil had in fact a four years' contract from the Viceroy in his pocket; though, as event shaped themselves, only three of those years were to be effective, the fourth being submerged in the turbulence and bloodshed of Partition. (Wheeler 1956, 186)

Working under this time constraint amidst the political turmoil surrounding the making of two new postcolonial nations, Wheeler restructured the ASI, because "in that theoretical four years, nearly everything had to be done;" it was not "merely a matter of reshaping, refinancing, revitalizing" but "the dead wood of obsolete and erroneous ideas had to be uprooted" (Wheeler 1956, 186). There was a need "to stir the activities of the Indian Archaeological Survey from its unworthy condition of lethargy and archaism to a new and modernized phase of archaeological research and methodology" (Wheeler 1976, 32). Wheeler's tenure paved the way for the firm establishment of the postcolonial ASI. Wheeler transformed the colonial bureaucracy from an administrative unit confined to maintaining and conserving monuments, running a few museums, collecting epigraphs, and conducting arbitrary excavations followed by intermittent publications, into a systematic academic bureaucracy. He did this through the creation of a national museum and the founding of a scholarly journal, *Ancient India* (1946–66).[6] During his tenure, new strategies and problem-oriented fieldwork were introduced, rejuvenating Indian archaeology (Wheeler 1949).

Alluding to the near impossible task that Wheeler accomplished and to the lethargic state of the ASI bureaucracy during the last years of British rule in India, Paddayya notes that Wheeler's "term of office lasting four years (1944–48) was marked by a series of developments which would normally take forty years" (Paddayya 1995, 134). Chakrabarti remarks that Wheeler's "sense of archaeological planning and the excavation took Indian archaeology to a new level of scientific awareness" (Chakrabarti 1988, 188). He also argues that contrary to popular perception, it would be an incorrect assessment to "imagine" that "Mortimer Wheeler gave a 'kiss of life' to Indian archaeology" because "Indian archaeology was not in its death-throes when he arrived in 1944 to stay on as the Director General" (Chakrabarti 1988, 188).[7]

The aura of Wheeler in the ASI was not principally consolidated and shaped by these historical appraisals but, instead, through oral tradition. Stories, anecdotes, and tales passed from teachers to students like a resplendent folklore. The oral narratives originated from archaeologists who had attended his famous training school in field archaeology in Taxila in 1944. Some of them such as Amalananda Ghosh, B. K. Thapar, B. B. Lal, S. R. Rao, and K. R. Srinivasan occupied senior positions in the postcolonial ASI.[8] During my fieldwork, several archaeologists asserted that they considered themselves to be direct descendants of Wheeler's intellectual heritage. At Baror, an assistant superintending archaeologist (ASA) who had joined the ASI more than 25 years ago stated: "We learnt archaeology the hard way, working day and night, excavating at sites like Kalibangan under Dr B. B. Lal; he learnt the same way under Wheeler, and that is what we are teaching our students here. We are continuing the age-old tradition of teacher-disciple tradition [*guru-shishya parampara*]." Archaeologists and the ASI technical staff were not ambivalent about the importance of Wheeler. A senior photographer at Baror, who was trained in the "art of archaeological photography" by his predecessor, who had learnt to take "archaeological photographs" during "Sir Wheeler's time," reverently told me: "What we do in the ASI is a ditto copy of what Sir Wheeler started. He was the finest archaeologist India ever saw. We merely follow his footstep. He was our *guru*." All my informants considered Wheeler's tenure as the most important period in the history of twentieth-century ASI. "Sir Wheeler transformed the face of ASI and the way archaeological excavation was conducted. He made it scientific and modern," asserted the senior photographer.

When Wheeler came to India, the presiding figurehead of the ASI was Sir John Marshall, who had headed the ASI for a staggering 26 years starting in 1902. Before he arrived, Wheeler knew of both the role that Marshall had played in the making of the ASI as well as his aura: "Certain it is that, when I reached India in 1944, Marshall was still a remote king-god of whom his worshippers had no intelligent comprehension, and sought none" (Wheeler 1956, 182). It was ironic to discover during my fieldwork, 60 years after Wheeler, that he now had a similar demi-god like status in the ASI. The foremost reason for this idolization was the overpowering impression on students he had in the 1944 paradigmatic archaeology field school. Organized by Wheeler, the "Taxila School of Archaeology" was one of the most influential field-training schools in the history of South Asian archaeology and the first such in the world (Paddayya 1995, 134). It focused on training young students in "the neglected arts of India's archaeological technology" (Wheeler 1976, 32). This event created the aura of Wheeler as not only a competent administrator but also as a great teacher of archaeological methods (Ghosh 1954, 43). At Taxila and the other sites where he worked—Arikemedu, Brahmagiri, and Harappa—Wheeler inscribed on Indian archaeology, which was largely ensconced within the paradigm of culture-history archaeology, ideas of scientific excavation, stratigraphy, and efficacious technical methods.

In India, Wheeler transformed a rather chaotic culture-history archaeology practice into a militaristic system influenced by the work of General Pitt Rivers (Bradley 1983; Bowden 1991), who at the end of the nineteenth century had advocated for excavating ancient sites scientifically (Wheeler 1954, 13; Lucas 2002, 36). To create a chain of command that would produce knowledge, Wheeler argued for a "basic factor of labor-control or in the quaint terminology of the army, 'Man-management,'" which was "very much the same thing" (Wheeler 1954, 173). In a prosaic style, he explicitly explained his ideological position:

> In one vital respect at least there is an analogy between archaeological and military field-work that is recurrent and illuminating. The analogy rests—strangely enough as between the dead and the deadly—in the under-lying *humanity* of both the disciplines. The soldier, for his part, is fighting not against a block of colored squares on a war-map; he is fighting against a fellow being, with different but discoverable idiosyncrasies, which must be understood and allowed for in every reaction and manoeuvre. Equally ... the archaeological excavator is not digging up *things*, he is digging up *people*. (Wheeler 1954, 16–17, emphasis in original)

This analogy between archaeology and militaristic exercise is a recurring theme in Wheeler's theory of practice. Wheeler used the military trope for transforming an incipient disciplinary practice, still regarded as a pseudo-scientific antiquarian's delight, into an empirical and scientific laboratory. Wheeler collapsed the ideas of scientific thought and military strategy into a single discursive ideology (Wheeler 1954, 18). For Wheeler, the archaeological project suffered from lethargy. It was a malaise that is cured by making it a professional mechanism of knowledge production, akin to the scientific enterprise. This is evident in his concern with "methodical digging for systematic information, not with the upturning of earth in a hunt for the bones of saints and giants or the armoury of heroes, or just plainly for treasure" (Wheeler 1954, 20). The genealogy of these concepts can be traced to Pitt Rivers, who was called the "first scientific British archaeologist" (Clark 1934, 414). Wheeler shaped and developed these ideas soon after World War I, when he commenced work on the Roman and Iron Age sites in Essex and Wales (Lucas 2002, 37). The need to gather meticulous data propelled him because the "knowledge of human achievement outside the historical field was dependent upon fresh and methodological discovery, and that fresh discovery in great measure meant fresh digging" (Wheeler 1956, 66). At the excavation of the prehistoric fortification of Maiden Castle in Dorset between 1934 and 1937, Wheeler, for the first time, used the technique of area excavation in regularized trenches with balks, along with the practice of meticulous mapping and recording of all significant features (Lucas 2002, 39). He used stratigraphy, a concept introduced into the archaeological domain from geology, in this excavation (Wheeler 1943). Pitt Rivers introduced this technique as an important means of retrieving accurate and comprehensive scientific knowledge from an excavation, to establish internal chronology and the relative sequence of ancient cultures (Trigger 1989, 199; Lucas 2002, 34). These principles were reflected in Wheeler's insistence on accurate recording of the archaeological sequences, the finds, and the structures in accordance with their stratigraphical indices, which transformed the previously chaotic knowledge production process into a scientific operation.

In the first among a series of Staff Memoranda with Technical Sections that Wheeler wrote as the DG of the ASI, he described the principles of his method in the following way: "The excavation of a site, like the ordering of the battle, must be thought and co-ordinated by a single present and directing mind. Otherwise chaos, waste, inefficiency is inevitable" (AACD, File No. 33/24/44; 1944). The genesis of the Technical Sections lay in the Staff Memoranda, meant for internal circulation, that Wheeler dispatched throughout the early part of his directorship between 1944 and 1945. These were his first attempts at disciplining the ASI. It is through these succinctly titled memos, "Conservations," "Research," "Museums," "Directives for Young Officers," and others, that he articulated his goal of putting to order a colonial bureaucracy in disarray by summoning virtues of science and discipline: "Once more you are a scientist, one with the initiative to acquire and enlarge knowledge. You are no longer a school-boy waiting to be taught. You are an officer, and the weight of your command will be proportionate to the effective weight of your knowledge and experience. Learn!" (AACD, File No. 33/24/44; 1944).

For Wheeler, science was imagined like a war:

> It has nothing to do with office hours. There is no such thing as "science from 10.30 am to 5.30 pm." Those are hours between which the administrating scientist has least time for his science. The real work begins when his routine work ceases. And archaeology is a branch of science. (AACD, File No. 33/24/44; 1944)

Although Wheeler pursued the project of making archaeology scientific, he accepts its inherent limitations: "As scientists, our life is founded on selection and decision. We like to think that selection and decision are objective and impersonal. What fools we are!" (Wheeler 1950, 122). His schemes were attempts to make excavation a rigorous process whereby the knowledge that could be gained from the site is not lost forever through the permanently destructive procedure of excavation. He believed that "archaeology is primarily a fact-finding discipline" and that an archaeologist is "primarily a fact-finder, but his facts are the material records of human achievement; he is also, by that token, a humanist, and his secondary task is that of revivifying or humanizing his materials with a controlled imagination that partakes of the qualities of art and philosophy" (Wheeler 1954, 228–29). It is this correspondence between the archaeologist as the scientific technician who gathered uncontaminated data and the archaeologist as the humanist interpreter that informs Wheeler's archaeology. His main aim was to grasp Man: "A subject which, being Men ourselves, we can never fully objectify. Our science is of all sciences the most subjective and selective" (Wheeler 1950, 122). It is this epistemic and philosophical concurrence that marks Wheeler's interventions. On the one hand, his work concentrates on disciplining the chaotic practice of excavation and, on the other, it inscribes an idea of the human past on the site and its people (Wheeler 1954, 80). It is in colonial India that both of these projects reached their logical conclusion. It was in this location that Wheeler controlled and trained the natives, while continuing the Indological project of inscribing on the colonial masses a past unknown to them (see, for example, Wheeler 1950, 1953, 1959, 1968, 1976).

The Rationality of Large-Scale Horizontal Excavation

The Wheelerian Grid, according to ASI archaeologists, was the most efficient way to dig a "large-scale" archaeological site, also called the open-area excavation—a method in which the full horizontal extent of a site is cleared and large areas are opened up. In the ASI, "large-scale" meant big excavation, both in terms of the financial and governmental resources that the ASI had at its disposal and the physical magnitude of the excavation.[9] "We are the ASI. We are a central governmental organization and we specialize in excavating large sites.

The University departments and the state departments just don't have enough money or the resources to conduct excavation how ASI does" (*Hum ASI hai. Hum central government organization hai aur hum bade excavations karte hai. Yehi hamari specialty hai*). The SA of the Delhi Ex. Br., who was in charge of the Hansi excavation, rather ebulliently justified the massive excavation of the multicultural mound. The official definition of large-scale excavation was: "[T]hose that carried out as problem-oriented excavation, involving excavation in a large area of a site which brought to light a huge quantity of pottery, antiquity, and other archaeological remains, etc., were put in the category of large-scale excavations" (AACD, File No. 1/6/2004-EE). A recurrent refrain I heard was: "If we don't do, who will? This is our duty" (*Agar hum nahi karenge toh kaun karega. Yeh hamaari duty hai*). This sense of obligatory encumbrance emerged from the ASI's self-perception that it was the only archaeological institution in India capable of undertaking large-scale excavation. "It's in our blood" (*Hamare khoon main hai*), an AA candidly asserted as we were sitting on a charpoy under the cool shade of a large banyan tree in the scorching heat at the site of Baror. In 1957, elucidating the objectives of a horizontal excavation, the then DG of the ASI writes in *Ancient India*:

> [T]o lay bare the relics of the newly-discovered cultures comprehensively, so that they can be viewed as the components of a coherent unit, as the trees constituting the wood, with is at present not seen. Without horizontal excavation, the early man will never reveal himself to us in his fullness, and our knowledge of the culture to which he belonged will remain circumscribed by the limitation imposed by the dominion of the trench. (Ghosh 1957, 3)

Ever since the days of Sir John Marshall (early 1900s), who had received his training at the large archaeological sites of the classical world in the Mediterranean, ASI excavations were monumental. It involved massive removal of earth to uncover the ruins of colossal urban settlements (Chakrabarti 1988, 122; Lahiri 2005, 46). Under Marshall, the ASI, following trends in early twentieth-century archaeology, was obsessed with excavating civilizational sites (Childe 1925, 1942). When the sites of Mohenjo-Daro and Harappa were discovered in the 1920s, these archaeological interventions caused large-scale excavations. This was logical for Marshall, who had excavated Taxila for more than a decade before the discovery of the Indus civilization (Marshall 1951). The excavation at Mohenjo-Daro under his leadership, with K. N. Dikshit, Madho Sarup Vats, and Harold Hargreaves, followed by Ernst Mackay (1927–31)[10] and Vats's (1926–31)[11] excavations at Harappa, were all large-scale endeavors, involving multi-year engagement, uncovering huge tracts of earth.[12] When Wheeler arrived, his archaeological intervention was no different—Taxila, Harappa (Wheeler 1947b), Brahmagiri (Wheeler 1947a), and Arikamedu (Wheeler, Ghosh, and Deva 1946) were all large-scale operations. This was followed by mimetic excavations by his students in postcolonial India—Maski in 1953–54 (Thapar 1957) and Prakash in 1954–55 (Thapar 1967) by B. K. Thapar; Hastinapur in 1950–52 (Lal 1954), Kalibangan from 1960 to 1962 (Lal et al. 2003), Sringaverpur from 1969 to 1977 (Lal 1993), and Purana Qila, Delhi, from 1954 to 1955 and from 1969 to 1973 by B. B. Lal. Large-scale excavations were the hallmark of ASI bureaucratic archaeology and contrasted with excavations conducted by Indian university departments, which were in most cases tiny and often characterized by "digging a few holes in the earth," as a young archaeologist from Deccan College noted. Only a couple of departments such as the Deccan College or the department at M.S. University in Vadodara conducted large-scale "ASI style" excavations, but could never match the scale of ASI excavations.

Some university-based archaeologists I spoke to complained that it was impossible for them to excavate larger and prestigious sites (such as Dholavira, for instance) because the Central Advisory Board of Archaeology (CABA) would not give them the license to excavate.[13] A senior university archaeologist explained:

> The ASI is a central government organization. They have a lot of power and money. Even if a University department had the organizational caliber to excavate large sites, it is almost impossible to get the license to excavate prestigious and large Harappan sites like Kalibangan, Dholavira, Rakhigarhi. You think we did not ask for permission to excavate there? A university department can only dig small Harappan villages but only the ASI has the historical right to dig Harappan cities!

The sarcasm reflected reality. University-led excavations over the past 50 years have only dug Harappan villages such as Padri, Rodji, Kuntasi, Bagasara, and Nageshwar, to name a few. In 2012, Deccan College archaeologist Vasant Shinde got a CABA license to undertake excavation at Rakhigarhi, but just to excavate a small section of the largest Harappan site in India—the necropolis (Shinde et al. 2012; Shinde et al. 2018; Woo et al. 2018).

Theoretically and methodologically, horizontal excavation contrasted with vertical excavation. Horizontal excavation focused on exposing the cultural layers of a large area of the landscape to study the cultural deposit of each period, whereas vertical excavation was a small surgical probe into the depth of the earth to comprehend the cultural history of a site (Barker 2005). The key conceptual difference between a vertical and a horizontal excavation was that the former had a temporal focus whereas the latter had a spatial emphasis (Simonetti 2013). Vertical excavation involved a 10-meter-by-10-meter trench that is laid at the topmost section of the mound and excavated until it reached the natural surface. The goal of vertical excavation was to uncover the chronological history of the site by correlating the artifacts discovered with the stratigraphical layers of the trench (Harris 1989). In contrast, horizontal excavation uncovered the complete area to expose the spatial spread of the site.

In an ASI excavation, I observed that both techniques of horizontal and vertical excavation are followed. Vertical excavation is undertaken at the beginning of the excavation to decipher the chronological history of the site while horizontal excavation is employed to expose the most monumental cultural layer of the site. This was as Wheeler had emphasized: "*vertical digging first, horizontal digging afterwards*, [that] must be the rule" (Wheeler 1954, 85, italics in the original). At Dholavira, the cultural layer most exposed at the site was the mature Harappan layer, which comprised monumental architectural remains like the fortification wall and houses and streets. At Bhirrana and Baror, it was the early and mature Harappan layers comprising mud-brick architecture that were exposed. Although the principal theoretical impetus of the excavations in these sites was the horizontal and spatial exposure of the Harappan layer, vertical excavation was used in various trenches.

Horizontal excavation comprised "opening-up" a few thousand square meters of earth, exposing multiple trenches spread over the landscape of the site. Here, the Wheelerian Grid with its balks was used as a means of controlling and regulating the mammoth data output. By the early part of the twentieth century, archaeologists such as Flinders Petrie (1904) and Leonard Woolley (1930) had perfected the technique of horizontal excavations at the monumental sites of Abydos and Amarna in Egypt and Ur in Mesopotamia. At the ASI, early excavations conducted under John Marshall's tenure at the large sites of Charsada, Taxila, and Mohenjo-Daro are good examples of horizontal excavation. The credit goes to Wheeler for introducing the gridded network of balks with stratigraphical matrices for efficacious and meticulous spatial and temporal recording. The ASI's practice of horizontal excavation in postcolonial India was a faithful continuity of the methodological innovations introduced by Marshall and Wheeler. It incorporated the methodological strategies of large-scale excavation of a village, town, or a fortification, introduced by Marshall and integrated into the scientific systematization and organization of the Wheelerian Grid.

ASI archaeologists considered horizontal excavation to be the standard technique of digging archaeological sites. "It is the most appropriate way [*sab se sahi tareeka*] of digging a large site in India—Harappan, Chalcolithic, Early Historic or Medieval," remarked an ASA. "Wheeler advocated the usage of horizontal excavation to dig large sites. The ASI is best at doing this.

Any large-scale excavation has to be dug in a horizontal manner if you want to know the complete cultural deposit of the site," the ASA continued to explicate. The ASI's predisposition to extensive uncovering through horizontal excavation turned the epistemological framework of the Wheelerian Grid into an efficacious bureaucratic tool for ensuring control and discipline of archaeological artifacts, material culture, and the knowledge produced at the excavation site, as well as managerial power over the people who worked at such a large site. By fragmenting the archaeological site into convenient units, Wheeler's method brought order into a chaotic system of knowledge production (Wheeler 1954, 82). Within the paradigmatic framework of ASI archaeology, horizontal excavation was the synthesis of the historical articulation of open-area excavation, the bureaucratic efficacy of the Wheelerian Grid, and the normative necessity of large-scale excavation. When Wheeler introduced his techniques in Indian archaeology, he characterized the Indian excavation practices followed before his time as chaotic, unsystematic, and reflecting "concentrated confusion" (Wheeler 1954, 80). By the time I was doing my ethnography, horizontal excavation represented the exemplary form of archaeological intervention for the ASI, practiced for over half a century, with no technological or technical evolution.[14]

The epistemological logic of a horizontal excavation was designed to produce an archaeological spatiality by removing vast amount of earth to expose and make explicit cultural deposits comprising of monumental architecture and features. Horizontal excavation was not directed toward the cultural sequence within a site but was concerned with the material culture of the "whole" archaeological area (Wheeler 1947c, 143). The direction of the trenches and the number of quadrants to be dug were determined by the presence and spread of structural features. For example, at Baror, more than 10 quadrants in a parallel sequence were opened in the second season of excavation to trace what the archaeologists assumed to be a mud-brick fortification of the Harappan village (*IAR 2004–05* 2014, 112). At Dholavira, the search for the monumental reservoirs around the citadel fortification had propelled much of the archaeological excavation in the 1990s (*IAR 1991–92* 1996, Plates XXI, XXII; *IAR 1997–98* 2003, Plates 13–14). An AA who had been a student during those years recounted:

> When Bisht sir found the rock-cut reservoirs south-east of the citadel, more than twenty trenches were opened. Around six to seven hundred laborers worked twenty-four hours a day in three shifts. Three diesel generators were used to light up the whole area at night while the excavation was being conducted. We were so excited that no one slept or ate for weeks. And Bisht sir was always in the trenches. We even got him his food in his trench.[15]

Horizontal excavation in the ASI sites was a "structural feature"–driven excavation, where the process of exposure of the cultural deposits depended on the form and nature of the structures found. The emphasis was on uncovering the architectural features of the site—a formidable technique for crafting monumental archaeological evidence. Horizontal excavation is executed with the aim of not merely *accumulating evidence* about an archaeological event but rather that of *manufacturing evidence* (Knorr-Cetina 1985) about an archaeological event. This manufactured evidence about material culture is documented by using an array of representational techniques—from traditional photography and drawings to digital mapping and now drone videography. Dholavira and Surkotada (Joshi 1990, Plate V) are iconic examples of this archaeological spatiality as manufactured evidence—shaped and produced by the archaeological intervention of the ASI's horizontal excavation. The exposed sites today comprise monumental architectural edifices, fortification walls, house foundations, streets, and drainage systems that are now preserved as permanent evidence of Harappan culture.

This excavation technique was thus not just an epistemological practice but also a process of creating archaeological spatiality as heritage. The most prominent aim of horizontal excavation in the ASI was "complete acquisition" (*poori pakad*) of knowledge about the most prominent cultural layer of a site and its final display as a heritage structure. Sometimes, a site is displayed for only a short period, during which a permanent record of the heritage is created and preserved via representational systems. The prime focus of the Saraswati Heritage Project (SHP) was always the Harappan cultural deposit, but most of these sites had multilayered cultural deposits. Oftentimes, the upper layers comprised early historic structures and cultural deposits, which were not the research objective of the project. At each site, the research aim of the excavation was to excavate and horizontally expose only the Harappan layers, unless the structures of the upper layers were monumental—for example, the Buddhist Stupa at the top of the mound in Mohenjo-Daro (now in Pakistan) is left intact, or in Dholavira Chalcolithic circular house structures are exposed and left intact on top of the monumental citadel. At Dholavira, I observed that the horizontal excavation was motivated by the need to create a heritage site, which was also an explicit intention of the SHP (see, for instance, AACD, File No. 1/4/2003-SP). Monumentality and antiquity governed the micro-process of excavation and its logic. The ASI had developed the pathology for excavating (Tilley 1989, 275) large monuments and objects with antiquarian value; epistemological concern was secondary.

Cartographic Ontology of the Wheelerian Grid

"How can excavation be possible without a survey of the site? You cannot dig wherever you like. It has to be done properly [*sahi tarike se karna padega*]," noted a surveyor of the Patna Ex. Br. at Baror. He was lecturing a group of students from the Institute about survey techniques and the importance of survey in archaeological excavation. We were all standing on the topmost part of the Harappan mound, surrounding an optical theodolite, as the surveyor was explaining the importance of "survey work." The "work" (*kaam*) of the surveying team, he explained to the students, "begins much before the excavation starts or even before the camp is set up." The task of the surveyor, he described, consisted of "first locating the topmost part of the mound, noting its elevation; positioning the exact coordinates of the extent of the site; mapping the site; creating a topographic map; gridding it; and then doing the layout of the trenches. This is survey-work." As he was explaining, one student after another was peering through the telescope of the optical theodolite. Each student was trying to note the marking on the 3-meter-tall wooden collapsible scale held by a laborer about 70 meters away, at the edge of an excavated trench. The ASI survey team at the site consisted of a surveyor, a draughtsman, and often two to three laborers who would help in moving the scale, using the measuring tape, hammering the trench peg, tying strings, or simply carrying the theodolite or the tripod.

Wheeler explicates the task of the surveyor and the surveying team: "[P]reparation of the site-plan, general contoured and often of considerable extent" (Wheeler 1954, 167). This was the process through which a known, unexcavated site was scientifically rationalized and prepared for excavation: "Through survey work we make the site ready for excavation" (*Survey kar ke ham site ko excavation ke liye* ready *karthe hai*), explained the draughtsman to me. The operative word here is the English word "ready," which referred to the task of situating in the landscape an area deemed fit for archaeological excavation (usually the mound). Before the landscape was inscribed with the "Wheelerian Grid," it was outlined on the "survey-map" of the landscape. The survey-map was the cartographical representation of the archaeological site. The surveyor at Bhirrana elaborated:

> Once the survey map was ready, with its coordinates, elevation, datum points, and extent set, our work in the field was completed. Then we went back to our office desk in the Branch office. We marked the location of the base line and then divided the map into a 10-meter-by-10-meter grid and numbered the trenches according to the quadrant system.

The end product of a pre-excavation survey-work was the site survey-map—the cartographical representation of the archaeological site that rendered the field portable. The survey was a scientific practice of domesticating the wild unknowable landscape into a legible representable universe. It involved encapsulating the archaeological site from a mass of landscape with scattered material culture remains into a representational system, which had a fixed matrix and absolute coordinates. It was a cartographic exercise of converting an area on a landscape into an epistemological spatiality suitable for excavation (see Bisht 2015, 88).

The archaeological site is first confined within a two-dimensional cartographical representation system and then fragmented via the Cartesian grid. The excavation cannot proceed before the landscape to be excavated is domesticated within a two-dimensional representation. As Bisht notes in his report on Dholavira: "For excavation, five rows of squares, criss-crossing the entire settlement in a tic-tac-toe fashion in order to cover principle features and divisions, etc., were chosen for excavation. Needless to say, it helped to conjure up an overall picture" (Bisht 2015, 89).[16]

Wheeler's most iconic images that had a deep impact on the disciplinarian trajectory of archaeology in India were two photographs he published in his pedagogic text, *Archaeology from the Earth* (Wheeler 1954, Plates IVA, IVB). About the first, he remarks without suppressing his condescension: "The first is an official photograph of a well-known excavation in the East, conducted by an archaeologist of considerable repute and long field-experience. Nevertheless, a mere novice might guess, and guess correctly, that chaos reigns" (Wheeler 1954, 80). This rhetorical strategy implies a civilizing mission that Wheeler imposes upon the process of excavation and its practitioners who are not conscious of the "scientific" enterprise they are taking part in. Wheeler achieves this by using a subtext of a double metaphor, which is played against the notion of an archaeologist of repute unable to conduct scientific practice, but is also an incapable colonial administrator who cannot control the natives. The imposing scientific ideal is further collapsed with the colonial project in an intricate and pedagogically instructive text—for instance, in the form of the Technical Section in the ASI journal *Ancient India* (Wheeler 1947c, 1948). In an introduction to one such Technical Section, Wheeler notes:

> This section may be prefaced by two quotations. The first is from the annual report of the archaeological department of one of the leading Indian States, and describes the recent excavation of some important megalithic tombs. It is as follows: "Where necessary, the dolmens were blasted, the circles of stones were

removed and cistvaens constructed with large flat slabs, were made available for study." As evidence of impartiality, the second quotation is taken from the annual report of the Archaeological Survey of India: "The maximum number of laborers employed at any one given time (in an excavation controlled by one supervisor) was something over thirteen hundred." These quotations are eloquent of all that an archaeological excavation should not be. (Wheeler 1948, 311)

To produce a sharp contrast, the photograph of the chaotic excavation is juxtaposed against a photograph of a scientific excavation with not only a representation of a controlled means of knowledge production but also one of controlling the knowledge producer. Under the caption: "Discipline: Excavation at Arikamedu, South India, 1945" (Wheeler 1954, Plate 4b), Wheeler comments:

> The second illustration, from the same subcontinent, unblushingly represents an excavation from my own, on the principle that the professor may properly be expected to practice. It shows a site neatly parceled out into readily controllable areas; small groups of workmen are directed by supervisors (distinguishable in the photographs by their sun-helmets); the basket carriers are working in orderly procession along clear pathways; and in the middle distance in the right, the survey-party is conveniently at work at a table shaded by an essential umbrella. (Wheeler 1954, 80)

This photograph has a canonical aura; in this gaze, the disciplinarian project of Wheeler dissolves into the colonial authority. The means of knowledge production, with its emphasis on epistemic certainty, is brought about by taming and controlling the disorderly—both the knowledge and the knowledge producer. It is not only the field that is transformed into a location of knowledge production tamed by cellular grids but also the undisciplined colonized workers. They are beyond the control of the incapable colonial master and are the graphic cause of the chaos of the earlier photograph. Their bodies need to be tempered and disciplined by the strict masters who direct the colonized bodies under the comfort of the shade. A statement appearing at the bottom of the same photograph in another text clarifies the relations among the location of the knowledge production, the knowledge producer, and the knowledge that is produced:

> The erratic cutting of our French predecessors on the scene was methodically superseded and extended by school-trained grids and graduated stratigraphy in the busy hands of students already trained to anticipate just this sort of situation— the emergence of familiar western products in meaningful association with the still-unknown and variable output of the east. (Wheeler 1976, 44)

This photograph transforms into a document that merges scientific, colonial, and military discourses in one instance, and exposes the "epistemic murk" (Taussig 1987, 1) of bureaucratic archaeology. In the attempts to increase the efficacy of the data-gathering process through epistemic control is inherent the colonial project of civilizing the native.

For Wheeler, the grid produced squares that were both the epistemological and ontological units of archaeological excavation (Wheeler 1954, 83). His strategy transformed the landscape into multiple scientific laboratories. Small cubicles driven into the earth, enclosed by the four walls of the balks, ontologically disciplined the epistemology of the excavation. This ordered and organized three-dimensional spatial mimesis of the two-dimensional cartographic constitution of the survey-map simulated the disciplinarian ontology necessary for epistemological action. This reorganization of the landscape into a disciplined scientific space was the most appealing aspect of the Wheeler Method for archaeologists throughout the world who adopted it. As Wheeler emphasizes:

> Be it repeated that a great merit of the "square" method is that it localizes both control and record. The supervisor's responsibilities are clearly defined, and the area covered by his field notebook is precise. The basis of his record is the careful identification, embodied in an accurate measured drawing of the stratigraphy of each of the four sides of his square and of such supplementary sections as may be required. (Wheeler 1954, 86)

Many ASI excavation reports since independence had multiple photographs of archaeological sites divided into these Cartesian grids. These grids had become synonymous with archaeological excavation as a scientific enterprise in India. Its symbolic valence is located not just in the pragmatic methodological possibilities offered but also in its affective power to transform the rugged, dusty, and wild landscape into a scientific and orderly one. The visual impact of a landscape divided into clear-cut squares separated by slender balks gave an aura of scientific legitimacy, stressed by the obvious manifestation of symmetry and balance (see, for example, the book cover of *IAR: 1954–55* 1954; *IAR: 1973–74* 1979; *IAR 1988–89* 1993; *IAR 1991–92* 1996; *IAR 1993–94* 2000; *IAR 2004–05* 2014; *IAR 2010–11* 2016). The ASI archaeologists deployed cartographic apparatus when confronted with territory with potential because it was only technology through which they could produce creditable knowledge by rationalizing it into a familiar conceptual universe. As Latour notes about soil scientists in his succinct ethnography of field scientists working in the Brazalian Savanna: "Yes, scientists master the world, but only if the world comes to them in the form of two-dimensional, superposable, combinable inscription" (Latour 1999, 29).

Thus, the act of surveying the landscape was a practice of deploying multiple epistemologies to reconstruct the physical spatiality into a visualized representation through which the world could be engaged with one's own conceptual vocabulary. This transformation of territoriality as an epistemic materiality has its genealogy in colonialism and it has been an operative mechanism thorough which postcolonial states transform landscape into commodified spatiality (see Duncan 1990; Mitchell 1991, 2002; Sluyter 1999, 2001, 2002).

In this cartographical universe, the 10-meter-by-10-meter square became the ontological embodiment of the gridded universe of the laboratory where scientific knowledge is produced through the application of a regulatory universe. The geometric affect of the Cartesian grid exemplified the epistemological bulwark of scientific rationality because the grid was not just a cartographic apparatus to consolidate an unknown landscape, but also an ontological framework for ordering and disciplining an undomesticated spatiality by rationalizing it within a mathematical discourse (see Motz and Weaver 1993; Akkerman 1998). Its imposition produced an abstract representational space, with a powerful ontological bearing. The ontological persuasion of the Cartesian grid was obvious in the street network of modern cites, arrangement of chairs and desks in a classroom, military formations, and other forms of disciplinarian spaces. The Cartesian grid was modernity's fetish with legibility and its desire to grasp the physical world producing a rationalized subjectivity, which rendered its worldview "normal," "neutral," and "objective"—features attractive both to science and bureaucracy. Scholars have argued that this normalizing gaze of the Cartesian grid was located in its usage as a disciplinary formation and an organizational schematization for capitalist commodification of the physical landscape (see Harvey 1990; Scott 1998; Pickles 2004). Colonial bureaucrats such as Wheeler were drawn toward the Cartesian grid not only because it provided control and a coherent epistemic universe but also because the Cartesian grid offered a bureaucratic rationality conducive to the spatial ordering of the everyday life of the subjects at the excavation site. Analogous to Foucault's critique of the technology of surveillance, personified by the panopticon and its encompassing gaze (Foucault 1977), the Cartesian grid has been labeled a repressive tool of social control (de Certeau 1984) (Figure 5.1).

Paradoxically, the earliest example of gridded spatiality was discovered in the Indus civilization (Guha 2011, 173). The gridded cityscape of Mohenjo-Daro and Harappa where the streets intersected at right angles and divided the towns into residential blocks have been suggested by historians as the earliest example of grid networks (Stanislawski 1946, 108–10). This irony of the double

Figure 5.1 Two 10 × 10 meter trenches divided into four quadrants each with
Wheelerian balks at Dholavira, adjacent to the Eastern Reservoir, 2004

Source: Photograph by the author.

inscription was not lost on me when, during my first site visit at Dholavira,
I was taken to the Lower Town and showed right-angled street intersections
discovered through the extractive deployment of the Wheelerian Grid in the
1990s (Bisht 2015, 132–35). The employment of one gridded conceptual
apparatus to unearth another gridded spatiality was not without ideological roots
(*IAR 1991–92* 1996, Plate XXII). Its operational mechanism was at the heart of
modernity's fetish with the acquisition of objective data and the production of
totalitarian knowledge. The application of Cartesian grids on natural wilderness
was not Wheeler's innovation. It emerged from a long history of privileging
geometrical uniformity as the preferred way for modernity to engage with the
physicality of a landscape. This imposition of the grid was an analytical export
from the cartographic framework of Cartesian perspectivalism into the spatiality
of the physical landscape.[17] It was also an ideological apparatus to make the
unknowable territory commensurable within the configurations of modernity's
own epistemological universe. It personified modernity's impetus for legibility,
organization, and rationality viewed by scholars of space and spatiality as the
"hallmark of modernity" (Krauss 1985, 10–12; Dimendberg 1998, 2). It was
modernity's instrumental apparatus to make unknown territory commensurable
within its own universe of comprehensible configurations.[18]

The "geo-power" of the Cartesian grid emerges from its employment in ordering space and in the production of geographic knowledge, both of which were central to the formation of modern governmentality.[19] The *ideological affect* of the Wheeler Method was in the Cartesian perspectivalism that encompassed a territory and transformed it into an epistemic landscape (Jay 1994). It applied the Cartesian grid from the confines of cartographical representation (the signifier) and imposed it on territoriality (the signified) for epistemic production. Imposing a Cartesian grid on a map was a conceptual survey tool to plot the site, and it was neatly transferred from the map into the landscape. The disciplinarian apparatus used to map the landscape ended up being inscribed on the landscape itself. The scientific practice of inscribing a Cartesian spatial regime provided Wheeler with an epistemological foundation on which the excavation site was rendered legible and decipherable. The ideological intentionality of the Wheeler method lay not only in its transformation of the site into a scientific zone that facilitated the performance of archaeology as a scientific practice, but also in its commanding a visual presence as a spatial formation with scientific resonance. The deployment of the Wheelerian Grid allowed the archaeological landscape to be reorganized as a materialized conceptual schematic framework through which the archaeologist-as-bureaucrat domesticated territoriality and organized it as epistemic materiality.

The popularity of the Wheelerian Grid in the ASI rested on its *bureaucratic efficacy* to administer and regulate the ontological universe of the subjects who inhabited the grid and not merely the epistemological output of the archaeological landscape it encompassed. ASI archaeologists would often describe the Wheelerian Grid in terms of its managerial efficiency and the supervisory capabilities it was endowed with (Adams and Carole 1995). It was a pragmatic bureaucratic tool that facilitated them to command subjects at the excavation site. All personnel involved at the site, from the director of the site to the laborer, were consciously and involuntarily ontologically ordered by the physical bounds of the Wheelerian balks. The grid was highly suitable for the postcolonial bureaucracy because it was a tool that contributed to the efficacious administration of wild landscapes (*jungli*) and also the native (*dehati*) laborer employed at the excavation site, referred to as the derogatory "coolie" by colonial ASI officers.[20] This rationality of regulation formed the central principle of the bureaucratic efficacy of the grid balks. Colonial scholar-bureaucrats like Wheeler were drawn toward the Cartesian grid not only because it provided control and a coherent epistemic universe but also because the Cartesian network provided an ontological control over the everyday life of the people producing the knowledge.

Pivotal to Wheeler's method was not just the practice of dividing the earth into a gridded spatiality, but also naming the grids. This was necessary to control the chaos of the excavation process, in terms of the knowledge produced. The gridded squares of the excavation site were sequentially numbered. Each artifact excavated was inscribed with the grid number in which they were discovered. For the Cartesian grid to have any scientific value, it had to be numerically coded (Wheeler 1954, 84). The logic of the Cartesian grid comprised two standard principles—rectilinear geometry and sequential numbering—which were instrumental in the production of an abstract spatialized universe (Rose-Redwood 2006, 8). The grid was a product of rectilinear geometric formation based upon the principles of orthogonal order and replication. Necessary to this formation was the coordinate system. It consisted of two central baselines (axes), where each baseline was numbered sequentially, forming the grid coordinates (Motz and Weaver 1993). This geometric and mathematical impetus gave the Cartesian grid an aura of efficacious neutrality. It became associated with the nineteenth-century emergence of large-scale scientific and engineering projects and in creating a "geo-coded world" (Pickles 2004). On this were imposed the sequentially numbered spatial regimes of an inscription that had an algebraic basis. This process of first fragmenting the physical landscape within a geometric spatiality and then naming the units using a comprehensible matrix of inscription helped to restructure the landscape into a materialized epistemic spatiality. The pattern of naming was the default framework of sequential numbering used in the ASI sites, with minor variations. In the field, the trench supervisor was given the name of his quadrant when the survey team pegged the trenches. The importance of the grid numbers was often underscored by ASI archaeologists during introductory lectures to the students: "You have to be very careful as this is how we will know while writing the report, what was what and what was where [*kya kya tha, aur kya kidhar tha*]." Trench numbers were also inscribed in bold fonts on the site notebook that each site supervisor was given.

The numbering, like the gridding, enabled the Cartesian grid to function as a knowledge extraction and categorization apparatus. This was a characteristic process for the production of an abstract spatiality that reduced qualitative attributes to a numerically coded quantitative sign system. Lefebvre has argued this quantitative imagination to be one of the distinguishing features of capitalist modes of production (Lefebvre 1991). Latour contends that such an inscriptive practice is central to the scientific project and refers to many transformative practices through which an object becomes an epistemological entity (Latour 1987). In his ethnography of geologists in the Brazilian Savannah forest, he shows that such an inscriptive universe of naming is essential for recognition and subsequent categorization of the knowledge produced. He asserts that if such an inscriptive universe is destabilized in any manner, then the scientific project loses its capacity to produce knowledge (Latour 1999).

Notes

1. There are only five metropolitan cities of the Harappan civilization—Mohenjo-Daro, Harappa, Rakhigarhi, Ganweriwala, and Dholavira. The rest of the sites are considered "satellite" or "rural" settlements (Parikh and Petrie 2019).

2. Although I have been associated with Indian archaeology since 1994, I first saw huge archaeological sites divided into Wheelerian Grids only during my fieldwork (2004–06) for this ethnographic research. My archaeological training in India had been at the Deccan College, which was critical of the large-scale horizontal excavation as practiced by the ASI. Methodologically, archaeologists at the Deccan College and other university departments in India loathed the Wheelerian Grid and accused the ASI archaeologists of being "slavish to Wheeler's method of archaeological excavation"—a remark I vividly remember being uttered by a professor of mine during a graduate course on archaeological methods.

3. It is important to note that the ASI follows the method Wheeler innovated and does not take into consideration the methodological advances of Mary Kenyon. For distinctions between the two methods, see Wheeler and Wheeler (1936); Kenyon (1960); Harris (1989, 11–13); and Lucas (2001, 36–43).

4. See Supreme Court (2019, 552) for an invocation of Wheeler in its judgment.

5. K. N. Dikshit, who was the DG of the ASI (1937–44) during the period when Woolley wrote the report, sought numerous academics and senior archaeologists to comment on the report and critique it. Among the most prominent archaeologists camping in India at that time was Aurel Stien, who responded to Dikshit's call and noted, in a handwritten letter on April 4, 1940, that Dikshit and his department should not be anxious about the negative impact of the report and encouraged that the report be published:

   > In conclusion I wish to assure you that I fully appreciate the apprehensions expressed in the latter part of your letter as to the effect which Sir L. Woolley's Report might have upon the future of the Archaeological Survey. But I feel encouraged to hope that the opportune publication of that exhaustive and carefully prepared review of its work presented in "Revealing India's Past" will remove any risk of serious set back in the attitude of Government towards the Survey. (AACD, File No. 1195/1940)

   For an extended commentary of the Woolley report, also see Possehl (1993b, 1); Wheeler (1956, 184); and Chakrabarti (1988, 174).

6. See AACD, File No. 25/4/1945 and File No. 25/4/1946 for the making of National Museum and File No. 21-I/3/1947 for *Ancient India*.

7. For an extended discussion on Wheeler's contribution to theory and practice of Indian archaeology from multiple perspectives, see Clark (1979); Chakrabarti (1988); Paddayya (1995); and Ray (2008). Some of these works are hagiographic and others have minor critical remarks, but they are all overwhelmed with Wheeler's charm and charisma.

8. The first three rose through the ranks to be the DG of the ASI: Amalananda Ghosh (1953–68), B. B. Lal (1968–72), and B. K. Thapar (1978–81). Also see Wheeler (1946a, Plate I).

9. The term was often contrasted with "small-scale" excavations that the university departments or the various regional state archaeological organizations carried out. In India, the semiotics of the term "large-scale" was rooted in the ideology underlying the post-independence Nehruvian paradigm of Soviet-inspired industrial development adopted by India, embodied in the form of big dams and large state-controlled industrial factories, mills, and manufacturing units. The term "small-scale" referred to village-based traditional industries advocated as the sustainable economic paradigm for India by Gandhi (Schumacher 1973).

10. Ernest J. H. Mackay was trained in Egyptology under Sir Flinders Petrie between 1907 and 1912. During World War I, Mackay was in the army, rising to the rank of captain and serving in the Middle East. Following the war, he was custodian of antiquities for the Palestine government (1919–22). He found an Indus seal at the site of Kish and began correspondence with John Marshall. Eventually, the ASI deputed him as a special officer between 1926 and 1931 (Possehl 2010). He became the field director of the excavations at Mohenjo-Daro, and played a significant role in the making of the two-volume report on the excavation. Also see Mackay (1937, 1943).

11. Madho Sarup Vats began his career at the ASI by deciphering the inscription found in Buddhist caves of Karle in Bombay (Vats 1925). He worked at Mohenjo-Daro excavations under Marshall and excavated Harappa and produced a two-volume report (Vats 1940) and finally retired as the DG of ASI (1950–54). Also see AACD, File No. 839/1925-34, on Vats's correspondence while writing his report on Harappa.

12. For instance, the Mohenjo-Daro mound covered an area of 240 acres and 1,000–1,200 laborers were employed during Marshall's excavation (Blakiston 1928, 74). See AACD, File No. 839/1925, for the correspondence between K. N. Dikshit and John Marshall on the shortage of laborers at the site.

13. Archaeological excavations in India can only be conducted after the DG of the ASI has granted a license on the recommendation of the Standing Committee

of CABA. All excavations in India are governed under Sections 21, 22, 23, and 24 of the Ancient Monuments Archaeological Sites and Remains Act, 1958 and 1959.

14. For examples, see *IAR 2003–04* (2011, 226) and *2004–05* (2014, 112) (Baror); *IAR 2003–04* (2011, 43) (Bhirrana); Bisht (2015, 126–27) (Dholavira); and Nath (2015, 125) (Rakhigarhi).

15. See *IAR 1997–98* (2003, 19–22); Bisht (2015, 164–69).

16. Bisht further describes deployment of the Wheeler Method in the Dholavira report as:

> For excavation and recording, in the first year of excavation, Wheeler's system of grid-plan was adopted.... One square kilometre of the area bearing antiquarian remains was brought within the GSQ system and divided into 100 grids—each measuring 100 × 100 m; each grid was further divided, into 100 squares of 10 × 10 m each; and each square, as usual, was subdivided into quadrants of 5 × 5 m each. Both grids and squares thus had rows of tens either way. Serial numbers denoted by Arabic numerals ran from north to south starting from the north-east. In case of quadrants, numbering was clock-wise from the north-east. To elucidate, 11 × 20 × 4 represents the 4th quadrant of 20th square of 11th grid. (Bisht 2015, 87)

17. Here I am referring to the earliest forms of mapping that begins with Ptolemy's *Cosmographica*. For over 1,400 years, it constituted the major map of the known earth and has defined the cartographic imagination of the western world. For a comprehensive history of influence of this text, see Berggren and Jones (2000). Also see Kostof (1991) for a study of cities that have adopted grids as their organizing principle.

18. Rose-Redwood shows that the grid functioned as a mechanism of disciplinary power. Employing Latour and Foucault, he argues that the Cartesian grid was instrumental in producing a "spatial regime of inscription," which in turn produced a materialized epistemic space epitomized by the Wheelerian Grid (Rose-Redwood 2006, 12).

19. Geároid Ó Tuathail defines geo-power as "the functioning of geographical knowledge not as an innocent body of knowledge and learning but as an ensemble of technologies of power concerned with the governmental production and management of territorial space" (Ó Tuathail 1996, 7).

20. See AACD, File No. 839/1925, for the correspondence between John Marshall and K. N. Dikshit in the context of procuring laborers to work at the site of Mohenjo-Daro, where they are referred to as "coolies."

6 Theory of Archaeological Excavation

For an ASI archaeologist, the trench is the micro-area "where real [*asli*] archaeology happens." The director of the Dholavira site underscored for me the ontological authenticity: "Real archaeology is done in the trench. It is in the trench you connect with the ancient civilization. The site is about the big picture. The trench is where you dirty your hands [*hum apne haath trench ki mitti mein gande karte hai*]." We were cautiously crouching on the floor of a trench in the citadel, with brushes in our hands, clearing up a little patch of earth where a small scatter of carnelian beads had been unearthed. We were on the floor of a mature Harappan room, surrounded on three sides by stone-cut bricks, parts of which were concealed in the balk that cut across the room (Figure 6.1). There was a hearth tucked in one corner of the northeastern wall of the room that had been excavated a few days ago. Half an hour earlier, I was sitting with the director in his mud and thatch hut (*boonga*) chatting about the state of cricket in India, when a young laborer, gasping for breath, barged into our room and informed us that a necklace had been discovered in the citadel. We rushed to the trench. Upon our arrival, the director pulled out the knife from the back pocket of his trousers and scraped the earth where a few "typical Harappan" carnelian beads were discovered.[1] After a few temperate jabs and mild scratching of the surface, he complimented the trench supervisor:

> Good job! I knew this was a very rich trench [English words used]. You will find more antiquity. Take the measurements properly [*sahi*] and expose this carefully [*dhyan se*]. Don't dig any more, just clean up. Prepare the subject for photography. I want an in situ picture. This is beautiful evidence [*bahut sundar evidence hai*].

Soon after, we sat on top of the balk of the half-meter-deep trench. The director had stepped back. He was observing as the trench supervisor got on her knees and carefully exposed the carnelian necklace with a tiny paintbrush and surgical instruments (part of a high school biology dissection-box). The laborers meanwhile were instructed by her to clear the floor of dirt and "prepare the subject for photography." As we were observing, the director explained, "*The trench is the whole and soul of archaeology* [English words used]. If you cannot dig the trench properly, then the whole site will get messy [*agar trench kharab tarike se khoda toh poore site ka satyanaash ho jaye ga*]." His conversation with me was often interrupted with rapid instructions to the laborers squatting with brushes and clearing the trench. He continued:

> I train students how to dig a trench correctly [*sahi dhang se*]. A good excavator is one who can control a trench systematically. Harappan sites are big. You cannot dig the site all at once. You have to do it bit-by-bit [*thoda-thoda karke*]. And that's why we need balks and trenches. However much you want to criticize Wheeler—this is the best method for Indian archaeology. It is fashionable for you, young people, to criticize Wheeler, but whatever said and done, his methods are the best for us in the ASI [*hamaare liye sabse badiya*]. Like him, I also try to teach my students to do *perfect archaeology* [English words used].

This idea of faultless practice echoed how the ASI imagined an archaeological excavation, as apparent in internal documents that circulated in their official correspondence. In one such official document, I read a rather impassioned description:

> An excavation is a scientific operation in which strata of occupation are removed one by one, just like unpacking of garments from a suitcase, and then those layers/strata along with their contents are studied in relation to structural activities, which go with a layer or a set of layers/strata. In a multicultural site, all such occupational strata are studied in a defined area of operation, pieces of information thus gleaned are put together, and then a sequential history of a given site is conjured up. (AACD, File No. 24/1/2003-EE)[2]

In the earlier chapter, I showed how the ASI archaeologists transformed a site with archaeological potential into an epistemological landscape prepared for excavation by employing the conceptual apparatus of the Wheelerian Grid as the organizing principle. In this chapter, we enter the microcosm of the archaeological trench where evidence is discovered, revealed, and exposed. Unlike the earlier chapter, in which I showed how the ASI conceived and construed an excavation site, this chapter and the next shift the focus of my ethnographic intervention from the site to the micro-practice of archaeology as science inside the trench where archaeological evidence is produced.

Ontology of the Trench

At the micro level, the daily activities of the ASI archaeologists, supervisors, students, and laborers were epistemologically and ontologically contained within the trench. The ontological role of the trench was that it ensured the jurisdiction of the excavation process while its epistemological functionality lay in facilitating discipline in the knowledge production mechanism. My informants regularly emphasized the importance of the trench within the Wheelerian Grid. During one conversation with a young assistant archaeologist (AA) who had just graduated from the ASI's Institute of Archaeology in Delhi, he proceeded to question me: "How can you excavate without trenches and balks? It is easy to say excavation should follow the logic of the structure. But look at Dholavira, you will get lost if we did not have balks." Such justification was common. All my informants believed it was not possible to dig a site without trenches locked in a grid.

The AA unequivocally retorted,

> You need trenches and balks. Or you will just dig for eternity [*sari zindagi*] and get confused [*kho jayenge*]. Trenches within balks are essential [*anivaarye hai*]. They are the most logical [*bhudimaan*] way to dig. You have to dig step-by-step [*ek-ek kar ke*]—trench-by-trench. It is impossible to just dig anywhere you find structure. Destroy the balks later on when you need to study the site or a structure as a whole. But you need the balks when you are just starting to dig. Or you will go crazy [*aap pagal ho jayenge*]. It is the only way to dig. There is no alternative [*koi alternative nahi hai*].[3]

Figure 6.1 The floor of a mature Harappan room on a Dholavira citadel where carnelian beads were found, 2004

Source: Photograph by the author.

I observed that the ASI archaeologists, who worked daily at the site, rarely engaged with the site in its entirety; they conceptualized it as an abstract entity. The ASI archaeologists reminded me that Dholavira was "by all definition [*har roop se*]" a mammoth site (*bhyankar badi site hai*) that was more than 70 hectares in area with half of that lying within the fortification of the city. "We don't know much about the site as a whole [*pooree tarah se*]. In these circumstances it is impossible to think about the site in physical terms," explained an AA. "We can only understand it bit-by-bit [*tukde-tukde kar ke*]." At the level of daily practice, archaeologists engaged only with a quadrant, a trench, or a few trenches at a time. "The whole picture is always missing," complained an AA. "Day in and day out, all you do is just focus on one quadrant or one trench. That is the discipline of research work but it can be boring at the same time." I was sitting with the AA, 7 meters below the surface, inside a deep vertical trench in Hansi that had been excavated to determine the stratigraphical history of the site. Since Hansi was a monumental mound, the site director had decided to first excavate a few vertical trial trenches before he began horizontal excavation. The AA was frustrated because for the past month and a half, they had been digging with the hope of "hitting" the Harappan layers, but even after 7 meters of digging, they had only reached the Painted Grey Ware (PGW) layers.[4] He enthusiastically explained:

> I know that only through working in a trench will you be able to create knowledge, but one feels a thirst [*pyass*] to dig up the whole site all at once [*ek hi bar main*]. But that would be unscientific—complete chaos [*ekdum gadbad*] will occur. You have to admit, Wheeler was right about the balks and trenches. It makes things so easy [*asan*].

The trench was the four-walled laboratory space, which exemplified archaeology as a scientific process. This is the zone where archaeological evidence in the form of artifacts, material culture, and ecofacts (faunal and botanical remains) are recognized, discovered, recorded, and transformed into evidence (see Thapar 1957, Plates IV, XVI). As Wheeler convincingly states about his method: "Be it repeated that a great merit of the 'square' method is that it localizes both control and record" (Wheeler 1954, 85). He referred to the trench as the "square" (Wheeler 1948, 315).

For Wheeler, the trench represented an unscientific method, an "old practice" of excavating an archaeological site. It reflected a process of excavating the earth determined by probability rather than an instrument of scientific intervention:

"… it was to a large extent 'shooting into the brown' on the off-chance of bringing down a bird" (Wheeler 1954, 81). The term "square" invokes a mathematical and exact universe that diminishes the "mess" that is symbolized in the term "trench." The use of this terminology instead of the word "trench" is rhetorical and alludes to the precision and the meticulousness of the Wheelerian Grid. Notations in the ASI site notebook used "square," bracketed in Devanagari script as *varg*—a Sanskrit word meaning section, division, or separation. The square accentuated the managerial efficacy of the Wheelerian Grid—its ability to fragment spatiality and to domesticate it within its regulatory grasp, to allow further spatial subdivision (Jones 2001, 41).

The ASI trench was a 10-meter-by-10-meter square divided into four equal quadrants, separated by a half-meter balk. A quadrant was the product of further fragmentation of the archaeological site to manage archaeological evidence (Wheeler 1954, 83). The smallest unit of such fragmentation was the 1-meter-by-1-meter control pit, which is excavated before a "dig." The control pit was an investigative micro-trench that was dug to gain information about material culture that was below the whole quadrant or the trench. Wheeler describes such a pit as "a small cutting, about two and a half feet square, split by the supervisor himself or by a trained man under his eye, to a depth of one and a half to two feet lower than the average level of the work" (Wheeler 1954, 84). Such an investigative square in a trench was necessary to "enable the supervisor, with a minimum disturbance of the strata, to anticipate the nature and the probable vertical extent of the layers which are being cleared by his main gang. It is a glimpse into the future of his stratigraphical work" (Wheeler 1954, 84). Thus, before any trench was dug, the ASI's practice was to fragment the quadrant into four 1-meter-by-1-meter control pits. The excavation would begin with digging in one of the control pits to test the nature of the deposit, followed by the rest of the quadrant (Wheeler 1948, 316). Once a quadrant had been excavated to about a meter in depth, the whole trench would be excavated. An AA at Bhirrana, where the Nagpur Excavation Branch was conducting the excavation, explained the process: "The quadrant is taken as the most important piece of the excavation. First, study each quadrant thoroughly and then divide the quadrant into four equal control-pits. Then dig one at a time. That is how you control the digging. This is the method that comes from Wheeler."

The disciplining ability of the trench emerged from its ability to control the three-dimensional excavated volume surrounded by the trench walls. Before the excavation, the trench was an inscribed space on the landscape, which was demarcated by the grid lines that encapsulated it. As the digging began, the two-dimensional inscribed space gained its third dimension—depth. Thus, the inscribed space became both physically and metaphorically deeper as the trench became a three-dimensional epistemological volume (Schiffer 1976, 42–43). The four walls of the trench served as the disciplining ontology within which archaeological volume was epistemologically fixed. It was this four-walled, three-dimensional volume embodied by the trench that bestowed archaeological excavation the aura of a scientific operation (Barker 2005, 25).

If the Wheelerian Grid transformed the archaeological landscape into an epistemic landscape, then the trench converted the excavated earth into an epistemic volume. Each trench then became its own ontological universe, with its own indicators of control and organization of the excavated material. Also, importantly, the ASI archaeologists used the trench to regulate the personnel excavating. A trench supervisor headed each unit. Under the trench supervisor were a "gang of laborers," which included a trench leader, who was always a male laborer. The key skill of the trench leader was that he was a literate subaltern worker who had the ability to recognize the artifacts or features found in the trench and inform the trench supervisor about discoveries in the trench. Under the trench leader were five or six laborers—men and women. The daily life of this group was ontologically bounded and contained by the trench. Each laborer had to take permission of the trench leader to get out of the quadrant—to drink water, to use the makeshift toilets, or to get beyond the confines of the trench for any other purpose.

The Wheelerian square commanded an ontological discipline that regulated the daily lives of the personnel involved at the site, especially the laborers—working for more than eight hours a day, where the confines of the trench curtailed their physical movements (Figure 6.2). The moment a laborer went outside the encapsulated unit of the trench, the trench leader or the trench supervisor marked them. The physical characteristics of the grid complemented the bureaucratic hierarchy of the ASI excavation team (see Wheeler 1946a, Plate IIB). Extraordinarily, the hierarchy of the postcolonial organization slipped comfortably into the disciplinary and controlling structure of the Wheelerian Grid. The grid, the square, and the organizational hierarchy at the site complimented each other's disciplinary regimes—making the excavation site both an administrative as well as an ontologically oppressive unit of knowledge production.

Figure 6.2 Examples of the ontological confinement by the Wheleerian square
of the workers at the site of Dholavira, 2004 (*top row*)
and Bhirrana, 2005 (*bottom row*)

Source: Photographs by the author.

Mortimer Wheeler and the Temporal Chronology of Indian Archaeology

The deployment of stratigraphy in Indian archaeology as an indispensable
system to determine the temporality of the cultural layers occurs with Wheeler.
Stratigraphy was known in Indian archaeology by the time Wheeler came, but he
provided an objectivistic and scientific agency to it. For Wheeler, only through
planned and disciplined excavations, with an emphasis on three-dimensional
recording, could a proper stratigraphic sequence of the site be created (Wheeler
1948, 313–15). Such a sequence functioned like a cartographic exercise with
the ability to map time. Before Wheeler, artifact typologies and classification
systems were a standardized means through which relative dating of an excavation
site and its cultural layers was done. This was a characteristic epistemological
strategy of culture-history archaeology (see Dunnell 1978; Lyman, O'Brien,
and Dunnell 1997; Lyman and O'Brien 2003). The principles of stratigraphy
were rudimentarily implemented, playing a secondary role in the dating of the
chronology of the site. It is with Wheeler that stratigraphy and its emphasis on
absolute chronology permeated into Indian archaeology:

It may seem reactionary and perverse to reaffirm, as I do, at the beginning of a book [*Archaeology from the Earth*] on archaeology in the field that mere dates are still of primary and ultimate and unrelenting importance. And by dates I mean not simply those nebulous phase and sequences, those dates-substitutes, with which archaeologists often enough try to bluff us. I mean time in hard figures. I mean Bradshaw.... It is important but not enough to know that in twentieth century A.D. an aeroplane flew from London to Singapore. It is almost equally important, in our estimate of human achievement, to know that in 1950 the aeroplane took 50 hours for the journey, and in 1999 only 50 minutes. Do not let us forget the significance of tempo; and that implies a time-table in the most literal sense, nothing less. (Wheeler 1954, 38–39)

It was not surprising that Wheeler framed his research program in India with a chronological focus. This attention led to the practice through which the stratification of layers in the excavation trench became the fecund location for mapping the temporality of the Indian past. In the absence of absolute dating techniques, Wheeler argued that proper stratigraphical recording is more robust than the relative dating obtained by studying artifact typologies and classification (Wheeler 1927, 824).

There were two principal objectives to Wheeler's intervention when he arrived in India in 1944. The first goal was to rectify the ills of the ASI as reported by Sir Leonard Woolley in his report on the state of Indian archaeology in 1939 (Possehl 1993b; Paddayya 1995). This goal, as I have discussed earlier, had a disciplinarian impetus and was aimed at restructuring the bureaucratic apparatus of the ASI. The second aim of Wheeler's intervention was epistemological and had a chronological focus, which was also lifted from Woolley's report (Boast 2002, 165). Wheeler aimed to solve the temporal dysfunction of the Indian past, both in north India where the Indo-Gangetic civilization thrived, and in the southern plateau and the coast where multiple kingdoms rose and fell (Staff Memorandum No. 1, AACD, File No. 33/24/44; 1944).

In both cases, Wheeler's epistemological intentionality was driven by a desire to uncover the chronological absence that marked the archaeology of these regions. The problems in north India, according to Wheeler, were simpler and involved the uncovering of a temporal hiatus between the Harappan civilization and the northwestern kingdoms of the sixth century BCE. The dates of both the periods were archaeologically available through comparative and analogical dating with the western world—the Indus civilization with the Mesopotamian and the later settlements with the Achaemenid Empire. For south India, the problem according to Wheeler was far greater; the settlements of south India had no comparative, temporal, or analogical relationship with the western world.

Correlating Indian sites with Greco-Roman artifacts became a programmatic agenda for Wheeler. He notes that, in order to deal with "the 'Dark Ages' of the Vedic period," the first requirement is "... to determine its delimiting phases with all possible exactitude" (Wheeler 1949, 5). In effect, the scholarly focus of all the excavations that Wheeler undertook in India (Taxila, Arikamedu, Brahmagiri, and Harappa) during his four-year tenure as the director general (DG) of the ASI was on solving this dysfunctional temporality of Indian archaeology.

Wheeler undertook two excavations in southern India—the Roman trading station in Arikamedu (Wheeler, Ghosh, and Deva 1946) and the megalithic site of Brahmagiri (Wheeler 1947a)—to provide south India with "concrete" dates.[5] The site of Arikamedu provides an extraordinary example of how colonial archaeology under Wheeler worked (Boast 2002), for the epistemological thrust of the ASI could only conceptualize an archaeological site in India within a chronological framework of a European temporality. This notion of European time in archaeology has been defined and constructed by a western fixation with classical archaeology and antiquity in oriental scholarship. In India, from the moment of the discovery of its ancient past, colonial scholars and antiquarians have attempted to fit it within the confines of European cartographical (see Edney 1997; Driver 2001; Barrow 2003) and chronological imagination (Cunningham 1871).

In its incipient stages, the ASI was also propelled by a dual necessity of cartographically mapping India and chronologically dating Indian monuments and sites through its contact with the west. Alexander Cunningham conducted archaeological surveys relying on the travel accounts of Chinese travelers of the fifth to the ninth centuries CE. He located the contemporary provenance of ancient Buddhist sites by comparing them with Chinese accounts. Cunningham then stripped *stupa*s and drilled holes to the bottom of the sites to locate Buddhist relics and caskets. As he assumed, he found Indo-Greek coins, which were valuable in dating other discoveries where the date was in doubt (Imam 1966). For Wheeler, and most of his earlier Orientalist predecessors, ancient India lacked historical imagination in the linear European temporality (Thapar 1996, 1). It was only possible to create a chronology of ancient India through its contact with the west; the Indian past was subsumed within the temporal hegemony of European chronology (Inden 1986).

It is in south India that Wheeler's fetish for fixating the chronology of the Indian past brings into clear focus the colonial subtext of his scholarly enterprise and the ideological subtext of stratigraphy as Wheeler used it. While in the north the chronology of Indian archaeology was fixed by correlating the artifacts and sites on the basis of the known contact with the west, Wheeler desired to establish a similar datum-line for south India. This was provided by the Roman trade contacts in coastal India. His search took him to the coastal site of Arikamedu in the French colony of Pondicherry. Along with a cache of Roman coins, Wheeler discovered Roman ceramics. As he shares his discovery in a note to M. V. Taylor, president of the Society of Antiquaries of London, Wheeler's excitement is noticeable:

> Today you will be faintly entertained to hear that we have found the first Arrentine pottery stamp known, so far as I am aware, from India [Pause for drums and trumpets]. The place being Arikamedu or Virapatnam, two miles south of Pondicherry. But seriously, it is slightly romantic to find out here under the coconut palms the identical stuff that you or I are used to in other climes. The beauty of it is of course, that we are getting hitherto wholly undated Indian culture in association with it, together with substantial brick buildings which are just beginning to make their appearances. (AACD, File No. 19/14/44; 1944, dated April 7, 1945)

Explaining the importance of the find to Lt. Col. Stuart Piggott, British Air Commander of Southeast Asia and New Delhi, Wheeler notes:

> The place [Arikamedu] clearly contained a Roman colony in the first half of the 1st century A.D., in connection with the semi-precious stone trade. The beauty of it, of course, is that here we shall get at last our synchronism with native Indian stuff, and a firm chronological datum line for South East India within a margin of 50 years. As I said before, don't laugh. (AACD, File No. 19/14/44; 1944 D.O. No. 517/C)

Wheeler conceptualized the significance of Arikamedu to the chronology of south India within a cryptographic metaphor. For him the site was a "bilingual" one, where "the unknown local culture is dated from the known foreign culture, just as Egyptian hieroglyphs were partly deciphered from the parallel Greek version on Rosetta stone, or Kharoshti from the bilingual inscriptions on the Indo-Bactrian coins" (Wheeler 1946b, 2). The subtext of the cryptographic metaphor is situated within the colonial ideology of taming the unknown (Chadha 2010). This process of framing and structuring the Indian archaeological past within the metanarrative of western civilization can also be seen in the nuances of an innocuous remark that Wheeler makes about the Arikamedu excavations:

> The erratic cuttings of our French predecessors on the scene were methodically superseded and extended by school-trained grids and graduated stratigraphy in the busy hands of students already trained to anticipate this sort of situation—the emergence of familiar western products in the meaningful association with the still unknown and variable output of the east. (Wheeler 1976, 44)

Wheeler does not conceptualize Arikamedu as an archaeological site in its own indigenous terms or within a southern Indian temporality, but instead historically situates it within the metanarrative of western history—Roman antiquities (Boast 2002, 166). In this hegemonic imagination, Arikamedu is relegated to the fringe of classical historiography—at best, named as a trading port beyond the frontiers of the Empire. By negating its Indian temporality, Arikamedu's past is seen as playing a peripheral role in the larger expansionist progression of the classical world. Benign trade and commerce were the framing configurations at Arikamedu, unlike in north India, which was framed within the invasion narratives of the west.[6]

In Wheeler's stratigraphic chronology, Roman Arrentine ware and amphorae from the Mediterranean were central to delineating the chronology of Arikamedu.[7] These two forms of material culture were used to provide a datum line not just to the site but also to the whole of south India: "… upon the imported Mediterranean wares the whole chronology of the site, and its special importance therefore to Indian archaeology depend" (Wheeler, Ghosh, and Deva 1946). Wheeler uses these two ceramic types as control devices—to discipline the atemporal artifacts of the native site:

> … subsequent to our date A.D. 50 there were, in the Southern Sector, several successive stages of construction and reconstruction, accompanied by some modification of the associated Indian pottery. These developments were controlled by two unifying factors: a general continuity in the main units of the plan, and the occurrence in all strata of shreds of Mediterranean amphora. (Wheeler, Ghosh, and Deva 1946, 24)

Stratigraphy under Wheeler thus transforms into an ideological practice of the past, which is framed as a scientific practice but is mediated through imposing narratives of western classical antiquity. This can be more acutely seen when, on the basis of the stratigraphical occurrence of Roman material culture (Ravitchandirane 2007), Wheeler not only demarcates Arikamedu's functional character as a peripheral trading post of the classical world but also transforms it into a colony of the Roman Empire. He claims: "The historical indications are that the consolidation and development of Roman trade with the east was a product of the unification of the western world under Augustus (23 B.C.–A.D. 14) … therefore, the Roman occupation of this site is unlikely to antedate the principate of Augustus" (Wheeler, Ghosh, and Deva 1946, 22). The usage of stratigraphy in ASI archaeology emerged from such a Wheelerian genealogy. During my conversations with ASI archaeologists in Harappan sites, the importance of stratigraphy and its usage in Arikamedu was often invoked.

For Wheeler, stratigraphy represented a practice through which the science of archaeology in the daily practice of excavation and discovery was made robust and systematic—in order to have more control and discipline over the temporal axis of archaeological practice (Lucas 2002, 39; Chapman and Wylie 2016, 77). The archaeological role of the trench in pre-Wheelerian archaeology in India was to excavate artifacts and expose structural features. With Wheelerian archaeology, the trench became both an epistemological unit that contributed to the unearthing of past material cultures and the location to situate the temporality of the site through stratigraphic correspondence. By emphasizing stratigraphy, Wheeler did not undermine the importance of the typological study of material culture but shifted the focus from establishing the chronology of the site from post-excavational typological analysis to the moment of archaeological excavation (Lucas 2012, 81). This shift had an instrumental impact on field archaeology as it weakened the role of the typological expert in the museum. It made the archaeologist in the field the dominant figure in defining the chronological sequence of the site.

The genealogy of deployment of stratigraphy as Wheeler employed begins with another military officer—General Pitt-Rivers, often called the "father of field archaeology" (Lucas 2002, 5). Prior to conducting archaeological excavations, he was involved in the study of firearms. He pursued the cartographic and the taxonomic goal of archaeological practice with military precision and is considered the father of British field archaeology. He believed that all material culture, very much like the natural world, could be ordered in a typological sequence, exhibiting evolutionary development. He emphatically emphasized that archaeology was primarily a study of objects, which could be retrieved, collected, and classified in taxonomic order: "Not for the purpose of surprising anyone, either by the beauty or value of the objects exhibited, but solely with a view to instruction" (Daniel 1981, 140). His diagram on the evolution of weaponry from Australasia is a characteristic example of imposing a taxonomic framework on material culture borrowing from Linnaeus's natural classification and merging it with Darwinian evolutionary progression. This allowed him to produce a scientific explanation for the variability and similarities that are exhibited in the material world. For Pitt-Rivers, the primitive material artifact was analogous to the natural world and can be differentiated and ordered in evolutionary terms, which has the "evidence of being derived from natural forms such as might have been employed by man before he had learnt the art of modifying them to his uses" (Pitt-Rivers cited in Lucas 2002, 71). This simplistic conflation between the natural and the artificial, which formed the basis of his museum collection at Oxford University, had substantial ramifications for the archaeological excavation that he carried out at his estate subsequently.

To Pitt-Rivers goes the credit for the transformation of archaeological excavation from a pleasant hobby pursued by gentleman scholars and retired civil servants to a professional discipline. He instilled a methodological rigor that made the excavation a mediating discourse that had the ability to produce scientific knowledge (Bowden 1991). This transformation was brought about by taking the cartographic, taxonomic, and cryptography conceptual elements to its disciplinarian and rigorous extremities, by conducting what he called "total excavation." The underlying methodological strategy was not so much in innovating original means of conducting excavation. It was an approach of ordering and regulating an unruly discipline by applying standardization techniques, with military precision and authority (Bradley 1983, 3). The rigor was initiated in order to produce objective data about the past that could stand the scrutiny of the larger scientific community and establish itself as a science in its own right. The total excavation was an efficient, exhaustive, and methodical mechanism in cartographic and taxonomic procedure to generate scientific evidence brought about by disciplinary and military precision. His practice was endowed with descriptive and statistical information to be arranged into a classificatory universe in order to provide knowledge that could be useful in deciphering the obscurities of antiquity. This knowledge was presented in an overwhelming fashion that was a graphic representation of empiricism, and objectivity, and instrumental in creating evidence as hard facts.

The text produced by Pitt-Rivers on the excavation that he conducted at Cranborne Chase, in North Dorset, had canonical implications for archaeology. The resultant format is still the customary way of producing scientific archaeological reports (Pitt-Rivers 1888). The visual rhetoric played a dominant part in the report, *Excavation of Cranborne Chase*. The visualization of data consisted of cartographical plans of the site, diagrams of archaeological features, and natural and cultural artifacts, fixed to three-dimensional measurements and plotted on graphs. The description of the site was then made suitable for statistical tabulation in the form of summaries called "Relic Tables" which gave detailed metrical information of each feature and artifact, bounded in a cartographic space, described in typological sequence, and enumerated in quantified metrics. Thus, a pseudo-legal, scientific document that attempted to explain the site and its chronology was created, and was positioned in the evolutionary universe of Pitt-Rivers.

Pitt-Rivers's impact on the archaeological method did not have a far-reaching influence on the burgeoning discipline of archaeology, but his methodological practice was picked up immediately by Flinders Petrie, who began the excavation of Egyptian sites around the turn of the nineteenth century and the early twentieth century. Petrie was unable to conduct the excavation of huge Egyptian sites with the precision of Pitt-Rivers, but he gave birth to the idea of "sequence dating," a process of statistical analysis that was used by him to order the vast quantity of Naqada ceramics from a cemetery in the Middle East.[8] Influenced by Pitt-Rivers's taxonomic project of evolutionary typology, Petrie's main focus was on creating a typology of pottery types that could help him to draw the chronology of a site, and utilize the knowledge gained through this, along with the stratigraphy of the site, to create a relative dating of the site (Petrie and Quibell 1896). This, in turn, would help him to comprehend the cultural evolution of the site. For Petrie, the archaeological excavation was primarily a typological and cartographical project that could help him generate the chronological sequence of a site and his objective was "to obtain plans and topographical information, and ... portable antiquities" (Petrie 1904, 33). Along with the cartographical and the taxonomic methods used in archaeology, he introduced metrical methods to push the cartographical project of archaeology into its modernistic phase. Here the cartographical methods of the Renaissance merged with the typological program of the Enlightenment to produce scientific knowledge about the past supported by statistical metrics to describe the evolutionary progress of human culture: "It would be, therefore no fallacy to portion out the past by the ratio of events rather than by seasons; and to measure history by the stages of thought and action of man rather than by its animate celestial motions" (Lucas 2002, 31).

The conceptual interplay between the ideas of "taxonomic classification," "cryptography," and "topographic cartography" as well as their historical unity is at the core of stratigraphy as a conceptual technique. By taxonomic classification, I allude to the mission in natural science of the sixteenth and seventeenth centuries of classifying and arranging the botanical and zoological specimens in orthodox nomenclatures. By cryptography, I allude to the philological project of studying, encoding, and deciphering ancient texts that was pursued by scholars during the Medieval and Renaissance eras (Chadha 2002). And lastly, by topographic cartography, I mean the project of making atlases, maps, and plans of the known world—representational strategies through which the known universe was objectified, suggesting an impartial, dispassionate, and unprejudiced vision—all these conceptual tools were portrayed as markers of truth that signified objectivity by their creators.

The appearance of stratigraphy as a statistical cartography occurred with Wheeler who resurrected stratigraphy as an essential tool of archaeological excavation. He rediscovered Pitts-Rivers's methods of the meticulous practice of three-dimensional recording and total excavation along with stratigraphy, and perfected the method with military zeal and made it into a canonical practice with massive scientific subtext. The use of quantification in stratigraphy had a metaphoric importance and it served as a means to regulate the method and the way the archaeological excavation could be homogenized to produce standardized data sets. Wheeler appropriated the cartographic technique of the day, of surveying landscape and topographic features, in a uniform grid to produce a standardized and quantifiable data that "once in place it permitted land claims to be registered and enforced from hundreds of miles away" (Porter 1995, 22). This he did by not just digging the earth at arbitrary archaeological locations, but by dividing the site into a standardized cartographic grid and conducting an excavation in each grid, and preparing a laboratory capable of producing objective facts about the past. Cartesian coordinates encased each excavated trench and any archaeological artifact or feature discovered was conceptually confined by a three-dimensional recording so that these discoveries could imitate scientific data and mimic its quantifiable markers. Wheeler was heavily influenced by the project of standardization because of his military training, and went on to inscribe on the discipline the importance of measurement that, as Porter argues, fundamentally introduces into the sciences a kind of objectivity that derived its empiricism by standardized metrics, and negated any kind of local knowledge. It was an attempt by Wheeler, following the trajectory of other scientific disciplines, to produce objective knowledge about the past that was separated from its local context of manufacture.

Wheeler first applied the idea of stratigraphy on the Roman sites in Wales. In 1927, in an address to the Royal Society of Arts, he proclaimed that the method pioneered in geology could be used to elaborate on the chronology of sites. For Wheeler, it was important to excavate a site in a scientific and a disciplined fashion, with the similar military rigor and precision of Pitt-Rivers. Wheeler produced magnificent photographic and stratigraphic representations in which similar symbolic mimetic devices were used to allude to the scientific nature of knowledge produced as objective data, which have statistical, scientific, and mathematic implications. It was as if the artifacts produced from a subterranean experimental process had equivalent epistemological status as those in the natural and physical sciences. The visual representation of the archaeological record produced by Wheeler and his colleagues was an extraordinarily neat diagrammatic representation of the stratigraphical section. According to one of his collaborators, it involved "the construction of technical cryptograms, and as in all ciphers these must be made according to rules carefully observed both by the transmitter and the recipient" (Piggot 1965, 165). Wheeler was interested in professionalizing archaeology, disciplining it, and endowing it with similar means of objective knowledge production capability that he witnessed in the hard sciences, but Wheeler's method were credulous adoption of the quantification methods, imitating the natural and physical sciences, and it was a symptom of disciplinarian envy.

Stratigraphy as Visualizing an Objective Past

During a post-lunch session one early afternoon in Dholavira, I was accompanying the director of the site as he went on his rounds, inspecting all the trenches. After several hours of touring trenches in the citadel and the Southern and Eastern Reservoirs, we came across a trench in the Middle Town. The quadrant was several meters deep and was "hitting" the early Harappan layers after penetrating through the habitational deposits of the mature Harappan layers. According to the co-director, this trench was crucial to the aim of the excavation, as it was dug to see "[w]hat remained below the complex structures of the mature Harappan township." Upon entering the quadrant, the director became suddenly enraged. In stern tones, he rebuked the trench supervisor:

> You have destroyed [*kharab*] my work. You cannot just mark lines on the section wherever you like. These lines have meaning [*matlab*]. You should not mark lines on the section if you do not know their significance [*mahatv*] or if you cannot explain the meaning of the lines. There should not be any useless lines on the section [*faltu lines nahi honi chahiye*].

The director was upset because the trench supervisor had scratched multiple lines with his knife to demarcate the stratigraphy on the section. He continued, "You cannot have lines on the section run like tree-roots and tributaries of a river. They have to be bold and strong [*bold aur majaboot*]. Your trench is now confusing [*tumhara trench gadbada gaya hai*]. It does not convey any meaning [*matlab*]." He then proceeded toward the trench walls and knelt down. Removing his spectacles—fitted with shortsighted lenses—he carefully peered into the surface of the section for a closer inspection. After a few seconds, reflexively, he pulled out his knife from the back-pocket of his trousers and erased the lines made on the section. He then told the trench supervisor, who was standing in one corner of the quadrant: "Ask your section cutter to redo the section. I want it to be done by the end of the day. I will come and show you how to make correct lines of the section tomorrow morning." As we came out of the quadrant to resume our site inspection, he remarked:

> You know how important [*mahatvapoorn*] stratigraphy is in archaeology. It cannot be taken lightly [*ise halke se nahin liya ja sakta hai*]. It is as important [*jaruri*] as finding antiquity. Even in trenches where we do not find any antiquity or structures, if we get good stratigraphical section—it is very useful evidence. It is important to teach these students the importance of stratigraphy. Archaeology is not just about things, it also about time.

The following morning we were back at the trench. Under the oblique light of the rising sun, the director examined the layers of the stratigraphy on the section. One by one, beginning from the uppermost surface (that is, the most recent layers chronologically), each layer was scanned and observed. With his knife, he examined each layer—jabbing the section surface to check its density and thickness. He removed the soil from the section and felt the texture between his fingers, pressing his thumb on the surface to check its compactness. He sprayed water on the surface to see how the color changed. Soon, he etched deep, bold lines on the surface of the section, where the layers of the strata separated (Figure 6.3). This process was repeated at each layer. After half an hour of meticulous inspections and demarcations of each visible layer on the section surface, he commented:

> Look, this is how stratigraphy has to be studied and made. You cannot have thin [*pathli*], unsure [*faltu*] lines. They have to be thick [*moti*] and bold [*majboot*]. Remember, you are the *master of the trench* [English phrase used]. No one else on the site knows your trench better than you do. So, when you are drawing stratigraphy lines you have to be confident of what you are doing. It is ok if you commit mistakes, we all do. But be sure of what you are doing. That's how you will learn.

Figure 6.3 An archaeologist marking the stratigraphy on the trench wall with his knife in Dholavira, 2004

Source: Photograph by the author.

In the gridded universe of the ASI excavation site, it is the walls of the trenches that provide the stratigraphic evidence of the site, which, in turn, provides the temporality of the material cultures excavated. These walls play an evidential role in delineating the stratigraphy of the site since the physical embodiment of the stratigraphy is the section—the vertical surface of the four walls (balks) of the trench that enclose it. The section is both a material and visual manifestation of the stratigraphy that reveals the layers of accumulation of earth on its surface. In the enclosed spatiality of the trench, it is the epistemological interplay between materiality and the visuality of the section through which is articulated the temporality of stratigraphy. For Wheelerian archaeology, the section was the vital location where the science of stratigraphy was practiced and performed: "The basis of scientific excavation is the accurately observed and adequately recorded section" (Wheeler 1954, 22). The wall surface is a material cross-section of the archaeological site, analogous to the section of a biological sample after dissection (Wheeler, Ghosh, and Deva 1946, 23; Wheeler 1947b, 68, 72, 73, 75, 77). The excavated trench is a surgical fissure into the landscape to expose the depositional content of the site on the section to situate its temporality. The surface of the trench walls materially reflects its chronology, as the section visually shows the various stages of cultural accumulation over time (Wheeler 1947b, Plate XIX). The section is the visual and material representation of temporality in the trench. It is by systematic study and recording of the section that the science of stratigraphy is carried out.[9] The science of archaeology for ASI archaeologists in the trench therefore consisted not just in excavating the trench in a codified manner to unearth and expose past material culture, but also to explicitly reveal the stratigraphy on the section. Wheeler had also emphasized that it was through the accurate observation of sections that the scientific practice of stratigraphy was performed:

> Observation in different lights at different times of the day may help. In a difficult and important section, observation may be continued over a period of days before certainty is reached. And finally an attempt must be made to "read" the section—discriminate, without prejudice, between the more significant strata and the less significant differentiation of strata ... it is not enough to identify layers, although that is, of course, the essential step; it is the task of the archaeologists to interpret them, to understand the sentence and transliterate it. (Wheeler 1954, 60)

The science of stratigraphy for ASI archaeologists was about the systematic practice of observation and the accurate process of recording—the interpretative moment was subsumed under these two practices. Through consensus-building in the trench—involving numerous actors with credibility—the interpretative analysis of stratigraphy was turned into an objective category. By observing the visuality of the section and the inscriptive act of lining the surface of the section with a knife, the stratigraphical section was transformed from an interpretative epistemic artifact to an objective sign. A considerable amount of time was spent in the trench in the daily micro-practice of archaeology to enable the reading, interpretation, and recording of the section. The emphasis on accurate observation, interpretation, and recording was an iterative practice of the daily science of archaeology that was dutifully followed by archaeologists as underscored in Wheeler's manual:

> In practice, the identification and correlation of the strata or layers which represent the successive phases in the archaeological "history" of a site is one of the principal tasks of the excavator and will occupy a major portion of his time.... The task is one which involves clear and logical thinking reinforced by experience and infinite patience. (Wheeler 1954, 60)

In the ASI trenches, the necessity of reading and observing the section began soon after the first dig, which ranged between 6 and 10 inches, where the habitation deposit was "dense" (*jyada*), and less depth if the habitation deposit was "thin" (*thoda*)—informed an assistant superintending archaeologist (ASA), who had many years of experience working on both Harappan and other historical sites. He explained that unlike Harappan sites, stratigraphic observation did not begin before at least a meter had been dug in historic or early historic sites, "where the habitational deposit was thick and deep [*moti aur gahari*]."[10] But at Early Harappan sites, where the total habitational deposit of a site might not exceed more than 2 meters and where mud-brick architectural features were prolific and difficult to differentiate from the soil, "close stratigraphic control had to be maintained. Constant observation of the layers and deposit in the section is essential in digging an Early Harappan site," explained the ASA.

The epistemological attention to stratigraphy began with interpreting the soil layers in the trench by the trench supervisor, who noted his readings in the trench notebook. Senior archaeologists encouraged him at the site to mark on the section surface the different layers with his knife. He did this through close observation of the layers over the course of a few days. Numerous techniques were used to read the layers. Most often, the stratification on the section was taken early in the morning or late in the evening when the sun was in the horizon. Another method was to spray the section surface with water to study the layers. Both of these processes were essential, as a trench supervisor informed me: "Due to extreme heat, the soil moisture evaporates fast. These two methods were not the only ways to observe the character of the layers." Reading stratigraphy was not focused on just visual observation but also included haptic procedures such as "feeling the texture of the soil," "touching the section with fingers," and "poking the section with knives." The layer in the trench was attributed with ontological agency and the only way to comprehend it was to "understand its behavior." During a lecture in the trench, an AA instructed the Institute's students that the most vital thing about the stratigraphic layer was to "observe its behavior. See where it goes. See how it moves. Feel its compactness. See how it changes color. Feel its texture. Taste it, if necessary. You have to remember that each layer is real. To understand it you need to see how it behaves." The epistemology of stratigraphy is based on an ontological approach of cognizing the layers in the section. By focusing on the "*behavior of the layer* [the English phrase was always used]," a dynamic agency is attributed to the layers in the section and the science of stratigraphy is emphasized as the accurate observation of the behavior of these layers and the process of marking them.

Once the trench supervisor was sure of his reading of the stratification, he would use the knife and mark on the surface of the section the various layers he had observed and studied—by scratching at the junction where two layers appeared to separate. The act of using the knife and marking each layer on the section was considered an essential practice for the ASI archaeologist in the trench. An AA explained: "These knife-drawn lines are used to tell the story [*kahani*] in the quadrant. If one has to convey any meaning about the trench, lines have to be drawn." Often, students in the trenches were instructed (when they could not differentiate between layers) to draw multiple lines to depict one layer on the section: "Be the master of these lines. For these lines are the basic referral points of the trench." Interpreting the stratigraphical section was not enough; it had to be inscribed and made concrete. These knife-drawn lines were considered powerful by the ASI archaeologists—they were definite visual inscription of temporality in the trench. Wheeler in his inimitable style underscored the importance of a knife in an archaeological excavation: "Knife (Hindi, Urdu and Bengali, *churri*; Tamil, Telegu, Malayalam and Kannada, *katti*). This is the indispensable and inseparable instrument of every supervisor and foreman. Indeed, it is almost a badge of rank; without it, the supervisor can scarcely begin upon his task" (Wheeler 1948, 319). Only ASI archaeologists (not the technical staff or the senior laborers) carried knives with them, often tucked in the back pockets of their trousers (even women archaeologists, who typically wore jeans). The knife for them was a symbol both of their bureaucratic authority and their epistemological expertise. "It is like our gun; we cannot move without it," explained an AA from Hansi, who secured his knife in a custom-made leather holster: "This is the symbol of our power."[11] Interpretation in ASI archaeology occurred at the "knife edge" and not at the "trowel's edge" (Hodder 1997, 693; Hodder 1999, 103; Edgeworth 2003, 30) as seen in the western world (Figure 6.4).

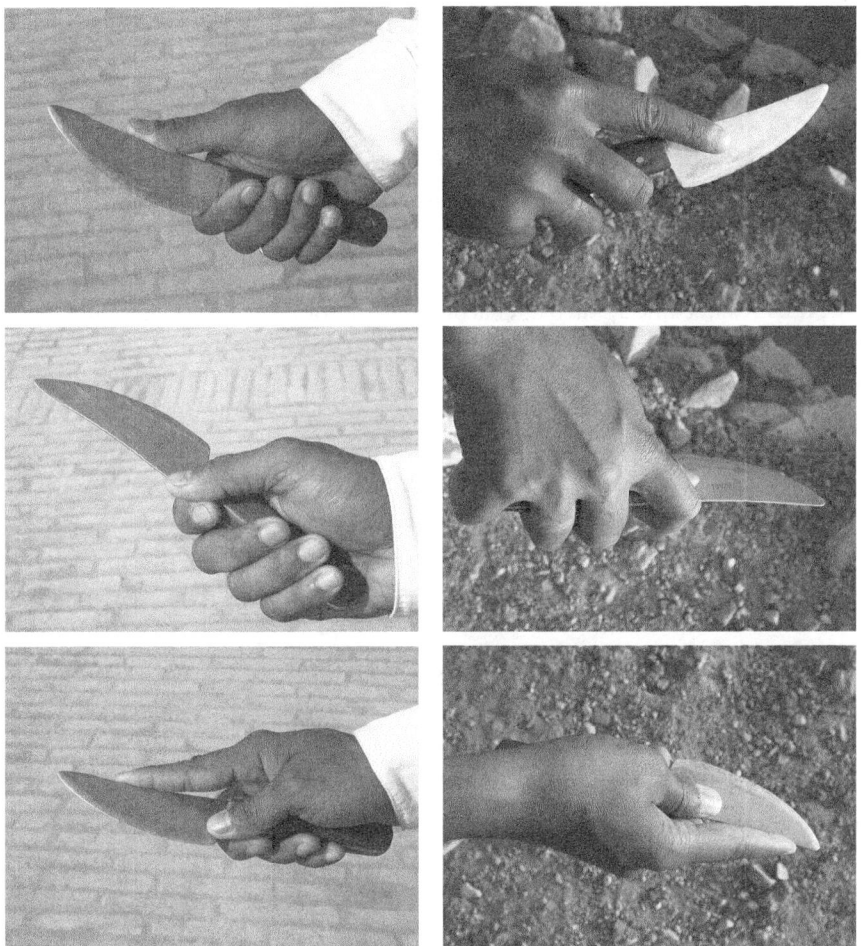

Figure 6.4 Archaeological ways of holding the knife to mark the layer, 2004

Source: Photographs by the author.

Once the knife lined the section, its depth and boldness reflected the confidence of the trench supervisor's interpretative abilities. He invited senior archaeologists during their inspection (AA, ASA, superintending archaeologist [SA], or even the site director) to study the markings on the section. The senior archaeologists would then pull out their knives to read, interpret, and (re)inscribe the stratification on the section. They would erase the markings the trench supervisor had made if they felt those to be incorrect, or re-scratch lines more deeply to emphasize the correctness of the markings of the layers. This process would be undertaken after discussions with the trench supervisor and once consensus had been reached. Within the hierarchical framework of the ASI, however, consensus would be disregarded if the decision was issued by an SA or the director who was inspecting the layers on the section. "The site director is the boss. He is the only one who understands the whole site. His stratigraphy marks are lines on stones [*pather per laqeer*]. So, no one can challenge his interpretation. We can question him, but we cannot contest his interpretation," explained an AA who had worked at Dholavira for multiple seasons. For ASI archaeologists, reading stratigraphy was considered to be the most technical skill of archaeological excavation. It was mandatory expert knowledge (Leighton 2015, 69). I observed that in the hierarchy of knowledge acquisition, it was not just the ability to recognize artifacts or the skill to excavate structures in the trench, but, more importantly, the competency to decipher the deposits of the soil in the section and the dexterity to demarcate the chronology of the trench on the basis of stratigraphy that were considered to the most highly specialized skills of an ASI archaeologist (Figure 6.5).

Figure 6.5 Layer inspection and discussion in a Dholavira trench, 2004

Source: Photograph by the author.

The surface of the section was crucial for observing the stratigraphy of the trench; an enormous amount of manpower was spent in the excavation trench to make "good" sections. The prominence of this skill was so indispensable that each trench had an expert "section-cutter." This expert was a laborer who had a "good hand" (*accha haath*) in cutting a clear and defined section. It had to be "ninety degrees to the floor" of the trench, with no bulges or depression. "The section has to be clear like a mirror [*sheeshe ki tarah saaf*], so that it can be properly [*thik tarah se*] drawn," explained a draughtsman. A site director informed me that until the mid-1980s, there had been a separate category of skilled laborer called the "section-cutter," who was given more daily wages than the lay workers. Although the section-cutters during the years of my ethnography were not given higher wages, this category of the laborer was sought after in an ASI excavation.

I observed the importance of the section-cutter's role in Baror, when an AA introduced me to an elderly laborer working in one trench as a section-cutter, who was trained during the Kalibangan excavation in the 1960s by B. B. Lal. He was summoned from his village near Kalibangan when excavation work started in Baror: "Only to cut sections and train other laborers to make proper sections." The job of the section-cutter commenced as soon as the first dig took place and the horizontal wall of the gridded trench emerged. Preparing a section was a time-consuming task. A section-cutter would often take a day just to turn the wall of the trench into a proper section. Wheeler also emphasized this:

> There are in practice various ways and means of dealing with the reluctant, sun-baked section of the Orient, or indeed with many sections in the West. Damping, and careful scraping with a knife or turf-cutter, will often provide the remedy by bringing out more subtle variations of color or material. (Wheeler 1954, 60)

Although some AAs I observed were very good section-cutters, it was not expected of the students to learn section-cutting; cutting the section was the responsibility of solely the subaltern laborers at the site. However, often the trench supervisor or an AA would jump into the trench and pull out the knife from his pocket to sharpen the section. I was also often told that to be a good archaeologist it was important to be a "fine section-cutter," but never in the training nor in the daily practice of ASI archaeology did I ever see section-cutting being done by any of the officers. Within the hierarchy of work (*kaam*) on the excavation site— "section-cutting" was relegated to the domain of the "skillful" laborers (Figure 6.6).

Figure 6.6 A trench on the citadel at Dholavira with labeled stratigraphy, 2004

Source: Photographs by the author.

Once the rituals of observation, inscription, inspection, and re-inscription were completed, the layers are labeled. Labeling the stratigraphy on the section was considered to be a performative aspect of the excavation of the trench analogous to the "preparation of the subject"—a practice that I discuss in Chapter 8. Each trench leader was given a series of white, square cardboard pieces with numbers inscribed in a circle. These were the layer numbers, which were pinned onto the section to identify each stratum. This practice had a sense of finality: "Once the layers have been labeled, it means that excavation in the trench has ended for the time being. Now the draughtsman and photographers can enter and do their work. Once they are done, then the excavation starts again," explained an experienced ASA. We were sitting cross-legged on the floor of a four-and-a-half-meter-deep vertical trench. He was directing a laborer, who was trying to pin the layer label on top of the trench by balancing on a bamboo ladder resting on one wall of the quadrant. Wheeler spends a considerable time discussing the value and importance of labeling the stratigraphic layers of the section:

> I like to see my sections plastered from head to foot with orderly arrays of labels, which serve three main purposes: they demand clear and decisive thought on the part of the supervisor who invents them, they show on the ground and on the drawing precisely what his small-find labels mean, and they make it possible for the director or a substitute-supervisor to understand at once the diagnosis up to date. (Wheeler 1954, 72)

It was through this process of labeling that stratigraphy transforms the interpretation of layers into *objective empirical evidence*. This practice of visually marking the various layers of stratigraphy is the definitive inscriptive process through which the layers on the section are accorded empirical value (Latour and Woolgar 1986, 88). Such a process of tagging makes the layers *factual artifacts* of the archaeological excavation. By creating various layers, an objective temporality is delineated. The messy epistemic practice of reading, interpreting, and forming consensus is erased. Instead, the strata/layer as a concrete factual category of archaeological science emerges. Once this objective inscription in the trench was completed, the excavator would end their task and the ASI technical staff—surveyors, draughtsmen, and photographers—would enter the trench to transform the epistemic spatiality of the trench with its layers and material culture evidence into a scientific representation.

Notes

1. For an extensive survey on the presence of carnelian beads in Harappan culture, see Kenoyer (2005, 2007). On Dholavira carnelian technology, see Prabhakar (2016, 2018).

2. A description that echoed Michael Shanks's objectifying portrayal of excavation as a "striptease" in which layers of earth, like clothes, are "peeled off slowly, tantalizing us with glimpses of something we hope to see completely exposed" (Shanks 1992, 192–93).

3. See Lal (1964, Plate XLV) for an elegant example.

4. Painted Grey Ware is a characteristic pottery that is considered the hallmark of Iron Age culture in north India (c. 1200 BCE–600 BCE), and has been diagnostically associated with post-Harappan cultures. For more details, see Hegde (1975); Joshi (1978); and Sharma (1978, 131–43).

5. For a reappraisal of the Brahmagiri chronology, as advocated by Wheeler, see Morrison (2005).

6. For a sustained critique of Wheeler's archaeological intervention in Arikamedu, see also Begley (1983).

7. For an alternative view on the Roman Arrentine ware, see Begley (1988, 1993).

8. Naqada culture is an archaeological culture of Chalcolithic Predynastic Egypt (ca. 4400–3000 BC). For the most recent discussion on the typological nature of Naqada pottery, see Hendrickx (1996).

9. See *IAR 2003–04* (2011, 232–33) (Baror); *IAR 2003–04* (2011, 33) (Juni Kuran); Bisht (2015, 101–02) (Dholavira); Nath (2015, 102) (Rakhigarhi).

10. See, for example, Lal (1949, Plates XXXII, XXXIII) for early historic habitation deposits at the site of Sisupalgarh, Orissa.

11. Most of the knives carried by the ASI archaeologists, I was told, were custom-made by a local ironsmith, often at the site at which they worked for the first time as student archaeologists.

7 Making of the Archaeological Artifact

The ASI was a "well-oiled" (*chalu aur chust*) bureaucratic postcolonial system—conducting an archaeological excavation with "as much scientific care as possible [*jitana sambhav*] for a governmental [*sarkari*] organization," an assistant archaeologist (AA) at Dholavira dryly told me during one of our conversations, as we walked in the excavated streets of the Lower Town. Every morning at the stroke of the bell, the laborers who had arrived earlier for the roll call would slowly walk toward the site and enter the excavation trenches. I would sometimes get up very early in the morning to see this ritual as hundreds of men and women, wrapped from head to toe in faded woolen blankets and shawls, emerged from the early morning mist. These workers would walk toward the excavation site in a regimental fashion, mostly barefoot, some in rubber flip-flops and others in worn-out plastic footwear—not with the military trot that Wheeler would have desired, but more like a ragtag army of tired subaltern rebels, despairingly carrying the tools of their trade (see Wheeler 1948, 318–21).

Men hauled pickaxes and spades on their shoulders, and women bore basketfuls of brushes, trowels, ropes, and pegs on their head. Around the same time, from the tents of the camp, the ASI supervisors, students, and the AA along with the site director would enter the excavation site attired very differently—jeans, cotton shirts, synthetic wind-cheaters, leather jackets, sweaters, cricket hats, baseball caps, and sneakers. They would be carrying nylon backpacks and bags stuffed with the tools of their trade—towels, plastic water bottles, rulers, pens, pencils, clipboards, measuring tapes, torchlights, brushes, a geometry box, and a knife. In a matter of minutes, the excavation trenches would teem with activity that seemed organized and coordinated—with each worker performing their pre-assigned duty, but, as I have shown earlier, encompassed within a social–cultural ecology that was riddled with caste, class, and professional hierarchy.

Each actor at the excavation site had a specific task, which was watchfully carried out in a synchronized manner. Looking from the top of the fortification mound at Dholavira or the top of the habitation mound at Baror and Bhirrana, I could not fail to realize the labor-intensiveness of an ASI archaeological excavation. It was different from the archaeological practice in the contemporary western world and uncannily similar to descriptions of archaeological excavation in the colony (Guha 2011, 159).[1] The men could be seen with pickaxes, digging the trenches and removing the earth into iron containers for the women, who would walk a few meters and throw the dirt in a dump. Some women could be seen sifting the excavated earth for artifacts; others could be seen on their haunches with a brush and trowel, going through the earth in the trenches searching for artifacts. The trench supervisors, with baseball caps and cricket hats, clutching notebooks in their hands, could be seen sitting and jotting down notes. The technical staff with their work-teams would be seen measuring the excavated structures and the ASI draughtsman drawing diagrams of these under the shade of a colorful umbrella. In the evening, under the slanting light of the setting sun, the photographers and their retinue of workers would be seen taking photographs of the artifacts discovered onsite or the structures or the floors exposed over the course of the day's excavation. For an outsider like me, the initial impact of such an activity, which reflected the organized might of a bureaucratic organization at work, was overwhelming. However, as I continued my anthropology of archaeological practice, the facade of this coordinated action crumbled to slowly reveal a gravely compromised epistemological process, which further jeopardized the artifact discovered and recovered in the trench.

The Artifact in the Trench

The excavation in an archaeological trench is enclosed by two planar surfaces: the horizontal floor of the trench and the vertical section of the trench. Through the co-relationship between these two surfaces, evidence is produced at the site. By triangulating an artifact or a structure between these two surfaces, the discovered material culture is transformed into empirical evidence. These are not static surfaces; they are constantly evolving and getting shaped in the trenches. With every dig, a new horizontal floor is uncovered, and a longer vertical section is exposed. In the trenches, the science of archaeology is to observe and record both of these surface features accurately and precisely. The micro-practice of science in an archaeological excavation is to uncover each horizontal layer and to co-relate the material culture on the floor to the stratigraphic layer of the section (Harris 1989).

In the ASI trenches, definite conventions were followed to optimize this process of knowledge production. These rules and regulations of scientific archaeology not only emerged from a collective wisdom of earlier archaeologists who had spent their life digging in Indian sites, but also by following and regurgitating Wheeler's stratigraphy method (Wheeler 1947c, 143–49). Although the general sets of norms adhered to were guidelines learned through textbooks, these processes were iterated on a daily basis: "Archaeology is not a *bookish subject*

[English word used]. It is a field science. What you will learn in the field you will never learn in the classroom," was the wisdom often emphasized by the site director of Dhalovira to his students. These methods and practices were taught to the students during their training at the excavation site. During my fieldwork, I spent a considerable amount of time observing how senior archaeologists trained the ASI Institute students in "ASI's ways [*ASI ka tareeka*] of digging"—which I was frequently reminded was "very different [*bahut alag*] from the way you dig in Deccan College," but identical to Wheeler's earliest account of the Taxila field school of 1944 (Wheeler 1946a, 1–2). The training was imparted through lectures by AAs and the technical staff, and sometimes even by the site directors. They were held at the excavation sites, trenches, and also in the evening after the excavation in the "antiquity class." It was during these lectures and classes that the students were trained not only in how one ought to dig and to read stratigraphy, but also how to measure, record, and write detailed reports in the site notebook.

According to a senior AA, who was lecturing to a group of students in a trench in Baror:

> Archaeology is not just about discovery. It is about knowledge. If you just dig and remove objects without recording and measuring, that is murder [*khoon*]. It is like killing [*maar*] the site. You must measure antiquities, where they were found, label them, and write notes about them. That is why you are given a trench notebook, and measuring tape.

This was one of the first days of fieldwork for a group of students from the ASI Institute who had come to Baror two days earlier for their "90 days" mandatory field training. We were all standing in a quadrant, as the senior AA at the site was explaining the importance of measurement in archaeological excavation:

> Accurate measurement and labeling is essential for each and every [*har ek*] antiquity that you discover, each structure you expose. If you don't label them or take measurements, then the site director can never write anything about your trench in the report. So, if you want your work to feature in the report, measure and label everything and write detailed notes in your site notebook.

Then he demonstrated how each artifact discovered in the quadrant was measured: "We usually follow 3D [three-dimensional] measurement. You triangulate and then measure the depth." He beckoned several trained laborers and showed the students, with their help, how three-dimensional measurements should be taken. The AA lectured: "Take the two quadrant pegs which are closest to the antiquity. Take the horizontal measurement using a string, spirit level, and the measuring tape. Then, take the vertical measurements using the plumb-bob."

It was through the process of triangulating the material culture in the quadrant, labeling, and making a record about it that archaeological evidence was transformed into archaeological fact. "Merely [*keval*] the discovery and recovery of the artifact does not make archaeology a scientific practice," the AA archaeologist frequently instructed. It is only through the process of fixating the artifacts and structures found in the trench within the larger gridded matrix of the site that archaeological science at the ASI is performed. Once the excavation is completed, the notes and recordings logged are summoned while creating a narrative of the site. During field-lectures, the Institute students would be regularly told, "Archaeology, as we all know, is a destructive process. The need for accurate recording and measurement is most crucial [*sabase mahatvapoorn*]. If you don't do that, then you do not differ from gravediggers and thieves. We are archaeologists because we work systematically."

Not every artifact discovered in the trench was measured with the meticulousness described above: "Only the antiquities have to be measured and recorded the way I have shown. For pottery and bones only measure the depth in which they are discovered," clarified the AA to the students. Archaeological intervention, for the ASI, was not the retrieval of material culture as *archaeological artifact* but as *archaeological antiquity*. The distinction between artifact and antiquity was an instrumental component of the ASI archaeological apparatus. All artifacts were not antiquities. Only those artifacts were considered antiquities that the ASI archaeologist believed were "precious and rare" (*keemti*)—fragments of metal objects, terracotta figures, shells objects, seals, beads, and other artifacts that were "extraordinary" (*ekdum alag*). The significance of antiquity was not subjective; it had a distinct legal definition in the ASI. According to the Antiquities and Art Treasures Act, 1972, "antiquity" comprised:

> (i) any coin, sculpture, painting, epigraph or other work of art or craftsmanship; (ii) any article, object or thing detached from a building or cave; (iii) any article, object or thing illustrative of science, art, crafts, literature, religion, customs, morals or politics in bygone ages; (iv) any article, object or thing of historical interest; (v) any article, object or thing declared by the Central Government, by notification in the Official Gazette, to be an antiquity for the purpose of this Act, which has been in existence for not less than one hundred years. (Tripathi 2007, 66)

This legal delineation informed the ASI archaeologist's comprehension of the value of the artifacts. Objects like ceramic fragments, faunal remains, and botanical remains, which were found in abundance at Harappan sites, did not fall within the definitional bounds of antiquity. These non-antiquity objects discovered in the excavation trenches were often given a dissimilar treatment that endangered the epistemological significance of the archaeological excavation.

"The antiquities go into the antiquity trunk," explained an AA at Bhirrana who was "in-charge" of all the antiquities discovered at the site. "These are objects that are eventually photographed and drawn, but only a few are eventually published and exhibited in the museum," he explained. The ASI archaeologists differentiated between seldom-found artifacts and the prolifically unearthed artifacts such as ceramics and bones. At the level of daily practice of knowledge production, this disparity was reflected in taking three-dimensional measurements—only the objects that were considered antiquities by the excavators were triangulated, recorded in the site notebook, and labeled. Detailed tabulations mentioning site, object, date, trench, quadrant, stratum, locus, depth, period, and material were marked on them. They were then placed in cotton "pottery bags," and labeled by the category, trench, quadrant, stratum, and depth. On the other hand, only the depth and layers of the ceramics and faunal remains were recorded.

The "antiquity class" was a daily post-excavation ritual at the ASI excavation site. It was mandatory for all the student excavators, trench supervisors, AAs, and technical staff to attend. The antiquity class was held in a special tent, which contained several padlocked tin trucks containing "significant" (*mahatvapoorn*) artifacts discovered over the season. The class started two hours after the excavation ended and continued until dinnertime. The antiquity class was a pedagogic ritual where the senior archaeologists at the site gave lectures about the "nitty-gritties [*dau-pach*] of the excavation method." The importance of this class was highlighted to the students who attended excavations for the first time, and required "compulsory attendance." While the overt goal of the antiquity class was pedagogical, it was also a practice of socialization into the minutiae of the archaeological method. During this class, students shared their experiences of the excavation and were socialized by senior ASI archaeologists into the technical nuances of the excavation process.

It was also during this evening ritual that the artifacts were handed over publicly to the AA by the excavator who would safely keep them in the antiquity trunk and lock it. During this meeting, various artifacts were passed around for other excavators to see, observe, and feel. On one occasion, in an exciting antiquity class during which the students could feel and touch "first hand" a Harappan seal that had been discovered in a trench in the Middle Town in Dholavira, the AA dejectedly noted, "This is the only time you will ever be able to see this artifact." The Indus seal was the rarest of any artifact found at a Harappan site (for instance, see Marshall 1931, 103; Mackay 1937, 325–49; Vats 1940,

316–36; Rao 1985, 305–18). It was considered to be the most "valuable antiquity" (*moolyavaan*) of Harappan excavation. "Only a couple are found each season," noted the AA. "If we are lucky, five. Anything more than that is a miracle."[2] To ontologically experience a Harappan seal was considered by many to be the highlight of an excavation season, but the AA remarked:

> The apathy of the ASI system is that after an excavation, an antiquity like a Harappan seal disappears into the tin trunks of Purana Qila. God knows how many seals are lost there. No one knows. This is the last time you will see this seal. If the seal is lucky, it might be published, and if it is very lucky, it will end up in the National Museum. But it is more or less out of reach for researchers because it is a precious antiquity and the ASI bureaucrats will let no one get any access to it.

In this context, the ritual of the antiquity class at the excavation site where the excavators have an opportunity to materially interact with archaeological artifacts becomes fetishized as the site of both an epistemological and an ontological engagement with archaeological artifacts. It is here that material culture is designated as an antiquity and an "epistemic artifact" is created akin to "epistemic things" (Rheinberger 1997, 28). During the "antiquity class," discussions were held about objects whose functions could not be determined. These discussions led to a consensual opinion about objects whose material or purpose was doubtful. Often, during this process, objects were relabeled. Each antiquity was registered and recorded in several archives. First, it was labeled and kept in a separate plastic or paper container. Then, it was logged in the trench notebook by the trench supervisor. Thereafter, it was recorded in the antiquity register. The epistemological significance of the antiquity class was that it was during this assembly that those artifacts designated as antiquities by the excavators were transformed into "epistemic artifacts" (Rheinberger 2005, 406–07).[3] Labeling artifacts in the trench was the first step in transforming archaeological artifacts into knowledge objects but it was in the antiquity class that an artifact's epistemic position was inscribed in primary representational texts—the site notebook and the antiquity record book. The director of the excavation later referred to these initial representational texts during the process of writing the final authoritative representational text—the site report. A vast number of antiquities are found in a Harrapan site. R. S. Bisht notes that 54,276 antiquities were discovered at Dholavira, consisting of a "multitude of varieties including seals and sealings, beads, bangles, blades, chisels, arrowheads, grinding stones, stone members, inlay pieces, etc. A variety of materials were used to fashion the artefacts at Dholavira" (Bisht 2015, 223).

The Practice of Discovery

The practice of discovery in the ASI archaeological trench was symbiotically linked to the "act of recognition" (Edgeworth 2003, 54). Theoretically, archaeological discovery is not possible unless the excavators are cognizant of what they are looking for. Archaeology, like any other disciplinary practice, is based on an epistemological acculturation of scholarship, research, and erudition. At the ASI, methodological training was mandatory for the making of an ASI archaeologist—by enrolling for a diploma in Archaeology at the Institute of Archaeology in New Delhi. Even students who had been trained as archaeologists at university departments across the country—with MA/MSc degrees—had to acquire a diploma from the Institute to join the ASI as an archaeologist. "The Institute was not just a school for training in archaeology, it is where we teach how to do ASI archaeology," explained an AA at Hansi.

It was paradoxical that with such a distinctive sense of training and scholarly socialization, the primary excavator at an ASI archaeological site was an untrained laborer. These "excavators" who dug the trench and cleared and shuffled the excavated earth were "illiterate" (*dehati*) men and women. They were neither trained as archaeologists nor conversant with the goals and objectives of the archaeological excavation. During my ethnography, I observed that the actors at the site who did most of the physical work (*kaam*) of excavation were the laborers, and not the trench supervisors or the ASI archaeologists. "That is what they are supposed to do, manual work [*kaam-kaaj*]—dig trenches, remove dirt, and carry excavated earth [*khodna, mithi uthana aur phekna*]," explained an assistant superintending archaeologist (ASA). Ironically, these "manual laborers" were the foremost actors who engaged with an artifact or a structural feature in the trench, but in the social hierarchy of the excavation site, they were the lowest. However, in the chronology of discovery, they were the principal actors. They were the first to discover an artifact in the trench, to notice something unusual and valuable, and to recognize its epistemological value.[4]

Once the quadrant had been inscribed on the landscape, the work of the laborer-excavator was to conduct the "first dig"—6 to 10 inches in depth. Both men and women did this with the help of small pickaxes (*choti gaithi*). After the ground had been dug, the laborers, with their bare hands or with trowels, brushes, or even pieces of iron scrap or plastic, would rummage through the excavated soil and search for artifacts (Figure 7.1). It was during this process of searching that the laborers and excavators would find objects that had archaeological value—potshards, animal bones, stone and metal objects, beads, micro-beads, and terracotta objects: "Anything they thought was unusual and different [*ajeeb aur alag*], they were told to pick it up," explained an AA.

The potshards and the bones were effortlessly identified by them and were kept in separate tin containers. Other objects would be handed over to the trench supervisor and stored separately. Fragile artifacts such as carnelian beads, metal objects, and terracotta figurines would be wrapped in cotton and stored in a polythene bag or a plastic container. Findings at this stage were only labeled with their layer number, depth, and the name of the object. Since the objects were found during the process of searching through the debris after excavation, three-dimensional recordings were not conducted. Only approximate recordings could be taken. This was just the depth of the horizontal surface of the dig—it was impossible to pinpoint the exact location of a find. Accurate measurements were only taken when the excavators had discovered a habitational floor with known precious Harappan artifacts such as seals with inscriptions, metal projectiles, complete terracotta figures, and complete carnelian beads.

The practice of deploying a laborer who had never been trained as an archaeologist to do a specialist's task was intriguing. However, my informants—both the laborers and the ASI archaeologists—considered it "commonsensical" (*buddhiman*) and were surprised when I asked them about this process. One site director explained:

Figure 7.1 Tool-kits for digging, excavating, cleaning, and marking in a trench at a site in Bhirrana, 2005

Source: Photographs by the author.

We train them [*hum unhe seekhate hai*]. It takes weeks and days of very careful schooling [*bahut dehyan se sikhate hai*]. We tell them what is essential and what is important. Look, these are hardworking people of the earth [*matti ke log*]. They know when something is unusual [*anokhi cheez*] and different [*alag cheez*]. They learn quickly [*jaldi seekh jate hai*]. We show them photographs of antiquities that are found in the Harappan sites. We carry a sample of potshards, steatite beads, and other found artifacts to show them. And they just get it. And there is no space for mistakes [*galatiyon ke lie jagah nahi hai*] for there are also the trench supervisors, AAs, and the technical staff. Everyone is in the trenches. So nothing gets lost or goes unseen [*kuch bhi khota ya gayeb nahi hota*]. We have full control [English phrase used].

For the site director, the key issue was that "they have to be taught and explained that these things are important [*mahatvapoorn*] and that we are searching [*khoj rahe hai*] for these objects. And then they do it." At the ASI, the process of discovery and recognition was controlled and regimented, with the laborer-excavator given the agency of identifying objects but not of discovery. Their epistemic agency was only acceptable until the moment of recognition, after that it was the job of the archaeologist: "To make the finding scientific, by measuring them, labeling them, cataloging them, and finally writing the reports," explained the AA, emphasizing the difference between the work he did and the task the laborers undertook. This division of epistemic labor was assiduously followed—the laborer dug and discovered; the archaeologists gave the discovery its epistemic worth.

The epistemic agency of discovery was attributed to various official actors at an excavation site through a chain of credibility and authority. At Baror, an ASA explained:

Look around [*dekhiye*], their village surrounds [*charo-taraf*] these archaeological mounds. Day in and day out they live with potshards scattered around their field and villages. So they know all the antiquities we are looking for. Harappan mounds, like most sites in India, are not hidden under the earth; they are visible mounds, with antiquities scattered hundreds of meters across the landscape. The mound and its antiquities are part of their daily lives [*unki roze ke zindagi*]. So these people are the best persons for digging. For they know the site better than us [*hum se aacha site ko jante hai*]. We don't even have to train them. We tell them to pick up potshards for us. We make the job of finding things scientific [*hum bus cheezo ko scientific bana dete hai*].

This was a characteristic justification for many ASI archaeologists who deployed a large number of members of the local population as laborers at archaeological sites.

I observed that most often the local laborers were able to identify artifacts much more efficiently than the ASI archaeologists.

Most of the ASI archaeologists acknowledged that some of the laborers were far superior field archaeologists than they were. An AA at Dholavira who had also worked at Rakhigarhi as a student described it thus:

> At Rakhigarhi, which, as you know, is the largest Harappan mound in India, the locals were already expert diggers by the time we came. There was a clever [*chaloo*] primary school teacher who knew the value [*keemat*] of the mound and its antiquities. He would pay a few rupees to his students to collect seals, beads, and other antiquities. You will not believe it [*aap vishwas nahi karoge*], but when we reached the site, we also asked those same students to do the primary exploration work for us. They were so good [*itne acche the*] that in the first few days we got a few seals and many carnelian beads. We could not employ children, as we are a government organization. But we did use the children to help us during the excavation.

I do not have any ethnographic evidence to support this anecdote; however, during my visit to Rakhigarhi, we were accosted several times by a bunch of kids cajoling us to buy beads and terracotta figurines they had collected. When I asked them how they had found these artifacts, a young boy remarked: "After every rain, a lot of these objects appear on the surface. We collect them. Everyone does. When foreign tourists come they give us a lot of money for them." At Baror, a young laborer said that they had known these mounds since they were kids:

> I see these potshards and bones every day. I know them since as far back as I can remember. We would take our animals to graze here. I never knew these potshards could be important for anyone. When I started work here, the *saheb*s told me to look for these potshards. It is easy for me.

He bicycled 10 kilometers every day in each direction in order to work at the Baror site: "It's even worth dropping school for a month." He was studying in a high school in the sub-divisional headquarters of Anoopgad (district Ganganagar, Rajasthan). For most of these laborers, working in the archaeological trench amounted to doing what the *saheb*s told them to do; it was work (*kaam*) for livelihood (*rozi-roti*).

Once, I was observing routine work at a new trench in the Lower Town of Dholavira. The Lower Town was a sprawling habitation deposit comprised of formidable architecture—domestic structures, elaborate drainage lines, and streets—which the excavators considered to be inhabited by the "working-class" members of Dholavira during Harappan times. It was a sprawling habitational deposit at the site, lower than the citadel, surrounded by the fortification wall and the Middle Town. The trench was inside a domestic habitation structure, and the excavation in the trench was conducted to locate the working floor of the room. This was the second dig in the quadrant; it was about 18 inches deep. Half of the quadrant had been excavated and three elderly women were sitting on their haunches, shuffling through the excavated earth looking for artifacts, while two men with small pickaxes were digging in the northwest part of the trench. One woman, who had been meticulously rummaging through the excavated earth with a trowel, gathered dirt in her hands and slowly walked toward us. She came and opened her palm and showed it to the trench supervisor, exclaiming: "Sir, see" (*Sir, dekho*). In the dirt were about a dozen micro-steatite beads (see Kenoyer 2001). "Very good! Very good! Find more" (*Bai, bahut acche! bahut acche! Aur khojo*), the supervisor excitedly replied. Pleased, the woman went back to her corner in the trench and rummaged through the excavated earth again separating the dirt with her dusty fingers. "Look at her. See, she is going through the dirt as if she is removing the gravel from the rice [*chawal se kankar nikal rahi hai*]. That's why you need local labor," he justified in a contented voice.

> Will you ever to do this? These are micro-beads. I can never find them in this much of dirt [*main kabhi nahi kar payunga*]. This is even more difficult than *finding a needle in the haystack* [English phrase used]. But these women do it every day [*har roz*]. It is in their genes [*unki rag-rag mai hai*]. They have been removing gravels [*kankar*] from tons and tons of rice all their lives, so to find beads in this dirt is natural [*svaabhaavik*] for them.

I found this narrative illustrative of ASI archaeologists' rationalizations for the deployment of local labor in the trenches. Local laborers were important at the archaeological site for the ASI because they not only provided the workforce to clear the vast tract of land that an ASI excavation site occupied, but also because they had a tacit skill (Polanyi and Sen 2009) effective for the excavation process.[5]

At Dholavira, archaeological work had a different meaning for the senior laborers at the site. Ganesh *bhai* (brother)—one of the first laborers to begin work at the site of Dholavira—was now a supervisor in the pottery yard. When I asked him how he had learned about ceramics categories at the site, he explained:

> Sir, I learned all about archaeology and Dholavira by following and observing Bisht sir. When he first came, I was one of earliest laborers at the site. He taught me all I know about archaeology [*sab kuch unhone seekhaya*]. I learned how to dig with him—with both big and small pickaxes. I learned to clear the earth with a brush, prepare subjects, and to use a knife properly on the floor and the section. I knew nothing. He taught me all. But most what I learned was by observing Bisht sir.

I would just tag him. If he were in the trench day and night, I would be with him without food or water. I would carefully see how he did things and I picked up [*kaam pakad liya*].

Ganesh *bhai* did not dig in the trenches anymore. We were sitting under a tree overlooking the massive Dholavira pottery yard, where a group of women were sitting with their *dupata*s (scarf) protecting their faces from the harsh mid-March sun. With heads bent down, they were washing the potshards with water and toothbrushes. He continued,

Sir*ji*, it was matter of survival. I had to learn things that Bisht sir, and other officers, did not teach. I had an inkling that ASI would work in Dholavira for a long-long time. So to get a job, I had to learn everything. And it is because of my knowledge that in a few years they made me full-time member of the excavation.

He was one of the few senior laborers at the site who did not dig, but instead worked as site supervisor. He oversaw the laborers working in the pottery yard. "Today, I can tell you the difference between pottery from the earliest level in Dholavira to the latest phase," he proudly told me. Another day, during my daily visit to the pottery yard, I asked him about the various kinds of ceramics found at the site.

Something Sir*ji*, please don't mind—even these young AAs with degrees cannot tell the difference between various kinds of pottery. All these are just kids fresh out of school [*kal ke chore hai*]. We have to listen to them because they are officers. But sir, they know little about the site or even about the Harappans.

Ganesh *bhai* confided in hushed tones, although there was no one within earshot. For Ganesh *bhai*, recognizing ceramics at the excavation site was a matter of both skill and pride, like many senior laborers at the site. Working at the ASI site was not just a means of earning a livelihood, but it was also a way to gather knowledge about the site that could be deployed for prestige. During the non-excavation season, senior laborers like Ganesh *bhai* would also work as tourist guides for the few tourists who would make the long journey from Bhuj or Ahmedabad to visit the site. If you go to Dholavira today, you will find some of these senior laborers still working as tourist guides at the site (Balasubramanian 2018; Iyer 2019).

Jaimal *bhai* was another senior laborer at the site, who had the reputation of being the unsurpassed "bone-expert". When I first came to Dholavira, I enquired among the ASI archaeologists working at the site if there was any archaeozoologist at the site. An AA told me that at the ASI animal bones have a secondary value: "The ASI has no archaeozoologist on its payroll. There are experts who are invited by Bisht on and off. The only person at the site who knows bones like the back of his hands is Jaimal *bhai*." Jaimal *bhai* was a Dalit farmer from the village of Dholavira, who, along with Ganesh *bhai* and four other senior laborers at the site, was a full-time *chowkidar*. They were daily-wage laborers employed by the ASI year-round as site custodians. During the months of excavation, they worked as site supervisors and did various specialized jobs—from recruiting laborers from adjoining villages to doing excavation and conservation work. When I asked Jaimal *bhai*, during one of my many conversations with him, how he became the "bone-expert," he explained,

> I don't clearly remember, but it was after two or three years of excavation I learned about bones. Once a white sahib [*gora saheb*] from your America came, and Bisht sir asked me to be his assistant. He was kind and taught me everything I know today. He was here for just a few weeks, then his student—a madam—worked at the site. She was also very nice, and I worked as her assistant whenever she came to the site. She also taught me a lot. But she has not returned for the past few years. Now I look at the bones. But sir, I have only studied till class five. What research can I do? I can only tell which bone belongs to which animal—cow, pig, and goat. But I cannot do anything more than that. No one here knows about animal bones. The officers and technicians don't know. I am the only one who knows—so they call me bone-expert. Sir, I am no expert. This is what they say. But if I have to work here I have to know all this. It is a matter of survival.

An AA who had worked at Dholavira for multiple seasons informed me that the only faunal expert who has spent time in Dholavira was a Harvard University doctoral student, Ajita K. Patel, an archaeozoologist who was studying with Richard H. Meadow.[6] These are the two individuals referred to by Jaimal *bhai*. One evening, standing on the citadel overlooking the Rann, over the setting sun, Jaimal *bhai* mused, "After all, sir, it is all about money. If it was not for this site, I would have been struggling in the city of Ahmedabad working as a rickshaw driver, or sweating in the salt pans of Gandhidham."

Ganesh *bhai* and Jaimal *bhai* were exceptions. There were very few laborers like them in Dholavira, and none at all at the newer sites. "Skilled laborers," as both these experts were called, were not many on ASI sites and existed "only at sites," I was told by a senior ASA, "which had a history of long excavation. I remember there were many like these in Kaliganban." This ASA had started his career as technical assistant (earlier designation for an AA) at Kalibangan working with B. B. Lal and B. K Thapar. "They played a very important role in the day-to-day workings of the archaeological site. They were local and understood our objectives as archaeologists. They were very helpful in training other laborers and getting work done," explained the ASA. But most laborers at the sites were unfamiliar with the practice of archaeology and their role in discovery and recognition of artifacts was very limited. The epistemic role of the laborer in the trench was restricted to recognizing the artifacts and structures. The information then moved to the next level of expertise which added credibility to the recognition of the laborer; then that material culture was considered officially discovered. The movement from recognition to discovery involved a chain of credibility. In the ASI trenches, the laborer's tacit skills were employed to excavate the artifact from the earth and recognize its value; they did not discover artifacts. For an artifact to be discovered, it had to have its significance ratified by a legitimate member of the ASI bureaucracy—the mere act of unearthing did not transform material culture into epistemic artifacts.

Discovery and Chain of Credibility

I was sitting in a quadrant digging with a student trench leader in Baror. In 2004, 20 trenches that had been opened for excavation in the lower part of the mound were destroyed by prior agricultural activity. The ASI archaeologists who led the excavation had decided that the destruction of the upper layer of the site "should be exploited" to examine the deeper Early Harappan layers (see *IAR 2003–04* 2011, 226). An AA explained the logic of this intervention:

> Although this site is partially destroyed, it is still useful. A local farmer had dug open a part of the mound, as he wanted to expand his agricultural field. But the same season his brother died. This was a bad omen. He abandoned his plans of expansion. This has been a godsend for us. Although he destroyed the upper layers of the site, the lowers layers are still intact because no regular agricultural work was done. So now it is faster for us to hit the Early Harappan levels here. In sites like Surkotada and Dholavira, early Harappan layers are four to five meters deep. Here we can reach it in a meter or two.

This trench was about a meter and a half deep and the excavation was done through "slow and small digs." The trench leader explained: "These trenches are barren; other than some Hakra ware and animal bones, nothing was discovered."[7]

While I was working on the excavation with the team—digging with small pickaxes—a laborer informed us that he seemed to have found mud bricks in his quadrant (for examples, see *IAR 2003–04* 2011, 233; *IAR 2004–05* 2014, 125). Excited, we proceeded to the quadrant. The laborer was a section-cutter, and he pointed out distinct mud-brick alignments that could be seen about 18 inches above the surface of the trench floor. The trench supervisor asked the laborer to take over our work in the quadrant we had abandoned. He then pulled out his knife and scraped the section slowly and delicately. After a few minutes, he asked: "Can you see it?" and marked with his knife the outline of a mud brick on the section. He continued: "This is a mud-brick wall. But look, it has been dug through. The student excavator could not notice this and dug through the whole wall." The trench supervisor was referring to the students of the Institute who had been digging this part of the mound for six weeks and who had now moved to another part of the site. "This has to continue on the floor," he observed, and then knelt down and scraped the floor of the wall. Soon it was possible to see the mud-brick wall he had mentioned. There was a distinct color change. To make it more apparent, he again used his knife and inscribed on the earthen floor the mud-brick wall. "We have to call the AAs for inspection." He directed one laborer to go to the camp and summon a senior officer. After a few minutes, one of the senior AAs working at the site arrived. He hopped into the trench and inspected the area where the mud bricks had been discovered. He also used his knife to re-mark on the surface the lines of the mud brick, and then told the trench supervisor: "Clear up the subject. This needs to be photographed before any further excavation. Please note the measurements carefully in the trench notebook." Before the day ended, the SA, other AAs, technicians, and trench supervisors had all observed the mud-brick wall. In the evening, during the antiquity class, it was announced to the students and all present in the camp that the team had found a mud-brick structure in the "early Harappan part of the mound" (see Thapar 1975; Datta 2001; Smith 2006).[8]

The distributive hierarchy of work at an ASI site is clearly demarcated in the "act of discovery" (Edgeworth 2003, xiii). The laborer is assigned the hard and menial task of digging the trenches—considered the simplest skill to acquire. The act of recognizing and discovering antiquities and structures is the next level of competence—considered to be an essential skill in the micro-practice of the excavation performed by the laborer under the guiding eye of a trench leader. The next level of expertise involves the ability in reading stratigraphical evidence of a quadrant and relating it to the trench floors that have been excavated. Only senior archaeologist officers of the ASI can do this, although, as part of their training, student archaeologists are also encouraged to identify and read stratigraphical sequences. Then comes the ability to create typologies of artifacts discovered—to divide them into classificatory indices; to co-relate the artifacts discovered with the stratigraphical evidence of each trench; and to narrate a chronological narrative of the whole site. This is considered to be the most complex task assigned to the senior-most members of the ASI archaeological team, led by the site director. The ability to excavate, recognize, and discover is the lowest in the hierarchy because, as an AA explained to me:

To recognize is easy, as one studies many books and learns what the various Harappan pottery are, or what a steatite bead, or lapis lazuli looks like. But learning what layers mean on the section, and what is the relation for instance, of layer 32 to a burnt floor, is a matter of practice and experience only. You cannot learn that in school. You need the experience in the trench for it. You have to know how to use your knife and dirty your fingers. There is no other way.

The linear movement from the moment of recognition to the moment of discovery is a development from the laborer who works in the trench to the trench supervisor who is the first to ratify the discovery by recording and labeling it.

This was that "chain of command," as a junior AA stated: "We are just cogs in a well-oiled machine where there is no room for disturbance [*galti ke lie koee jagah nahin hai*]." The discovered object—an antiquity, structure, or a stratigraphic layer—gains epistemological credibility only after a chain of authority ratifies its existence. The laborer unearths the artifact, the trench leader measures and labels it, and consigns it to the realm of *epistemological inscription*, whereas the senior members of the ASI team who study these artifacts finally suture them into a narrative of the site as *epistemological evidence*. "The ASI excavations are so systematic that other governmental agencies are awed by our scientific methodological streamline way of doing things when they come to our sites for visits," proudly pronounced an AA while we were working in a trench in Dholavira. He continued:

Once a bunch of junior army officers came to the site. This was during the Indo-Pak build up in 2001–2002. I took them around the whole site. They were very inquisitive and so it was fun. I gave them a tour of the site for a whole day. And at the end, they were so impressed that they told me: "You guys work like us in the army. Everything is so perfect and organized."

Pottery Yard and Ceramic Classification

The most abundant type of artifacts unearthed in any Harappan excavation are ceramic fragments—potshards of different sizes, texture, color, shapes, and material. For culture-history archaeologists, the ceramics excavated are vital *artifactual* building blocks through which they construct factual knowledge about the site (Shepard 1956; Rye 1981; Rice 2015). In culture-history paradigm, the ceramic evidence unearthed at the site is used to construct the cultural sequence of the site; they are analyzed to relatively date each cultural layer (Arnold 1988; Neff 1992). The proper collection, classification, and documentation of ceramic artifacts were the heart of post-excavation work in a culture-history archaeological site (Gifford 1960; Sabloff and Smith 1969). The sheer magnitude of ceramic artifacts at a Harappan site caused an elaborate sequence of processes for their organization, compilation, and categorization (see Dales, Kenoyer, and Alcock 1986). Although ceramic artifacts found at the site during excavations were equally "antique," they were not considered valuable because they were discovered in abundant quantities. Unlike other artifacts unearthed during an excavation, it was only through painstaking study of the ceramic artifacts that the ASI archaeologists created a chronological history of the site.[9]

Each "dig" in a quadrant produced a vast number of ceramic artifacts. The potshards excavated were shattered fragments, and, in rare cases, complete ceramic vessels were found. In habitational deposits and living spaces in the citadel of Dholavira, dated to the Mature Harappan period, around 100 to 150 ceramic fragments of various types and shapes would be discovered in each quadrant, in every dig. In Bhirrana, where the excavation was being conducted in habitational deposits categorized as Early Harappan, each dig would generate less than 100 ceramic fragments. In both cases, each dig would be around 6 inches deep. In a site like Hansi where the excavators were digging through early medieval and historical layers in quadrants of similar sizes, each dig would be about a foot deep, and the ceramic count would be between 200 and 300. The ceramic count depended on two factors—the type of cultural deposit and the depth of the dig. In Dholavira, where between two and three dozen quadrants were excavated every season, the total number of pottery fragments unearthed would be more than 100,000. To manage, sort, classify, categorize, document, and then study them gave rise to the conceptual and epistemological architecture of the pottery yard.

The pottery yard was the two-dimensional simulacrum of the three-dimensional excavation site. Here, all the ceramic material culture and animal bones were stored, and they were categorized according to the quadrants and layers from which they had been unearthed. Each square was neatly made up of lined stone pieces and brickbats, daubed with white lime to indicate their official legitimacy. These lime-smeared pieces of stone architecture on the landscape consisted of hundreds of 1-meter-by-1-meter squares laid out in a grid. Each trench was represented by four squares corresponding to the four quadrants of the trench. Similar to the Wheelerian balk, groups of four squares, representing trenches, were separated by a balk-pathway. The squares were tagged with an iron peg stating both the trench and the quadrant number. In each square of the grid there were numerous heaps of ceramic fragments, representing one layer of the quadrant (Figure 7.2). Tucked under the heap would be a label, specifying the quadrant number, the layer number with depth, and the name of the trench supervisor.[10]

Figure 7.2 Examples of pottery yards: *clockwise, from top left*—Dholavira yard with exposed pottery; Dholavira yard with pottery in bags from excavations from earlier seasons, 2004; Bhirrana and Hansi pottery yards, 2005

Source: Photographs by the author.

An AA would be given the charge of the pottery yard with two or three technical staff members manning the laborers in the yard. Every evening, after the excavation ended, each trench supervisor came to the pottery yard accompanied by laborers carrying ceramic and faunal remains found on that day. They deposited the contents of these baskets into the square representing the quadrant. Subsequently, each ceramic fragment would be cleaned and labeled before sorting and classification. Cleaning the ceramic fragments and then labeling them was continuous, as the flow of potshards never stopped. In one corner of the pottery yard, a group of women of varying ages, in their colorful printed attire covering their whole bodies and their heads, with their faces barely visible, would squat together and scrub ceramic fragments with water and toothbrushes. An AA told me that the women had been trained to scrub the potshards gently so that pattern or design on its surface would not get erased. Once dried, one of the women would take the potshards batch by batch and cart them to the pottery shed. Here, young men, sitting cross-legged, would label each ceramic fragment. In black or white indelible ink they would write on the inner surface of each fragment the abbreviated name of the site, the trench number, the quadrant number, and the year of the excavation season (Figure 7.3).

Figure 7.3 Marked ceramic fragments from Bhirrana, 2005

Source: Photographs by the author.

The laborers considered work in the pottery yard to be relaxed (*aaram ka kaam*) as it involved little labor (*halka kaam*), unlike other tasks at the excavation site. Writing and labeling potshards was awarded to the educated laborers at the site, as it involved a "minimum proficiency in English" to read the labels, and then copy the information onto the ceramic fragment. Most of these were young boys who had studied up to eighth grade. The AA who was in charge of the pottery yard in Bhirrana was not a ceramic specialist but was "interested in pottery." Describing the work he did at the pottery yard, he explained:

> Specialists are in a short supply at the ASI. You have to be *jack of all trades, master of none* [English phrase used] in the ASI. An archaeologist in the ASI has to be everything. First and foremost, he is a bureaucrat. Then he is an archaeologist. And as an archaeologist, he has to learn to be a pottery specialist, bone specialist, excavation specialist, everything. To tell you the truth, they don't encourage specialization in the ASI.[11]

There were few specialists in the ASI. There were neither any archaeozoologists, archaeobotanists, or archaeometallurgists,[12] nor were there any lithic or ceramic specialists—often the site director invited experts from various university departments in India to do this kind of specialized work.[13] They were given access to the artifacts and then later requested to contribute in the final excavation report when it was written. Since such university specialists were in short supply, PhD students did the work requiring such specialization pertaining to ceramic and faunal remains at the site (Figure 7.4).[14]

At Baror, I observed one such specialist archaeologist who had recently completely his PhD and was working on the ceramic assemblage of the site. He was not an employee of the ASI, but had been deputed by the site director to work and study the pottery at the site, since his PhD focused on Harappan ceramics. We were sitting close to the corner of the pottery yard, on colorful molded plastic chairs, shaded by a rainbow-colored field umbrella that was just big enough to provide shade to the two of us. Explaining his status at the site, he confided:

Figure 7.4 Examples of Harappan ceramic fragments found during my ethnography at Dholavira, 2004; *clockwise, from top left*: Black and Red ware; Red ware; Perforated ware; Reserve Slip ware

Source: Photographs by the author.

I am just a glorified daily wager. They pay me a fixed amount, along with a tent to stay in. There is no value for my PhD here. They wanted someone to take care of the pottery. I did not have a job and I wanted excavation experience, so I am here.

On the adjacent white plastic molded table was a lazy cluster of pottery fragments, which two standing laborers were carefully counting. A third laborer was going back and forth between the pottery yard and the table, ferrying pottery fragments. The ceramic specialist was sitting at the table with a sheet titled "Frequency Chart of the Pottery." This was a handwritten chart with 32 columns divided into 4 clusters. The first cluster contained columns for trench number, quadrant number, layer number, and depth. The second described the type of fragment: rim, belly, and base. The third cluster had columns for the type of pottery: bi-chrome, rusticated, deluxe, incised, buff ware, gray ware, red ware, Hakra ware, perforated, cream slip ware, chocolate slip ware, and black and red ware. The fourth cluster of columns was related to the shape: *lota*, vase, basin, bowl, disc, storage jar, trough, *handi*, miniature, goblet, flowerpot, and tumbler.

The laborers counted the number of pottery fragments in each heap—representing a layer in a particular quadrant. The ceramic specialist noted the number of fragments and their traits and characteristics in the chart he had spread on the table. After the notation of the entire set of ceramic fragments was completed, only the "diagnostic" pottery was collected and separated from the rest, which were eventually discarded. The fragments retained were set aside because of their distinct shape, size, or design; most of the discarded fragments were considered "too small [*bahut chota*], too useless [*bahut bekar*] for any analysis." During my ethnography, I observed that the ASI's engagement with a huge volume of archaeological evidence was driven by a bureaucratic rationality, rather than a epistemological logic—instrumentally, functionally, and pragmatically. The vast amounts of ceramic artifacts being unearthed at the excavation site were "both a curse and boon to the process of the archaeological excavation," wearily noted an AA in Dholavira. "These sites produce so many potshards it becomes a management problem. All we require for the site report is some diagnostic pottery. The rest end up in the Purana Qila godown."

The Purana Qila was a famed sixteenth-century medieval fort in Delhi. The Central Antiquity Collection (CAC) of the ASI was within its ramparts. The CAC was the central storage location of the explored and excavated pottery and other antiquities of the ASI.[15] The CAC was created in the 1910s to house the antiquities discovered by Sir Aurel Stein during his Central Asian Expeditions.[16] In ASI lore, the Purana Qila was, as an AA at Dholavira expressively noted, "the final resting place for ASI artifacts." He further elaborated, "Once an artifact ends up in Purana Qila, it requires an enormous amount of paperwork even for senior ASI archaeologists to get it for examination. Purana Qila is the death bed of the ASI artifact."[17] This emotion was also echoed by the CAG report, which bemoaned: "The storage condition of antiquities kept at CAC, Purana Qila and Safdarjung Tomb were found deplorable.... The artifacts of CAC were scattered and spread over four different locations. In the absence of appropriate documentation, it was not possible to ascertain the location of specific artifacts" (CAG 2013, 133). Pointing to the dismal state of antiquity preservation with regard to Dholavira, the CAG report also observed:

> In some cases, when excavators were relocated, they had been allowed to carry these antiquities from one place to another e.g. Excavation work at site of Dholavira, Vadodara Circle and Sirpur, Raipur Circle, the excavated material was not handed over even after a lapse of upto 12 years. In such a situation damage and loss of antiquities lying with the excavators without proper insurance and security, could not be ruled out. (CAG 2013, 116)

The report damningly continued:

> We noticed that as with protected monuments, the ASI was not aware of the total number of antiquities in its possession as no database or inventory of antiquities had been prepared by the ASI. Branch wise lists were also not available with the antiquity Branch at the ASI HQ. In the absence of any centralized information, there was a high risk of loss of antiquities. (CAG 2013, 142)

I also distressingly observed that the trajectory of ceramics from the quadrant and trenches in an ASI excavation site to rusted tin trunks in the Purana Qila involved numerous intermediary stages that were devastating for archaeological practice.

It was one hot afternoon in Dholavira when I noticed that behind the mud hut of the director was a 5-meter-by-5-meter trench in which a massive amount of ceramic fragments had been dumped in white nylon gunny bags. Upon inquiry, the AA who was accompanying me explained, "This is useless [*bekar*] pottery, we don't need it. At the end of every season, we throw away all the potshards that are of no use to us [*koi kaam ki nahi hai*]." Upon further prodding, the AA explained:

> These are pottery pieces which serve no function [*koi matlab nahi hai*]. You know well how much of pottery is excavated in a season. It is impossible to keep all. In the pottery yard, the important fragments are sorted out and the rest are thrown here [*yahaan phenk dete hai*].

This was called the "pottery-dump." This was a regular feature at ASI excavation sites—ceramic fragments that were deemed to lack *artifactual* status were discarded here. In the pottery yard, during the sorting and the classification process, diagnostic potshards were separated and categorized within the legal definition of "antiquity." These were those ceramic fragments which either belonged to a vessel that could be reconstructed in the pottery shed, or were fragments with distinctive fabric, shape, artwork, and design repertoire on them—which had "some uniqueness." The rest of the ceramic artifacts that were not believed to be diagnostic by the archaeologists were discarded in the pottery dump.

The notion of diagnostic ceramic was the theoretical bulwark of the epistemological structure of culture-history archaeology. Diagnostic ceramic consisted of those ceramic fragments or complete vessels that defined the cultural period of the layer. The material culture sequence of the site was drawn by their typological characteristic.[18] Stratigraphical layers of every quadrant were culturally delineated by the typological classification of these "diagnostic pottery." In ASI archaeology, only a few of these diagnostic ceramic fragments had "unique value" attached to them and even fewer reached the table of the artist of the pottery yard for representational purpose. The unique value of the potshard was defined thus, as an ASI artist in Dholavira explained to me: "We only select those pieces of pottery which can give us a clear idea of the unusual make, distinct shape of the period, those that have good designs on them or those that have some sort of inscription on them." Therefore, diagnostic ceramic fragments were those that fulfilled the definition of "antiquity" and those that were considered valuable. The rest were discarded and reburied in the pottery dump. An AA at Dholavira dejectedly confided: "This is the burial ground of Dholavira pottery. Hundreds of years later when archaeologists again dig Dholavira they will excavate this pottery dump. They will wonder what kind of unscientific archaeologists we were. They will think we were bad archaeologists [*bakwas archaeologist*]."

Notes

1. Before I began my ethnography in India, I had an opportunity to observe and participate in two international archaeological projects. In 2000, I worked at the site of Monte Polizzo, a native Sicilian site from the age of Greek colonization (c. 900–400 BCE), and at the Andean site of Chavín de Huantar in Peru (c. 1200–500 BCE). Excavation at Monte Polizzo was a multinational excavation with archaeologists from Stanford University, Cambridge University, Northern Illinois University, University of Oslo, University of Naples, and Göteborg University. Launched in 1998 as a Sicilian-Scandinavian Archaeological Project, led by Sebastiano Tusa and Kristian Kristiansen,

the excavation continued until 2006 under the leadership of Ian Morris (Morris et al. 2003). Excavation at Chavín de Huantar was led by John Rick of Stanford University with the goal of mapping the site using theodolite surveying technology to construct a three-dimensional computer model of the monumental ritual site (Rick 2008).

2. According to R. S. Bisht, during the course of excavation at Dholavira, 225 seals and 60 sealings were recovered. These were chiefly found in the site's Stage IV (c. 3800–3200 BCE) and Stage V (c. 3200–2600 BCE). Bisht notes that a "phenomenal increase in seals, bearing iconography and inscriptions, and usually executed deftfully showing all such features, which mark the Harappan sigillography everywhere else in the mature phase at a number of contemporary sites" (Bisht 2015, 233). For a recent and exhaustive account containing a summary of the history of scholarships on the Harappan seals, debates, controversies regarding interpretation, and their importance in the economy of the civilization, see Green (2015).

3. In a rebuttal to David Bloor who had critiqued his book *Toward a History of Epistemic Things Synthesizing Proteins in the Test Tube*, Rheinberger provides an eloquent description of epistemic objects, which I have found very valuable in my work:

> My goal was to provide an object-centered, materially founded account of knowledge production. According to my position, scientific or epistemic objects are clearly material things. They function as scientific or epistemic objects by virtue of their opacity, their surplus, their material transcendence, if you like, which is what arouses interest in them and keeps them alive as targets of research.... They are epistemic by virtue of their preliminarity, of what we do not yet know about them, not by virtue of what we already know about them. They are epistemic because it has not yet been determined whether they will become obsolete as targets of research, or whether they will become transformed into stable, technical objects that may define the boundary conditions of further epistemic objects. (Rheinberger 2005, 406–07)

4. Even in heavily funded European archaeological projects (like Monte Polizzo), I observed that the first actors to discover and engage with an archaeological artifact were untrained undergraduate students from the universities mentioned earlier or the local laborers that constituted the bulk of the workforce at the site. For a fascinating ethnography of the site of Mount Polizzo, Sicily, that focuses on the "life" of a potshard and its journey from the trenches to the laboratory, see Holtorf (2002). Also see my short essay film, *Rummaging for the Past: Excavating Sicily, Digging Bombay* (Avikunthak 2001), shot at Mount

Polizzo that juxtaposes the politics of material culture archaeology and media archaeology.

5. I am employing the concept of "tacit" from Michael Polanyi's idea of tacit knowledge which can be defined as personal knowledge entrenched in a singular experience and encompasses abstracts influences, like personal beliefs, perspective, and the value system. This form of knowledge is difficult to enunciate in linguistic formulations and contains subjective perceptions, intuitions, and hunches. Polanyi states: "Tacit knowing is shown to account (1) for a valid knowledge of a problem, (2) for the scientist's capacity to pursue it, guided by his sense of approaching his solutions, and (3) for a valid anticipation of the yet indeterminate implications of the discovery arrived at in the end" (Polanyi and Sen 2009, 24). Amartya Sen in a lucid introduction to Michael Polyani's book explains: "Polanyi argues that if tacit knowledge is a central part of knowledge in general, then we can both (1) know what to look for, and (2) have some idea about what else we may want to know" (Polanyi and Sen 2009, xi).

6. See Patel (1997) and Meadow and Patel (2002), and a section of the Dholavira report with Patel's analysis of faunal remains at Dholavira (Bisht 2015, 838–57).

7. Hakra Ware culture is a material culture contemporaneous with the early Harappan Ravi phase culture (3300–2800 BCE).

8. "Early Harappan" as a temporal phase in Harappan archaeology is not standardized, but in ASI trenches it was employed as a normative term. It has been contested by archaeologists because of its evolutionary teleology that fails to take into account regional differences or the material diversity within the sprawling Harappan landscape (Possehl 1999).

9. For instance, see Joshi (1990, 60–251) (Surkotada); Nath (2015, 168–204) (Rakhigarhi); Bisht (2015, 170–222) (Dholavira); *IAR 2003–04* (2011, 47–54), *IAR 2004–05* (2014, 44–47) (Bhirrana).

10. See Wheeler, Ghosh, and Deva (1946, Plate XIB) for a photograph of a pottery yard in Arikamedu; Lal (1954, Plate I) for a photograph of a pottery yard in the Hastinapur excavation.

11. The ceramic assemblage excavated in Bhirrana were classified as:

> mud appliqué ware, Grey ware, Red ware, Red ware with black slip, Red ware (incised), painted Red ware, Painted Red ware (slipped), Red ware with buff slip, Deep Red ware, Red ware/buff painting (combed pattern), Red ware (combed pattern), Buff-slipped Red ware, Chocolate-slipped ware, Bichrome ware, deep incised ware and Tan slipped ware. (Krishnan et al. 2012, 18)

12. For instance, during the high-profile excavations at Ayodhya in 2003, the High Court took note of the lack of specialization in the ASI and ordered it to locate external specialists for analysis of faunal and botanical remains. ASI archaeologists wrote furious requests to a number of institutions throughout the country for analysis of the material it did not have expertise in. Some of these were institutes that the ASI regularly relied upon for analytical assistance—National Geophysical Institute, Hyderabad; Physical Research Laboratory, Ahmedabad; Birbal Sahni Institute of Palaeobotany, Lucknow; Zoological Survey of India; Geological Survey of India; and Deccan College (AACD, File No. 29/1/1995/EE-Part IV (F); AACD, File No. 29/1/1995-EE/Part-VII).

13. For the SHP, a tentative list of scholars and scientists proposed to collaborate. It included:

> i. Palaeobotany—Dr. K.S. Saraswat, BSIP, Lucknow; Dr. M.D. Kajale, Deccan College, Pune; ii. Anthropology—Dr. S.R. Walimbe, Deccan College, Pune, Prof. D.K. Bhattarcharya, (retd.) Delhi University; iii. Archaeozoology—Dr. P.K. Thomas, Dr. Joglekar Deccan College, Pune; iv. Archaeometallurgy—Prof. R. Balasubramaniam, IIT, Kanpur, Dr. Sharada Srinivasan, Indian Institute of Science, Bangalore; v. Palaeontology—Prof. G.L. Badam, (retd.) Deccan College, Pune; vi. Geoarchaeology—Prof. V.N. Mishra, Prof. Rajaguru, (retd.) Deccan College, Pune; Dr. D.P. Agrawal, (retd.) PRL, Ahmedabad; vii. Geology—Nominees from GSI; viii. Soil Analysis—Dr. Y.S. Farswan, JNU; ix. Palaeoclimate—Dept. of Metereology, GOI; x. Ethnology—Anthropological Survey of India; xi. Digital Imaging of excavated remains—IIT or other IT agency; GIS—National Remote Sensing Agency, GOI. (AACD, F. No. 9/6/2003-EE)

14. These were student interns who had just finished their PhDs. They were paid a fixed salary and hired on a contractual basis, and in the site hierarchy were considered on a par with the Institute ex-students. The use of such specialists who were recent PhD students was far more common than inviting university professors as specialists, and it reflected not only the desperation of the students working but also the intellectually impoverished state of the ASI.

15. The CAC, in the 2007 document "National Mission on Monuments and Antiquities", is officially described as:

> The Central Antiquity Collection of the Archaeological Survey of India is supposed to be the largest repository of antiquities in the country. It has over 3 Lac antiquities in its collection. The nature of collection include antiquities from excavations and explorations carried out from

time to time, confiscated and seized antiquities, purchased and donated antiquities etc. The composition of these collections includes objects of stone, terracotta, glass, ivory, bone, metal and paintings etc. The antiquities from foreign origin are also housed here. (CAG 2013, 14)

16. The CAG report notes:

> The collection of Aurel Stein is perhaps the biggest collection of Central Asian art including Chinese, Tibetan and Tangut manuscripts, paintings, textile fragments, ceramic, Buddhist art objects, Prakrit wooden tablets, thousands of other art objects and documents. Presently this collection was located at the National Museum, New Delhi, Indian Museum, Kolkata and Srinagar Museum in India. A part of this collection consisting of 700 objects was loaned to V&A Museum, UK by the ASI between 1923 and 1933. As per records, these antiquities were still "owned by Archaeological Survey of India" and were on loan. However, we did not find evidence of any efforts by the ASI to retrieve them. (CAG 2013, 142)

17. Archaeological artifacts from ASI excavations were also stored in Ghiyasuddin Tuglaq's Tomb, Humayun's Tomb, and Safdarjung Tomb in New Delhi.

18. On the history and theory of ceramic diagnostic and analysis, see Bishop, Rands, and Holley (1982); Sinopoli (1991); and Stoltman (2001).

8 Performance of Archaeological Representations

It was a big day for the archaeologists at Dholavira. The chief minister of Gujarat and a national level politician were going to visit the site. "The nearest we have ever got to such a *darshan* (divine glimpse) of a politician was when Rajiv Gandhi visited us. He came to Rapar during an election campaign many years ago," remarked a senior laborer. We were in the site director's mud hut in Dholavira—students, assistant archaeologists (AAs), technical staff, the director, along with the superintending archaeologist (SA) of the Vadodara Circle and his staff, sitting on red, yellow, and white molded plastic chairs, sipping endless cups of sweet tea and munching on Parle biscuits. We had been waiting since early morning. It was noon now and there was still no sign of the dignitaries. It was getting hot and the desert sun was blazing on a winter December day. The SA of the Vadodara Circle, drying the perspiration over his forehead with a white handkerchief, complained in muted annoyance: "These VVIPs are never on time. There is no difference between a film star and these politicians. They are always late." Soon a flurry of anecdotes about different VIP visits was flying back and forth across the plastic table. Stories of conceited petty politicians, petulant district magistrates, nondescript members of the Legislative Assembly (MLAs), imperious former members of Parliament (MPs), arrogant district police commissioners, complacent secretaries of the state, their haughty wives, frivolous daughters, and brash relatives were recounted with a familiar candor, amusement, and scorn. "Everyone wants to see an archaeological excavation. They think it is a circus or a zoo. Too much of Discovery Channel and National Geographic Channel has made them think they will see gold jewelry and mummies here," remarked a senior AA. "For their *touristy* fun we have to sweat," he complained. "It is not just a waste of our time. It is also a sheer waste of money and energy of the nation." No one raised an eyebrow at this outburst; we were all tired from waiting for the VVIPs.

It was after almost another hour of "time-pass" (Craig 2010) that we heard the sound we were all waiting for—the distant hum of army helicopters—the chief minister and his entourage had arrived. The SA of Vadodara Circle, the Dholavira site director, the AAs perspiring in their formal attire—ties, blazers, and trousers—raced toward the helipad next to the site. During the 2001

India–Pakistan war build-up, the army had leveled a piece of agricultural land adjacent to the site and constructed a helipad. It was rarely used; I was informed during my initial exploration of the site: "Nowadays it is only used when a minister or any other VVIPs comes to visit the site." The disused helipad was now trimmed of its overgrown grass and a fresh coat of white lime was painted over the rugged desert landscape for the VVIP visit.

As soon as the helicopters landed, the chief minister of Gujarat, Narendra Modi, jumped out—then a well-built, stout man in his early fifties, with a round face and a close-trimmed salt and pepper beard. He sported a short-sleeved pink-and-white checkered *kurta* and donned Bulgari glasses.[1] Along with him emerged Pramod Mahajan—a short-statured man with a dark moustache, dressed in white *kurta-pajama*. He was the high-profile BJP Rajya Sabha MP, a former minister of telecommunication, parliamentary affairs minister, and the-then general secretary of the BJP, considered by many to be the most influential power broker in the government.[2] Along with them also emerged their family members and some state officials, who were in turn followed by a group of the famed Black Cat commandos—security men dressed in their ubiquitous grey safari suits and dark Ray-Ban sunglasses, and armed with automatic guns. From a distance, I observed the SA of the Vadodara Circle, the site director, the headman of Dholavira—one by one, they garlanded the two leaders who seemed to be in an unusual haste, in the midst of a minor sandstorm raised by the still-rotating fans of the two dusty helicopters. With this began "*the mother of all site-tour* [English phrase used]"—as an AA standing next to me mockingly whispered in my ears.

The primary purpose of Modi and Mahajan's visit was not to see the archaeological heritage, but to inaugurate a new neighborhood of Dholavira christened Pandit Deendayal Nagar.[3] This was a new village that had been constructed with the MP relief fund of Pramod Mahajan after the Bhuj earthquake of 2001, when most of the villages in Kutch district had been flattened.[4] Pramod Mahajan had adopted Dholavira because of its archaeological visibility. His wish was, as he announced during a political reception held in the village: "To do something for such a great and ancient village of the nation." The district government had erected a large, colorful *shamiyana* (ceremonial tent) for the reception at the edge of the village. The first part of their visit comprised presiding over the reception, attended by more than 3,000 people from Dholavira and neighboring villages, who came in tractors and buses a day earlier. During the reception they gave the keys to the new owners, and Modi inaugurated Pandit Deendayal Nagar. A long-drawn political meeting followed the reception. It began with a nationalist song, sung by young schoolgirls who had come from the district headquarters, Bhuj. They were dressed in blue and white school uniforms with pigtails tied with red ribbons, and the song was set to the tune of a popular Bollywood song. This was followed by speeches about Gujarat's pride (*gaurav*) and the greatness (*mahaantha*) of the Saraswati civilization, given by a host of local politicians and culminating in an emotionally charged speech by Narendra Modi. He emphasized his government's responsibility of protecting and projecting the importance of Dholavira's valuable treasure (*mulyavan khazana*). It was after this formal ceremony of the state—coupled with the demonstration of political exuberance at the fringes of the country—had concluded that the site visit began.

The VVIP entourage was first taken to the monumental Eastern Reservoir of Dholavira where the site director explained the significance of the site to a gathering of about a hundred people—the VVIPs, their relatives, aides, and assistants, their Black Cat security personnel, the senior district level officials, such as the district magistrate, the district collector, the director general of police, and the block development officer, members of the Dholavira elite, and village officials from nearby villages. The crowd was boisterous. Amidst the jostling, uproar, and din, the site director narrated the significance of the site in non-technical terms, spoken mainly in Hindi with a sprinkling of English words. Often, he had to yell at the top of his voice. Perspiring, he was at once official, stern, and erudite but also sometimes incoherent. Occasionally, an AA would jump in to add details to the descriptive account of the site. The two leaders distractedly listened to the narratives, frequently talking with each other as the ASI archaeologists illuminated the importance of the site. An AA later confessed they were unhappy with the way they had conducted the site tour: "It was lackadaisically done. There is so much of drama in a site like Dholavira. Nothing came out. It is only on the site tour that these VVIPs are under your command—one should exploit the potentiality."

The site visit lasted close to an hour during which the entourage was shown the key architectural features of the site—the monumental fortification, rock-cut reservoir, houses on the citadel, and the main street of the Middle Town. They then took the VVIPs to the camp site where the "antiquities" discovered at the site had been displayed on a molded plastic table covered with a white cloth. Metal and stone artifacts tucked in cotton wads and sealed in plastic containers were neatly arranged here. The site director described the archaeological value of each object and explained its functions. Only the VVIPs could pick up and experience the tactility of the material objects. The important members of the VVIP entourage were taken to the director's mud hut, served tea and biscuits in "special" porcelain cups and plates, as the site's photographic album was circulated among the visitors. The album consisted of photographs of the site in a chronological order. The wall of the mud hut was transformed into a museum where large photographic blowups of the site were displayed in laminated frames. The site visit ended with a group photograph of the ASI staff with the two VVIPS.

The "site visit" or the "site tour" was a pervasive display of postcolonial archaeology, regularly enacted at the ASI site. It was a ritual of authoritative performance through which archaeologists as bureaucrats asserted their knowledge—for statist actors as a privilege; for laity as a burden. There was a consistent stream of local visitors and curious onlookers at an archaeological excavation site. The ASI staff at the site considered most to be minor irritants. I observed that the site tour for lay people visiting the site was not conducted with either generosity or sincerity. In the eyes of the ASI, the local community was subsumed under the categories of the "illiterate native" (*dehati*) or a "minor *touristy* irritant." More often than not, I observed that the ASI archaeologists would not take the initiative in showing the site to local community members who would occasionally visit the site (Figure 8.1), but would go "beyond the call of their duty" to please the statist actors who visited the site.

The term "site visit" was especially reserved for the occasional visit of a local state official or a politician; or in the case of Dholavira, also senior army officers. It was through these events that the ASI archaeologists would showcase the excavation site, both as a scientific enterprise and as a feat of ASI bureaucratic efficacy. The statist officials were vital to the ASI archaeologists because, in their eyes, these officials were of their "class" and their bureaucratic peers. An AA in Dholavira once mentioned:

> It is very important to do a good site visit for army officers because they have to know that by digging the ground we are also serving the nation as much as they are [*hum bhi desh ki seva main lage hue hai*]. It is like an assistant archaeologist of the Archaeological Survey of India talking to a captain of the Artillery Regiment of the Indian Army on equal terms.

He said this soon after a site visit that he had conducted for a group of young army artillery captains and their subordinates, on their way to the India–Pakistan border. I had followed the energetic AA, as he diligently spent nearly half a day with the army officers giving them the most detailed site tour that I had observed during my entire ethnography. The AA also commented in despair about the pittance of a salary he got as an AA: "Although we both are of the same rank, and from a similar school and college, I dare not tell him my salary. He will then know my true status [*asli auqat*]." The site tour was not just a performance of epistemology but also played an important role in reinvigorating the self-esteem of archaeologists as bureaucrats in the service of the nation.

Figure 8.1 Local schoolchildren peering into an archaeological trench at the site of Hansi, 2005

Source: Photograph by the author.

Subject Preparation

One afternoon, a few days before the aforementioned VVIP site visit, along with the site director, I reached a "rich" habitation trench on the citadel. Numerous artifacts were being discovered at a rather consistent frequency in this trench. A large red slipware ceramic vessel had been freshly unearthed. The excavation had stopped and the trench leader, together with the laborers, was cleaning the trench for photography. She had scooped all the soil from the vessel and had kept it in a labeled plastic container. When we arrived at the trench for inspection, the site director noticed that this ceramic vessel was empty. He was irritated, and rebuked the female trench leader:

> This is not a scientific way of digging or exposing antiquity. You should only remove half the earth from the vessel for analysis and leave the rest of the earth in vessel. Dig in such a way that a vertical section is exposed inside the vessel. That is the scientific way of exposing.

However, since the trench leader had scooped out all the soil from the inside the vessel and kept it for analysis, the site director instructed her to now get "similar looking earth" (*vaiasi hi mitti*) from elsewhere and put it in "such a way" (*usihi tarah*) inside the vessel that a vertical section would be visible. "It is essential they learn the importance of presentation," he remarked later, as we continued our inspection of the trenches. As we walked down the steps of the fortification and trotted toward the Middle Town of Dholavira, he gravely said:

> Students should learn not only to dig scientifically, but also learn that archaeological excavation has to be done aesthetically [*sundar*]. Excavation is not just about digging for antiquities and structures. Presentation is also essential. Along with the chief minister, there will be other archaeologists coming from the Vadodara circle, and even the director general might come. And if they see that the subject has been dug incorrectly, they will laugh at us. We have to do a little bit of performance [*thoda bahut to dihkawa karna padata hai*].

Just before the impending visit of the VVIPs, it was decided by the director of Dholavira, based on consultation with the other archaeologists at the site, that the excavation work should cease. The trench leaders were instructed that "all time and energy should be devoted to subject preparation." The motivation behind this instruction was to "groom" (*sajna-savarna*) the excavation site for the visit of the VVIPs. For the next four days, excavation work ceased and the laborers, trench leaders, and archaeologist officers got involved in the subject preparation of the site. Two hundred and fifty laborers at the site got involved in cleaning the trenches; clearing debris, repairing broken balk walls, making flat, sharp, and neat section walls, and removing dirt. The goal of this effort was to erase the disorderliness of the excavation process and to transform the trench into a "newly married bride" (*nayi-naveli dulhan*). Such fixation on presentation was noticeable not only when VVIPS came to the site, but was in fact a regular feature at the site. "Subject preparation" was a standardized, aesthetically driven practice of ASI archaeological excavation. Trench, stratigraphic section, structure, or artifact, after its excavation and discovery, underwent a process of subject preparation—cleaning, labeling, and preparation for presentation, display, drawing, or photography.

Subject preparation was the first act that marked the end of the excavation and the beginning of documentation. It was an indispensable representation practice in ASI archaeology through which the material culture discovered was transformed into evidence—neat, legible, and presentable. This was the theory of practice that transformed an excavated object, quadrant, or trench into an evidential artifact by erasing the disarray and the disorder of the archaeological process. It was to give "finishing touches" to the trench, as an AA explained— an obsessive practice of cleaning the trench floor, the excavated structures, the exposed artifacts, and the section wall; of cutting and re-cutting the section wall with an emphasis on keeping the angle between the floor of the trench and the section wall at 90 degrees. The aesthetics of legibility drove the logic of subject preparation—the goal was to display archaeology as a "neat and clean" scientific enterprise, done in a "beautiful and proper way" (*sunder aur sahi*). A photographer at Baror, on being questioned about the essentiality of subject preparation, gave a gendered analogy: "In fashion photography, a woman has to have her complete make-up done before she can be shot. In the same way, in archaeological photography, the subject has to be prepared, cleaned up, and given a 'make-up' before the photograph can be taken." The feminization of the excavation site was not an uncommon trope among my informants. For them the site represented a female form that had to be "uncovered," "exposed," "laid bare," "revealed," "opened," and finally "displayed" for exhibition. In such a gendered rhetorical imagination, the aesthetic fetishizing of the excavation site was customary, since the overwhelming majority of ASI archaeologists, staff members, and technicians were male. During my ethnography, I met only two women archaeologists—an AA and an SA—whereas in sites such as Dholavira there were more female laborers than male laborers; however, none of the female laborers were given positions of responsibility.

Subject preparation was a performative representational practice whose necessity had been underscored by Wheeler and followed by the ASI archaeologists as a maxim:

> No amount of mechanical skill is a substitute for the careful preparation of the subject. Clean, sharp angles between the divergent planes of a section, carefully and emphatically cut with trowel, knife, or edging-tool, are essential if the section is to tell its story with the minimum confusion. Furthermore, a spotlessly clean trench is no mere "eye-wash," if only because it gives the spectator a justifiable trust in the orderliness and accuracy of the work. Even the top edges of a trench should be neatly trimmed and the grass cut and swept along them; a stray blade of grass in the foreground of the picture may be overlooked by the eye but may loom embarrassingly in the lens. (Wheeler 1954, 200)

Wheeler emphasized the spectatorial effect of the excavation site and the performative impact of the archaeological trench as a scientific representation zone. This performance of representation was affected through the cosmetic creation of a "spotlessly clean trench." For Wheeler, this was indispensable for the creation of a non-ambivalent narrative of the trench, which had no trace of epistemological clutter. Here, a causality-based link is pursued between the tidy physicality of the trench and the orderly archaeological narrative that the trench corresponds to. For the ASI, the emphasis was on negating the disjuncture, disturbances, and the disorderliness associated with the archaeological project and to assemble its subject within a disciplined matrix. This performative and spectatorial subtext was essential not only for the process of documentation but also for displaying the archaeological site as a scientific site (Figure 8.2).

Figure 8.2 "Subject preparation" at the edge of the Lower Town in Dholavira, 2004

Source: Photograph by the author.

Photography and the Epistemic Marker

"Excavation is all about photography. We dig because we can shoot it. In archaeology, everything is destroyed; all that is left are the photographs. The only real proof that remains of an excavation is the photographs. So ours is a great responsibility," earnestly explained a senior photographer at the site of Bhirrana. He was a placid, soft-spoken man in his mid-fifties, working as a photographer for the ASI for more than 25 years. We were sitting atop the photography tower—a wood and iron contraption, 5 meters tall. It stood at the southwest corner of the excavation site, used for taking pictures from a height. Each ASI excavation site had a photography tower. It was considered to be an essential piece of equipment in any ASI archaeological excavation. The tower was used to get "bird's eye perspective" of the excavation trench—a standard visual trope, customarily employed in archaeological photography since the nineteenth century (Reeves 1936).

> I did a year-long diploma in photography. But it was my father who taught me everything—from preparing a subject in the trench to developing and printing negatives in the darkroom. The diploma was just to get the job in the ASI, because the SA told my father that some degree in photography was needed.

The photographer disclosed the above as we attempted to balance ourselves between two tripods on which a medium format Mamiya camera and a 35 mm Nikon SLR camera were positioned respectively, to take pictures of the trenches below.

There were four mature Harappan trenches that were opened up to expose a part of the fortification wall of the habitation. The Wheelerian balks had been removed and an area of 20 by 20 meters had been carefully dressed for photography. "It will take one full day; only in the evening, when the harsh sunlight has gone, and the features of the trench are clearly visible [*saaf dikhe*] that we will take the photograph," the AA mentioned to me early in the morning of a day I spent with the photography crew. "The Nagpur Excavation Branch is not only the oldest but also the best Excavation Branch," he noted with a subdued pride. "You have to see how the senior photographer *saheb* [sir] takes pictures. This is the perfect way to do archaeological photography. This is the best it gets in the ASI," he announced decisively. The importance of photography as a means of *manufacturing* evidence about archaeological material culture was as old as the technology (Shanks 1997; Bohrer 2011). The ubiquity of its usage was so widespread that in 1904, Flinders Petrie devotes an entire chapter on photographic technique in his textbook on archaeological method. As early as the 1870s, the ASI employed photographers to make images of the monumental architectural heritage of India for documentary purposes (Guha 2002, 97), but by the early twentieth century, with the excavation at Harappan sites, photography became an authoritative means of projecting the scientific impetus of ASI archaeology (Chadha 2002).

Since morning, I had been trailing the senior photographer and a group of laborers carrying the photography equipment. Along with them was the photographer's assistant. He was a young gruff looking short man in jeans and sneakers. "He is a fourth-class office peon, but has always assisted me," explained the senior photographer. He lamented,

> He is better than most photographers in the ASI. He does not have a degree or formal training, so he cannot become an ASI photographer. But you tell me, does one need a degree to do photography? It is all about experience. But how will the government understand that? They only know how to follow rules.

Early in the morning, the senior AA relieved laborers working in four quadrants in the northern part of the excavation site. He informed the trench team leaders: "Today we have to prepare the subject. So, there will not be any digging. You and your mates will only take orders from the Photographer *saheb*." And soon, around 40 laborers, both men and women, picked up the tools—brushes of different types, scrapers, and trowels. They slowly followed the photographer and his assistant toward the trench that had to be prepared. By midday, most of the site was cleaned. Every excavated structure in the trench looked "spotless" (*chaka-chak*). During this process, the workers first used large brushes to clean the area. After lunch, it was "time for the small brushes, to make the subject spic and span [*saaf-sutra*]." Now the laborers used fine brushes and cleaned up dirt from the crevices of small objects and structures in the trenches. Meanwhile, "section-cutters" perfected the section, removing bulges and depressions, using multiple shapes and sizes of iron scrapers, made for this purpose by the local ironsmith. With the help of a plum-bob and spirit level, they labored to make the vertical wall of the section perpendicular to the horizontal floor of the trench.

The photographer and his assistant began a coordinated series of activities. The photographer, perched on his tower, looked through the viewfinder of the camera and instructed his assistant to convey to the laborers instructions to clean up areas that he thought looked unprepared or messy (Figure 8.3). The assistant would direct the laborers to the particular spot that needed attention. Often the photographer also instructed the assistant to use his knife to deepen the marks on the floor or of the stratigraphical layers on the section walls, or the bricks of the mud-brick fortification. His assistant would make those marks, which were visible through the camera viewfinder—solid and conspicuous. On my questioning about the necessity of this process, the photographer explained:

> We are not making any new marks. The archaeologist had made them. We cannot tamper [*chheda-chhaad*] with that. We make them more visible [*saaf*]. It is a different thing when you take a photograph. If one cannot see the marks in the viewfinder, make them deeper [*gehera*]; this is what will remain. So we have to make sure that the markings made by the archaeologists are seen and obvious in the photograph. If it cannot be seen in the photograph, then the director will get upset.

Figure 8.3 The photographer on the tower taking the photograph of a prepared subject in Bhirrana, 2005

Source: Photograph by the author.

He explained this with irritation because he said his reasoning was "commonsensical" (*commonsense ki baath hai*) and my query unwarranted.

Shortly, the photographer was looking through the viewfinder, directing the assistant who removed the labels marking the stratigraphical layers and substituting them with special labels that were used by the photography team. These were larger, made up of thick cardboard and with the numbers etched in dark black ink. He pinned the labels on the layers in alignment with the floor. The assistant worked according to the instructions of the photographer. He placed a black and white meter-scale at a specific location, as the photographer yelled commands peering through the viewfinder of the camera (Figure 8.4). The meter-scale was the epistemic marker that played an important role in transforming archaeological materiality into archaeological evidence. It framed the archaeological evidence within the apparatus of a scientific representation.[5] This practice, the photographer explained to me later, was to make sure that the "scale has to be parallel to the plane of the camera, or it looks terrible [*bahut kharab lagega*]." He further explained: "The biggest difference between archaeological photography and any other photography is the scale. This makes the archaeological photograph scientific. If the scale is missing, then it is like any other photograph. Both the labels and the scale are key elements of archaeological photography."[6]

Figure 8.4 A photography session in a trench on the citadel of Dholavira, 2004

Source: Photograph by the author.

This method of archaeological photography with an overt emphasis on creation of epistemic evidence had a Wheelerian genealogy. In *Archaeology for the Earth*, Wheeler notes, "The overriding difficulty of an archaeological photographer is to induce his camera to tell the truth" (Wheeler 1954, 200). The job of the photographer in the ASI was to produce images through which the "truth" of archaeology could be captured and reproduced. The skill of the photographer was exhibited in the degree to which his photographic representation had the ability to produce the truth. As Wheeler noted: "The quality is as much a matter of proper emphasis of accumulative statement, and not a little of the photographer's time and skill, both in the field and in the studio, are devoted to the rescue of the more from the less significant" (Wheeler 1954, 200). For ASI photographers following Wheeler, the act of taking photographs was a process through which "truth" had to be transformed into a "fact." This was "commonsensically" within a structured convention of emphasizing the truth that negated the disorderliness of an archaeological excavation. Fact in an archaeological photograph was a performative truth (Shanks 1992, 145–46).

Like most archaeologists of his time, the photographic record formed an essential part of Wheeler's representational oeuvre. It played a central role in the discursive practice of his numerous published texts (see Wheeler, Ghosh, and Deva 1946; Wheeler 1947a, 1947b, 1947c, 1950, 1962, 1966, 1968, 1976). Wheeler transformed photographs into factual documents that provided empirical knowledge about the past. This was orchestrated by introducing an epistemic marker—the scale: "Every archaeological photograph should include a scale, either in the form of a graduated rule or rod or in that of a human figure. (Adult human skeletons provide their own scale with as much accuracy as may be expected from a photograph.)" (Wheeler 1954, 201). The use of the scale as an epistemic marker in archaeological photographs is a common means of transforming an arbitrary sign of the past into scientific knowledge. Wheeler with consummate aplomb emphasizes its importance:

> Scale (Hindi and Urdu, *paimana*; Bengali, *map kathi*; Tamil, *adikkol*; Telugu, *kolatabadda*; Malayam, *asarikkol*; Kannada, *adikolu*). This is a scale of two feet, one foot being subdivided into inches. The use of a scale proportionate to the size of the subject, is an elementary necessity of every photograph and need not be further discussed. (Wheeler 1948, 320)

Using the scale as an epistemic marker in archaeological photographs was a "commonsensical" means of transforming an arbitrary sign of the past into scientific knowledge that inscribes an epistemic certainty. The scale inscribes an epistemic certainty in the photograph, which cannot be challenged.

This is aggravated in archaeological excavation, as it is a destructive means of knowledge production that can never be tested at that trench or location (Jones 2001, 40). The photographic document with an epistemic marker transforms the location of discovery into an empirical fact. The scale then becomes the most important scientific signifier of an archaeological photograph. Wheeler doubtless shows its importance: "The scale should normally be parallel with the plane of the camera-plate; if the latter is tilted the graduated scale should be correspondingly tilted, other-wise the graduations are in perspective and of variable length" (Wheeler 1954, 201). The centrality of the scale and its importance in the transformation of an arbitrary subject is so overwhelming that Wheeler is forced to add a note of caution: "On the other hand, the scale should not monopolize the attention of the spectator. A central scale is, for this reason, usually bad" (Wheeler 1954, 202).

Photography and the Ethnic Marker

One late afternoon at the massive citadel wall of Dholavira, the chief photographer and a team of assistants were preparing to take photographs of the entire monumental structure. The Dholavira citadel fortification wall was understandably called "a monumental structure." Made of "stone bricks," it enclosed the entire citadel mound. It had an awe-inspiring presence, and along with the rock-cut reservoir and the huge Eastern Reservoir lined with rock-bricks, comprised the monumental spatiality that made up the site of Dholavira. The chief photographer conducted his work with a series of assistants—a peon and a group of four laborers carrying tripods, camera bag, scale, black cloth, brushes, scrapers, and other photographic paraphernalia.[7] These laborers had been handpicked by the chief photographer because "they were experts in subject preparation" and had been trained by him over the years. Whenever he came to Dholavira to take pictures, these four laborers were relieved of their work in the trenches to assist him. They began work early in the morning and used the entire day for preparing the subject. In the "angled light" of the setting sun, well after the laborers had left the excavation site for home, the photographer made images. Standing on top of a soaring collapsible aluminum tower, bought from Ahmedabad and transported to Dholavira in a truck a few years ago, the chief photographer yelled orders in Hindi while a laborer assistant translated them into Kutchi. He instructed around two dozen laborers cleaning and preparing the monumental subject. The sight was spectacular. The chief photographer, a short and bulky man, donning a white cricket hat, blue jeans, grey-white sneakers, and a brown photographer's jacket, was precariously balancing on top of the 15-meter-tall collapsible aluminum photographic tower fully stretched. Strapped across his chest were three 35 mm

Cannon SLR cameras with a black and white roll, a color roll, and a transparency roll. The cameras were fitted with zoom lenses of various focal lengths. On the ground, there were 30 men holding up the aluminum tower, perilously bent under the weight of the chief photographer, with three thick ropes.

After the monumental architectural "subject" had been cleaned and prepared, the chief photographer instructed his assistant from atop his 15-meter-high tower: "Get me a man in a *dhoti* and turban [*pagdi*].[8] I don't want a man in trousers [*pantwala admi nahi chahiye*]. And also get a woman with bangles [*churiwali aurat*]." Since the subject—the citadel fortification wall—was so enormous, instead of the black and white meter-scale found in an archetypal ASI representation style, a human scale was needed. In a few minutes, the assistant had assembled a couple of women dressed in typical rural Kutchi attire of *ghagra-choli*, with both their arms adorned with white plastic bangles. But there was no man with a *dhoti*. When the chief photographer inquired about the absence of a man in the attire he had demanded, his assistant informed him that the only man who wore a *dhoti* on the site was not present. It was at this moment that the chief photographer cautiously climbed down the aluminum tower and tentatively walked toward me with a distinct resolve.

I was standing and observing the proceedings from under the shade of a tree. He came up close to me and politely requested: "Sir, will you be our scale? You are the only one on the site wearing a *dhoti*." At first I refused, but after a little cajoling from the photographer and an AA who was standing beside me, I hesitatingly agreed to be their human scale. For me, it was a moment of epistemic epiphany. Two years ago, I had written an article critiquing the use of a human scale in the photographic presentation of the colonial ASI (Chadha 2002).[9] As fate would have it, I was now standing on the steps of the citadel fortification wall of Dholavira, posing with a brush, looking away from the camera, in my *dhoti-kurta*. I was not the rustic (*dehati*) Kutchi laborer the chief photographer was hoping for, but I looked "ethnic" enough to be made part of the ASI photograph of an archaeological monument. The chief photographer had also requested me to remove my spectacles to look "authentic." I posed for nearly an hour as the setting sun cast its long shadows on the Harappan site. The chief photographer on top of the elevated aluminum tower bellowed multiple instructions at the two Kutchi women and me. One of them was given a brush and asked to squat and pose as if she was cleaning the floor of the fortification wall. The other woman was ordered to stand in one corner of the fortification wall with a wicker basket on her head. I was instructed to stand in the stairwell, at the center of the citadel's fortification. The chief photographer tutored each of the women to stand, squat, look, and hold the brush in a particular style. If he was not satisfied, then one of his assistants would go to the women and give them further instructions. Once he was "satisfied," under the lengthening shadows of the setting sun, atop a 15-meter-tall collapsible tower, he clicked pictures with each of the three cameras. Below him, 30 laborers kept the chief photographer aloft. Another few dozen laborers stared at the elaborate performance. And I, together with the two women from Dholavira, became forever inscribed on the scientific representation of the Dholavira fortification wall.

After the hour-long ordeal, he discharged me. On the way back to the camp, I questioned the chief photographer about the process. He explained:

> Whenever I use a human scale, I make it a point to use the local laborers. I try avoiding the laborers dressed in modern western clothes. The more traditional attire the better it is. Dholavira is an ancient site; we know little of what the people wore. But we know they did not wear pants and shirts, like these menfolk today.

He disparagingly remarked about the western dresses worn by most men in Dholavira.

> The closest we can get to the original [*asliyat*] is by putting people dressed in their traditional attire in the picture. That is why I want women with bangles. Because we find so many shell bangles in the Dholavira and these womenfolk here wear bangles till their shoulders. They are like the Harappan dancing girl. That is how you make the photograph look authentic [*asli*].

But when I responded, "Isn't the human used just a scale?" He replied: "Yes, their primary purpose is that of a scale but they are not inanimate objects—they have a character so we exploit that to the fullest [*hume pooree tarah se unke character ka phaayada uthana chaiye*]" (Figure 8.5). [10]

The juxtaposition of the human body and the measuring scale in archaeology produces a scientific representation of the past, which has a colonial genealogy. It can be traced to the practice of the colonial anthropometric project of measuring the cranial features of the human subject as a means of objectifying it as a scientific fact (Tanner 1981; Sekula 1986; Spencer 1992; Hamilton and Hargreaves 2001). The racial process of codifying and disciplining the body of the primitive native is evidenced in photographs taken in the late nineteenth century in India, where the primitive native was represented as the *object* of scientific discourse (Risley 1969 [1915]; Pinney 1992, 1997; Ryan 1997). The photograph became a performative space, akin to the museum for colonial science, to stage its articulation of power through which the scientific gaze compared, identified, differentiated, and categorized the native subject. Colonial ethnologists such as

Figure 8.5 An ASI photographer in Dholavira making images with human epistemic and ethnic markers, 2004

Source: Photographs by the author.

Edgar Thurston, the superintendent of the Madras Central Museum, stalked the museum in pursuit of his anthropometrical interests by keeping his calipers and other scientific instruments ready to measure native visitors (Prakash 1999, 156). Native subjects thus apprehended were represented in anthropometrical photographs where the measuring scale as the anthropometrist's talisman was not only used as a studio prop but also transformed into a symbolic scientific instrument (Pinney 1997, 48). It not only provided useful information but also played the role of scientifically controlling the native body. Innate in Wheeler's practice of using the native and the scale was the subtext of disciplining the native and using him as an epistemic marker in order to validate his own position as the colonial master capable of controlling the native through the discourse of science that was already prevalent in colonial India. The measuring scale as a pseudo-scientific device was substituted as a studio prop by the girded backdrop of graph paper in these photographs of the native (Pinney 1997, 51). A reflection of such a grid occurs in the excavation methods of Wheeler, which were marked by the characteristic cellular trenches that were inscribed on the earth to gain more control of the process of generating scientific knowledge (Wheeler 1946a, Plate IIb).

Wheeler continued this earlier practice and actively used human figures as scales to produce an epistemologically sound representation of the past and to legitimize his practice: "Where the scale is a human being, as is often desirable in large subjects, the individual thus honored must remember that he is a mere accessory, just so many feet of bone and muscle" (Wheeler 1954, 202). The human figure is transformed by Wheeler from a producer of knowledge—an active member of the means of knowledge production—to a passive accessory of the knowledge production project because "(1) the figure shall not occupy a disproportionately large portion of the picture and (2) … the figure shall not look at the camera but shall ostensibly be employed in as impersonal a manner as possible" (Wheeler 1954, 202). It is not coincidental that Wheeler never appears as the human epistemic marker in any of the images. It is the nondescript workman or woman, the subaltern, who plays the dual role of the human epistemic marker and the ethnic marker—an anthropological motif imperative for an "authentic" visual representation of colonial archaeological projects. The tradition of utilizing the subaltern human marker was widely practiced in Indian archaeology before Wheeler, but he provides the marker with a set of epistemological semantics that had scientific credence.

The subaltern laborers, both men and women, were objectified in the representational lexicon of archaeological knowledge by colonial archaeology, and utilized as an ethnic marker to legitimize the colonial undertaking of inscribing on the subalterns their past. The past is discovered by colonial authority, but not known to the subalterns, who are incapable of discovering themselves. It is only through the participation in the colonial project that they can engage with it. The encounter with their glorious heritage, the experience with their ancient ancestors is only possible through an intermediary—the colonial knowledge producing agency, the ASI. The subaltern subjects were subverted because, in spite of being given a place of pride in the knowledge production process, they were simultaneously appropriated to authenticate the Enlightenment project of civilizing the native. They are always shown in these photographs as the industrious workmen or women, attired in native robes and clothes, who experience the past provided to them and are deeply engaged with it while doing menial labor—usually cleaning. This representation of the natives by fixing them with work that they did, in their traditional attire, along with their tools of trade, was a marker of typicality that signified their ethnicity (Pinney 1997, 53).

Wheeler's visual vocabulary borrowed these tropes from the depiction of native workers in the service of the Raj, where they performed the role not of a primitive symbol but rather of a tame and adaptive labor force (Pinney 1997, 57). The representation of the prototypical natives with occupational gear and clothing, participating in the colonial task, had wide currency, as these images were mass-produced in the form of phototype postcards. The native bodies were not only objectified in Wheeler's images, but these representations also played the dual role of inscribing the colonial discourse with the legitimacy that it lacked. In the process, the subaltern workmen/women were reduced to motifs in a photographic document and became nothing but a necessary nuisance that had to be controlled and disciplined for the efficacy of the archaeological project:

> I have seen, towards the end of the day, the lines of young native basket-carriers, upon whose speed and regularity depends in great measure the general *tempo* of an Eastern excavation, falter and chatter and play truant in spite of the despairing efforts of the strong-minded foreman. Basket carriers are never the most responsible members of the party, and they are necessarily numerous and elusive. (Wheeler 1954, 175–76)

Wheeler undermined the identity of the subaltern men and women by objectifying them as auxiliary items in scientific discourse. Subaltern subjects were simultaneously disciplined not just by the appropriation of their bodies as the primary means to carry out the knowledge production process, but also by the utilization of their bodies as symbols to humanize the representation of knowledge, thus making it an "authentic" and "legitimate" discourse.

During his work in India, Wheeler produced numerous illustrations depicting stratigraphy, which represented "the successive phases in the archaeological 'history' of a site" (Wheeler 1954, 59). They were prepared by differentiating strata on the basis of "variation in colors or material and content" which "particularly under the bleaching influences of an African or Asian sun, present difficulty to an experienced eye" (Wheeler 1954, 60). These diagrams were neatly illustrated with clearly demarcated strata and layers and they transformed the "observation in different lights and different times of the day" into illustrations of scientific knowledge. These diagrammatic constructions were attempts to "read the sections—to discriminate without prejudice, between the more significant and less significant differentiation of the strata" (Wheeler 1954, 60). Thus, after the first step in the Wheeler Method had been inscribed over the mound, with cellular grids as adequate techniques of scientific knowledge production, the second step was initiated through stratification. Cultural layers were identified, codified, and also utilized to "interpret them, to understand the sentence and transliterate it" in order to sufficiently inscribe the dug earth with a chronology (Wheeler 1954, 60). This knowledge was given a firm and fixed shape in two-dimensional illustrations embellished with Wheeler's motif of the subaltern workers (*coolie*), once again represented as disciplined, industrious, and proud natives playing the dual roles of the epistemic and the ethnic marker. They usually occupy the fringe of the dramatic display, reduced to diminutive figures in the vast stratigraphical performance put together by the colonial masters. Awed by the past inscribed upon them, they are finally controlled and reduced to symbols in a diagram like the other symbols in depicting stratigraphical sections "for the easy and conventional representations" as "they have no special merit but [are] reasonably expressive" (Wheeler 1954, 77). The dead, non-human stratigraphical illustration is given life: "[A]n intelligently drawn section is far more than a diagram; it is, as I say, a picture, representing not merely the skeleton but also something of the vital flesh and blood of its subject" (Wheeler 1954, 76).

In these illustrations of stratigraphy, Wheeler is appropriating key Enlightenment aesthetic notions of the picturesque and the sublime that dominated most of the earlier representation of Indian art and architecture throughout the eighteenth and nineteenth centuries. Colonial travelers, artists, and administrators, overwhelmed by the natural surroundings and the architectural richness of the country, created romantic images of India that had a lasting influence on the way Indian art, architecture, and antiquities were represented to the European world (Mitter 1977, 1994; Dirks 1994; Ray 2008). The aesthetics of these images were dominated by eighteenth-century European tastes and ideas, shaped by romantic sensibilities (Drew 1987; Labbe 1998) and erotica, which viewed the image of native people as collectible objects (Dennis 1994, 23). The emergence of these ideas was linked to the discoveries of ancient monuments in Greece and the European Middle Ages, and led to a revivalist fervor in art and aesthetics affected by the notion of the picturesque and the sublime (Mitter 1977, 120). The picturesque has been designed as the nineteenth century's modality of viewing the universe that was situated in the period of transition from classical formalism to a state of romantic disorder that challenged the Renaissance ideas of beauty and aesthetics (Bermingham 1987; Andrews 1989; Labbe 1998). It is an artificially and socially constructed mode of viewing landscape, where nature is objectified and transformed into the basis of scientific and aesthetic appropriation (Ryan 1996, 59). On the other hand, the idea of the sublime was linked to a growing interest in nature, evoking a sensation of pleasure in the beholder due to the inability of the human mind to comprehend it (Hipple 1957; Twitchell 1983; Labbe 1998). This, in turn, was aroused by the monumental size of the subject (Mitter 1977, 121). In India, this notion is closely connected to early antiquarian ideas of colonial officials, administrators, and travelers who first encountered the traditional monuments, architecture, and edifices. These were illustrated with a typical romantic treatment, exploiting the idea of the picturesque and the sublime to create images of famous monuments for consumption by a European audience. These earliest depictions of archaeological sites of India in the west presented the monumentality of the site in a dramatic fashion that was brought about by situating the performance of the monument in a vast space, contrasting it with the image of the native, attired in a native costume, diminutively performing his role as the ethnic marker (Mitter 1977; Dirks 1994; Ray 2008).

In Wheeler's diagrammatic representation of stratigraphy in India in the form of folding plans, especially of the huge Indus valley sites of Harappa (Wheeler 1947b, 66, 1968, 31) and Mohenjo-Daro (Wheeler 1968, 44) and the early historic site of Charsada (Wheeler 1966, 22), he uses a similar visual rhetoric to magnify the monumentality of the site. He contrasts these representations with the diminutive figures of the subaltern workers in native costumes as they are forced to stand at the corner of these large folding plans, in the symbolic role of the ethnic marker. The subtext implied in these representations, very much like the photographs discussed earlier, is that of double inscription. The inscription on native bodies of the past that they are unaware of, and therefore in need to be civilized into its knowledge, and the inscription of the archaeological project by these same bodies to authenticate and legitimize the patronizing, civilizing project of the colonial archaeologist. The ethnic markers are the subaltern workmen/ women, the laborers with the basket or pickaxe forced on them, appreciating the workmanship that they have created for their master and for themselves.

Today, in the photographic documentation of the ASI's numerous excavations, the epistemic marker and the ethnic marker are ubiquitous (for instance, seen in every *IAR*). The visual vocabulary used by the ASI still expresses the ideological subtext of the colonial mission of inscribing the landscape with its statist power, and continues the project of producing the past for the natives. The bureaucratic gaze of the ASI objectifies the landscape through the same colonial apparatus of knowledge production, steeped in a similar ideological framework and using identical methods of extraction, codification, and dissemination of archaeological knowledge. Like most institutions of colonial bureaucracy, the change that occurred in the ASI after the transference of power in 1947 was symbolic, devoid of any substantive transformation in the ideological apparatus of the system, its reach, and its power to inscribe a scientific and an "objective past" on the people of India.

The human epistemic and ethnic marker is thus an expression of the "body politic" in the disciplinarian discourse of ASI archaeology, where the bodies of the subaltern (*dehati*) are the sites for the articulation of the nexus of power and knowledge. Here, the ASI as a postcolonial bureaucracy operates as an ideological apparatus exerting its power over the subaltern bodies by appropriating their symbolic valence and attributing them with an epistemological significance. This process subverts the subaltern bodies for the knowledge production objective of the colonial project, and simultaneously legitimizes its oppressive power. The body of the subaltern (*dehati*) is directly involved in a political field as an epistemological category, where the power relations between the dominant and the oppressed are performed in the knowledge production process. The ASI not only exploits the subaltern bodies as a labor force, but also transforms them into a representational idiom, through which it articulates its power over the knowledge about India's past. The resulting domination of the ASI is exercised by investing in the subaltern an epistemological valence that is exploited by manipulating it to validate the ASI's power to generate knowledge. The photographic archive of ASI archaeology is thus a discursive system in which the scientific, the bureaucratic, and the archaeological processes collapse to produce a narrative of domination, exploitation, and legitimization. Here, the political function of the archaeological project coalesces with the epistemological authority of the postcolonial bureaucracy, where through the application of scientific technologies, identities are normalized, domesticated, and controlled.

Notes

1. By this time, Narendra Modi had already become an extraordinarily influential figure in Indian politics. He was considered to be the younger and more virulent face of Hindu fundamentalism in India. He became the prime minister of India in 2014. During my ethnographic years, his claim to infamy was his government's central role in actively orchestrating the Gujarat pogrom in early 2002, in which nearly 2,000 Muslims were killed.

2. Pramod Mahajan was a senior leader of the BJP from Maharashtra, a much milder figure, but was often touted as a future PM of India in certain circles of the BJP. Unfortunately, in May 2006, he was killed by his brother Pravin Mahajan over a family dispute.

3. Deendayal Upadhyaya (1916–68) was a political ideologue of Hindu fundamentalism in India. He was the founder of the Bharatiya Jana Sangh, the forerunner of the present-day Bharatiya Janata Party, and is considered a symbolic figurehead of the party.

4. Nearly 20,000 people were killed in this earthquake with a magnitude of 7.7, which caused widespread damage in Kutch and the adjoining areas in Gujarat and Pakistan.

5. For examples, see *IAR 2003–04* (2011, 232–33) (Baror); *IAR 2003–04* (2011, 33) (Juni Kuran); *IAR 2004–05* (2014, 42) (Bhirrana); *IAR 2004–05* (2014, 126) (Baror); Bisht (2015, 90–91) (Dholavira).

6. See *IAR 2003–04* (2011, 43, 46, 48) and *IAR 2004–05* (2014, 42, 49, 51) for the photographs made at Bhirrana. For photographs at Baror, see *IAR 2003–04* (2011, 226) and *IAR 2004–05* (2014, 112).

7. In the context of Indian bureaucracy, the term "peon" is an official occupational designation, not a pejorative noun.

8. A *dhoti* is an unstitched cotton cloth worn by men in India, usually 15 feet long and around 3 feet wide that is wrapped around the abdomen and the legs and knotted at the waist.

9. I have worn a *khadi dhoti* since my high school days as a political statement, since I got involved with Gandhian environmental movements in the late 1980s. Recently, my choice of attire catapulted me into national news in India. On July 14, 2017, I was denied entry into an upmarket mall in Kolkata because I was wearing a *dhoti*. For more details, see Avikunthak (2017a, 2017b).

10. For examples at Dholavira, see *IAR 1990–91* (1995, Plates X, XI, XII, XIV); *IAR 1991–92* (1996, Plates XXI, XXII); *IAR 1992–93* (1997, cover page); Bisht (2015, 90–91, 101–02, 109, 114–15, 117–22, 126–27, 152–53, 165–68).

9   The Absent Excavation Reports

It was in the dry winter of 2003 at Dholavira when I met ASI archaeologists and technical staff who had excavated the disputed site of the Ram Janmabhoomi–Babri Masjid complex in Ayodhya. Speaking about the Ayodhya excavation was prohibited. It was not a mere taboo, but illegal. Everyone who had worked at Ayodhya had signed a High Court prohibitory order—it was forbidden to divulge any details about the excavation. A draughtsman—a 15 years' veteran of the ASI—in hushed tones rebuked me: "Why are you troubling [*taqleef*] me? I have to support my children, sir [*bibi-bache hai, saheb*]. The court has forbidden [*mana hai*] us to talk about the excavation. It is too sensitive [English word used]."[1] It was less than four months after the Ayodhya excavation and trepid reluctance was in the air. Most of my informants were frightened to speak, but some whose confidence I had gained did communicate. For the next two years, as I conducted my fieldwork, I had a series of conversations with some members of the Ayodhya excavation whom I met during my fieldwork at ASI sites. All of them refused my request for a formal interview. But in the slow and languorous pace of an ASI archaeological excavation, time is not at a premium; gradually my informants opened up and candidly shared their experiences at the Ayodhya excavations of 2003.

"This was the most terrifying archaeological excavation in the history of the ASI. *Full of tension* [English phrase used]," he continued. On nudging further, he explained:

> Now what should I tell you? [*Ab kya bathae aapko?*] First, no one digs in the summer. Second, this is archaeology and not red tape [*babugiri*]. We dig history [*itihas*]. We make history. We make the nation [*rashtra*]. And we need time [*waqt*]. Archaeology is about patience. Archaeology is a science. Archaeology is an art. You cannot do archaeology under the pressure. But who will tell the High Court? They gave us the order and we did the work [*Unhone order diya. Aur hamne kaam kiya*]. After all we are government servant[s] [*sarkari naukar hai*]. If the court tells us to dig on the moon, we will have to do it.

The ASI, like most bureaucratic organizations in India, had an ambivalent relationship with the judicial system in India. During my fieldwork, I observed that a large volume of the daily office practice of ASI branches dealt with incessant court cases—site encroachments, minor corruptions, disgruntled employees, property disputes, and others. "We are used to dealing with court cases. This is our daily bread-and-butter [*hamri rozi-roti hain*]," retorted the assistant archaeologist (AA) with a sense of despondency. He had experience working in proto-historic, early historic, and medieval sites in north India. He was one of the most experienced AAs in the ASI. "Excavating in the summer under excruciating heat is a terrible idea [*bada hi kharab plan hai*]. But then excavating in the monsoon is disaster [*musibath*]," he continued his diatribe.

The timing of the Ayodhya excavation ran counterintuitively to over 100 years of wisdom that Indian archaeologists had accumulated. The Ayodhya excavation started in March—around the time of the year when most excavations are wrapped up throughout South Asia. The piercing heat of over 40-degree centigrade makes it virtually unbearable to work in the vast open landscapes, especially in north India. Archaeological sites are excavated during the most climatically agreeable months of the year—"between Diwali and Holi." One of my informants parenthetically bracketed the temporal location of the arduous archaeological fieldwork between two of the most popular festivals of the Hindu calendar. During these dry winter months from November to February, not only is it pleasant to work for long hours in the outdoors but it also prevents the deep excavation trenches from collapsing (as it was common in the wet season). The Ayodhya excavation began in March 2003 and continued during the monsoon months, which by all standards of archaeological acumen was unfavorable. The Ayodhya excavation at its inception began as an inappropriate archaeological intervention, under pressure from an obdurate judiciary.

By now we were sitting on the edge of a trench in the Middle Town of Dholavira. We observed a dozen women attired in traditional Kutchi *ghagra-choli* industriously cleaning the floor of a trench with plastic paintbrushes, exposing a layer that had recently being excavated. He wryly recounted:

> In Ayodhya we worked for 16 hours a day in two shifts—day and night. Once the rains started falling, the trenches were covered under multi-colored plastic sheets. We worked under the agonizing heat of halogen light's glare, descending 20 meters under the earth, just digging. Only sweat, humidity, dirt and darkness. It was terribly hot. They used huge fans that would only churn out more hot air. We could not see anything, let alone do archaeology. We were just digging and collecting objects. This was not archaeology, it was donkey-labor [*gaddha-mazdoori*]. All we found was tons of potshards, burnt bones, shattered ceramics tiles, unidentified terracotta pieces, and fragments of unknown idols that looked like someone's God, but no one's Ram or Rahim [*na kisi ka Ram, na kisi ka Rahim*].

The work conditions at Ayodhya were so unusually non-normative that it is mentioned in the ASI excavation report—a genre of archaeological text that is usually reticent and discreet and has no place for even subdued belligerence. Dr B. R. Mani, one of the directors of the Ayodhya excavation, in a rare exception made an extra-special note in the introductory chapter of the report in a section succinctly titled "Constraints." He rather distressingly, but in restrained terms, notes: "Working conditions worsened at the onslaught of the monsoon … creating heat and humidity besides total darkness in a number of deep trenches. One team member fell down and fractured his hand and leg while others including some casual laborers received electric shocks by touching pedestal fans fixed on baulks." However, in the spirit of bureaucratic determinism, Dr B. R. Mani continues in a formidable vein: "In spite of all such constraints the team of the Archaeological Survey of India worked vigorously with full devotion and sprit" (Manjhi and Mani 2003, 11).

The Ayodhya excavation of 2003 was the most unusual excavation in the history of the 142-year-old organization. It was an archaeological excavation to find the remains of a Hindu temple buried under an Islamic mosque ordered by the court. "The premise of the excavation was unscientific. This was [a] property dispute [*property ka lafda*]. It had political [*raajaneetik*] and communal [*saampradaayik*] overtones but the court unnecessarily [*befazool*] pulled in [the] ASI [*khama-kha court ne ASI ko iss main ghasite liya*]," complained another AA. With the High Court's summon, the listless bureaucracy of the ASI was jolted and pushed into the center of the most distressing events of postcolonial Indian history since the partition of 1947. The Special Full Bench of the Allahabad High Court, Lucknow, had taken recourse to the scientific framework of archaeology to adjudicate a case with huge political valence.[2] The court summoned the ASI as an "expert body of the government" (Khan, Agarwal, and Sharma 2010, 2181) and ordered excavations on March 5, 2003, because "extraordinary situations demand extraordinary steps and strategy" (Khan, Agarwal, and Sharma 2010, 2142). "We came to the rescue of the court. This case needed a civil judgment, at worst a political judgment. The court instead decided on an archaeological judgment," resentfully explained my informant as we sat under the clear night sky outside our tent in Dholavira.

In comparison to the vast airy expanse of Dholavira, especially in the cool winter months, where, at the end of the day, one could admire the mesmerizing sunset reflecting beautifully on the shimmering waters of the Rann of Kutch, the excavation at Ayodhya was ostensibly "disturbed" (Khan, Agarwal, and Sharma 2010, 2212). An ASI archaeological excavation is a relaxed bureaucratic exercise—tedious, monotonous, and repetitive with occasional discoveries, done at a relatively calm, nonchalant pace, without excessive haste or stress. Years are spent languorously excavating the site layer by layer—artifacts are cautiously removed, structures are leisurely exposed.[3] They are mapped, drawn, photographed, classified, and, sometimes, analyzed. Archaeologists on field sites live in spacious and comfortable tents with a large retinue of servants and laborers at their disposal. The Ayodhya excavation of 2003, in contrast, was an excavation in "fast forward" mode, as an AA eloquently explained. "Doing an archaeological excavation under the direct orders of the High Court was [a] different ball game [*alagh hi kehla tha*]. Excavation is [a] five-day match. [The] Court forced us to play a one-day match [*Excavation five-day match hota hai. Court ne toh humese one day khilaya*]," expressively explained the AA. He smartly employed the allegory of a cricket match to distinguish between a usual ASI excavation and the Ayodhya excavation. He compared the slow moving, languid pace of a five-day genre of cricket to the regular ASI excavation and sharply contrasted it with the much faster one-day version of the game to the Ayodhya excavation. It was the most rushed archaeological excavation in the history of the ASI. What would have taken any ASI Excavation Branch (Ex. Br.) in an analogous medieval site in north India nearly four to five seasons (around 500–700 days of excavation) was hurriedly excavated in less than 150 days from March to August of 2003.[4] When the excavation ended, the ASI had unearthed a staggering 90 trenches, some of which were 20 meters deep, and recovered many thousands of antiquities, ceramics of different periods, coins, architectural fragments, terracotta objects, figurines, and bones.[5]

The flawed nature of the Ayodhya excavation not only emerged from the inappropriate temporality of the excavation or the sluggish bureaucratic juggernaut that the ASI was, but the culpability was greatly exacerbated by another postcolonial institutional behemoth—the Indian judiciary. The Allahabad High Court "remote-controlled" the daily practice of archaeological excavation and, even by the disheartening ASI standards, made the Ayodhya excavation of 2003 a logistical mess (Mandal and Ratnagar 2007; Varma and Menon 2010; Varghese 2018). For instance, one of the major concerns of the court that caused considerable anxiety amongst the senior officers at the director general's (DG) headquarters in the ASI was the equal representation of Muslims and Hindus in the ASI workforce at Ayodhya (Khan, Agarwal, and Sharma 2010, 235–38). After considerable jugglery, the office of the Exploration & Excavation of the ASI's DG headquarters handpicked its most energetic officers and technical staff from the five Ex. Brs. throughout India (see AACD, File No. 29/1/95-Pt IV). Not all were happy to be working at Ayodhya. Some of my informants confided to me that they were reluctant participants of the Ayodhya excavation.

A surveyor who was able to evade the Ayodhya excavation dramatically explained: "The Court prodded the DG. The DG prodded us. Those who were ordered they had to go" (*Court ka danda pade DG pe. Aur DG ka dande pade ham pe. Jinko order mila, unhe toh jana hi pada*). Finally, 51 ASI personnel with cautious Muslim representation proportionate to their population according to the 1991 Indian census records, along with 131 laborers, including 29 Muslims, were chosen to excavate the site.[6] Two excavation directors—Hari Manjhi, director (Antiquity), and B. R. Mani, superintending archaeologist (SA)—led the motley group of industrious excavators. B. R. Mani was the sole team leader of the excavation when it began and Manjhi was deputed later (Khan, Agarwal, and Sharma 2010, 234–37) because a large number of complaints were filed against the ASI excavation practices at Ayodhya (Varma and Menon 2010, 65).

The High Court's intervention was not just confined to the constitution of the workforce of the excavation team but percolated more penetratingly (see AACD, File No. 29/1/1995-EE [Part-V]). One of my informants asserted that the constant "interference" by the High Court with its multiple orders and counter-orders made the Ayodhya excavation the "ultimate bureaucratic circus" (*ekdum sarkari circus*). The constant vigilance and daily "irritating" intrusion of the various representatives of the feuding parties overseeing the minute details of the excavation were stressful, further aggravated by the national media reporting every potshard discovered. "The excavation site looked like an army operation with the PAC (Provincial Armed Constabulary) and the CRPF (Central Reserve Police Force) constantly guarding us," described an AA in Bhirrana. The stress level was so high that some archaeologists abandoned the excavation midway.[7]

D. Mandal, a retired professor of the Department of Ancient History and Archaeology, Allahabad University, was one of the few independent observers who had visited the site during the excavation. He poignantly noted in his critique of the Ayodhya report in the journal *Social Science Probings* published in 2004: "The worst aspect of the working environment was a considerable absence of mutual trust. It was of course from both sides, and whatever it was, it was very sad indeed" (Mandal 2004, 38). Furthermore, the numerous anxious parties of the court case would file injunctions, which radically transformed the usual placid pace of ASI archaeological excavation. The court's intrusion was so disruptive that every minor action of the archaeological excavation was strictly monitored.[8] As soon as artifacts would emerge from the surface of the excavated earth, it would be transformed into an incriminating evidence of postcolonial bureaucratic jurisprudence rather than a material culture having an archaeological credence.[9] B. R. Mani in his introduction to the report notes with mild annoyance that the court's emphasis on following the protocol of juridical bureaucracy greatly hindered the ASI's investigative efficacy (Manjhi and Mani 2003, 10). Objects were understudied, analysis was hastened, proper diagnosis was hampered, and these greatly impeded the making of the Ayodhya report (Varma and Menon 2010).

The "scientific investigation" (Khan, Agarwal, and Sharma 2010, 2169; Supreme Court 2019, 552) that the three judges of the Lucknow Bench of the Allahabad High Court (Sudhir Agarwal, Sibghat Ullah Khan, and Dharam Veer Sharma) depended upon in the adjudication of the case was itself a product of an extremely compromised archaeological excavation.[10] An AA, who had worked at Ayodhya for the first few weeks, sardonically narrated his frustrations of working at the site: "None of us cared if under the Masjid was [a] Hindu temple, a Buddhist Vihara, or a Jain temple. We just wanted to leave the site as soon as we could." He, like many of the 53 ASI employees, had been in the field for nearly six months—first from November 2002 to March 2003 working at sites that their various Ex. Brs. were digging and then since March 2003 "on deputation" at Ayodhya. We were sitting and sipping tea at Baror. He scornfully continued to air his annoyance:

> Who can work with a group of anxious *maulvi*s, nervous *pundit*s, suspicious RSS *swayamsevak*s (volunteers), and the skeptical communists, voyeuristically gazing at every act we did in the trench. They even followed us when we went to relive ourselves. As if we will smuggle something incriminating from the toilet into the trenches. The Muslims wanted us to find Babur's name plate and the Hindus wanted us to find Ram's *paduka* (shoes)![11]

Finally, after painstakingly answering my innumerable queries, with a heavy sigh he said:

> Sir*ji* … we did all we could. We did our best. Like the army, we work for the country. They told us to dig Ayodhya. We did that. They told us to write the report. We did that. Now those above have to decide if it was good or bad [*Hamne toh apana kaam kar diya, baki upurwale ki marzi*].

I did not further question my informant but I suspect the *uparwale* (those above) in this case was both the High Court and the God that the ASI was searching for at Ayodhya.

The excavation report titled *Ayodhya: 2002–04—Excavations at the Disputed Site* consists of two volumes—the first volume is the text, the second consists of plates of images, diagrams, drawings, and photographs.[12] Hari Manjhi and B. R. Mani edited the report, with 23 other contributors to volume 1, who penned the 10 chapters—4 SAs, 2 deputy superintending archaeologists (Dy SAs), 4 assistant superintending archaeologists (ASAs), 12 AAs, and 1 assistant superintending epigraphist. Manjhi is not named as an author of any chapter of the report. He was a symbolic head to placate the Muslim parties of the court case who had accused B. R. Mani of being close to the Hindu parties and not without reason. B. R. Mani's reputation as a saffron (*bhagwa*) archaeologist was common knowledge among the archaeological community in India.[13] He and R. S. Bisht, the excavator of Dholavira, were known to be close to S. P. Gupta and B. B. Lal, who had been unambiguously instrumental in the formation of a Hindutva archaeology. The year 2003 was also when Jagmohan—the BJP leader and the then minister for tourism and culture—was persuasively pushing for a Hindutva agenda in the ASI, especially in the context of the Saraswati Heritage Project (SHP). It was not a surprise that Mani was appointed the team leader since the pre-excavation stage in September 2002.

If the Ayodhya excavation was the most rushed archaeological excavation in the history of the ASI, then the Ayodhya report was the most hastily written excavation report in the history of archaeology. It was a record of sorts. The Ayodhya excavation ended on August 12, 2003, and the report was submitted to the High Court on August 22, 2003. The two-volume, 574-page report was written in 10 days. An informant who had worked at the excavation and was closely involved at the writing of the report informed me that they had started working on the report simultaneously with the excavation (also see Khan, Agarwal, and Sharma 2010, 230). Explaining the process of report-writing, he excitedly narrated:

> There was tension all around. Everyone worked without complaining. We knew we were making history. The photographer took the photographs. The draughtsmen drew furiously. Everyone did over time. We were sleeping less than three hours a day. It was excruciating [*dardnak*]. Teams were made for each chapter. We worked very hard [*hamane bahut mehanat ki*]. The Court had given us two extensions. We submitted the report just on time. It was such a relief [*aaram*] when everything was over [*sab kuch khatam ho gaya tha*].

This is not how archaeologists write site-reports, especially ASI archaeologists. If the excavation is a premeditated and measured form of knowledge production, then writing an archaeological report is a deliberative, pensive, and time-consuming process (Sinclair 1989; Hodder 1989; Tilley 1989; Joyce 2002). The act of representing material cultural formation into an epistemic narrative is looked upon in the ASI with as much dread and trepidation as the adventurous excitement of archaeological fieldwork is looked upon in favorable anticipation.

This two-volume report was the most secretive text ever written by the ASI. Only the top brass had seen the report—even those who had worked at Ayodhya had not seen it. It came to a very limited public domain when copies of the report were given to the parties of the court case, and not yet published. [14] The non-publication of the Ayodhya report after more than 15 years of excavation signals not just that fact that it consisted of state secrets but also that it was poorly written. As I have shown earlier, the ASI archaeologists were very unhappy with the working conditions at the site and the production of enormous amount of material culture was done in conditions that were substandard and impossible. B. R. Mani in his "Constraints" section of the "Introduction" to the report further elaborates:

> Monkeys started damaging the sheets as a result of which several layers of sheets were spread over bamboo and wooden poles. They created further darkness. Photography was also affected due to bad light and natural colors were not easily obtained as multi-colored sheets reflected their colors on the surface and sections. Much difficulty was felt for the stratigraphical observations particularly for determining layers. (Manjhi and Mani 2003, 10)[15]

This alarming disclaimer in the body of the report makes the evidential basis of the report suspect (see Khan, Agarwal, and Sharma 2010, 572–73). Fueled by the fact that very little time was spent to do a nominal analysis of the artifacts excavated, the ensuing report had to be kept unpublished because it was truly "a[n] inferior [*ghatiya*] piece of work," as a senior university archaeologist told me. "It is a good thing that report is not published, we are ourselves very embarrassed of it," an AA who worked at site once confided. The practice of writing site-reports has a checkered history in the ASI. ASI archaeologists are notoriously known for taking decades to write archaeological reports, if they write any. A senior archaeologist who had also worked at Ayodhya, during a dinner conversation in an ASI field camp, without sarcasm and with profound seriousness remarked: "It normally takes twenty-five years to write an archaeological report in ASI. But the Ayodhya report was written in less than 10 days." He contemptuously continued: "The High Court had kept the gun [*bandook*] on our forehead [*kanpati*], so we worked like mad men [*pagalo ki tarah*]—day and night without sleep and rest, to produce a report which reads less than [a] scientific report but more like a court testimony [*adalt ki gawahi*]."

If the Ayodhya excavation was a flawed project—a product of postcolonial juridical anxiety—then the ASI report that formed the empirical grounds for the court to adjudicate that a temple existed under the Babri Masjid was an even greater anomaly.[16] It was written in an innocuous lackluster style, more dreary and staid than the usually written ASI archaeological site-reports (for example, see Lal 1954; Thapar 1967, 1957; Rao 1985; Joshi 1990, 1993; Lal et al. 2003), which were bland clones of the nineteenth-century archaeological derivative (Hodder 1989, 270–71; Hamilton 1999), rather than exemplars of contemporary archaeological practice. Finally, the most controversial inconsistency of the text is the mysterious un-authored tenth chapter of the report which provocatively and without much empirical basis asserted for the presence of the temple under the disputed site. Each of the nine chapters has two or more authors, whereas the last chapter, unexpectedly, has been written anonymously.

This last chapter of the report is called "Summary of Results" (Manjhi and Mani 2003, 268–72) and is the most assertively interpretative section of the report—generously quoted by the High Court and Supreme Court judges. My informants told me that this chapter was ghostwritten by the late S. P. Gupta—the card-carrying member of the Hindu fundamentalist organization the Rashtriya Swayamsevak Sangh (RSS).[17] He forcefully noted in the report that the monumental pillared structure under the mosque was a temple. It is in the last paragraph of the chapter of the report that the ASI gives its parting Hindutva shot:

> Now viewing in totality and taking into account the archaeological evidence of a massive structure just below the disputed structure and evidence of continuity in structural phases from the tenth century onwards up to the construction of the disputed structure along with the yield of stone and decorated bricks as well as mutilated sculpture of divine couple and carved architectural members including foliage patterns, *amalaka*, *kapotapali*, doorjamb with semi-circular pilaster, broken octagonal shaft of black schist pillar, locus motif, circular shrines having *pranala* (waterchut) in the north, fifty pillar bases in association of huge structure, are indicative of remains which are distinctive features found associated with temples of north India.[18]

This assertion of a monumental structure having characteristics of a Hindu temple was usurped by the judges to adjudicate that a temple did exist under the Babri Masjid. The importance of this section can be judged by the fact that it has been cited twice in the Supreme Court judgment (Supreme Court 2019, 524 and 563). Significantly, this chapter is generously quoted by Justice Sudhir Agarwal (Khan, Agarwal, and Sharma 2010, 2442–45) for adjudicating the case in favor of the Hindu parties in 2010.[19] However, as critics have pointed out both in court and in the public sphere, the ASI report suffers from many serious lacunas. It had failed to take into account many elements of the site in the writing of the report (see Gupta 2010; Mani 2010; Varma and Menon 2010;

Anwer 2011; Varghese 2018). Both the judgments provide a legal sanction for the construction of the temple over the obliterated mosque, but also for the first time in the history of modern judiciary it provides a legal rationale for the presence of God. And most problematically, it imparts a powerful juridical validation for the destruction of the Babri Masjid (see Supreme Court 2019, 505–99).

The Ayodhya excavation represented a stark and a highly controversial instance of an ASI archaeological excavation—a peculiar product of postcolonial bureaucracy and postcolonial science. Although the Ayodhya excavation was one of the most important excavations in the history of postcolonial India, it was also one of the most disturbingly ineffective excavations ever conducted— as evidenced from the contestations, objections, and criticism, remarkably documented in excruciating details in the judgment of Justice Sudhir Agarwal (Khan, Agarwal, and Sharma 2010, 117–2912). However, for the bureaucratic archaeologists of the ASI, the Ayodhya excavation was only an irritant in its routine work. It impeded their normal customary schedule of managing, excavating, and preserving the rich archaeological heritage of India. They viewed the 1992 demolition as a problem of law and order, while the Ayodhya excavation of 2003 was regarded as an incident of bureaucratic duty exercised under the astonishing pressure of the judiciary.[20]

Unpublished Excavation Report

One night, after dinner, I was sitting with a technical staff member of the Dholavira excavation camp. A day earlier, a photographer had chided me for spending too much time with the *saheb*s. "Spend time with us too" (*Hamare saath bhi thoda bahut waqt beetaiye*), he remarked. That evening I sat with them until midnight. The conversation at one point veered toward the archaeologist *saheb*s. "Once I was watching the rerun of the Ramayana serial on TV with my wife," narrated the photographer, who was the star of the evening's gathering, cracking jokes (*chutkule*) one after another.

> It was the scene in the school [*gurukul*] in the forest, the guru [*rishi*] was training Lord Rama [*Bhagawan Ramji*] and other heavenly figures [*devata*] in the fine art of archery. The guru asked all the *devata*s to take aim at a mango on a tree far away. But before they aimed, they were asked how far the target was. The first *devata* noted that "it was approximately [*shayad*] 40 meters away," the next *devata* said the target was "*shayad* 50 meters away," then another said the mango was "*shayad* 35 meters away." Then it was the turn of Lord Rama. He gravely peered at the mango and calmly declared that the target was "exactly 43.987 meters way." "Superb!" [*shabaash*], the guru praised Lord Rama and let him take aim.

It was then that my wife asked me a question—"so because Lord Rama gave the right answer, he became a God [*bhagwan*]. So what happened to the rest of the *devata*s?" I replied, "They all became archaeologists."

This provoked a peal of laughter. The photographer then concluded: "See, that is the difference between archaeologists and normal people. They are always about approximation [*shayad-yeh shayad-voh*]—they will never tell you anything straight [*kabhi sahi uttar nahi dethe*]." It was through this kind of jocularity that it became obvious to me several times during my ethnography[21] that an ASI archaeological excavation was "everything else but research." As a disgruntled ASA once remarked: "It is about money, corruption, public performance, politics, favoritism, personal gains, and everything else. Research is just an excuse. Go ask any archaeologist what research is and you will know that it means nothing to him." And this is what I did. To ask various members of the archaeological team what their research program or scholarly motive was in taking part in such a large-scale archaeological excavation.

"The research questions for the SHP have already been decided by the bosses in the DG office," noted an AA in Baror, who was disenchanted with the ASI excavation process after having been in the ASI for more than a decade and a half.

> We come here to just dig holes. There are smaller day-to-day research questions— such as which trenches to open, which quadrants to dig, and so on. But these are minor questions [*choti baathye*]. At the end of the season, we see that all the money that has been allocated to us for the excavation has been spent, and that we have enough data for the annual report. That is our primary aim.[22]

However, when I spoke to the site director at Baror, he was more precise. His aim was to excavate the early Harappan layers and demarcate the extent of the habitation deposit, to trace the fortification wall, to get the complete sequence of the culture-history of the site, and to expose at least one complete house structure. His narrative about the SHP research design was the "official answer," according to an AA who was also sitting with me while I was talking to the site director. He said,

> As you can see, the excavation is in a mess. They are just digging arbitrarily. In two seasons there have been three site directors. The first was an absentee [*loopth*] site director, who came here only for the inauguration of the excavation. She also had joint assignment as the SA of the Circle. Then there was the onsite director who would only sit in his tent. He only wanted to ensure that the money allocated to the excavation was finished [*khatam*] by the end of the season. He could then

pocket some in the process [*thoda paise pocket mein bhar le*]. Now there is a new site director, who is the present SA of the Ex. Br. He has been here just a few weeks, and this is the first time he is digging a Harappan site. He is a Buddhist specialist from eastern India. He cannot make out the difference between red slipware and black and red ware. He does not have any clue about what is going on here. We know what is happening here. It is PWD [Public Works Department] work. Dig because there is a site [*khodo kyonki site hai*]. The only research questions involve day-to-day problem solving and management problems. That's all.

At Dholavira, when asked about the research design, a veteran AA told me:

It has been the same thing for the past 10 seasons. The important thing is just to dig. Now that Bisht sir is busy in the DG office, he does not care about the day-to-day workings at the site. The report is nowhere in sight. All we are told to do is to dig. Find more reservoirs. Dig the Middle Town. Dig the citadel. You tell me how much more can you find after having worked for more than 12 years. I think this is just glorified treasure hunting. Dig antiquities from the earth and then lock them up in trunks in Purana Qila. Nothing more.

Questions about research design and research plans would almost always elicit such dismissive replies from informants who could confide in me. Others would give me the standard official reply: "The need to search for Saraswati at a macro-level and the necessity of defining the cultural sequence at the micro-level of the site." For most of the junior-level officers and the staff, day-to-day management of the archaeological excavation dictated the research question. These micro-research questions were considered to be administrative issues rather than academic queries with scholarly implications.

In his "Third Staff Memorandum" in August 1944, Wheeler, in his inimitable style, notes the conceptual inconsequentiality of research in the ASI during his days:

Here I will insert a true story, in the hope that by smiling at ourselves we may begin to take ourselves seriously. At the conclusion of an inspection, I discussed a number of points with the official in charge who, to each of my suggestions, replied emphatically and very properly, "Sir, I will do it tomorrow". At last, I came to the question of research. I remarked that although he had been there many years, I could not find that he had produced any evidence of research into the many problems that lay to the hand. His eyes lit up with the fires of eager intent. "Sir" he said earnestly, "I will do researches tomorrow." And there is no doubt that he sincerely meant it. (AACD, File No. 33/24/1944)

Although I cannot narrate a similar tale from my own ethnography, this "true story," as Wheeler describes it, is instructive in understanding the functional role that research and research design had for ASI archaeologists. It was subsumed under the discourse on scholarly mentality, corruption, the inner workings of the Central Advisory Board of Archaeology (CABA) and the institutional hierarchy of the ASI. For the ASI excavation team, the research design was primarily "given from above [*upper-se*]," and they were only expected to "work at the bottom [*neeche-se*]." Who frames the research question was also a question of professional hierarchy and therefore the responses I have noted earlier were disparate and contradictory. The larger research objectives were defined in abstract terms, in a few terse pages, when the director of the excavation submitted a proposal for excavation to the CABA.[23]

The lack of direction in the research impetus of the ASI had reached such an acute level by 2009 that during the 34th meeting of the CABA, the prime minister of India indicated a necessity for the formulation of the "National Policy on Archaeological Excavation and Explorations." After the formation of five sub-committees, a draft policy was submitted to the Ministry of Culture, which was not approved until 2020 (Niti Aayog 2020, 97). In 2012, the Comptroller and Auditor General (CAG) report, in a rather acerbic tone, observed the paucity of any research plans at the ASI and said that it

> did not have any laid down policy or guidelines for selection of sites for excavation. There was no priority list or perspective plan for completion of projects within a given period. We found that excavation licenses were not being given in a systematic manner to solve cultural or historical debates or questions pertaining to different parts of the country. (CAG 2013, 102–03)

It is this lack of research objectives that was the root of the greatest malaise of the ASI excavation machinery—the non-publication of excavation reports.

The excavation report is the final epistemological representation of any archaeological excavation (Tilley 1989; Jones 2001, 44; Lucas 2019). Its importance in the disciplinary discourse of archaeology has been underscored since the birth of the discipline in the eighteenth century (Hodder 1989). Discursively, the excavation report is an epistemological artifact of an event that involves the destruction of evidence (Lucas 2001, 35). Therefore, the need to record the complete nature of evidence—its physical and material proprieties, its spatial position, its stratigraphical location, and other characteristics, with as many representational media as possible (Drewett 2011)—has been a distinct part of the disciplinary practice of archaeology (Olsen et al. 2012, 48). An excavation report is a compilation of such a multifarious record—photographs, maps, diagrams, drawings, and statistical charts—that are sutured within a narrative, purportedly empirical (Zimmerman 2003). Depending on the site, the time taken for excavation, the quantum of material culture unearthed, and the area exposed, an excavation report can run from a few pages to many volumes.

At the ASI, excavations are first reported in the annual publication of the ASI called *Indian Archaeology—A Review* (*IAR*) started in 1953–54 where the key characteristics of the site are noted and the main material cultural discoveries are announced. It is mandated by the rules of the Ancient Monuments and Archaeological Sites and Remains Act of 1959 that after an archaeological excavation, a report has to be submitted to the Government of India:

> The licensee shall, within three months of the completion of the excavation operations submit to the Director General a summary report of the results of the excavation, and where the operations are carried on for a period of more than three months such report shall be submitted every quarter, and it shall be open to the Director General to publish the report in his reports or reviews. (Tripathi 2007, 30)

Within this legal framework, the ASI publishes a short report on all the excavations carried out by it in the *IAR*—enumerating the valuable artifacts found at various sites and the structural features that had been exposed. It is obligatory that a detailed, book-length report is submitted and published, especially of large monumental sites. The ASI regarded the excavation report as the requisite intellectual result of a scholarly pursuit, and its indispensability was framed in terms of the moral responsibility of a statist institution to provide information to its citizen. The evidential paradigm followed in the report is a mimesis of juridical logic and, therefore, for the ASI, it had a quasi-legal valence. The excavation report was bestowed not just with an overpowering cultural and epistemological credence but it also epitomized the quintessence of the scientific and statist authority of the ASI. It is the official document of an archaeological excavation, which, as we have seen in the case of the Ayodhya excavation, also has a legal status.

By 2003–04, when I began my ethnography, there was a simmering discontent among the rank and file of the ASI regarding a large backlog of unpublished excavation reports. The ASI rapidly carried out excavations but few reports were being written and published. By 2002, the ASI had excavated 292 sites and out of these 102 had been identified as those for which detailed reports should have been written. However, only 45 reports had been published, with 56 others pending.[24] Out of these 56 pending sites, 17 sites were identified as large-scale excavations and 39 sites were identified as small-scale excavations.[25] The 2001 Lal Review Committee report had also noted that unpublished reports of major excavations were a big embarrassment to the ASI. It admonished:

"It is acknowledged on all hands that excavation is nothing but destruction if it is not published in detail. It is just not enough to publish brief notes here and there"—referring to the mandatory synopsis of excavations published in the *IAR* (Lal 2001, 184). In addition, harsh opinions were openly voiced during the years I was doing my fieldwork. "It is our public duty to publish the report," rationalized an AA in Hansi. He elaborated:

> After all, we are spending public money. If we do not publish, it would be a criminal waste of these resources. The public has the right to know what we have excavated and recovered. We are doing all this for the national good. If the public does not know what we have dug up, then the government should stop [*bandh kare de*] all these excavations! The ASI should then just concentrate on preserving monuments and heritage. We should stop digging. We should cease to be a research institute and become only a heritage management organization.

The parliamentary committee on the functioning of the ASI, headed by Nilotpal Basu, similarly observed: "The Committee is of the view that if excavation reports are not written, then all the taxpayers' money spent on them goes to waste. Also, in absence of the timely publication of excavation reports, the achievements of the Archaeological Survey of India largely remain unnoticed by the public" (Basu 2005, 16). It was common knowledge in the ASI community that there was a huge gap between actual excavation and the publication of excavation reports:

> Regarding delay in writing the excavation reports, the Archaeological Survey of India informed that the delay is due to their nature and scope, as these are supposed to be comprehensive research documents, containing information on excavated structures, stratigraphical features, supported by maps, illustrations—photo-documentation and line-drawings of excavated structures, potteries, artifacts, and other materials. The report also would have to incorporate detailed technical and scientific reports and bibliographical references. Since a huge body of data is generated in course of excavation, it takes time to organize and describe that exhaustive database on factual and interpretative lines. For report writing, a team of excavators, who participated in that very excavation, is required to discuss, prepare research notes, and correlate the excavation findings for description in terms of time and space. This is true in the case of all excavations. (Basu 2005, 15)

However, the gap between the actual excavations and the reports was so long that the above rationality of delayed reports by the ASI was not an adequate explanation. One famous example that would often be cited during my conversations was the report of the Harappan site of Kalibangan, published a staggering 33 years after the excavation. B. B. Lal, one of the excavators and editors of the report, wrote with anguish in the preface:

In presenting this report to readers, so many years after the excavations, we feel really small, nay even ashamed. The only umbrella under which we can cover our heads is the saying "Better late than never." We hope that the academic community will accept this much-belated report for whatever it is worth. (Lal et al. 2003, v)

I was often told that the Dholavira report would also meet with a similar fate. An AA at Dholavira noted:

I am not even sure if the Dholavira report will ever be written. After more than a dozen years of excavation, we only have some articles by Bisht sir, and the insignificant mentions in the Annual Review—which is also delayed by more than five years. Now Bisht sir is retiring in less than six months—he will also have similar problems like Lal sir. Before he retires, he should at least start the Dholavira Cell to begin the process of collecting and assembling the excavation material and artifacts. It will be a monumental miscarriage of responsibility if the Dholavira report is not published. But the way things are going, I will be surprised if it is ever published.

Such concerns were not unwarranted, as most people I asked about the status of the Dholavira report would wave their hands dismissively. A photographer wryly commented, "Only God knows if the report will ever be published. I really hope Bisht lives for another 20–30 years—only then we will see the face of the report." This fear was not unfounded, as a number of excavators of large-scale excavations had passed away before the publication of the excavation reports. As one of my informants movingly articulated, "With them, the site reports have also been cremated" (*Unke saath, site report ki bhi chita jal gayi hai*).[26] In 2015, a PDF of the 396-page Rakhigarhi report was uploaded on the ASI website, followed by a 940-page PDF of the Dholavira report; however, both were soon removed. In 2019, my informant told me that the internal review of both reports had been scathing. Their publication has been stalled due to the poor quality of the work submitted, and they are yet to be published.

The delay in the publication of excavation reports is a norm in archaeology throughout the world, but it has taken on grave proportions at the ASI. It was Wheeler who was the earliest to notice that unpublished reports of the ASI had become a problem in postcolonial India. In the first post-independence review of the ASI in 1965, headed by Wheeler, more than 25 years after the damning Woolley report, he mentions:

During the past ten years, no fewer than 64 sites have been thus examined, and in March 1965, eight sites are actually under investigation. The total effort, in quality as in quantity, is impressive; as a result of it, we now have appreciably more information about several aspects of Indian culture than we had ten years ago....

More serious is the accumulation of *un-published* excavations; at present moment no fewer than 14 excavation-reports are outstanding, some of them (including one of the most important) going back to 1955. This is wrong, whatever the cause. It cannot be too often emphasized that *unpublishable excavation is destruction*, and is therefore wholly unjustified. (Wheeler 1965, 16–17, emphasis in original)

In 1984, the Ram Niwas Mirdha Committee report also observed a dismal situation, but it was only in 2001 that the Lal Committee report mentioned that the non-publication of the excavations report had reached epidemic proportions. By 2005, more than three parliamentary committees had observed the gravity of the state of affairs. The *49th Parliamentary Committee Report on the Demands for Grant (2001–02) of the Department of Culture* stated, while mincing no words, that the "practice of excavating something and not publishing reports had become a chronic malaise" (Mukherjee 2001, 15). The *56th Report on the Demands for Grant (2002–03) of the Department of Culture* observed that it was "aghast to find that final reports on excavation works have been pending for more than fifty years. Some of the excavation work had been taken up during 1947.... The Committee feels the Department was having a lackadaisical approach in the matter" (Mukherjee 2002, 14). The staggering magnitude of non-published excavation reports by the ASI had become a common topic of discussion and conversation by the time I was doing my ethnography. In 2013, the CAG report observed the following: "We found reports pending for 57 years in some cases. For some of the major excavations, like Mathura, Saravasti and Ropar the report writing work for the excavations carried out in 1954–55, 1958–59 and 1953–54 respectively, were yet to be completed" (CAG 2013, 116).[27]

For those in the ASI, this was a matter of embarrassment, as illustrated by B. B. Lal's apology in the Kalibangan report cited earlier, but no one could adequately pinpoint the cause of the delay. There were various theories regarding the non-publication of excavation reports and everyone contributed their insights. The director of the Dholavira excavation explained,

There is no point in blaming excavators for not writing the report. It is the system. Please remember, first and foremost we are bureaucrats and not archaeologists [*sabse phele aur sabse aage hum sarkari karamchari hai*]. The government wants us to be like archaeologist, but it treats us like a bureaucrat [*government chahati hai ke hum archaeologist bane, per hume treat karte hai karmachari ki tarah*]. They want us to dig a site, and then go back to the office and write an excavation report right away. When we reach office, we get drowned with so much bureaucratic work [*babugiri*] that there is no room to breathe—files, redundant paperwork, court cases, financial accounts, budgets, parliament questions, hundreds of pointless queries from the ministry or the DG office. It is just back-breaking.

Everyone I spoke to echoed this emotion. The daily functioning of a bureaucracy had made the archaeologists "paper-pushers," as one senior ASA, using the English expression, illuminated. The archaeologist-bureaucrat poignantly narrated:

> When I first joined the ASI, I loved to sign official paper. It made me feel important. I would sign my full name [*pura naam ka sign karta tha*]. But soon I saw that the number of times I had to sign my full name every day; I had to shorten my signature [*sign hi chota kar diya*]. Now I only use my initials [*ab keval initial karta hoon*].

When I first met the director of the Dholavira site at the DG office in New Delhi, to get permission to work in Dholavira, he had asked me, after a cup of tea, if it was possible for him to get a grant to work in an American university to "peacefully [*itminan se*] write an excavation report." Later on, in the field, he further explained as we were sitting in his *boonga* in Dholavira, one evening after dinner:

> Those excavators interested in writing reports are unreasonably [*bematlab ke*] transferred. The system ensures that they cannot write their reports. Tell me how can one write a report if the antiquities of the site are all locked up in Delhi, all the trench notebooks, the site drawings, and photographs are in Nagpur and you are sitting in Agra trying to write a report of a site that is in Gujarat. It is madness [*pagalpan*]. Can you imagine how much paperwork and time it takes just to get access to a site notebook from an office where you are no longer the boss?

This wearying state of affairs is obvious in a letter appended to the unpublished Rakhigarhi report. Amarendra Nath, the excavator of the site, complains to the-then DG of the ASI, Rakesh Tewari, that his work was impeded due to a lack of assistance from the ASI:

> You may be aware of the fact that the ground staff available to this section is too meager to cope up the work of report writing. The services of only one semiskilled casual labour engaged to this section has been withdrawn vide F. No. 9/66/2014-15/EB-II496 Dated 01.12.2014. The Assistant Archaeologist who is holding the charge antiquities and records of Rakhigarhi is available only when he is free from his office duty in the Branch. The services of a draftsman accorded to this unit are hardly available. Under the circumstances it is requested to restore the services of one semiskilled casual labour earlier attached to this unit and draftsman of the Excavation Branch II Purana Quila so as to enable the unit to function smoothly with limited hands and achieve the target. Necessary instructions may kindly be issued at your level for restoring the same. (Nath 2015, 2)

This excuse of ineffective bureaucratic machinery was not novel. It had already been brought to light by the Lal Committee report, which pointed out that one of the major reasons for the non-publication of the excavation reports was, the indiscriminate transfers of officers in charge of excavations, which did not give them time to finish writing the reports: "The shifting of excavators from one office to another, without seeing to it that the reports are completed before the shifting, has resulted in a major backlog" (Lal 2001, 184).

The CAG report in 2013 also notes the debilitating effect that incessant transfers of archaeologists have on the timely completion of the excavation reports. Taking a stern view, it says, in a reprimanding tone:

> We noticed that no time was given to the officers of the ASI doing excavation, exclusively for Report writing work and as such there was no specified timeframe. The report writing work was undertaken much after the excavations and for the ASI's own excavations, sometimes after the retirement of the main excavators. This resulted in pending report writing work and also extra expenditure on remuneration of retired officers. We found that expenditure of 63.75 lakh had been incurred as expenditure for such delayed report writing works…. The ASI replied (May 2012) that taking stringent measures against unusual delays of report writing by the ASI on officers could not be justified as the officers were overburdened by other administrative activities and untimely transfers which resulted in delay. The reply of the ASI is not convincing, as the primary responsibility of report writing by excavators cannot be compromised.[28]

Indiscriminate transfers and its effect on the non-publication of the excavation reports was a real problem and the blame for this was put on the Administration Department of the ASI by almost all ASI officers. They believed the ASI Administration was the major cause of the "mess" (*gadabad*) that the ASI had gotten into. A Dy SA in Baror explained:

> These administrators [*babus*] are not archaeologists and are not sensitive to needs in the field and neither are they aware how archaeology works. They are basically administrators. They are good at management [*babugiri*] but they do not understand that archaeology is not just about digging holes but also about writing, which is an extremely important and time-consuming process. So they cannot understand how harmful indiscriminate transfers are.

The Nilotpal Basu Parliamentary Committee also noted that the untimely transfer of excavation directors caused significant delays in the report's writing:

The Committee recommends that the Archaeological Survey of India should enforce a fixed time frame for writing excavation reports after the excavation work has been completed, so that the public at large is not deprived of the vital right to information. The Committee also recommends that the ASI should ensure that officials engaged in a particular excavation work are not transferred till such time that they complete the excavations and submit their reports. (Basu 2005, 16)

The official explanations for the non-publication of reports placed the blame on the "system" and the "administration." In the narratives I heard, it was common to allocate agency to the postcolonial bureaucratic system for the present state of the ASI. I empathized with this narrative, as it was effective. It allowed the victims to be a Kafkaesque casualty of the "system." For instance, as early as 1968, this issue was being discussed with considerable seriousness. During the 22nd meeting of the CABA in 1968, the principal of Deccan College, Dr H. D. Sankalia, notes:

It has been found in experience over the last so many years that the Superintending Archaeologists and the Dy. Superintending Archaeologists of the various Circles of the Survey have got to do things, viz. look after the monuments which is their main charge and also carry out research. This they are unable to do and the worst part of it is that they are transferred from time to time that the research they have done suffers terribly. (AACD, File No. 13/6/1/68-M; 1968)

For the ASI and its archaeologists who prided themselves as custodians of the vast wealth of the archaeological heritage of India, large-scale excavations seemed only fitting to their status, or as one site director matter-of-factly stated it: "*Its natural* [English phrase used]." Not once during my conversations and interviews with the archaeologists and the staff at various excavation sites was I was given an academic justification for large-scale excavation. Large-scale excavation was always framed as a given. It was the normative and naturalistic outcome of the very being of the institutional and bureaucratic ontology of the ASI. An AA in Baror who had been involved in the excavation and report writing at Ayodhya told me,

If the ASI can produce an excavation report on Ayodhya, it can do so for any site in India. The Ayodhya report came out because of the court's pressure [*court ka danda*]. If there is pressure like that, all the excavation reports will be published in less than a year. It is just a matter of discipline, which is lacking in the ASI.

The unpublished excavation reports of the ASI were an illustration of the broader malaise of bureaucratic archaeology in India. The excavation report in archaeology is not just the final epistemological act of an archaeological event, but it also symbolizes the fruition of the archaeological project. Its publication signifies the fact that the excavators are willing to share their insights with the scholarly world and the larger public. The ASI is aware of the epistemological valence of the excavation report, and, therefore, its chronic non-publication is an embarrassment to the organization. Somewhere—jostling between systemic incompetence and individual weariness—has been a systemic and structural failure. Everyone has someone or something they could blame for it. That is the ontology of bureaucracy in India.

Theories of Corruption

One somber evening, in Dholavira, I was in the tent of an AA. I was chatting with him as he was logging the artifacts discovered into the antiquity register, sitting cross-legged on his foldable metal cot. Fragile steatite micro-beads, delicate fragments of terracotta figurines, exquisite pieces of lapis lazuli, and weathered carnelian beads, carefully stored in labeled zipper storage bags were scattered all over his bed. He was painstakingly copying the details of the labels into the antiquity register. In the shadow of the flickering incandescent bulb and in the background of the humming diesel generator, he told me in a low voice that the trench numbers and stratigraphical measurements on innumerable artifacts discovered in the early years of Dholavira excavation had been obliterated due to poor storage:

> Those artifacts, mostly ceramics and non-precious metal, steatite and terracotta antiquities are of no use. They are now without context [*unka koi context nahi hai*]. They would have been essential to construct a deep cultural history of the site. I don't know how it happened. In some trunks the termites [*dimak*] have eaten the site-cards. In other trunks the pottery bags have withered. We have lost them. They are all trash now [*ab yeh sab kura ho gaya hai*].

Latour belabors this point in his poignant ethnography of soil scientists working in the thick tropical jungles of the Amazon. He asserts that if such a destabilization of the inscriptive universe occurs, then the scientist would be lost in the landscape.[29] In Dholavira, and with the archaeological excavations of the ASI, such obliteration of the inscriptive universe was a persistent problem. Its adverse impact on the knowledge production capacity of the archaeological project was indelible. My informants admitted that this problem was one factor resulting in the non-publication of archaeological reports. B. B Lal, in the preface to the Kalibangan report, notes with regret the difficulty in obtaining Harappan seals from the excavation he directed. He implies that those artifacts were lost forever:

In 1972, the writer took voluntary retirement from the post of the Director General of the Survey and joined Jiwaji University, Gwalior, as Professor and head of the School of Ancient Indian History, Culture and Archaeology. During the summer vacation at the university in 1973, he came to Delhi with the specific objective of writing the report on the excavations at Kalibangan. He wanted to begin the work by analyzing the data regarding the seals. The idea was to find out if seals with a given motif occurred in any particular context or not. And if they did, what could be its implications. He had already made some eye-copies of the seals during fieldwork. All that he wanted was to examine the plans and sections of the trenches wherein the seals concerned had been found. He requested the authorities to make the relevant drawings available to him. He waited for more than a month, sweating in the sultry room at the Survey's Safdarjung office, but nothing was done. Excuses of one kind or another were produced. Completely disappointed, he had to go back to Gwalior, informing the authorities of the situation and adding that as and when the records were made available, he would come back and resume the work. That day never came and the report-writing was thus at a standstill for quite some time. (Lal et al. 2003, v)

This overt public condemnation by an ex-DG of the ASI reveals the inadequacies of the bureaucratic process. Artifacts excavated at the site disappear into the unknown crevices of postcolonial bureaucratic archives, never to be found. In the confines of the small tent in Dholavira, under the gentle darkness of the night sky, the AA, without looking at me as he was carefully writing in the antiquity register, in soft tones, scorned: "Data is dead [*data hi khatam ho gaya hai*]. On what basis will they write a report [*aab kis basis per report likhenge*]?"

The poor quality of the excavation report published by the ASI reflects such a lost inscriptive epistemic universe, which was a product of a professional malaise that was endemic in the bureaucratic ecology. "For them [the excavators], digging is just another routine-work. They dig because they are supposed to dig. Report writing is a different issue and most of these senior officers just don't have the patience to sit, think, and write," elucidated a draughtsman in Bhirrana one evening while sipping tea after the day's excavation. Continuing further, he said in an unsympathetic tenor:

First, most of these excavators are not academic. They have PhDs but their mentality is that of an administrator [*babu*]. They are happier signing infinite [*ungeenath*] files rather than sitting and writing something intellectually worthwhile. Also, you have to understand [*aap ko samajna padega*] excavation is now just a means of making money [*paisa banana*]. As you know, corruption is rampant [*charo taraf corruption hai*]. Everyone wants to make more money than they have [*sab koi paisa banana chahate hai*], and for those who run the excavation branches, there is no other way than digging sites [*unke pass aur koi rasta nahi hai*]. So what they want is to dig sites so they can show in their annual expenditure budgets they have spent the entire allocated amount for excavations. Writing reports is not so profitable. So, there is no inclination for doing that [*unki koi iccha nahi hai*].[30]

The archaeological process that I have described in this book was driven by the necessity to expose large archaeological spatiality rather than determined by a coherent research objective; here, excavation reports took a back seat, as it did not have a possibility of "making money" (*paisa banana*).

The decision to excavate an archaeological site and when the actual excavation begins is a long and arduous process, even for an ASI archaeologist. An AA in Hansi explained:

> Only an ASI archaeologist of the rank of Dy SA can apply for the license to excavate. So we as AA, even if we have PhDs from reputed universities, cannot write a proposal to excavate even a small site on our own. We have to work under an SA or a Dy SA.[31]

This statement also revealed the disenchantment of the AA working at the site under a senior officer. Many junior officers were working under officers they believed were incompetent, dishonest, or lacked a "scholarly mentality." I learned that "scholarly mentality" (always the English phrase was used) encompassed not just the ability to excavate a site, or to have a research plan or design, but also the ethical disposition of an individual officer. As a senior AA clarified, "Scholarly mentality is not about digging holes in a stratigraphic manner. It is the larger worldview of an excavator. In the ASI, it has to do with honesty [*imandari*]. The honesty to not only excavate a site, but also to be *non-corrupt* [English word used]."[32] He further elaborated:

> I think there is clear link between good scholars and non-corrupt scholars. First, according to me, a good scholar [*badiya scholar*] is one who digs sites with some research question(s) in mind. Who excavates a site thoughtfully [*sohch-samjh kar*] and does not rip open the whole site [*poori site ko nahi uqharte hai*]. Who makes attempts to write the report soon. He is also a good taskmaster. He also is not corrupt. Now it is difficult to say, as you know, who is corrupt and who is not. But let us say they don't have CBI cases registered against them. And according to my theory—a good scholar is most likely a non-corrupt person.

In this description of the "scholarly mentality" of an ASI archaeologist, my informant took the qualities he believed epitomized an academic-archaeologist and combined them with those of a bureaucrat-archaeologist—an unblemished professional. "Scholarly mentality" was also tied to other social characteristics; it was not merely about astute academic and intellectual capability. This combined quality of an academic-archaeologist and an administrator-archaeologist made up an ASI officer and differentiated him/her from normal university-trained archaeologists. It is in between this tension of an administrator and the academic that the career biographies of senior archaeologists were narrated. Most of my informants noted that there were less than a handful of ASI archaeologists who could be said to have a "scholarly mentality." A Dy SA lamented: "Where are those people [*ab vayse log kahan*]? They were all the old timers [*woh sab purane jamane ke log the*]. Nowadays you cannot become the director at the ASI without having a CBI case against you."

In Bhirrana, one wintry night after a sumptuous meal, during a rather warm conversation with a group of AAs and some staff members huddled in a canvas tent, I was told the "real reason" for the ASI's obsession with large-scale excavation. It did not come as a surprise to be told: "The real reason [*asli karan*] ASI does large-scale excavations was not because all these sites needed [*zaoorat*] huge digs. But big [*bada*] excavations, lengthy [*lamba-samay wala*] excavation, large [*fhhela hua*] excavations meant, money [*ka matlab hai, paisa*]. And that is the real reason, sir*ji*." The political economy of a large-scale excavation made it the preferred intervention for ASI archaeologists working in the Ex. Br.—the least funded of all the units of the ASI. The Circle was the most heavily funded division of the ASI, where most of the funds were allocated to conduct conservation work. Deputation in the Circle was considered to be the most lucrative of all jobs at the ASI. Numerous informants told me that to be the SA of a Circle was the most "money-making position in the ASI [*sabse paisa banana wala post hai*]." This was because a huge amount of funds was allocated for conservation work, which provided a "ready-made setting" for pilfering funds by either using sub-standard restoration materials or through "kickbacks" involved in buying materials and supplies for conservation work. The only way of "making money" in the Ex. Br. was to conduct an excavation and "what better way than having a large-scale excavation [*bada aur lamba excavation se accha aur kya ho sakta hai?*], which went on for many years, which required hundreds and hundreds of labor, and tons of material and supplies [*maal-pathar*]."

One of the most common cases of corruption that was often discussed with me in hushed tones during my ethnography was about Dr Amarendra Nath, who had excavated Rakhigarhi from 1997–98 to 1999–2000. He was the director of the Institute of Archaeology when he excavated this important Harappan site. He was considered to be an impeccable ASI archaeologist, who was endowed with a "scholarly mentality." My informants held him in high esteem, some of whom had learnt the craft of archaeology under his tutelage at the Rakhigarhi excavation.[33] However, in 2001, the CBI filed a case of corruption against him. He was charged with forging and fabricating bills of non-existent shops, showrooms, and firms. In 2015, a special CBI court in Haryana found him guilty in three cases and sentenced him to two and a half years' rigorous imprisonment.[34] I heard instances of many other narratives of corruption throughout my fieldwork—their orality encompassed my ethnographic world—it was not difficult for me to make the connection between the ASI's fetish for large-scale excavations and its political economy. For instance, the total budget of the SHP for the year 2003–04 was INR 53.35 million, and for the year 2004–05 it was INR 23.98 million. This included conservation, excavations, and building of heritage complexes. For the year 2003–04, the money allocated for the excavation work at Dholavira was INR 6 million, for Baror it was INR 4 million, while for Bhirrana and Juni Kuran it was INR 2 million.

In a moment of rare self-reflexivity, at another time, another location, another informant—an ASA—confessed to me, while relaxing in a mud hut on a very hot afternoon in Baror:

> We in the Ex. Br. love excavations. We all benefit [*fayada*] from it. Some make huge amounts of money while others make a small sum of money. But we all benefit from it. From fixing muster rolls to making false receipts for travel, to buying unnecessary supplies. We are all corrupt. This system is corrupt [*hum sab corrupt hai. Yeh system hi corrupt hai*]. But then, you cannot blame anyone [*aap kisi ko blame nahi kar sakte*]. Look [*dekhiye*], when you see everyone in the Circle making money because of the huge conservation projects, from the SA to the mere peon [*chaprasi*], what do you expect us to do? When you see that a conservation assistant drives a Santro to work every day, then what do you do?[35] It becomes difficult when you realize that you have been in the ASI for 15 years and you don't own even a scooter and the conservation assistant is just a young lad who has just arrived [*kal ka chokra*].

The CAG report also alluded to these kinds of corruption in the ASI:

> In Chandigarh Circle, during 2007–08, a proposal for excavation work (Buddhist Stupa, Asand, Haryana) was approved but could not be commenced due to non-availability of labour. We found that even though no excavation was undertaken, an expenditure of 14.98 lakh was incurred on acquiring computer camera, photo-material, stationery and kitchen articles, etc. from the funds allotted for excavation. (CAG 2013, 105)

This form of corruption that is assembled on the modality of accumulating, generating, and siphoning of bureaucratic capital by "making money" (*paisa banana*) is instrumentally incommensurable from "eating money" (Mathur 2018) or "leaky states" (Anand 2015), as has been discussed in recent anthropological literature of corruption in India. In the ASI, money is made by manufacturing the past—in the dusty and forlorn trenches of large-scale horizontal excavation in the margins of India; in the tattered tents of campsite; in the forged receipts and fabricated bills. This past-making is furthered compromised in the dumped pottery fragments; faded and obliterated antiquity labels; in the lost and forgotten artifacts stored in the rugged ramparts of medieval forts in Delhi; in the unwritten site-reports, never published. Here corrupt bureaucracy produces corrupt epistemology.

Notes

1. In a letter dated August 27, 2003, the joint director general (Jt DG) instructed the excavation directors (called team leaders) of Ayodhya to maintain secrecy:

    > Unless and until the Hon'ble Court gives its verdict on the case, it is imperative that every team member strictly follow the Conduct Rules, and maintain absolute silence on the matter. Under no circumstance, any team member should divulge to anyone any fact regarding the excavation, and its findings, contents and interpretation of the Report, etc. The letter is being circulated to all the team members individually too. However, you may also ensure the instructions contained herein are strictly followed in both letter and spirit. The Team Members are instructed to strictly adhere to the above instructions. (AACD, File No. 29/1/1995-EE/Part V)

2. Justice Sudhir Agrawal argues,

    > Archaeology provides scientific factual data for reconstructing ancient historical material culture, understanding, archaeology for the past is a multi disciplinary scientific subject and requires a team of workers for effective results. Excavation of ancient sites is one of the major works of Archaeologists. As it is a scientific discipline, it uses scientific methods in its working. (Khan, Agarwal, and Sharma 2010, 2375)

3. For instance, some of the longest ASI excavations have been: Dholavira—12 years (1989–95 and 1996–2004); Kalibangan—9 years (1960–69); Shringverpur—8 years (1977–85); Burzahom—9 years (1960–68 and 1971–72); Sannati—7 years (1986–89 and 1994–98); Lothal—7 years (1955–62).

4. The excavation was conducted over a total area of 1,200 square meters from March 12, 2003, to August 7, 2003.

5. In total, 98 trenches were excavated of 4-metre-by-4-metre dimension with a 50-centimeter balk in between the trenches. Out of these, 84 trenches were recommended for excavation by M/s Tojo-Vikas International (Pvt.) Ltd. Out of the 84 trenches recommended, only 70 could be excavated and the remaining 14 could not be excavated due to the presence of barriers and other obstructions on the site and subsequently another 14 trenches were excavated (AACD, File No. 29/1/1995-EE-Part-V).

6. The excavations began with a 14-member team and the latter swelled to a 51-member team. As on the final day, 51 members were in the Excavation Team. This included 1 director, 5 superintending archaeologists, 2 deputy superintending archaeologists, 1 deputy superintending epigraphist, 5 assistant superintending archaeologists, 4 assistant superintending chemists, 11 assistant archaeologists, 1 senior artist, 1 surveyor, 6 draughtsman, 5 photographers, 1 LDC, 1 work assistant III, 1 storekeeper, 2 foreman, 3 attendants, and 1 T/S casual worker (AACD, File No. 29/1/1995-EE/Part-IV).

7. The problem of ASI staff abandoning the site seemed common enough for Gauri Chatterjee, the then DG of the ASI, to notify Hari Manhji on July 4, 2003: "No ASI official of the excavation team shall leave excavation camp or the site without the express permission of DG or Jt. DG. This may be brought to the notice of all concerned and complied with strictly" (AACD File No. 29/1/95-Pt IV).

8. An internal note circulated in the ASI showed the degree of intrusion the court-led excavation was to the normal ASI methodology:

> The contesting parties sought direction that the ASI should not give a wrong description about the identity of a find and if something is beyond identification in terms of function or otherwise, then the safe method of describing it by morphology ... should be adopted. The description given by ASI team may not be conclusive and if the applicants find that the description is not correct, it will be open to them to file objection to such entry at a proper stage in regard to description made by the ASI team in the register. (AACD, File No. 29/1/1995-EE [Part-V])

9. My informant told me that each artifact discovered from the trenches was subjected to inspection of the observers of the court and counsels and nominees of the contesting parties. The artifacts were sealed in the presence of these observers and counsels on a daily basis. The sealed artifacts were later opened in the presence of the available nominees for photography and drawing purposes. In the same note mentioned above, there is clear instruction as to

how to deal with discrepancies that occur at the moment of recording and sealing of the artifacts:

> Regarding the allegation that ASI does not mention the number of bones, glazed pottery, etc. found during the excavation by the contesting parties, the Hon'ble observed that as mentioned earlier in their order dated 26.03.2003 the ASI should specify the nature of finds, i.e. bones, glazed wares, etc. ... and should be recorded in the register of day to day work. As regards giving the number and size of bones and glazed wares, etc., if they are sealed in the presence of the parties and duly numbered, it may not be necessary to give the size and number. It is, however, open to the ASI team to make specification of the finds by measurement of size if there is no difficulty. (AACD, F. No. 29/1/1995-EE [Part-V])

10. In his judgment, Justice Khan did not rely on the ASI report (Supreme Court 2019, 526).

11. The court reported that "[b]etween 14th April, 2003 to 26th July, 2003, thirty four" objections against the ASI excavation were filed in the court (Khan, Agarwal, and Sharma 2010, 2143). For more details on the objections on the practice of ASI's archaeology see Khan, Agarwal, and Sharma (2010, 2143–67).

12. Including: 47 field note books; 182 drawing/maps; 7,777 color negatives and 1,510 black and white negatives; 4,293 photographs in 46 albums; 10 video cassettes; along with registers of pottery, unsealed bones, architectural objects stored in tin-shed at the excavated site, individual list of 9 boxes containing bones, glazed-wares, antiquities, and so on, day to day registers, antiquity registers (Khan, Agarwal, and Sharma 2010, 251).

13. Often a refined synonym of the word "saffron"—*kesariya*—would be used instead of *bhagwa*.

14. In a letter to the director of the Ayodhya excavation, the Jt DG ordered extreme caution and secrecy:

> All records pertaining to the excavation should immediately be sealed and submitted to the Superintending Archaeologist, Lucknow Circle. It is also learnt that certain records still remain in the computer at Ayodhya. All these records should also be properly recorded in CD or Floppy and immediately deleted from the computer. Any loose records lying with any Team Member should also be immediately destroyed. (AACD, File No. 29/1/1995-EE/Part-V)

15. In a letter dated July 3, 2003, Gauri Chatterjee, the DG of the ASI, writes to Rajeev Kumar, District Commissioner of Faizabad:

... you are requested to ensure that there is proper height of "Shamiyana" so that there is enough light and air for persons working in excavation trenches. You may in consultation with Shri Hari Manjhi, Director, ASI, Team Leader, Ayodhya Excavation, remove these from northern, western and eastern sides so that there is sufficient light in recognizing stratigraphical features and details on cuttings. (AACD, File No. 29/1/95-Pt IV)

16. For an extensive examination of the objections in the report by Justice Sudhir Agarwal's assessment, see Khan, Agarwal, and Sharma (2010, 2182–211).

17. See Khan, Agarwal, and Sharma (2010, 517–34) for a detailed cross-examination of S. P. Gupta that gives evidence of his Hindutva background.

18. Page numbers are missing in this section of the report, which suggests that it was appended after all the chapters of the report were written (Manjhi and Mani 2003, XX).

19. During an interview with Justice Sudhir Agrawal, he affirmed that his judgment relied heavily on the ASI report, including the unauthored last chapter. During the interview with me, he also shared that he was under "tremendous pressure from higher powers" to postpone the judgment and delay the matter as long as possible. This he said was because the "higher powers" wanted to keep the political religious matter simmering as much as possible. He used an eloquent Hindi proverb, *unki daal galti rahi* (keep the lentil curry simmering as long as possible), to express the situation. He also was under a "moral pressure" because he said that he did not want a bloodshed, but at the same time he did not want to go outside the frame of jurisprudence. He claimed he was "walking a razor's edge" (*chaku ki dhaar per*). He asserted he did not care if he did not become the hero, but he was cautious that he did not want to become a villain. That was his most central concern while writing the judgment. This interview was held at Justice Agarwal's residence in Allahabad on January 20, 2013. It was made possible with the gracious support of Justice Suneet Kumar of the Allahabad High Court. I also met Justice Khan, but he refused to divulge much and asserted that whatever he had to say is written in the judgment.

20. The ASI provided an honorarium between INR 3,500 and 5,000 for "(strenuous) conditions under which the entire team has worked round the clock to complete the onerous task by being away from their family for months together continuously in the excavation camp" (AACD, File No. 29/1/1995-Pt. V [i]).

21. On the analytical and semiotic meaning of jokes in ethnographic research, see Johnson (1978) and Carty and Musharbash (2008).

22. In a letter to all the excavation directors of the SHP, R. S. Bisht noted that he expected to have within 45 days after the end of the excavation

    > a research article on the excavation with concise, pointed and focused data on the following lines and duly supported with photographs and line-drawings may be submitted for publication: Location; Natural Setting of the site; Objectives of the excavation; Strategy and Planning; Stratigraphy; Structural Remains; Pottery; Antiquities; Scientific samples and Conclusion. (AACD, File No. 1/3/2003-SP/EE)

    This was the standardized format for an excavation report in the ASI, which was derived from Wheeler's reports (Wheeler, Ghosh, and Deva 1946; Wheeler 1947a, 1947b).

23. A total of £728 proposals for excavations were received by the CABA from 2007 to 2012, out of which the ASI proposed 138 and the remaining 458 were proposed by university departments and various state archaeology departments (CAG 2013, 103).

24. One report was in press at that time (AACD, File No. 1/6/2004-EE). Out of these 56 reports, by 2012, only 25 were submitted (CAG 2013, 114).

25. Some of the most significant unpublished large-scale excavations were: Ramapuram, Andra Pradesh (1980–81 to 1983–84) by B. Narasimhaiah; Banawali, Haryana (1983–84 to 1986–87) by R. S. Bisht; Harsh-ka-Tila, Haryana (1987–88 to 1989–90) by B. M. Pande; Burzahom, Kashmir (1960–61 to 1968–69, 1971–72, 1973–74) by T. N. Khazanchi; Sanghol, Punjab (1986–87 to 1990–91) by C. Margabandhu; Lalitgiri, Orissa (1985–86 to 1991–92) by G.C. Chauley; Ayodhya, Uttar Pradesh (1976–77 to 1979–80) by B. B. Lal; and Hulas, Uttar Pradesh (1978–79 to 1982–83) by K. N. Dikshit. This list also includes sites that had multiple site directors, changing over the course of the years: Hampi, Karnataka (1975–76, 1976–77, 1978–79 to 2000–01), Sravasti, Uttar Pradesh (1958–59, 1986–87 to 1998–99, 2000–01 to 2001–02); Mathura, Uttar Pradesh (1954–55, 1973–74 to 1976–77); Udaigiri, Orissa (1985–86, 1986–87, 1987–88, 1988–89, 1997–98 to 2001–02); and Banahalli, Karnataka (1973–74, 1983–84, 1985–86, 1986). For a complete and detailed list, see AACD, File No. 1/6/2004-EE.

26. Some of these senior archaeologists were B. K. Thapar and M. C. Joshi (both of them served as the DG of the ASI); the excavator of Lothal, S. R. Rao, also led the excavations at Hampi but did not work at publishing the report; and G. C. Chauley, who excavated the monumental Buddhist site of Laitgiri, among other archaeologists.

27. On the same page, the CAG report also observes:

In 2005, a decision was taken to complete the pending excavation reports within a period of 24 months. Accordingly, the ASI identified pending 56 excavation reports pertaining to the period prior to 2007–08 for completion by 2007 but only 25 reports were submitted as of September 2012.... Besides 56 cases discussed in para 5.8.1, for the 113 excavations/ exploration works that were undertaken by the ASI during 2007–08 to 2011–12, report had been submitted in only 12 cases; out of which only one report had been published in the Indian Archeology-A Review (IAR). Details are given in Annex-5.3. (CAG, 116)

28.   The CAG report further noted:

We also found that 10 excavators, from whom reports were pending, were no more/incapacitated due to ill health and old age and one excavator had left the ASI to join some other organisation. The ASI failed to take effective measures against unusual delays in report writing by its own officers. (CAG 2013, 116)

29.   Remove both maps, confuse cartographic conventions, erase the tens of thousands of hours invested in Radambrasil's atlas, interfere with the radar of planes, and our four scientists would be lost in the landscape and obliged once more to begin all the work of exploration, reference marking, triangulation, and squaring performed by their hundreds of predecessors. Yes, scientists master the world, but only the world comes to them in the form of two-dimensional, superposable, combinable inscriptions. (Latour 1999, 29)

30.   The excavation budgets in 2003–04 for Bhirrana was INR 2,099,572; for Baror, it was INR 3,160,000; for Hansi, it was INR 2,100,000; for Chak 86 and Tarkhanewala Dera it was INR 941,119; and for Juni Kuran it was INR 1,851,000 (AACD, File No. 1/6/2004-EE).

31.   The CAG report noted in 2013:

In the ASI, officers of the rank of Deputy Superintending Archaeologist (Dy. SA)/Superintending Archaeologist (SA) or above were eligible to apply for licenses for excavation. We found that the ASI's own proposals depended on the individual initiative of the SA/Deputy SA of the Circle rather than any overall departmental perspective. (CAG 2013, 103)

32.   My informants rarely used the Hindi word for corruption, *bhrashtachar*; they would always use the English word "corruption" or would often talk in terms of *chori* (theft) and *loot*.

33. Amarendra Nath is one of the few ASI archaeologists who have published reports on all the sites he directed, excluding Rakhigarhi, which is yet to be published. See Nath (1998, 2016).

34. The Central Bureau of Investigation (CBI) special court in Haryana held former ASI director Dr Amarnedar Nath, who had excavated Rakhigarhi from 1997–98 and 1999–2000, guilty in three cases and sentenced him to two and a half years' rigorous imprisonment (RI) for forging bills during the excavation of the Harappan site at Rakhigarhi (1997–98, 1998–99, and 1999–2000). He was held guilty of forging and fabricating bills of non-existent shops, showrooms, and firms (*Hindustan Times*, October 15, 2015). The budget of the Rakhigarhi excavation for the year 1999–2000 was INR 2,950,000.

35. The Santro was a small car made by the South Korean manufacturer Hyundai that had become a new status symbol for middle-class India during the years I was doing my fieldwork. It had replaced the earlier middle-class vehicular status symbol—the Maruti car, which had been the preferred car for nuclear middle-class Indians for nearly a decade and a half starting in the mid-1980s.

Conclusion

Twenty-eight years after the illegal demolition of the Babri Masjid, two events marked a discouraging and an uncomfortable denouement of the narrative. In August 2020, the prime minister of India laid a 40-kilogram silver brick as the foundation stone for the construction of the Ram temple in Ayodhya, and a few weeks later, in September of the same year, the Supreme Court of India acquitted all 32 conspirators accused in the destruction of the *masjid* on December 2, 2020. After the Supreme Court adjudication of 2019 that upheld the findings of the ASI's specious archaeological excavation, and paved the pathway for the temple's construction, both these events were a forgone conclusion for me. The unempirical assertion of a monumental structure having characteristics of a Hindu temple in an un-authored chapter, of an unpublished report, of an epistemologically compromised archaeological excavation, conducted in constrained circumstances by the ASI was usurped by judges of the High Court and the Supreme Court to adjudicate that a temple did exist under the Babri Masjid. And it should not come as a surprise that like this un-authored chapter of the Ayodhya excavation report, the 1,045-page Supreme Court judgment does not have an author.

The covert epistemological sleight of hand in the case of the ASI report and the juridical appropriation of spurious archaeological evidence has once again given strength to the old slogans, for this is not the end. Hindu fundamentalists, who in 1992 shrieked hoarsely: "Give another push/Break the Babri Masjid" (*Ek dhakka aur do/Babri Masjid tod do*), are again screaming in the congested and clogged streets of India (now also on Facebook and Twitter): "This was the beginning/Kashi and Mathura are still left" (*Yeh to ek jhanki hai/Kashi Mathura abhi baki hai*), referring to two prominent archaeological sites of contestation and dispute among many others spread throughout India (including the Taj Mahal). In Kashi (another name for Varanasi in Uttar Pradesh) and in Mathura, the Hindu fundamentalists intend to demolish the mosques allegedly built by the Mughal emperor Aurangzeb after destroying Hindu temples—a meta-narrative not unfamiliar. The doors of the court have been knocked, but archaeological evidence has not yet been summoned; but I will not be surprised if that occurs, because the past is not a "foreign country" (Lowenthal 1999) in India; its epistemic vibrations continue to reverberate resoundingly in the ontology of the present.

My attempt in this book has been to call into question, and theoretically challenge, the hegemony of the ASI's epistemological legitimacy that is deployed by the state and employed by the judiciary in India to construct an infallible imagination of the past. As I write these lines (in September 2020), the Ministry of Culture announced the creation of an "Expert Committee" to study the "origin and evolution of Indian culture since 12000 years before present" (Nath 2020). Among the 16 members of this committee were retired archaeologists of the ASI, some of whom have featured in this book, including R. S. Bisht and B. R. Mani—yet another attempt by the state to invoke science and archaeology to construct a specious chronology of the nation. However, now big science in the form of archaeogenetic data is being assembled to trace an unadulterated genealogy of an Indian past, unambiguously reconstructed as a Hindu identity.

When I conceived of this project, I had framed it as an ethnographic investigation of archaeology as a scientific enterprise in postcolonial India. I considered the culture-history archaeology of the ASI as a fertile ground to examine the epistemological practice of archaeology as a science. I had chosen postcolonial India because I was interested in investigating how archaeology functions in a non-western setting, which I expected would make a meaningful contribution to the global discourse on the theory and practice of archaeology. I believed it was crucial to shift the geographical focus of the theoretical debates in archaeology, typically fixated on the Euro-American world, and to produce new insights into the disciplinary discourse of archaeology from a non-western geopolitical universe. The ASI was not just one of the oldest archaeological organizations in the world, but was a statist institution and one of the largest of its kind. Its extraordinary history of archaeological interventions, its deep colonial legacy, and its overwhelming presence in postcolonial India made it an ideal site to painstakingly examine not just the discursive practice of archaeology as a postcolonial science, but also as a rich site to investigate the political, theoretical, and methodological crisis that archaeology, as a modern discipline, was struggling with.

I began my fieldwork in the summer of 2003, and soon observed that archaeology for the ASI was not about science, nationalism, or patriotism. Some of my informants suggested repeatedly that the practice of "doing" archaeology was an act of patriotism (*desh ke liye* or *bharatiyata*), but I observed that the rhetoric of nationalism was a disingenuous rationalization for routine bureaucratic work (*sarkari kaam*). As I spent more time at the excavation sites observing the archaeological practices of the ASI, I came to another recognition:

ASI archaeology was not merely a scientific enterprise or a "craft"—a learned trade, a practice inherited from experienced members, or a continuation and transference of tradition from predecessor or master to disciple or apprentice—which, if applied as directed and learned, is expected to generate evidence, as theoretical archaeologists (Shanks and McGuire 1996; Walker and Saitta 2002) and ethnographers (Edgeworth 2003, 26) have argued. Instead, as I have shown in this book, ASI archaeology was, theoretically and functionally, overwhelmingly an ideologically driven postcolonial bureaucratic epistemological intervention—panoptical, compromised, oppressive, exploitative, and corrupt.

The ASI bureaucracy assiduously assembles this craft of science, with a penetrating colonial genealogy, to manufacture postcolonial knowledge. As I have argued in this book, the choice of Wheelerian archaeology was not because the ASI was caught in a time warp. Rather, Wheelerian archaeology was the preferred mode of the ASI as it was an ideological apparatus that was not only efficacious in the manufacture, control, and regulation of facts about the past, but it also had a bureaucratic rationality designed to control and manage the people working at the site. Succinctly put, the ASI bureaucratic archaeology perpetuates the colonial epistemological project reinforced by an authoritarian bureaucratic regime in a postcolonial ecology. It is this ideological morphology, which accentuates the bureaucratic efficacy of archaeology as a scientific craft, that gives archaeology and especially ASI archaeology—particularly during times of ultra-nationalism (Hindutva) and statist hegemony (neoliberal)—unparalleled authority in postcolonial India.[1]

ASI archaeologists primarily imagined themselves as bureaucrats in the state's service (*sabse pehle aur sabse aage hum sarkari karamchari hai*). This archaeology was driven by the thrust of managerial rationality of its bureaucracy rather than by the epistemological objectives. Thus, archaeology was dexterously usurped by a bureaucratic impulse to govern, manage, and regulate—it deployed epistemological predispositions, arrogated by bureaucratic predilections. Furthermore, with this form of postcolonial bureaucracy inevitably came corruption—having epistemological consequences. Failing to publish timely was symptomatic of this epistemological corruption that had percolated into the sinews of the ASI. Scientific inquiry for the ASI was a perfunctory mimesis of an unbridled colonial legacy, which, even in its Wheelerian form, was disingenuous. This form of epistemological practice was further enveloped in a stranglehold of a postcolonial bureaucratic apparatus; it had colonized the ASI's already compromised scientific practice with entrenched hierarchy, systemic oppression, and endemic corruption. ASI archaeology was plagued by onerous administrative apparatus, exacerbated by an obdurate institutional structure—colonial in its conception and firmly entrenched in copious postcolonial hierarchies. Its epistemological functions were articulated as an indifferent obligation of postcolonial bureaucracy that also institutionally beleaguered its own subjects. The knowledge-production enterprise of the ASI was a mere by-product of its bureaucratic apathy and rationality. For the ASI, archaeology was a manifest instantiation of the statist bureaucratic apparatus rather than a nationalist or scientific act.

Nationalistic narratives of the Indus or the Saraswati populated the discursive pronunciation of ASI archaeology, but at the level of daily routine practice, such nationalistic subtext was absent, even in such politicized projects like the Saraswati Heritage Project (SHP). My observations and arguments would have been no different if these were early historic, medieval, or Buddhist sites, or even if I was at the Ayodhya excavations of 2003. Nationalist or Hindutva narratives about the past were not framed or even expressed during the daily practice of archaeology in the trenches. It emerged surreptitiously in written texts—for instance, Chapter 10 of the Ayodhya report (Manjhi and Mani 2003, 268–72), or Chapter 12 of the Dholavira report where Bisht alludes to an Aryan origin of Harappan civilization (Bisht 2015, 870–89).

The ASI archaeologists viewed excavations in theory as a bureaucratic *act* of gathering *artifacts* to produce *facts*. As I have shown in the preceding pages, this act of gathering *artifacts* to produce *facts* was always and everywhere compromised, corrupted, and adulterated. The nationalistic narratives emerged only in the interpretative leaps of imagination while writing a report or an article. In this practice of knowledge production, the theoretical, ethical, and methodological influence of processual and post-processual archaeology was minimal, if not non-existent. Excavations for the ASI archaeologists were an act as elementary as "unpacking of garments from a suitcase."[2] The archaeologists as bureaucrats are unconcerned by methodological innovations or theoretical nuances of the disciplinary discourse, or even by the historical discordances and nationalistic pride that riddled the Indian past—it was overt bureaucratic production of data.

Archaeology, unlike any other discipline in the social sciences or humanities, is a complex hybrid conceptual apparatus—allowing for permutations and combinations of practices and theories to be imbibed on to its disciplinarian armature (Olsen et al. 2012; Rathje, Shanks, and Christopher Witmore 2013; Buccellati 2017; Lucas 2019). In India, we see one such combination— embroiled in colonial science, postcolonial history, hyper-nationalism, and hierarchical bureaucracy. However, to put the entire blame on the bureaucratic malfeasance of the postcolonial state for the state of archaeology in India would be disproportionate—as I show in this book, it is archaeology's theory of practice (Bourdieu 1977) that makes it susceptible to such a debilitating distortion. The disciplinary subjectivity of archaeology facilitates such a desecration of its theory of practice. This book challenges the belief in the fixity of archaeological practice that has been fed into the disciplinarian discourse of archaeology since the early twentieth century (Petrie 1904; Woolley 1930; Wheeler 1954) and still continues (Clark 1968; Harris 1989; Hodder 1999; Barker 2005; Buccellati 2017). Through the articulation of archaeology as a bureaucratic practice, I have revealed the theoretical fissure of its methodological practice and problematized the epistemological homogeneity of its disciplinary discourse.

Since the obsession with theory began in archaeology with the rise of processual archaeology, there has been an unquestioned premise about the apparent homogeneity of archaeological practice and method. Other than minute differences between American and European archaeology, it has been largely believed the epistemology of archaeology is standardized and homologous. This is largely a product of a widespread disciplinary fetish with Euro-American epistemic traditions, which have ignored the trajectory of archaeology outside its temporal and geographical ambit. That it is only through excavation that the evidential empirics of archaeological knowledge are produced has rarely been questioned other than in analytical discussions centered on archaeology in the philosophy of science. This premise has been an elementary assumption in the fidelity of scientific practice even among radical post-processualists (for instance, see Hodder 2013, 2014). The theoretical and meta-theoretical debates about method and theory in the past few decades have also presumed such homogeneity of archaeology's disciplinary discourse (Johnson 2019). In this book, I question this assumption. I argue that archaeology, as a knowledge production enterprise with specific acts of practice, comprises, in fact, a heterogeneous set of modalities—and the bureaucratic archaeology of the ASI is one attenuated variant of the archaeological theory of practice.

Peter Ucko, in 1995, attempted to break this assumption of homogeneity, but theory-building in archaeology is still constrained by the Euro-American practice of archaeology. This is not unusual as the space devoted to non-western practices in the history of archaeology is limited and incorporated within the rubric of an extension of the colonial exploits of the metropole. It is because of this geographic and ideological domination that, in this book, I have shifted the focus of the location of enquiry from the western world to the postcolony. I contend that in order to meta-theorize the universality of archaeological theory of practice, its disciplinary discourse needs to reinvestigate the practice and nature of knowledge production beyond the west. The incapacitating impasse between the processual, post-processual, and new variants of archaeology (Witmore 2007; Olsen et al. 2012) that is persistent in the contemporary discursive ecology of archaeology can gain from this investigation of the heterogeneity of archaeology from a non-western location of practice. This can be fructified in the form of examining the trajectory that archaeology in the colony took and the nature of its practice in the postcolony or in the non-western world (Liebmann and Rizvi 2010; Lydon and Rizvi 2016).

A case could be made that archaeology as a bureaucratic practice in the ASI is all that archaeology is not about. This practice of knowledge production epitomizes marginal modernity, but to ridicule it as bad archaeology would be to miss the point of this book, as well as to misrecognize the monumental work that the ASI has in fact carried out over the past several decades. ASI archaeology is a science as viewed by both its practitioners and those who consume it in India, including the highest courts of the land. To relegate it to the universe of bad practice would be to disparage the epistemological authority it wields in the fractured historical and political space of postcolonial India. Archaeology, like any scientific practice, is principally a social and cultural practice entrenched in the historical and political structures of the location it functions in. The authority of its claims does not derive from the scientific method of its practices, as claimed by the processual archaeologists, nor does it derive from the interpretative nature of its knowledge construction processes, as argued by the post-processual archaeologists. Neither is archaeology a practice subverted by political and nationalistic goals of the location of its performance.

Instead, as I show in this book, archaeology is itself an ideological and cultural practice—vulnerable to its own discursive ontology—the boundaries between construction of scientific evidence and its ideological or interpretative creation of knowledge are non-existent. The epistemological process of archaeology is itself a subjective practice that employs science as a methodological rhetoric and eventually applies interpretative techniques to create a scientific narrative about the past. The bureaucratic archaeology of the ASI is analogously a product of the social and cultural politics of its ruptured location. My ethnographic focus on daily practice has been to emphasize that even in a bureaucratic ecology like the ASI excavation site, archaeology works as a science—albeit a fractured science but a science nonetheless. The appalling state of ASI archaeology is simultaneously a product of science in archaeology and the statist oppression in the postcolonial bureaucracy.

Finally, in this book, I employ the ASI as a metonym for postcolonial governmentality—a bureaucratic site of relative postcolonial calm. It is outside

Agamben's ideological precincts of "state of exception" (Agamben 2005). Unlike other parts of the Indian state's bureaucratic machinery, the ASI does not perform its work in sites of extraordinary tension and hostility, where the postcolonial state exhibits its brute power—in zones of military occupation in insurgency-affected areas in northeastern India, Kashmir, or Punjab, where extra-judicial killings are a daily routine; in regions of perpetual administrative emergency, such as in tribal belts of central India, for example, where people's resistance is eliminated with ruthless aggression; or in sites of development or corporate projects where forcible removal of citizens without due compensation is customary. The archaeological sites of the ASI are dissimilar to these zones of exceptions. These are staid locations of postcolonial statist authority. Here, through the daily practice of epistemological activity, the state machinery directs its bureaucratic force in controlling and managing the lives of the people under its jurisdiction—from senior officers to local laborers. It works within the logic of factory time and military control—an authoritarian practice—and within its structural formation, oppression is intrinsic. As I have shown in this book, the power relations between the state and subaltern subjects, who formed the foundational labor force in ASI archaeological excavations, do not differ from the militarized, colonial bureaucracy that had been in place before decolonization. The hierarchical nature of ASI archaeology; the dominant mechanism of its statist organization as it penetrated the peripheral territory in the margins of India; and the transformation of a rural landscape into state-occupied epistemological terrestriality—were not only located in the colonial genealogy of the ASI, but were also products of a postcolonial bureaucratic project conceived of as a scientific mission, integral to it is systemic oppression. During my fieldwork, I recognized that the excavations done by the ASI were not a mere "pathology" (Tilley 1989, 275); instead, archaeological excavations are a manifestation of a widespread colonial ideology at work with its apparatus of oppression intact—even further perfected and sharpened. Its hegemony is uniform and impacts all, including the epistemological texts it produces. In this bureaucratic intervention, the colonial natives (*coolie*) are viewed as postcolonial illiterates (*dehati*), and brown *saheb*s have come to substitute the white *saheb*s.

I end this book with the first couplet of a political song I learned while working in the tribal areas of western India in the early 1990s (Chadha 1999) as an activist with an anti-dam environmental agitation—Save the Narmada Movement (Narmada Bachao Andolan). This song was often sung during political gatherings and protest meetings. It agonizingly expresses the postcolonial predicament we live in India: "The white rulers have gone, but the black masters have come instead! The keys have changed, but the locks remain the same!" (*Gore haakim gayo re bhaiya, aageya haakim kaale! Badel gayi hai chabi lekin, badle nahi hai taale!*)

Notes

1. The Action Plan of the Niti Aayog report of 2020 categorically exposes the neoliberal impetus of the postcolonial state when it recommends the adoption of the "Revenue Generation Model" and to treat each site as a "separate profit centre" (Niti Aayog 2020, 225–26). The Niti Aayog under the present BJP regime intends to reconceptualize the past as heritage to be consumed and managed in order to capitalize and produce surplus and suggests renaming the ASI to Archaeological Survey and Heritage Management of India (Niti Aayog 2020, 15).

2. This extract is from "Note on the Points Raised by the Members of the Parliamentary Committee on Transport, Tourism and Culture" (AACD, File No. 24/1/2003-EE).

Bibliography

Unpublished References

Basu, Nilotpal. 2005. *Ninety-First Report on the Functioning of the Archaeological Survey of India*. New Delhi: Rajya Sabha Secretariat.

Bisht, Ravi Singh. 2015. *Excavations at Dholavira (1989–90 to 2004–05)*. New Delhi: Archaeological Survey of India.

Comptroller and Auditor General of India (CAG). *Report of the Comptroller and Auditor General of India on Performance Audit of Preservation and Conservation of Monuments and Antiquities (Report No. 18 of 2013)*. 2013. New Delhi: Union Government (Civil), Ministry of Culture.

Files from the ASI Archive Collection, New Delhi (AACD).

Green, Adam. 2015. "Stamp Seals in the Political Economy of South Asia's Earliest Cities." Unpublished PhD dissertation, New York University.

Lal, Braj Basi. 2001. *Report of the Review Committee on the Functioning of Archaeological Survey of India*. New Delhi: Archaeological Survey of India.

Manjhi, Hari, and B. R. Mani. 2003. *Ayodhya: 2002–03, Excavations at the Disputed Site*. Report Submitted to the Special Full Bench, Lucknow of the Hon'ble High Court, Allahabad. 2 vols. New Delhi: Archaeological Survey of India.

Mirdha, Ram Niwas. 1984. *Report on the Working of on the Functioning of Archaeological Survey of India*. New Delhi: Archaeological Survey of India.

Mukherjee, Dipankar. 2001. 49th Demands for Grants (2001–2002) of the Department of Tourism. New Delhi: Rajya Sabha Secretariat.

———. 2002. *Fifty-Sixth Report on Demands for Grants (2002–2003), (Demand No. 80) of the Department of Culture*. New Delhi: Rajya Sabha Secretariat.

Nath, Amarendra. 2015. *Excavations at Rakhigarhi (1997–98 to 1999–2000)*. New Delhi: Archaeological Survey of India.

Niti Aayog. 2020. *Working Group Report on Improving Heritage Management in India*. New Delhi: Niti Aayog. Available at https://niti.gov.in/sites/default/files/2020-06/Improving-HeritageManagement-in-India.pdf, accessed on September 23, 2020.

Ram, Silak. 1972. "Archaeology of Rohtak and Hissar Districts (Haryana)." Unpublished PhD dissertation, Kurukshetra University.

Rose-Redwood, Ruben. 2006. "Governmentality, the Grid, and the Beginnings of a Critical Spatial History of the Geo-Coded World." Unpublished PhD dissertation.

Singh, Amar. 1981. "Archaeology of Karbal and Jind Districts (Haryana)." Unpublished PhD dissertation, Kurukshetra University.

Singh, K. D. 2017. *233rd Report of the Department-Related Parliamentary Standing Committee of Transport, Tourism and Culture.* New Delhi: Rajya Sabha Secretariat.

Wheeler, Robert Eric Mortimer. 1965. *Review Committee Report.* New Delhi: Archaeological Survey of India.

Published References

Abraham, Itty. 1998. *The Making of the Indian Atomic Bomb: Science, Secrecy and the Postcolonial State.* London: Zed Books.

Adams, Max, and Carole Brooke. 1995. "Unmanaging the Past: Truth, Data and the Human Being." *Norwegian Archaeological Review* 28, no. 2: 93–104.

Agamben, Giorgio. 1998. *Homo Sacer: Sovereign Power and Bare Life.* Translated by Daniel Heller-Roazen. Stanford: Stanford University Press.

———. 2005. *State of Exception.* Chicago: University of Chicago Press.

Agrawal, Arun. 2005. *Environmentality: Technologies of Government and the Making of Subjects.* Durham: Duke University Press Books.

Akkerman, Abraham. 1998. *Place and Thought: The Built Environment in Early European Philosophy.* London: Woodbridge.

Allchin, Bridget, and Frank Raymond Allchin. 1997. *Origins of a Civilization: The Prehistory and Early Archaeology of South Asia.* New Delhi: Viking.

Allen, John. 2016. *Topologies of Power: Beyond Territory and Networks.* London and New York, NY: Routledge.

Alvares, Claude. 1992. *Science, Development and Violence: The Revolt against Modernity.* Delhi: Oxford University Press.

Amrute, Sareeta. 2016. *Encoding Race, Encoding Class: Indian IT Workers in Berlin.* Durham: Duke University Press.

Anand, Nikhil. 2015. "Leaky States: Water Audits, Ignorance, and the Politics of Infrastructure." *Public Culture* 27, no. 2 (76): 305–30.

Andrews, Gill, John C. Barrett, and John S. C. Lewis. 2000. "Interpretation Not Record: The Practice of Archaeology." *Antiquity* 74, no. 285: 525–30.

Andrews, Malcolm. 1989. *The Search for the Picturesque: Landscape Aesthetics and Tourism, in Britain, 1760–1800.* New ed. Stanford, California: Stanford University Press.

Aneesh, A. 2006. *Virtual Migration: The Programming of Globalization.* Durham: Duke University Press.

Anthony, David W. 1991. "The Archaeology of Indo-European Origins." *The Archaeology of Indo-European Origins* 19, nos. 3–4: 193–222.

————. 1995. "Horse, Wagon and Chariot: Indo-European Languages and Archaeology." *Antiquity* 69, no. 264: 554–65.

————. 2007. *The Horse, the Wheel, and Language: How Bronze-Age Riders from the Eurasian Steppes Shaped the Modern World.* Princeton, NJ: Princeton University Press.

Anthony, David W., Peter Bogucki, Eugen Comşa, Marija Gimbutas, Borislav Jovanović, J. P. Mallory, and Sarunas Milisaukas. 1986. "The 'Kurgan Culture,' Indo-European Origins, and the Domestication of the Horse: A Reconsideration [and Comments and Replies]." *Current Anthropology* 27, no. 4: 291–313.

Anwer, Ahmer Nadeem. 2011. "NOTE/Judgment and Misjudgment." *Social Scientist* 39, no. 1/2: 60–73.

Appadurai, A. 1991. "Global Ethnoscapes: Notes and Queries for a Transnational Anthropology." In *Recapturing Anthropology: Working in the Present*, edited by Richard G. Fox, 191–210. Sante Fe: School of American Research Press.

Archaeological Survey of India. *Archaeological Works Code*. 2017. New Delhi: Archaeological Survey of India.

Arnold, Bettina. 1990. "The Past as Propaganda: Totalitarian Archaeology in Nazi Germany." *Antiquity* 64, no. 244: 464–78.

————. 1992. "The Past as Propaganda: How Hitler's Archaeologists Distorted European Prehistory to Justify Racist and Territorial Goals." *The Past as Propaganda: How Hitler's Archaeologists Distorted European Prehistory to Justify Racist and Territorial Goals* 45, no. 4: 30–37.

Arnold, David. 2000. *Science, Technology, and Medicine in Colonial India.* Cambridge: Cambridge University Press.

Arnold, Dean E. 1988. *Ceramic Theory and Cultural Process.* Cambridge: Cambridge University Press.

Atalay, S. 2006. "Indigenous Archaeology as Decolonizing Practice." *American Indian Quarterly* 30, nos 3 and 4: 280–310.

Atre, Shubhangana. 1987. *The Archetypal Mother: A Systemic Approach to Harappan Religion.* Pune: Ravish Publishers.

Avikunthak, Ashish, dir. 2001. *Rummaging for Pasts: Excavating Sicily, Digging Bombay.* Digital.

————. 2017a. "Denied Entry to Kolkata Mall in Dhoti: Filmmaker Ashish Avikunthak on 'Public Space.'" *DailyO*, August 4. Available at https://www.dailyo.in/voices/kolkata-quest-mall-denies-entry-dhoti-filmmaker-public-spaces-racial-profiling/story/1/18776.html, accessed on October 17, 2020.

————. 2017b. "Social Apartheid: I Was Barred from Entering a Kolkata Mall Because I Was Wearing a Dhoti." *Scroll.in,* July 17. Available at https://scroll.in/article/844091/social-apartheid-i-was-barred-from-entering-a-kolkata-mall-because-i-was-wearing-a-dhoti, accessed on October 17, 2020.

Baber, Zaheer. 1996. *The Science of Empire: Scientific Knowledge, Civilization, and Colonial Rule in India*. Albany: State University of New York Press.

Bagchi, Sanjoy. 2007. *The Changing Face of Bureaucracy: Fifty Years of the Indian Administrative Service*. New Delhi: Rupa.

Bailey, Catherine. 2019. "Waiting in Organisations." *Time and Society* 28, no. 2: 587–612.

Baker, W. E. 1840. "Report on the Line Levels between the Jumna and Sutlej Rivers." *Journal of the Asiatic Society of Bengal* 9, no. 2: 688–94.

Bakliwal, P. C., and A. K. Grover. 1988. "Signature and Migration of Sarasvati River in Thar Desert, Western India." *Records of the Geological Survey* 116, no. 3–8: 77–86.

Bakliwal, P. C., and S. B. Sharma. 1980. "On the Migration of the River Yamuna." *Journal of the Geological Society of India* 21, no. 9: 461–63.

Balasubramanian, Sridhar. 2018. "Dholavira: Where the Remains of the Harappan Civilisation Exist." *The Hindu*, August 22. Available at https://www.thehindu.com/life-and-style/travel/the-immortals-of-harappa/article24751437.ece, accessed on September 18, 2020.

Bamshad, Michael, Alexander E. Fraley, Michael H. Crawford, Rebecca L. Cann, Baskara R. Busi, J. Mastan Naidu, and Lynn B. Jorde. 1996. "MtDNA Variation in Caste Populations of Andhra Pradesh, India." *Human Biology* 68, no. 1: 1–28.

Bamshad, Michael J., W. Scott Watkins, Mary E. Dixon, Lynn B. Jorde, B. Bhaskara Rao, J. Mastan Naidu, B. V. Ravi Prasad, Arani Rasanayagam, and Mike F. Hammer. 1998. "Female Gene Flow Stratifies Hindu Castes." *Nature* 395, no. 6703: 651–52.

Banerjee, Somaditya. 2020. *The Making of Modern Physics in Colonial India*. London: Routledge.

Bapty, Ian, and Tim Yates. 1990. *Archaeology After Structuralism: Post-Structuralism and the Practice of Archaeology*. London: Routledge.

Barker, Philip. 2005. *Techniques of Archaeological Excavation*. London: B. T. Batsford Ltd.

Barnes, Barry. 1974. *Scientific Knowledge and Sociological Theory*. London: Routledge and K. Paul.

Barnes, Barry, and Steven Shapin. 1979. *Natural Order: Historical Studies of Scientific Culture*. Beverly Hills: Sage Publications.

Barrow, Ian J. 2003. *Making History, Drawing Territory: British Mapping in India, c. 1756–1905*. New Delhi: Oxford University Press.

Barry, Andrew, Thomas Osborne, and Nikolas Rose, eds. 1996. *Foucault and Political Reason: Liberalism, Neo-Liberalism, and Rationalities of Government*. Chicago: University of Chicago Press.

Bartu, Ayfer. 2000. "Where Is Çatalhöyük? Multiple Sites in the Construction of an Archaeological Site." In *Towards a Reflexive Method in Archaeology: The Example at Çatalhöyük*, edited by Ian Hodder, 101–09. Cambridge and London: McDonald Institute for Archaeological Research and British Institute of Archaeology at Ankara.

Basu, Analabha, Namita Mukherjee, Sangita Roy, Sanghamitra Sengupta, Sanat Banerjee, Madan Chakraborty, Badal Dey, Monami Roy, Bidyut Roy, and Nitai P. Bhattacharyya. 2003. "Ethnic India: A Genomic View, with Special Reference to Peopling and Structure." *Genome Research* 13, no. 10: 2277–90.

Basu, Analabha, Neeta Sarkar-Roy, and Partha P. Majumder. 2016. "Genomic Reconstruction of the History of Extant Populations of India Reveals Five Distinct Ancestral Components and a Complex Structure." *Proceedings of the National Academy of Sciences* 113, no. 6: 1594–99.

Basu, Nilotpal. 2005. *91st Report of the Department-Related Parliamentary Standing Committee of Transport, Tourism and Culture*. New Delhi: Rajya Sabha Secretariat.

Bayly, Christopher. 1988. *India Society and the Making of the British Empire*. Cambridge: Cambridge University Press.

Begley, Vimala. 1983. "Arikamedu Reconsidered." *American Journal of Archaeology* 87, no. 4: 461–81.

———. 1988. "Rouletted Ware at Arikamedu: A New Approach." *American Journal of Archaeology* 92, no. 3: 427–40.

———. 1993. "New Investigations at the Port of Arikamedu." *Journal of Roman Archaeology* 6: 93–108.

Berggren, Asa. 2001. "Swedish Archaeology in Perspective and the Possibility of Reflexivity." *Current Swedish Archaeology* 9: 9–23.

Berggren, Åsa, and Ian Hodder. 2003. "Social Practice, Method, and Some Problems of Field Archaeology." *American Antiquity* 68, no. 3: 421–34.

Berggren, J. Lennart, and Alexander Jones. 2000. *Ptolemy's Geography: An Annotated Translation of the Theoretical Chapters*. Princeton: Princeton University Press.

Bermingham, Ann. 1987. *Landscape and Ideology: The English Rustic Tradition, 1740–1860*. London: Thames and Hudson Ltd.

Bhan, Suraj. 1973. "The Sequence and Spread of Prehistoric Cultures in the Upper Sarasvati Basin." In *Radiocarbon and Indian Archaeology*, edited by D. P. Agrawal and A. Ghosh, 252–63. Bombay: Tata Institute of Fundamental Research.

———. 1997. "Recent Trends in Indian Archaeology." *Social Scientist* 25, nos 1–2: 3–15.

———. 2001. "Aryanization of the Indus Civilization." In *The Making of History*, edited by K. N. Panikkar, Terence J. Byres, and Utsa Patnaik, 41–55. New Delhi: Tulika.

Binford, Lewis Roberts. 1962. "Archaeology as Anthropology." *American Antiquity* 28, no. 2: 217–25.

———. 1965. "Archaeological Systematics and the Study of Culture Process." *American Antiquity* 31, no. 2: 203–10.

———. 1968. "Archaeological Perspective." In *New Perspectives in Archaeology*, edited by Sally R. Binford, 5–33. Chicago: Aldine Press.

———, ed. 1977. *For Theory Building in Archaeology: Essays on Faunal Remains, Aquatic Resources, Spatial Analysis, and Systemic Modeling.* Academic Press.

Binford, Lewis Roberts, and George Irving Quimby. 1972. *An Archaeological Perspective.* New York: Seminar Press.

Bishop, Ronald L., Robert L. Rands, and George R. Holley. 1982. "Ceramic Compositional Analysis in Archaeological Perspective." In *Advances in Archaeological Method and Theory*, edited by Michael B. Schiffer, 275–330. San Diego: Academic Press.

Bisht, Ravi Singh. 1978. "Banawali: A New Harappan Site in Haryana." *Man and Environment* 2: 86–88.

———. 1999. "Harappans and the Rgveda: Points of Convergence." In *The Dawn of Indian Civilization (upto c. 600 BC)*, edited by G. C. Pande, 393–442. New Delhi: Centre for Studies in Civilizations.

Bisht, Ravi Singh, and Shashi Asthana. 1979. "Banawali and Some Other Recently Excavated Harappan Sites in India." In *South Asian Archaeology 1977. Vol. 1*, edited by M. Taddei, 223–40. Naples: Instituto Universitario Orientale Seminario Di Studi Asiatici.

Blake, David M. 1991. "Colin Mackenzie: Collector Extraordinary." *The British Library Journal* 17, no. 2: 128–50.

Blakiston, J. F. 1928. *Annual Report of the Archaeological Survey of India, 1925–26.* Calcutta: Government of India Central Publication Branch.

Bloor, David. 1976. *Knowledge and Social Imagery.* London: Routledge and K. Paul.

Boast, Robin. 2002. "Mortimer Wheeler's Science of Order: The Tradition of Accuracy at Arikamedu." *Antiquity* 76, no. 291: 165–70.

Bohrer, Frederick Nathaniel. 2011. *Photography and Archaeology.* London: Reaktion Books.

Bourdieu, Pierre. 1977. *Outline of a Theory of Practice.* Translated by Richard Nice. Cambridge Studies in Social and Cultural Anthropology. Cambridge: Cambridge University Press.

Bowden, Mark. 1991. *Pitt Rivers: The Life and Archaeological Work of Lieutenant-General Augustus Henry Lane Fox Pitt Rivers, DCL, FRS, FSA.* Cambridge, England: Cambridge University Press.

Bowker, G. C., and S. L. Star. 1999. *Sorting Things out: Classification and Its Consequences.* Cambridge, MA: MIT Press.

Bradley, Richard. 1983. "Archaeology, Evolution and the Public Good: The Intellectual Development of General Pitt Rivers." *Archaeological Journal* 140: 1–9.

Bratich, Jack Z., Jeremy Packer, and Cameron McCarthy. 2003. *Foucault, Cultural Studies, and Governmentality.* Albany, NY: SUNY Press.

Braun, Bruce. 2000. "Producing Vertical Territory: Geology and Governmentality in Late Victorian Canada." *Ecumene* 7, no. 1: 7–46.

Bray, Tamara L., ed. 2001. *The Future of the Past: Archaeologists, Native Americans, and Repatriation.* London: Routledge.

Breglia, Lisa. 2006. *Monumental Ambivalence: The Politics of Heritage.* Austin: University of Texas Press.

Briers, Michael, and Wai Fong Chua. 2001. "The Role of Actor-Networks and Boundary Objects in Management Accounting Change: A Field Study of an Implementation of Activity-Based Costing." *Accounting Organizations and Society* 26, no. 3: 237–69.

Brodie, Neil, Jennifer Doole, Colin Renfrew, and McDonald Institute for Archaeological Research. 2001. *Trade in Illicit Antiquities: The Destruction of the World's Archaeological Heritage.* Cambridge: McDonald Institute for Archaeological Research.

Bronkhorst, Johannes, and Madhav Deshpande. 1999. *Aryan and Non-Aryan In South Asia: Evidence, Interpretation and Ideology.* Columbia: South Asia Books.

Bryant, Edwin F. 2001. *The Quest for the Origins of Vedic Culture: The Indo-Aryan Migration Debate.* Oxford: Oxford University Press.

Bryant, Edwin F., and Laurie L. Patton. 2005. *The Indo-Aryan Controversy: Evidence and Inference in Indian History.* London: Routledge.

Buccellati, Giorgio. 2017. *A Critique of Archaeological Reason: Structural, Digital, and Philosophical Aspects of the Excavated Record.* Cambridge: Cambridge University Press.

Burnes, Alexander. 1834a. "Memoir on the Eastern Branch of the River Indus, Giving an Account of the Alterations Produced on It by an Earthquake, also a Theory of the Formation of the Runn, and Some Conjectures on the Route of Alexander the Great; Drawn up in the Years 1827–1828." *Transactions of the Royal Asiatic Society of Great Britain and Ireland* 3, no. 3: 550–88.

———. 1834b. *Travels into Bokhara: Being the Account of a Journey from India to Cabool, Tartary, and Persia; Also, Narrative of a Voyage on the Indus, from the Sea to Lahore.* 3 vols. London: John Murray.

Callaway, Ewen. 2018. "Divided by DNA: The Uneasy Relationship between Archaeology and Ancient Genomics." *Nature* 555, no. 7698: 573–76.

Cannon, Garland. 1994. "Oriental Jones: Scholarship, Literature, Multiculturalism, and Humankind." *Bulletin of the Deccan College Research Institute* 54: 3–22.

Carty, John, and Yasmine Musharbash. 2008. "You've Got to Be Joking: Asserting the Analytical Value of Humour and Laughter in Contemporary Anthropology." *Anthropological Forum* 18, no. 3: 209–17.

Carver, Geoff. 2011. "Reflections on the Archaeology of Archaeological Excavation." *Archaeological Dialogues* 18, no. 1: 18.

Carver, Martin O. H. 1990. "Digging for Data: Archaeological Approaches to Data Definition, Acquisition and Analysis." In *Lo Scavo Archeologico. Dalla Diagnosi All'edizione. III Ciclo Di Lezioni Sulla Ricerca Applicata in Archeologia*, edited by Riccardo Francovich and Daniele Manacorda, 45–120. Florence: Edizioni all'Insegna del Giglio.

Castañeda, Quetzil E. 1996. *In the Museum of Maya Culture*. Minneapolis: University of Minnesota Press.

Castañeda, Quetzil E., and Christopher N. Matthews. 2008. "Introduction: Ethnography and the Social Construction of Archaeology." In *Ethnographic Archaeologies: Reflections on Stakeholders and Archaeological Practices*, edited by Quetzil E. Castañeda and Christopher N. Matthews, 1–23. Lanham, MD: Alta Mira Press.

Chadha, Ashish. 1999. "The Anatomy of Dispossession: A Study in the Displacement of the Tribals from Their Traditional Landscape in the Narmada Valley Due to the Sardar Sarovar Project." In *The Archaeology and Anthropology of Landscape*, edited by Robert Layton and Peter Ucko, 148–60. London: Routledge.

———. 2002. "Visions of Discipline: Sir Mortimer Wheeler and the Archaeological Method in India (1944–1948)." *Journal of Social Archaeology* 2, no. 3: 378–401.

———. 2010. "Cryptographic Imagination: Indus Script and the Project of Scientific Decipherment." *The Indian Economic and Social History Review* 47, no. 2: 141–77.

———. 2011. "Conjuring a River, Imagining Civilisation: Saraswati, Archaeology and Science in India." *Contributions to Indian Sociology* 45, no. 1: 55–83.

Chadwick, Adrian. 2003. "Post-Processualism, Professionalization and Archaeological Methodologies. Towards Reflective and Radical Practice." *Archaeological Dialogues* 10, no. 1: 97–117.

Chakrabarti, Dilip. 1979. "Robert Bruce Foote and Indian Prehistory." *East and West* 29, no. 1/4: 11–26.

———. 1988. *A History of Indian Archaeology from the Beginning to 1947*. New Delhi: Munshiram Manoharlal Publishers.

———. 1989. *Theoretical Issues in Indian Archaeology*. New Delhi: Munshiram Manoharlal Publishers.

———. 1997. *Colonial Indology: Sociopolitics of the Ancient Indian Past*. New Delhi: Munshiram Manoharlal Publishers.

———. 2003. *Archaeology in the Third World: A History of Indian Archaeology since 1947.* New Delhi: D. K. Printworld.

Chakrabarti, Pratik. 2004. *Western Science in Modern India: Metropolitan Methods, Colonial Practices.* Delhi: Orient Blackswan.

———. 2010. "Beasts of Burden: Animals and Laboratory Research in Colonial India." *History of Science* 48, no. 2: 125–51.

Chakravarti, Niranjan Prasad. 1950. "Notes." *Ancient India* 6: 1–3.

Chakravorty, Sanjoy. 2016. "Land Acquisition in India: The Political-Economy of Changing the Law." *Area Development and Policy* 1, no. 1: 48–62.

Chambers, David Wade, and Richard Gillespie. 2000. "Locality in the History of Science: Colonial Science, Technoscience, and Indigenous Knowledge." *Osiris* 15, no. 1: 221–40.

Chapman, Robert, and Alison Wylie. 2016. *Evidential Reasoning in Archaeology.* London and New York: Bloomsbury Academic.

Chatterjee, Anirban, and Jyotiranjan S. Ray. 2018. "Geochemistry of Harappan Potteries from Kalibangan and Sediments in the Ghaggar River: Clues for a Dying River." *Geoscience Frontiers* 9, no. 4: 1203–11.

Chatterjee, Partha. 2012. "After Subaltern Studies." *Economic and Political Weekly* 47, no. 35: 44–49.

Chattopadhyay, Swati. 2016. "Traverse, Territory and the Ecological Uncanny: James Rennell and the Mapping of the Gangetic Plains." In *Cartographies of Exile: A New Spatial Literacy*, edited by Karen Elizabeth Bishop, 89–110. London: Routledge.

Cherry, John F. 2011. "Still Not Digging, Much." *Archaeological Dialogues* 18, no. 1: 10.

Chia, R. 2000. "Discourse Analysis as Organizational Analysis." *Organization* 7, no. 3: 513–18.

Childe, V. Gordon. 1925. *The Dawn of European Civilization.* London: Kegan Paul.

———. 1926. *The Aryans. A Study of Indo-European Origins.* London: Kegan Paul.

———. 1942. *What Happened in History.* London: Penguin.

Chowdhury, Indira. 2016. *Growing the Tree of Science: Homi Bhabha and the Tata Institute of Fundamental Research.* Delhi: Oxford University Press.

Christenson, Andrew, ed. 1989. *Tracing Archaeology's Past: The Historiography of Archaeology.* Carbondale: Southern Illinois University Press.

Clark, Grahame. 1934. "Archaeology and the State." *Antiquity* 8, no. 32: 414–28.

———. 1979. *Sir Mortimer and Indian Archaeology.* New Delhi: Archaeological Survey of India.

———. 1989. *Prehistory at Cambridge and beyond.* Cambridge: Cambridge University Press.

Clark, Grahame, and John Grahame Douglas Clark. 1989. *Prehistory at Cambridge and beyond.* Cambridge: Cambridge University Press Archive.

Clark, Gregory. 1994. "Factory Discipline." *Journal of Economic History* 54, no. 1: 128–63.

Clarke, David L. 1968. *Analytical Archaeology*. London: Methuen.

————. 1973. "Archaeology Loss of Innocence." *Antiquity* 47, no. 185: 6–18.

Clift, Peter D., Andrew Carter, Liviu Giosan, Julie Durcan, Geoff A. T. Duller, Mark G. Macklin, Anwar Alizai, Ali R. Tabrez, Mohammed Danish, and Sam Van Laningham. 2012. "U-Pb Zircon Dating Evidence for a Pleistocene Sarasvati River and Capture of the Yamuna River." *Geology* 40, no. 3: 211–14.

Cohn, Bernard. 1996. *Colonialism and Its Form of Knowledge: The British in India*. Princeton: Princeton University Press.

Colebrooke, H. T. 1812. "On the Sources of the Ganges, in the Himadri or Emodus." *Asiatic Researches, or, Transactions of the Society Instituted in Bengal for Inquiring into the History and Antiquities, the Arts, Sciences and Literature of Asia* 11: 429–45.

Colley, Sarah. 1995. "What Happened at WAC-3?" *Antiquity* 69, no. 1: 16–18.

Collins, Harry M., and Robert Evans. 2002. "The Third Wave of Science Studies: Studies of Expertise and Experience." *Social Studies of Science* 32, no. 2: 235–96.

Collins, Harry M., and Trevor Pinch. 1979. "The Construction of the Paranormal: Nothing Unscientific Is Happening." In *On the Margins of Science: The Social Construction of Rejected Knowledge*, edited by Roy Wallis, 237–70. Keele: University of Keele.

Coningham, Robin, and Mark Manuel. 2009. "Priest-Kings or Puritans? Childe and Willing Subordination in the Indus." *European Journal of Archaeology* 12, nos 1–3: 167–80.

Conkey, M., and R. Tringham. 1996. "Archaeology and The Goddess: Exploring the Contours of Feminist Archaeology." In *Feminisms in the Academy: Rethinking the Disciplines*, edited by A. Stewart and D. Stanton, 199–247. Ann Arbor: University of Michigan Press.

Constable, Philip. 1997. "Early Dalit Literature and Culture in Late Nineteenth- and Early Twentieth-Century Western India." *Modern Asian Studies* 31, no. 2: 317–38.

Copeman, Jacob, and Dwaipayan Banerjee. 2020. *Hematologies: The Political Life of Blood in India*. Ithaca: Cornell University Press.

Coronil, Fernando. 1994. "Listening to the Subaltern: The Poetics of Neocolonial States." *Poetics Today* 15, no. 4: 643–58.

Cowell, Christopher. 2016. "The Kacchā-Pakkā Divide: Material, Space and Architecture in the Military Cantonments of British India (1765–1889)." *ABE Journal: Architecture beyond Europe*, nos. 9–10.

Cunningham, Alexander. 1871. *The Ancient Geography of India: The Buddhist Period, Including the Campaigns of Alexander, and the Travels of Hwen-Thsang*. London: Trubner & Co.

————. 1875. "Harappa." In *Archaeological Survey of India, Report for the Year 1872–73, Volume V*, 105–08 and plates XXXII–XXXIII. Calcutta: Government of India Press.

————. 1877. *Inscription of Asoka. Corpus Inscriptionum Indicarium*. Vol. 1. Calcutta: Office of the Superintendent of Government Printing.

Dales, G. F. 1964. "The Mythical Massacre at Mohenjodaro." *Expedition* 6, no. 3: 36–43.

Dales, George, Jonathan Mark Kenoyer, and Leslie Alcock. 1986. *Excavations at Mohenjo Daro, Pakistan: The Pottery, with an Account of the Pottery from the 1950 Excavations of Sir Mortimer Wheeler*. Philadelphia: UPenn Museum of Archaeology.

Dani, Ahmad Hasan. 1981. *Indus Civilization: New Perspectives*. Lahore: Centre for the Study of the Civilization of Central Asia, Quaid-i-Azam University.

Daniel, Glyn Edmund. 1950. *A Hundred Years of Archaeology*. London: Duckworth.

————. 1976. *Cambridge and the Back-Looking Curiosity: An Inaugural Lecture*. Cambridge: Cambridge University Press.

————. 1981. *A Short History of Archaeology*. London: Thames and Hudson.

Danino, Michel. 2010. *Lost River: On the Trail of the Sarasvati*. New Delhi: Penguin Books.

————. 2019. "Methodological Issues in the Indo-European Debate." *Journal of Biosciences* 44, no. 3: 68.

Danino, Michel, and Sujata Nahar. 1996. *The Invasion That Never Was*. Delhi: Mother's Institute of Research.

Das, S. K. 2000. *Public Office, Private Interest: Bureaucracy and Corruption in India*. New Delhi: Oxford University Press.

Das, Veena, and Deborah Poole. 2004. *Anthropology in the Margins of the State*. Santa Fe, NM: School of American Research Press.

Dasgupta, Simanti. 2015. *BITS of Belonging: Information Technology, Water, and Neoliberal Governance in India*. Philadelphia, Pennsylvania: Temple University Press.

Datta, Asok. 2001. "Evolution of Brick Technology in India." *Indian Museum Bulletin* 36: 11–33.

Dave, Aditi Krishna, Marie-Agnes Courty, Kathryn E. Fitzsimmons, and Ashok Kumar Singhvi. 2019. "Revisiting the Contemporaneity of a Mighty River and the Harappans: Archaeological, Stratigraphic and Chronometric Constraints." *Quaternary Geochronology* 49: 230–35.

David, Nicholas. 1992. "Integrating Ethnoarchaeology: A Subtle Realist Perspective." *Journal of Anthropological Archaeology* 11, no. 4: 330–59.

De Certeau, Michel. 1984. *The Practice of Everyday Life*. Berkeley: University of California Press.

Dean, Mitchel. 1999. *Governmentality: Power and Rule in Modern Society.* Thousand Oaks: Sage Publications.

Dennis, Kelly. 1994. "Ethno-Pornography: Veiling the Dark Continent." *History of Photography* 18, no. 1: 22–28.

Deo, S. B., and S. Kamath. 1993. *The Aryan Problem.* Pune: Bharatiya Itihasa Sankalana Samiti.

Deshpande, Madhav, and Peter Edwin Hook. 1979. *Aryan and Non-Aryan in India.* Ann Arbor: University of Michigan.

Dickey, Sara. 2012. "The Pleasures and Anxieties of Being in the Middle: Emerging Middle-Class Identities in Urban South India." *Modern Asian Studies* 46, no. 3: 559–99.

Diken, Bülent. 2004. "From Refugee Camps to Gated Communities: Biopolitics and the End of the City." *Citizenship Studies* 8, no. 1: 83–106.

Diken, Bülent, and Carsten Bagge Laustsen. 2005. *The Culture of Exception: Sociology Facing the Camp.* London: Routledge.

Dikshit, K. N. 1967. "Exploration along the Right Bank of River Sutlej in Punjab." *Journal of Indian History* 45, no. 2: 561–68.

———. 1982. "The Neolithic Cultural Frontiers of Kashmir." *Man and Environment* 6: 30.

———. 2013. "Origin of Early Harappan Cultures in the Sarasvati Valley: Recent Archaeological Evidence and Radiometric Dates." *Journal of Indian Ocean Archaeology* 9: 87–141.

Dimendberg, Edward. 1998. "Henri Lefebvre on Abstract Space." In *Philosophy and Geography II: The Production of Public Space*, edited by Andrew Light and Jonathan Smith, 17–47. New York: New York: Rowman and Littlefield Publishers, Inc.

Dirks, Nicholas B. 1994. "Guiltless Spoliations: Picturesque Beauty, Colonial Knowledge, and Colin Mackenzie's Survey of India." In *Perceptions of South Asia's Visual Past*, edited by Catherine B. Asher and Thomas Metcalf, 211–32. New Delhi: Oxford University Press.

———. 2001. *Castes of Mind: Colonialism and the Making of Modern India.* Princeton, NJ: Princeton University Press.

Dodson, Michael S. 2007. *Orientalism, Empire, and National Culture: India, 1770–1880.* New York: Springer.

———. 2020. *Bureaucracy, Belonging, and the City in North India: 1870–1930.* Abingdon, Oxon, and New York, NY: Routledge.

Doniger, Wendy, and Brian K. Smith. 1989. "Sacrifice and Substitution: Ritual Mystification and Mythical Demystification." *Numen* 36, no. 2: 189–224.

Donner, Henrike. 2012. *Being Middle-Class in India: A Way of Life.* London: Routledge.

Drew, John. 1987. *India and the Romantic Imagination.* Delhi: Oxford University Press.

Drewett, Peter. 2011. *Field Archaeology: An Introduction*. London: Routledge.

Driver, Felix. 2001. *Geography Militant: Cultures of Exploration and Empire*. Oxford, Malden: Blackwell Publishers.

Dumont, Louis. 1980. *Homo Hierarchicus: The Caste System and Its Implications*. Chicago: University of Chicago Press.

Duncan, James S. 1990. *The City as Text: The Politics of Landscape Interpretation in the Kandyan Kingdom*. Cambridge: Cambridge University Press.

———. 2007. *In the Shadows of the Tropics: Climate, Race and Biopower in Nineteenth Century Ceylon*. Aldershot, England and Burlington, VT: Routledge.

Dunnell, Robert C. 1978. "Style and Function: A Fundamental Dichotomy." *American Antiquity* 43, no. 2: 192–202.

———. 1980. "Evolutionary Theory and Archaeology." In *Advances in Archaeological Method and Theory*, edited by Michael B. Schiffer, 35–99. San Diego: Academic Press.

Durcan, Julie A., David S. G. Thomas, Sanjeev Gupta, Vikas Pawar, Ravindra N. Singh, and Cameron A. Petrie. 2019. "Holocene Landscape Dynamics in the Ghaggar–Hakra Palaeochannel Region at the Northern Edge of the Thar Desert, Northwest India." *Quaternary International* 501, January: 317–27.

Edgeworth, Matt. 1990. "Analogy as Practical Reason: The Perception of Objects in Excavation Practice." *Archaeological Review from Cambridge* 9, no. 2: 243–52.

———. 2003. *Acts of Discovery: An Ethnography of Archaeological Practice*. Oxford, England: Archaeopress.

———, ed. 2006. *Ethnographies of Archaeological Practice: Cultural Encounters, Material Transformations*. Lanham, MD: Alta Mira Press.

———. 2010. "On the Boundary: New Perspectives from Ethnography of Archaeology." In *Archaeology and Anthropology: Understanding Similarity, Exploring Difference*, edited by Duncan Garrow and Thomas Yarrow, 54–68. Oxford: Oxbow Books.

———. 2011. "Excavation as a Ground of Archaeological Knowledge." *Archaeological Dialogues* 18, no. 1: 44–46.

Edney, Matthew H. 1997. *Mapping an Empire: The Geographical Construction of British India 1765–1843*. Chicago: University of Chicago Press.

El-Haj, Nadia Abu. 2001. *Facts on the Ground: Archaeological Practice and Territorial Self-Fashioning in Israeli Society*. Chicago: University of Chicago Press.

Elst, Koenraad. 1999. *Update on the Aryan Invasion Debate*. New Delhi: Aditya Prakashan.

Engineer, Asghar Ali. 1991. *Mandal Commission Controversy*. Delhi: Ajanta Publications.

———. 1993. "Bombay Riots: Second Phase." *Economic and Political Weekly* 28, nos. 12–13: 505–08.

Erdosy, George. 1995. *The Indo-Aryans of Ancient South Asia: Language, Material Culture and Ethnicity*. Berlin: Walter de Gruyter.

Fabian, Johannes. 2000. *Out of Our Minds: Reason and Madness in the Exploration of Central Africa*. Berkeley: University of California Press.

Fairclough, Norman. 2005. "Peripheral Vision: Discourse Analysis in Organization Studies: The Case for Critical Realism." *Organization Studies* 26, no. 6: 915–39.

Ferguson, James, and Akhil Gupta. 2002. "Spatializing States: Toward an Ethnography of Neoliberal Governmentality." *American Ethnologist* 29, no. 4: 981–1002.

Fernandes, Daniel M., Kendra A. Sirak, Harald Ringbauer, Jakob Sedig, Nadin Rohland, Olivia Cheronet, Matthew Mah, Swapan Mallick, Iñigo Olalde, and Brendan J. Culleton. 2021. "A Genetic History of the Pre-Contact Caribbean." *Nature* 590, no. 7844: 103–10.

Fernandes, Leela, and Patrick Heller. 2006. "Hegemonic Aspirations: New Middle Class Politics and India's Democracy in Comparative Perspective." *Critical Asian Studies* 38, no. 4: 495–522.

Fernandes, Walter. 2004. "Rehabilitation Policy for the Displaced." *Economic and Political Weekly* 39, no. 12: 1191–93.

Fine-Dare, Kathleen Sue. 2002. *Grave Injustice: The American Indian Repatriation Movement and NAGPRA*. Lincoln: University of Nebraska Press.

Flannery, K. V. 1967. "Culture History v. Cultural Process: A Debate in American Archaeology." *Scientific American* 217, no. 2: 119–22.

Fleming, Andrew, and Matthew Johnson. 1990. "The Theoretical Archaeology Group (TAG): Origins, Retrospect, Prospect." *Antiquity* 64, no. 243: 303–6.

Fleming, John. 1812. "A Catalogue of Indian Medicinal Plants and Drugs, with Their Names in the Hindustani and Sanscrit Languages." *Asiatic Researches, or, Transactions of the Society Instituted in Bengal for Inquiring into the History and Antiquities, the Arts, Sciences and Literature of Asia* 11: 153–96.

Foote, Robert Bruce. 1866. "On the Occurrence of Stone Implements in Laterite Formations in Various Parts of the Madras and North Arcot Districts." *Madras Journal of Literature and Science*, 3rd Series, Part II: 1–35.

———. 1916. *The Foote Collection of Indian Prehistoric and Protohistoric Antiquities: Notes on Their Ages and Distribution*. Madras: Government Museum Madras.

Forth, Aidan. 2017. *Barbed-Wire Imperialism: Britain's Empire of Camps, 1876–1903*. Berkeley: University of California Press.

Fotiadis, M. 1993. "Regions of the Imagination: Archaeologists, Local People, and the Archaeological Record in Fieldwork, Greece." *Journal of European Archaeology* 1, no. 2: 151–68.

Foucault, Michel. 1977. *Discipline and Punish: The Birth of the Prison*. London and New York: Penguin Books.

———. 1991. *The Foucault Effect: Studies in Governmentality*. Chicago: University of Chicago Press.

Frankel, David. 1993. "The Excavator: Creator or Destroyer?" *Antiquity* 67, no. 257: 875–77.

Franklin, Michael J. 2011. *"Orientalist Jones: Sir William Jones, Poet, Lawyer, and Linguist, 1746–1794."* Oxford and New York: Oxford University Press.

Frawley, David. 1994. *The Myth of the Aryan Invasion of India*. New Delhi: Voice of India.

Fuller, C. J. 2017. "Ethnographic Inquiry in Colonial India: Herbert Risley, William Crooke, and the Study of Tribes and Castes." *Journal of the Royal Anthropological Institute* 23, no. 3: 603–21.

Fuller, Christopher J., and Veronique Benei. 2009. *The Everyday State and Society in Modern India*. New Delhi: Social Science Press.

Fuller, Dorian Q., and Nicole Boivin. 2002. "Beyond Description and Diffusion: A History of Processual Theory in the Archaeology of South Asia." In *Archaeology and Historiography*, edited by S. Settar and Ravi Korisettar, 159–90. New Delhi: Manohar.

Fuller, Steve. 1993. *Philosophy of Science and Its Discontents*. New York: Guilford Press.

———. 1997. *Science*. Minneapolis: University of Minnesota Press.

Fujimara, Joan. H. 1992. "Crafting Science: Standardized Packages, Boundary Objects, and 'Translation.'" In *Science as Practice and Culture*, edited by A. Pickering, 168–211. Chicago: University of Chicago Press.

Gamkrelidze, T. V., and V. V. Ivanov. 1995. *Indo-European and the Indo-Europeans: A Reconstruction and Historical Analysis of a Proto-Language and a Proto-Culture*. Berlin: M. de Gruyter.

Gathercole, Peter, and David Lowenthal. 1990. *The Politics of the Past*. London: Unwin Hyman.

Geertz, Clifford. 1973. *The Interpretation of Cultures: Selected Essays*. New York: Basic Books.

Gero, Joan M. 1985. "Socio-Politics and the Woman-at-Home Ideology." *American Antiquity* 50, no. 2: 342–50.

———. 1994. "Gender Division of Labor in the Construction of Archaeological Knowledge in the United States." In *Social Construction of the Past: Representation as Power*, edited by G. C. Bond and A. Gilliam, 144–53. London: Routledge.

———. 1996. "Archaeological Practice and Gendered Encounters with Field Data." In *Gender and Archaeology*, edited by R. Wright, 251–79. Philadelphia: University of Pennsylvania Press.

Ghatak, Maitreesh, and Parikshit Ghosh. 2011. "The Land Acquisition Bill: A Critique and a Proposal." *Economic and Political Weekly* 46, no. 41: 65–72.

Ghose, Bimal, Amal Kar, and Zahid Hussain. 1979. "The Lost Courses of the Sarasvati River in the Great Indian Desert: New Evidence from the Landsat Imagery." *The Geographical Journal, London* 145, no. 3: 446–51.

————. 1980. "Comparative Role of Aravalli and the Himalayan River Systems in the Fluvial Sedimentation of the Rajasthan Desert." *Man and Environment* 4: 8–12.

Ghosh, Amalananda. 1952. "The Rajputana Dessert: Its Archaeological Aspect." *Bulletin of the National Institute of Sciences of India* 1: 37–42.

————. 1953. "Exploration in Bikaner." *East and West* 4, no. 1: 31–34.

————. 1954. "Fifty Years of Archaeological Survey of India." *Ancient India* 9: 29–52.

————. 1956. "Exploration in Bikaner, India." *Miscellanea Asiatica Occidentalis* 18: 102–15.

————. 1957. "Notes." *Ancient India* 13: 1–3.

————. 1959. "Exploration in Bikaner." In *An Anthropological Reconnaissance in West Pakistan, 1955*, edited by Henry Field, 121–61. Cambridge: Papers of the Peabody Museum of Archaeology and Ethnology, Harvard University.

————. 1960. "Notes." *Ancient India* 16: 1–3.

Gifford, James C. 1960. "The Type-Variety Method of Ceramic Classification as an Indicator of Cultural Phenomena." *American Antiquity* 25, no. 3: 341–47.

Gilroy, Paul. 2000. *Between Camps: Race, Identity and Nationalism at the End of the Colour Line*. London: Allen Lane.

Gokcumen, Omer, and Michael Frachetti. 2020. "The Impact of Ancient Genome Studies in Archaeology." *Annual Review of Anthropology* 49: 277–98.

Golson, Jack. 1996. "What Went Wrong with WAC 3 and an Attempt to Understand Why." *WAC News* 4, no. 1: 3–9.

Golwalkar, Madhav Sadashiv. 1939. *We or Our Nationhood Defined*. Nagpur: Bharat Prakashan.

Gopinath, Vrinda. 2003. "Mythical Saraswati? Welcome to the Official Discovery." *The Indian Express*, October.

Gosden, Chris. 2001. "Postcolonial Archaeology: Issues of Culture, Identity, and Knowledge." In *Archaeological Theory Today*, edited by I. Hodder, 241–61. Cambridge: Polity Press.

Graham, Stephen, and Simon Marvin. 2001. *Splintering Urbanism*. London and New York: Routledge.

Graves-Brown, P., S. Jones, and C. S. Gamble. 1996. *Cultural Identity and Archaeology: The Construction of European Communities*. London: Routledge.

Griffith, Ralph T.H. 1889. *The Hymns of the Rigveda*. Vol. 1. Benares: E.J. Lazarus and Co.

————. 1890. *The Hymns of the Rigveda*. Vol. 2. Benares: E.J. Lazarus and Co.

————. 1897. *The Hymns of the Rigveda*. Vol. 2. Benares: E.J. Lazarus and Co.

Guha, Sudeshna. 2002. "The Visual in Archaeology: Photographic Representation of Archaeological Practice in British India." *Antiquity* 76, no. 291: 93–100.

———. 2003. "Imposing the Habit of Science: Sir Mortimer Wheeler and Indian Archaeology." *Bulletin of the History of Archaeology* 13, no. 1: 4–10.

———. 2005. "Negotiating Evidence: History, Archaeology and the Indus Civilization." *Modern Asian Studies* 39, no. 2: 399–426.

———. 2011. *The Marshall Albums: Photography and Archaeology*. London and New Delhi, Ocean Township, NJ: Mapin Publishing Gp Pty Ltd.

Guha-Thakurta, Tapati. 2005. *Monuments, Objects, Histories: Institutions of Art in Colonial and Postcolonial India*. New York: Columbia University Press.

Gupta, A. K., J. R. Sharma, and G. Sreenivasan. 2011. "Using Satellite Imagery to Reveal the Course of an Extinct River below the Thar Desert in the Indo-Pak Region." *International Journal of Remote Sensing* 32, no. 18: 5197–5216.

Gupta, Akhil. 1995. "Blurred Boundaries: The Discourse of Corruption, the Culture of Politics, and the Imagined State." *American Ethnologist* 22, no. 2: 375–402.

———. 2005. "Narratives of Corruption: Anthropological and Fictional Accounts of the Indian State." *Ethnography* 6, no. 1: 5.

———. 2012. *Red Tape: Bureaucracy, Structural Violence, and Poverty in India*. Durham: Duke University Press Books.

Gupta, Akhil, and James Ferguson. 1997. *Anthropological Locations: Boundaries and Grounds of a Field Science*. Berkeley: University of California Press.

Gupta, Anupam. 2010. "Dissecting the Ayodhya Judgment." *Economic and Political Weekly* 45, no. 50: 33–37, 39–41.

Gupta, Swaraj Prakash. 1994. "Government Sitting Tight over Clinching Archaeological Evidence?" *Organiser* 46, no. 18: 3.

———. 1995. *The "Lost" Sarasvati and the Indus Civilization*. Jodhpur: Kusumanjali Prakashan.

———. 1996. *The Indus-Saraswati Civilization: Origins, Problems, and Issues*. Delhi: Pratibha Prakashan.

———. 2001. "River Sarasvati in History, Archaeology and Geology." *Puratattva* 31: 30–35.

Haak, Wolfgang, Iosif Lazaridis, Nick Patterson, Nadin Rohland, Swapan Mallick, Bastien Llamas, Guido Brandt, Susanne Nordenfelt, Eadaoin Harney, and Kristin Stewardson. 2015. "Massive Migration from the Steppe Was a Source for Indo-European Languages in Europe." *Nature* 522, no. 7555: 207–11.

Habib, Irfan. 1997. "Unreason and Archaeology: The 'Painted Grey-Ware' and Beyond." *Social Scientist* 24, no. 1–2: 16–24.

———. 2001. "Imaging River Sarasvati: A Defense of Commonsense." *Social Scientist* 29, nos. 1–2: 46–74.

Hailey, Charlie. 2009. *Camps: A Guide to 21st-Century Space*. Cambridge, MA: The MIT Press.

Hamilakis, Yannis. 1996. "Through the Looking Glass: Nationalism, Archaeology and the Politics of Identity." *Antiquity* 70: 975–978.

———. 2011. "Archaeological Ethnography: A Multitemporal Meeting Ground for Archaeology and Anthropology." *Annual Review of Anthropology* 40: 399–414.

Hamilakis, Yannis, and Aris Anagnostopoulos. 2009. "What Is Archaeological Ethnography?" *Public Archaeology* 8, no. 2–3: 65–87.

Hamilton, Peter, and Roger Hargreaves. 2001. *Beautiful and the Damned: The Creation of Identity in Nineteenth-Century Photography.* 1st ed. Aldershot, Hampshire, UK, and Burlington, VT: Lund Humphries Pub Ltd.

Hamilton, Sue. 1999. "Lost in Translation? A Comment on the Excavation Report." *Papers of the Institute of Archaeology* 10: 1–8.

Handler, Richard, and Eric Gable. 1997. *The New History in an Old Museum: Creating the Past at Colonial Williamsburg.* Durham: Duke University Press.

Hansen, Thomas Blom, and Finn Stepputat. 2001. *States of Imagination: Ethnographic Exploration of the Postcolonial State.* Durham: Duke University Press.

Haraway, Donna Jeanne. 1989. *Primate Visions: Gender, Race, and Nature in the World of Modern Science.* New York: Routledge.

———. 1991. *Simians, Cyborg and Women: The Reinvention of Nature.* New York: Routledge.

Harding, Sandra. 1991. *Whose Science? Whose Knowledge? Thinking from Women's Lives.* Ithaca: Cornell University Press.

———. 2006. *Science and Social Inequality: Feminist and Postcolonial Issues.* Urbana and Chicago: University of Illinois Press.

———. 2008. *Sciences from below: Feminisms, Postcolonialities, and Modernities.* Durham, NC: Duke University Press.

Hardt, Michael, and Antonio Negri. 2009. *Commonwealth.* Cambridge, MA: Belknap Press.

Harris, Edward C. 1989. *Principles of Archaeological Stratigraphy.* San Diego: Academic Press.

Harvey, David. 1990. *The Condition of Postmodernity: An Enquiry into the Origins of Cultural Change.* Cambridge: Blackwell.

Hassan, F. 1995. "The World Archaeological Congress in India: Politicizing the Past." *Antiquity* 69, no. 266: 874–77.

Hegde, K. T. M. 1975. "The Painted Grey Ware of India." *Antiquity* 49, no. 195: 187–90.

Hendrickx, Stan. 1996. "The Relative Chronology of the Naqada Culture: Problems and Possibilities." In *Aspects of Early Egypt,* edited by Spencer Jeffrey A., 36–69. London: British Museum Press.

Heras, Henery. 1953. *Studies in Proto-Indo-Mediterranean Culture, Vol. 1.* Bombay: Indian Historical Research Institute.

Heyd, Volker. 2017. "Kossinna's Smile." *Antiquity* 91, no. 356: 348–59.

Hipple, Walter John. 1957. *The Beautiful, the Sublime, and the Picturesque in Eighteenth-Century British Aesthetic Theory.* Carbondale: Southern Illinois University Press.

Hodder, Ian. 1982. *Symbolic and Structural Archaeology*. Cambridge: Cambridge University Press.

———. 1984. "Archaeology in 1984." *Antiquity* 58, no. 222: 25–32.

———. 1986. *Reading the Past: Current Approaches to Interpretation in Archaeology*. Cambridge: Cambridge University Press.

———. 1989. "Writing Archaeology: Site Reports in Context." *Antiquity* 63, no. 239: 268–74.

———. 1991. *Archaeological Theory in Europe: The Last Three Decades*. London: Routledge.

———. 1992. *Theory and Practice in Archaeology*. London: Routledge.

———. 1997. "'Always Momentary, Fluid and Flexible': Towards a Reflexive Excavation Methodology." *Antiquity* 71, no. 273: 691–700.

———. 1999. *The Archaeological Process*. Oxford: Blackwell.

———. 2000. *Towards Reflexive Method in Archaeology: The Example at Çatalhöyük*. Cambridge: McDonald Institute of Archaeological Research.

———. 2002. "Ethics and Archaeology: The Attempt at Catalhoyuk." *Near Eastern Archaeology* 65, no. 3: 174–81.

———. 2003. "Archaeological Reflexivity and the 'Local' Voice." *Anthropological Quarterly* 76, no. 1: 55–69.

———, ed. 2013. *Humans and Landscapes of Çatalhöyük: Reports from the 2000–2008 Seasons. Çatalhöyük Reseach Project Series Vol- Ume 8; British Institute at Ankara Monograph No. 47; Mon-Umenta Archaeologica 30*. Los Angeles: Cotsen Institute of Archaeology.

———, ed. 2014. *Çatalhöyük Excavations: The 2000–2008 Seasons. Çatal- Höyük Reseach Project Series Volume 7; British Institute at Ankara Monograph No. 46; Monumenta Archaeologica 29*. Los Angeles: Cotsen Institute of Archaeology.

Hodder, Ian, Alexandra Alexandri, Michael Shanks, Victor Buchli, John Carman, Jonathan Last, and Gavin Lucas. 1995. *Interpreting Archaeology: Finding Meaning in the Past*. London: Psychology Press.

Hole, Frank, and Robert F. Heizer. 1969. *An Introduction to Prehistoric Archeology*. New York: Holt, Rinehart and Winston.

Hollowell, Julie, and George Nicholas. 2008. "A Critical Assessment of Ethnography in Archaeology." In *Ethnographic Archaeologies: Reflections on Stakeholders and Archaeological Practices*, edited by Quetzil E. Castañeda, Richard Handler, Julie Hollowell, Mark P. Leone, George Nicholas, K. Anne Pyburn, and Larry J. Zimmerman, 63–94. Lanham, MD: AltaMira Press.

Hollowell, Julie, and Lena Mortensen, eds. 2009. *Ethnographies and Archaeologies: Iterations of the Past*. Illustrated ed. Gainesville, FL: University Press of Florida.

Holtorf, Cornelius. 2002. "Notes on the Life History of a Pot Sherd." *Journal of Material Culture* 7, no. 1: 49–71.

Hull, Matthew S. 2012. *Government of Paper: The Materiality of Bureaucracy in Urban Pakistan*. Berkeley: University of California Press.

Imam, Abu. 1966. *Sir Alexander Cunningham and the Beginnings of Indian Archaeology*. Dacca: Asiatic Society of Pakistan.

Inden, Ronald. 1986. "Orientalist Constructions of India." *Modern Asian Studies* 20, no. 3: 401–46.

Indian Archaeology 1954–55: A Review. 1954. New Delhi: Archaeological Survey of India.

Indian Archaeology 1967–68: A Review. 1968. New Delhi: Archaeological Survey of India.

Indian Archaeology 1969–70: A Review. 1973. New Delhi: Archaeological Survey of India.

Indian Archaeology 1973–74: A Review. 1979. New Delhi: Archaeological Survey of India.

Indian Archaeology 1976–77: A Review. 1980. New Delhi: Archaeological Survey of India.

Indian Archaeology 1978–79: A Review. 1980. New Delhi: Archaeological Survey of India.

Indian Archaeology 1979–80: A Review. 1983. New Delhi: Archaeological Survey of India.

Indian Archaeology 1983–84: A Review. 1986. New Delhi: Archaeological Survey of India.

Indian Archaeology 1984–85: A Review. 1987. New Delhi: Archaeological Survey of India.

Indian Archaeology 1987–88: A Review. 1993. New Delhi: Archaeological Survey of India.

Indian Archaeology 1988–89: A Review. 1993. New Delhi: Archaeological Survey of India.

Indian Archaeology 1989–90: A Review. 1994. New Delhi: Archaeological Survey of India.

Indian Archaeology 1990–91: A Review. 1995. New Delhi: Archaeological Survey of India.

Indian Archaeology 1991–92: A Review. 1996. New Delhi: Archaeological Survey of India.

Indian Archaeology 1992–93: A Review. 1997. New Delhi: Archaeological Survey of India.

Indian Archaeology 1993–94: A Review. 2000. New Delhi: Archaeological Survey of India.

Indian Archaeology 1997–98: A Review. 2003. New Delhi: Archaeological Survey of India.

Indian Archaeology 2003–04: A Review. 2011. New Delhi: Archaeological Survey of India.

Indian Archaeology 2004–05: A Review. 2014. New Delhi: Archaeological Survey of India.

Indian Archaeology 2010–11: A Review. 2016. New Delhi: Archaeological Survey of India.

Iyer, Meera. 2019. "The Best Laid Plans." *Deccan Herald*, January 20. Available at https://www.deccanherald.com/sunday-herald/best-laid-plans-713650.html, accessed on September 23, 2020.

Jacob, T. 1994. *Cantonments in India: Evolution and Growth.* New Delhi: Reliance Publishing House.

Jacobson, J. 1986. "The Harappan Civilization: An Early State." In *Studies in the Archaeology of India and Pakistan*, edited by J. Jacobson, 137–74. Delhi: Oxford University Press and IBH.

Jay, Martin. 1994. *Downcast Eyes: The Denigration of Vision in Twentieth-Century French Thought.* Berkeley: University of California Press.

Jeffrey, Craig. 2008. "Guest Editorial." *Environment and Planning D: Society and Space* 26, no. 6: 954–58.

———. 2010. *Timepass: Youth, Class, and the Politics of Waiting in India.* Stanford: Stanford University Press.

Jha, D. N. 1998. *Ancient India in Historical Outline.* New Delhi: Manohar.

Jha, Natwar, and N. S. Rajaram. 2000. *The Deciphered Indus Script.* New Delhi: Aditya Prakashan.

Joffe, A.H. 2003. "Identity/Crisis." *Archaeological Dialogues* 10, no. 01: 77–95.

John, J. 2014. "Brick Kilns and Slave Labour: Observations from Punjab." *Labour File* 9, nos. 1–2: 15–26.

Johnson, Matthew. 2019. *Archaeological Theory: An Introduction.* 3rd ed. Hoboken, NJ: Wiley-Blackwell.

Johnson, Ragnar. 1978. "Jokes, Theories, Anthropology." *Semiotica* 22, nos. 3–4: 309–34.

Johnson-Roehr, Susan. 2008. "The Archaeological Survey of India and Communal Violence in Post-independence India." *International Journal of Heritage Studies* 14, no. 6: 506–23.

Jones, Andrew. 2001. *Archaeological Theory and Scientific Practice.* Cambridge and New York: Cambridge University Press.

Jones, Siân. 1997. *The Archaeology of Ethnicity: Constructing Identities in the Past and Present.* London and New York: Routledge.

Jones, Sir William. 1807. "Third Anniversary Discourse: 'On the Hindus.'" Reprinted in *The Collected Works of Sir William Jones, Volume II*, 23–46. London: John Stockdale.

Joseph, Helen. 2000. "Salokha: A Response to Communal Riots, a Social Disaster." *Indian Journal of Social Work* 61, no. 4: 664–74.

Joshi, Jagat Pati. 1978. "Interlocking of Late Harappan Culture and Painted Grey Ware Culture in the Light of Recent Excavations." *Man and Environment* 2: 98–101.

———. 1984. "The Indus Civilisation: A Reconsideration on the Basis of Distribution Maps." In *Frontiers of the Indus Civilisation*, edited by Braj Basi Lal and Swaraj Prakash Gupta, 511–30. New Delhi: Books and Books.

———. 1990. *Excavation at Surkotada and Exploration in Kutch*. New Delhi: Archaeological Survey of India.

———. 1993. *Excavations at Bhagwanpura 1975–76, and Other Explorations and Excavations 1975–81, in Haryana, Jammu and Kashmir and Punjab*. New Delhi: Archaeological Survey of India.

Joshi, Sanjay. 2010. *The Middle Class in Colonial India*. New Delhi and New York: Oxford University Press.

Joyce, Rosemary. 2002. *The Languages of Archaeology: Dialogue, Narrative, and Writing*. Oxford and Malden, MA: Wiley-Blackwell.

Kalyanaraman, S. 1999. *The River Sarasvati: Legend, Myth, and Reality*. Chennai: All India Saraswat Foundation.

Kar, Amal. 1983. "Drainage Desiccation, Water Erosion and Desertification in Northwest India." In *Desertification in Thar, Sahara and Sahel Regions*, edited by A. K. Sen, 49–72. Jodhpur: Scientific Publishers.

———. 1989. "Terrain Characteristics of Jaisalmer District." *Geographical Review of India* 55, no. 1: 48–59.

———. 1994. "Lineament Control on Channel Behavior during the 1990 Flood in the South-Eastern Thar Desert." *International Journal of Remote Sensing* 15, no. 13: 2521–30.

Kar, Amal. 1998. "Possible Neotectonic Activities in the Luni-Jawai Plains, Rajasthan." *Journal of the Geological Society of India* 32, no. 12: 522–26.

———. 1999. "A Hitherto Unknown Palaeodrainage System from the Radar Imagery of Southeastern Thar Desert and Its Significance." In *Vedic Sarasvati: Evolutionary History of a Lost River of Northwestern India*, Memoir Geological Society of India, Bangalore, No. 42, B. P. Radhakrishna and S. S. Merh, 229–35. Bangalore: Geological Society of India.

Kar, Amal, and Bimal Ghose. 1984. "The Drishadvati River System of India: An Assessment and New Findings." *The Geographical Journal* 150, no. 2: 221–29.

Kehoe, Alice Beck. 1998. *The Land of Prehistory: A Critical History of American Archaeology*. New York: Routledge.

Kejariwal, O. P. 1988. *The Asiatic Society of Bengal and the Discovery of India's Past 1784–1838*. Delhi and New York: Oxford University Press.

Kennedy, Kenneth Adrian Raine. 1994. "Identification of Sacrificial and Massacre Victims in Archaeological Sites: The Skeletal Evidence." *Man and Environment* 19, nos. 1–2: 247–51.

Kenoyer, Jonathan Mark. 1997. "Trade and Technology of the Indus Valley: New Insights from Harappa, Pakistan." *World Archaeology* 29, no. 2: 262–80.

———. 1998. *Ancient Cities of the Indus Valley Civilization.* Karachi and Islamabad: Oxford University Press and American Institute of Pakistan Studies.

———. 2005. "Bead Technologies at Harappa, 3300–1900 BC: A Comparison of Tools, Techniques and Finished Beads from the Ravi to the Late Harappan Period." In *South Asian Archaeology,* edited by Catherine Jarrige and Vincent Lefevre, 157–70. Paris: Editions Recherche sur les Civilisations.

———. 2007. "Stone Beads in Ancient South Asia-7000–600 BC: A Comparative Approach to Technology, Style, and Ideology." In *The Global Perspective of Beads and Beadwork: History, Manufacture, Trade, and Adornment,* edited by J. Allen and V. Hector, 1–12. Istanbul: Kadir Has University.

Kenyon, Kathleen M. 1960. *Excavations at Jericho. Volume 1. The Tombs Excavated in 1952–54.* London: Brit. School of Archeology in Jerusalem.

Khan, S. U., Sudhir Agarwal, and D. V. Sharma. 2010. *Ayodhya Matter Ram Janam Bhoomi-Babri Masjid Disputes.* Allahabad: Malhotra Law House.

Kivisild, Toomas, Michael J. Bamshad, Katrin Kaldma, Mait Metspalu, Ene Metspalu, Maere Reidla, S. Laos, Jüri Parik, W. Scott Watkins, and Mary E. Dixon. 1999. "Deep Common Ancestry of Indian and Western-Eurasian Mitochondrial DNA Lineages." *Current Biology* 9, no. 22: 1331–34.

Kivisild, Toomas, S. Rootsi, Mait Metspalu, S. Mastana, K. Kaldma, J. Parik, E. Metspalu, M. Adojaan, H-V Tolk, and V. Stepanov. 2003. "The Genetic Heritage of the Earliest Settlers Persists Both in Indian Tribal and Caste Populations." *The American Journal of Human Genetics* 72, no. 2: 313–32.

Knorr-Cetina, Karin. 1981. *The Manufacture of Knowledge: An Essay on the Constructivist and Contextual Nature of Science.* Oxford and New York: Elsevier Science.

———. 1999. *Epistemic Cultures: How the Sciences Make Knowledge.* Cambridge, Mass.: Harvard University Press.

Kochhar, Rajesh. 1999. *The Vedic People: Their History and Geography.* Delhi: Orient Longman.

Kohl, Philip L., Clare P. Fawcett. 1995. *Nationalism, Politics, and the Practice of Archaeology.* Cambridge: Cambridge University Press.

Kostof, Spiro. 1991. *The City Shaped: Urban Patterns and Meanings through History.* Boston: Bulfinch Press.

Krauss, Rosalind. 1985. *The Originality of the Avant-Garde and Other Modernist Myth.* Cambridge: MIT Press.

Krishna, Anirudh. 2010. "Continuity and Change: The Indian Administrative Service 30 Years Ago and Today." *Commonwealth and Comparative Politics* 48, no. 4: 433–44.

Krishnan, K, L. S. Rao, V. Vinod, Smitha S. Kumar, Prabhin Sukumaran, and Dilip Kumar Kushwaha. 2012. "Petrography of Ceramics from Bhirrana: A Preliminary Study." *Man and Environment.* 37, no. 2: 18–27.

Kuhn, Thomas S. 1965. *The Structure of Scientific Revolutions.* Chicago: University of Chicago Press.

Kuklick, H. 1991. "Contested Monuments: The Politics of Archeology in Southern Africa." In *Colonial Situations: Essays on the Contextualization of Ethnographic Knowledge,* edited by G. W. Stocking, 135–69. Madison: University of Wisconsin Press.

Kumar, Ashish. 2018. "Aryans versus Non-Aryans: A Study of Dalit Narratives of India's Ancient Past." *Contemporary Voice of Dalit* 10, no. 2: 127–37.

Kumar, Deepak. 1995. *Science and the Raj, 1857–1905.* Delhi: Oxford University Press.

Kumar, Prakash. 2013. *Indigo Plantations and Science in Colonial India.* New Delhi: Cambridge University Press.

Labbe, Jacqueline. 1998. *Romantic Visualities: Landscape, Gender and Romanticism.* New York: Macmillan Press.

Lahiri, Nayanjot. 2000. "Archaeology and Identity in Colonial India." *Antiquity* 74, no. 285: 687–92.

———. 2005. *Finding Forgotten Cities: How the Indus Civilization Was Discovered.* New Delhi: Permanent Black.

———. 2012. *Marshalling the Past: Ancient India and Its Modern Histories.* New Delhi: Permanent Black.

———. 2017. "Are Archaeological Discoveries like Scientific Discoveries? The Curious Case of the Indus Civilization." *World Archaeology* 49, no. 2: 174–86.

Lal, Braj Basi. 1949. "Sisupalgarh, 1948: An Early Historical Fort in Eastern India." *Ancient India* 5: 62–105.

———. 1954. "Excavations at Hastinapura and Other Explorations in the Upper Ganga and Sutlej Basins 1950–52." *Ancient India* 10 and 11: 4–151.

———. 1964. "On Excavating a House That Was Never Built!" *Ancient India* 20 and 21: 206–09.

———. 1975. "In Search of India's Traditional Past: Light from the Excavations at Hastinapura and Ayodhya." *India International Centre Quarterly* 2, no. 4: 311–14.

———. 1978. "The Indian Aryan Hypothesis and Vis-a-Vis Indian Archaeology." *Journal of Central Asia* 1, no. 1: 21–41.

————. 1980. "Archaeology of the Ramayana Sites: Its Genesis and a Summary of Its Results." *Manthan* 11, no. 10: 9–12.

————. 1984. "Some Reflections on the Structural Remains at Kalibangan." In *Frontiers of the Indus Civilization*, edited by Braj Basi Lal and Swaraj Prakash Gupta, 55–62. New Delhi: Books and Books.

————. 1993. *Excavations at Sringaverapura, 1977–86*. New Delhi: Archaeological Survey of India.

————. 1997. *The Earliest Civilization of South Asia*. New Delhi: Aryan Books International.

————. 1998. *India 1947–1997: New Light on the Indus Civilization*. New Delhi: Aryan Books International.

————. 2001. "A Note on the Excavations at Ayodhya with Reference to the Mandir-Masjid Issue." In *Destruction and Conservation of Cultural Property*, edited by Robert Layton, Peter G. Stone, and Julian Thomas, 117–26. London: Routledge.

————. 2002a. "Historicity of the Mahabharata and the Ramayana: What Has Archaeology to Say in the Matter?" In *Indian Archaeology in Retrospect, Vol. 4, Archaeology and Historiography*, edited by S. Settar and R. Korisettar, 29–70. New Delhi: Manohar and Indian Council of Historical Research.

————. 2002b. *The Sarasvati Flows on: The Contiguity of Indian Culture*. New Delhi: Aryan Books International.

————. 2008. *Rāma, His Historicity, Mandir, and Setu: Evidence of Literature, Archaeology, and Other Sciences*. New Delhi: Aryan Books International.

Lal, Braj Basi, Jagat Pati Joshi, Bal Krishen Thapar, and Madhu Bala. 2003. *Excavations at Kalibangan: The Early Harappans (1961–69)*. New Delhi: Archaeological Survey of India.

Lamberg-Karlovsky, C. C. 1997. "Politics and Archaeology, Colonialism, Nationalism, Ethnicity, and Archaeology." *Review of Archaeology* 18: 1–14.

————. 2002. "Archaeology and Language." *Current Anthropology* 43, no. 1: 63–88.

Latour, Bruno. 1987. *Science in Action: How to Follow Scientist and Engineer through Society*. Cambridge, MA: Harvard University Press.

————. 1999. *Pandora's Hope: Essays on the Reality of Science Studies*. Cambridge, MA: Harvard University Press.

Latour, Bruno, and Steve Woolgar. 1986. *Laboratory Life*. New Jersey: Princeton University Press.

Laudan, Rachel. 1987. *From Mineralogy to Geology: The Foundations of a Science, 1650–1830*. Chicago: University of Chicago Press.

Layton, Robert. 1989. *Conflict in the Archaeology of Living Traditions*. London: U. Hyman.

Lazar, Sian. 2008. *El Alto, Rebel City: Self and Citizenship in Andean Bolivia*. Durham: Duke University Press Books.

Lazaridis, Iosif, Alissa Mittnik, Nick Patterson, Swapan Mallick, Nadin Rohland, Saskia Pfrengle, Anja Furtwängler, Alexander Peltzer, Cosimo Posth, and Andonis Vasilakis. 2017. "Genetic Origins of the Minoans and Mycenaeans." *Nature* 548, no. 7666: 214–18.

Lazaridis, Iosif, Dani Nadel, Gary Rollefson, Deborah C. Merrett, Nadin Rohland, Swapan Mallick, Daniel Fernandes, Mario Novak, Beatriz Gamarra, and Kendra Sirak. 2016. "Genomic Insights into the Origin of Farming in the Ancient Near East." *Nature* 536, no. 7617: 419–24.

Leach, Edmund. 1990. "Aryan Invasion over Four Millennia." In *Culture through Time: Anthropological Approaches*, edited by Ohnuki-Tierney, 227–45. Stanford: Stanford University Press.

Lees, James. 2019. *Bureaucratic Culture in Early Colonial India: District Officials, Armed Forces, and Personal Interest under the East India Company, 1760–1830.* London and New York: Routledge India.

Lefebvre, Henri. 1991. *Critique of Everyday Life: Vol. 1.* London: Verso.

Legg, Stephen. 2007. *Spaces of Colonialism: Delhi's Urban Governmentalities.* Malden, MA: Wiley-Blackwell.

Leighton, Mary. 2015. "Excavation Methodologies and Labour as Epistemic Concerns in the Practice of Archaeology. Comparing Examples from British and Andean Archaeology." *Archaeological Dialogues* 22, no. 1: 65.

Lenoir, Tim. 1997. *Instituting Science: The Cultural Production of Scientific Disciplines.* Stanford: Stanford University Press.

Leonard, Karen Isaksen. 1978. *Social History of an Indian Caste: The Kayasths of Hyderabad.* Berkeley: University of California Press.

Leoshko, Janice. 2003. *Sacred Traces: British Explorations of Buddhism in South Asia.* London: Routledge.

Li, Tania Murray. 2007. *The Will to Improve: Governmentality, Development, and the Practice of Politics.* Durham: Duke University Press Books.

Liberhan, Manmohan Singh. 2009. *Report of the Liberhan Ayodhya Commission of Inquiry.* New Delhi: Ministry of Home Affairs, Government of India.

Liebmann, Matthew, and Uzma Z. Rizvi, eds. 2008. *Archaeology and the Postcolonial Critique.* Lanham, MD: AltaMira Press.

Lommel, Herman. 1927. *Die Yasts Des Awesta.* Göttingen-Leipzig: Vandenhoeck and Ruprecht/JC Hinrichs.

———. 1954. "Anahita-Sarasvati." In *Asiatica: Festschrift Friedrich Weller Zum 65*, edited by Johannes Schubert and Ulrich Schneider, 405–13. Geburtstag, Leipzig: Otto Harrassowitz.

Lowenthal, David. 1998. "Fabricating Heritage." *History and Memory* 10, no. 1: 5–24.

———. 1999. *The Past Is a Foreign Country.* Cambridge: Cambridge University Press.

Lucas, Gavin. 2001. "Destruction and the Rhetoric of Excavation." *Norwegian Archaeological Review* 34, no. 1: 35–46.

———. 2002. *Critical Approaches to Fieldwork: Contemporary and Historical Archaeological Practice*. London and New York: Routledge.

———. 2012. *Understanding the Archaeological Record*. Cambridge and New York: Cambridge University Press.

———. 2019. *Writing the Past: Knowledge and Literary Production in Archaeology*. New York: Routledge.

Lydon, Jane, and Uzma Z. Rizvi, ed. 2016. *Handbook of Postcolonial Archaeology*. London: Routledge.

Lyman, R. Lee, and Michael J. O'Brien. 2003. "Cultural Traits: Units of Analysis in Early Twentieth-Century Anthropology" 59, no. 2: 225–50.

Lyman, R. Lee, Michael J. O'Brien, and Robert C. Dunnell. 1997. *The Rise and Fall of Culture History*. New York: Plenum Press.

Lynch, Michael. 1993. *Scientific Practice and Ordinary Action: Ethnomethodology and Social Studies of Science*. Cambridge, UK: Cambridge University Press.

Mackay, Ernest J. H. 1937. *Further Excavations at Mohenjo-Daro, Being an Official Account of Archaeological Excavations at Mohenjo-Daro Carried Out by the Government of India between the Years 1927–1931. 2 Vols*. Delhi: Government of India Press.

———. 1943. *Chanhu-Daro Excavations 1935–36*. New Haven: American Oriental Society.

MacLagan, R. 1885. "The Rivers of the Punjab." *Proceedings of the Royal Geographic Society and Monthly Record of Geography* 7, no. 11: 705–19.

MacMurdo, James. 1834. "Dissertation on the River Indus." *Journal of the Royal Asiatic Society of Great Britain and Ireland* 1: 21–44.

———. 1839. "Observations of the Sindhoo, or River Indus." *Transactions of the Bombay Geographical Society* 5: 124–35.

Madella, Marco, and Dorian Q. Fuller. 2006. "Palaeoecology and the Harappan Civilisation of South Asia: A Reconsideration." *Quaternary Science Reviews Quaternary Science Reviews* 25, nos. 11–12: 1283–1301.

Maheshwari, Shriram. 1995. *Mandal Commission Revisited: Reservation Bureaucracy in India*. New Delhi: Jawahar Publishers and Distributors.

Majumdar, Nani Gopal. 1934. *Memoirs of the Archaeological Survey of India. NO. 48. Explorations in Sind: Being a Report of the Exploratory Survey Carried out during the Years 1927–28, 1929–30 and 1930–31*. Delhi: Manager of Publications.

———. 1999. *Explorations in Sind: Being a Report of the Exploratory Survey Carried out during the Years 1927–28, 1929–30 and 1930–31*. New Delhi: Archaeological Survey of India.

Mallory, J. P. 1989. *In Search of the Indo-Europeans: Language, Archaeology and Myth*. London: Thames and Hudson.

Mandal, D. 2003. *Ayodhya: Archaeology after Demolition*. New Delhi: Orient Longman.

———. 2004. "Report of the Ayodhya Excavation (2002–03): A Document of Unscientific Archaeology." *Social Science Probing* 16, no. 1: 37–65.

Mandal, D., and Shereen Ratnagar. 2007. *Ayodhya: Archaeology After Excavation*. New Delhi: Tulika.

Mani, Lata. 2010. "Where Angels Fear to Tread: The Ayodhya Verdict." *Economic and Political Weekly* 45, no. 42: 10–12.

Margarita Díaz-Andreu, and Timothy Champion. 1996. *Nationalism and Archaeology in Europe*. London: UCL Press.

Marshall, John. 1923. *Conservation Manual: A Handbook for the Use of Archaeological Officers and Others Entrusted with the Care of Ancient Monuments*. Calcutta: Archaeological Survey of India.

———. 1924. "First Light on a Long-Forgotten Civilization: New Discoveries of an Unknown Prehistoric Past in India." *Illustrated London News*, September 20, 528–31, 548.

———. 1931. *Mohenjo-Daro and the Indus Civilization*. Vol. 1, 2, and 3. London: Arthur Probsthain.

———. 1951. *Taxila: An Illustrated Account of Archaeological Excavations Carried out at Taxila under the Orders of the Government of India between the Years 1913 and 1934: In Three Volumes*. Cambridge: Cambridge University Press.

Masselos, Jim. 1994. "The Bombay Riots of January 1993: The Politics of Urban Conflagration." *South Asia: Journal of South Asian Studies* 17, no. s1: 79–95.

Masson, Charles. 1844. *Narrative of Various Journeys in Balochistan, Afghanistan, the Panjab, and Kalât, during a Residence in Those Countries: To Which Is Added an Account of the Insurrection at Kalât, and a Memoir on Eastern Balochistan*. 4 vols. London: Richard Bentley.

Mathur, Nayanika. 2016. *Paper Tiger: Law, Bureaucracy and the Developmental State in Himalayan India*. Cambridge, UK: Cambridge University Press.

———. 2018. "Eating Money: Corruption and Its Categorical 'Other' in the Leaky Indian State." *Modern Asian Studies* 51, no. 6: 1796–817.

Mbembe, Achile. 1992. "Provisional Notes on the Postcolony." *Africa: Journal of the International African Institute* 62, no. 1: 3–37.

———. 2000. *On the Postcolony*. Berkeley: University of California Press.

McIntosh, Jane R. 2008. *The Ancient Indus Valley: New Perspectives*. Santa Barbara, CA: ABC-CLIO.

Meadow, Richard H. 1996. "The Origins and Spread of Agriculture and Pastoralism in Northwestern South Asia." In *The Origins and Spread of Agriculture and Pastoralism in Eurasia*, edited by D. R. Harris, 390–412. London: UCL Press.

Meadow, Richard H., and Ajita K. Patel. 2002. "From Mehrgarh to Harappa and Dholavira: Prehistoric Pastoralism in North-Western South Asia through the Harappan Period." In *Indian Archaeology in Retrospect. Protohistory, vol. II*, edited by S. Settar and R. Korisettar, 391–408. New Delhi: Manohar.

Meskell, Lynn. 1998. *Archaeology under Fire: Nationalism, Politics and Heritage in the Eastern Mediterranean and Middle East*. London: Routledge.

———. 2002. "Negative Heritage and Past Mastering in Archaeology." *Anthropological Quarterly* 75, no. 3: 557–74.

———. 2005. "Archaeological Ethnography: Conversations around Kruger National Park." *Archaeologies* 1, no. 1: 81–100.

———. 2007. "Falling Walls and Mending Fences: Archaeological Ethnography in the Limpopo." *Journal of Southern African Studies* 33, no. 2: 383–400.

Metcalf, Thomas R. 1997. *Ideologies of the Raj*. Cambridge: Cambridge University Press.

Mihesuah, Devon A. 2000. *Repatriation Reader Who Owns American Indian Remains?* Lincoln: University of Nebraska Press.

Miller, P., and N. Rose. 1988. "The Tavistock Programme: The Government of Subjectivity and Social Life." *Sociology* 22, no. 2: 171.

Mishra, Siddhartha. 2019. "The Press Conference on Rakhigarhi Findings Throws Up More Questions Than Answers." *Outlook*, September 6, 2019. Available at https://www.outlookindia.com/website/story/india-news-the-press-conference-on-rakhigarhi-findings-throws-up-more-questions-than-answers/338052, accessed on October 13, 2020.

Misra, V. N. 1994. "Indus Civilisation and the Rgvedic Saraswati." In *South Asian Archaeology 1993*, edited by A. Parpola and P. Koshikallio, 511–25. Helsinki: Suomalainen Tiedeakatemia.

Mitchell, Timothy. 1991. *Colonising Egypt*. Berkely: University of California Press.

———. 2002. *Rule of Experts Egypt, Techno-Politics, Modernity*. Berkeley: University of California Press.

Mitter, Partha. 1977. *Much Maligned Monsters: History of European Reactions to Indian Art*. Oxford: Clarendon Press.

———. 1994. *Art and Nationalism in Colonial India: Occidental Orientations*. Cambridge, UK: Cambridge University Press.

Moorjani, Priya, Kumarasamy Thangaraj, Nick Patterson, Mark Lipson, Po-Ru Loh, Periyasamy Govindaraj, Bonnie Berger, David Reich, and Lalji Singh. 2013. "Genetic Evidence for Recent Population Mixture in India." *The American Journal of Human Genetics* 93, no. 3: 422–38.

Morris, Ian, Trinity Jackman, Emma Blake, Brien Garnand, Sebastiano Tusa, Tara Hnatiuk, Wendy Matthews, and Hans-Peter Stika. 2003. "Stanford University Excavations on the Acropolis of Monte Polizzo, Sicily, III: Preliminary Report on the 2002 Season." *Memoirs of the American Academy in Rome* 48: 243–315.

Morrison, Kathleen D. 2005. "Brahmagiri Revisited: A Re-Analysis of the South Indian Sequence." In *South Asian Archaeology 2001*, edited by Catherine Jarrige and Vincent Lefevre, 257–62. Paris: Editions Recherche sur les Civilisations.

Moser, Stephanie. 2007. "On Disciplinary Culture: Archaeology as Fieldwork and Its Gendered Associations." *Journal of Archaeological Method and Theory* 14, no. 3: 235–63.

Motz, Lloyd, and Jefferson Hane Weaver. 1993. *The Story of Mathematics*. New York: Avon Books.

Mountain, Joanna L., Joan M. Hebert, Silanjan Bhattacharyya, Peter A. Underhill, Chris Ottolenghi, Madhav Gadgil, and L. Luca Cavalli-Sforza. 1995. "Demographic History of India and MtDNA-Sequence Diversity." *American Journal of Human Genetics* 56, no. 4: 979.

Mughal, Mohammad Rafique. 1992. "The Consequences of River Changes for the Harappan Settlements in Cholistan." *The Eastern Anthropologist* 45, nos. 1–2: 105–16.

———. 1997. *Ancient Cholistan: Archaeology and Architecture*. Rawalpindi: Ferozsons.

Mukerjee, Soumyendra Nath. 1968. *Sir William Jones: A Study in Eighteen Century British Attitudes to India*. Cambridge: Cambridge University Press.

Mukherjee, Ashoke. 2001. "RigVedic Sarasvati: Myth and Reality." *Breakthrough* 9, no. 1: 1–10.

Mukherjee, S. N. 1968. *Sir William Jones: A Study in Eighteenth-Century British Attitudes to India*. Cambridge: Cambridge University Press.

Müller, Friedrich Max. 1869. *Rig-Veda-Sanhita: The Sacred Hymns of the Brahmans*. London: Trübner and Co.

Muralidharan, S. 1994. "Questions of Ethics: World Archaeological Congress, Delhi." *Frontline*, November 19.

Murray, A. 1998. *Sir William Jones 1746–94: A Commemoration*. Oxford: Oxford University Press.

Nakatsuka, Nathan, Iosif Lazaridis, Chiara Barbieri, Pontus Skoglund, Nadin Rohland, Swapan Mallick, Cosimo Posth, Kelly Harkins-Kinkaid, Matthew Ferry, and Éadaoin Harney. 2020. "A Paleogenomic Reconstruction of the Deep Population History of the Andes." *Cell* 181, no. 5: 1131–45.

Nandan, Aniket, and R. Santhosh. 2019. "Exploring the Changing Forms of Caste-Violence: A Study of Bhumihars in Bihar, India." *European Journal of Cultural and Political Sociology* 6, no. 4: 421–47.

Nandy, Ashis. 1988. *Science, Hegemony and Violence: A Requiem for Modernity*. New Delhi: Oxford University Press.

Narasimhan, Vagheesh M., Nick Patterson, Priya Moorjani, Nadin Rohland, Rebecca Bernardos, Swapan Mallick, Iosif Lazaridis, Nathan Nakatsuka, Iñigo Olalde, and Mark Lipson. 2019. "The Formation of Human Populations in South and Central Asia." *Science* 365, no. 6457: eaat7487.

Nath, Amarendra. 1998. *Further Excavations at Pauni 1994.* New Delhi: Archaeological Survey of India.

———. 2016. *Excavations at Adam (1988–1992): A City of Asika Janapada.* New Delhi: Archaeological Survey of India.

Nath, Damini. 2020. "Government Likely to Re-Constitute Panel to Study 'Origins of Indian Culture'." *The Hindu*, September 20. Available at https://www.thehindu.com/news/national/government-likely-to-re-constitute-panel-to-study-origins-of-indian-culture/article32704962.ece, accessed on September 22, 2020.

Navlakha, G. 1984. "Recovering, Uncovering or Forfeiting the Past?" *Economic and Political Weekly* 29, no. 47: 2961–63.

Nearchus. 1875. "The Lost River of the Indian Desert." *Calcutta Review* 60: 323–57.

Neff, Hector. 1992. "Ceramics and Evolution." *Archaeological Method and Theory* 4: 141–93.

Netz, Reviel. 2009. *Barbed Wire: An Ecology of Modernity.* Middletown, CT: Wesleyan University Press.

Ó Tuathail, Gear. 1996. *Critical Geopolitics: The Politics of Writing Global Space.* Minneapolis: University of Minnesota Press.

Obaidullah, Mohammed. 2016. "A Framework for Analysis of Islamic Endowment (Waqf) Laws." *International Journal of Not-for-Profit Law* 18, no. 1: 54–64.

Ogle, Vanessa. 2015. *The Global Transformation of Time: 1870–1950.* Cambridge, MA: Harvard University Press.

Ola Bergström, and David Knights. 2006. "Organizational Discourse and Subjectivity: Subjectification during Processes of Recruitment." *Human Relations* 59, no. 3: 351–77.

Oldenburg, Veena Talwar. 1989. *The Making of Colonial Lucknow.* New Delhi: Oxford University Press.

Oldham, C.F. 1893. "The Sarasvati and the Lost River of the Indian Desert." *Journal of the Asiatic Society of Great Britain and Ireland* 45: 49–76.

Oldham, R. D. 1874. "Notes on the Lost River of the Indian Desert." *Calcutta Review* 59: 1–27.

———. 1886. "On Probable Changes in the Geography of the Punjab and Its Rivers: An Historical-Geographical Study." *Journal of the Asiatic Society of Bengal* 55, no. 2: 322–43.

Olivelle, Patrick. 1999. *The Dharmasutras : The Law Codes of Apastamba, Gautama, Baudhayana, and Vasistha.* Oxford: Oxford University Press.

Olsen, Bjørnar, Michael Shanks, Timothy Webmoor, and Christopher Witmore. 2012. *Archaeology: The Discipline of Things.* Berkeley: University of California Press.

Omvedt, Gail. 2006. *Dalit Visions: The Anti-Caste Movement and the Construction of an Indian Identity.* New Delhi: Orient Longman.

Orengo, Hector A., and Cameron A. Petrie. 2017. "Large-Scale, Multi-Temporal Remote Sensing of Palaeo-River Networks: A Case Study from Northwest India and Its Implications for the Indus Civilisation." *Remote Sensing* 9, no. 7: 735.

Paddayya, K. 1974. "Mesolithic Culture of the Shorapur Doab, Peninsular India." *Anthropos* 69, no. 3/4: 590–607.

———. 1978. "New Research Designs and Field Techniques in the Palaeolithic Archaeology of India." *World Archaeology* 10, no. 1: 94–110.

———. 1987. "The Place of the Study of Site Formation Processes in Prehistoric Research in India." In *Natural Formation Processes and the Archaeological Record,* edited by D. T. Nash and Michael Petraglia, 74–85. Oxford: British Archaeological Reports International Series.

———. 1990. *The New Archaeology and Aftermath: A View from Outside the Anglo-American World.* Pune: Ravish.

———. 1995. "Theoretical Perspectives in Indian Archaeology." In *Theory in Archaeology: A World Perspective,* edited by Peter Ucko, 110–49. London: Routledge.

———. 2016. *Revitalizing Indian Archaeology: Further Theoretical Essays.* New Delhi: Aryan Books International.

Pande, B. M. 1982. "History of Research on the Harappan Culture." In *Harappan Civilization: A Contemporary Perspective,* edited by Gregory Possehl, 395–403. New Delhi: Oxford University Press and IBH.

Parapola, Asko. 1994. *Deciphering Indus Script.* Cambridge, UK: Cambridge University Press.

Pardy, Maree. 2009. "The Shame of Waiting." In *Waiting,* edited by Ghassan Hage, 195–209. Melbourne: Melbourne University Press.

Parikh, Danika, and Cameron A. Petrie. 2019. "'We Are Inheritors of a Rural Civilisation': Rural Complexity and the Ceramic Economy in the Indus Civilisation in Northwest India." *World Archaeology* 51, no. 2: 252–72.

Parpola, Asko. 1988. "The Coming of the Aryans to Iran and India and the Cultural and Ethnic Identity of the Dåsas." *Studia Orientalia* 64: 195–302.

———. 1997. "The Dāsas and the Coming of the Aryans." In *Inside the Texts, Beyond the Texts. New Approaches to the Study of the Vedas,* edited by Michael Witzel, 193–202. Harvard Oriental Series, Opera Minora 2. Cambridge, MA: Harvard University Department of Sanskrit and Indian Studies.

———. 2015. *The Roots of Hinduism: The Early Aryans and the Indus Civilization.* New York: Oxford University Press.

Patel, Ajita. 1998. "The Pastoral Economy of Dholavira: A First Look at Animals and Urban Life in Third Millennium Kutch." In *South Asian Archaeology 1995,* edited by R. Allchin and B. Allchin, 101–13. New Delhi: Oxford and IBH.

Petrie, Flinders W. M. 1904. *Methods and Aims in Archaeology*. New York: MacMillian and Company.

Petrie, William Matthew Flinders, and James Edward Quibell. 1896. *Naqada and Ballas: 1895*. Warminster: Aris and Phillips.

Phalkey, Jahnavi. 2013. *Atomic State: Big Science in Twentieth-Century India*. New Delhi: Permanent Black.

Pickering, Andrew. 1992. *Science as Practice and Culture*. Chicago: Chicago University Press.

Pickles, John. 2004. *A History of Spaces: Cartographic Reason, Mapping, and the Geo-Coded World*. New York: Routledge.

Pinney, Christopher. 1992. "The Parallel Histories of Anthropology and Photography." In *Anthropology and Photography, 1860–1920*, edited by Elizabeth Edwards, 74–95. New Haven, London: Yale University Press and Royal Anthropological Institute.

———. 1997. *Camera Indica: The Social Life of Indian Photographs*. London: Reaktion Books.

Piggott, Stuart. 1950. *Prehistoric India to 1000 B.C.* London: Cassel.

———. 1965. "Archaeological Draughtsmanship: Principles and Practice Part I: Principles and Retrospect." *Antiquity* 39, no. 155: 165–76.

Pitt-Rivers, Augustus Henry Lane-Fox. 1888. *Excavations in Cranborne Chase, near Rushmore, on the Borders of Dorset and Wilts: 1880–88. Volumes I–IV*. London: Harrison and Sons, Printers [Printed privately].

Plemmons, Dena, and Alex W. Barker. 2017. *Anthropological Ethics in Context: An Ongoing Dialogue*. London: Routledge.

Polanyi, Michael, and Amartya Sen. 2009. *The Tacit Dimension*, rev. ed. Chicago and London: University of Chicago Press.

Politis, G. 2001. "On Archaeological Praxis, Gender Bias and Indigenous Peoples in South America." *Journal of Social Archaeology* 1, no. 1: 90.

Porter, Theodore M. 1995. *Trust in Numbers the Pursuit of Objectivity in Science and Public Life*. Princeton, NJ: Princeton University Press.

Possehl, Gregory L. 1982. "Discovering Ancient India's Earliest Cities: The First Phase of Research." In *Harappan Civilization: A Contemporary Perspective*, edited by Gregory Possehl, 405–13. New Delhi: Oxford University Press and IBH.

———. 1993a. *Harappan Civilization: A Recent Perspective*. New Delhi: Oxford University Press and IBH.

———. 1993b. "Sir Leonrad Wooley Evaluates Indian Archaeology." *Harappan Studies* 1: 1–56.

———. 1999. *Indus Age: The Beginnings*. New Delhi: Oxford University Press and IBH.

———. 2002. *The Indus Civilization: A Contemporary Perspective*. Walnut Creek, CA: Alta Mira Press.

———. 2010. "Ernest JH Mackay and the Penn Museum." *Expedition* 52, no. 1: 40–43.

Potter, David C. 1986. *India's Political Administrators 1919–1983*. Oxford: Clarendon Press.

Prabhakar, V. N. 2016. "An Overview of the Stone Bead Drilling Technology in South Asia from Earliest Times to Harappans." *Heritage: Journal of Multidisciplinary Studies in Archaeology* 4: 47–74.

———. 2018. "Decorated Carnelian Beads from the Indus Civilization Site of Dholavira (Great Rann of Kachchha, Gujarat)." In *Walking with the Unicorn: Social Organization and Material Culture in Ancient South Asia: Jonathan Mark Kenoyer Felicitation Volume*, edited by Dennys Frenez, Gregg M. Jamison, Randall W. Law, Massimo Vidale, and Richard H. Meadow, 477–89. Oxford: Archaeopress.

Prakash, Gyan. 1999. *Another Reason: Science and the Imagination of Modern India*. Princeton, NJ: Princeton University Press.

Pramanik, Shubhra. 2004a. "Excavations at Juni Kuran 2003–04: A Preliminary Report." *Puratattva* 34: 45–57.

———. 2004b. "Hathab: An Early Historic Port on the Gulf of Khambhat." *Journal of Indian Ocean Archaeology* 1: 133–40.

Prasad, Amit. 2014. *Imperial Technoscience: Transnational Histories of MRI in the United States, Britain, and India*. Cambridge: MIT Press.

Pratt, Mary Louise. 1992. *Imperial Eyes: Travel Writing and Transculturation*. London: Routledge.

Preucel, R. W. 1995. "The Postprocessual Condition." *Journal of Archaeological Research* 3, no. 2: 147–75.

Puri, V. M. K. 2001. "Origin and Course of Vedic Saraswati River in Himalaya: Its Secular Desiccation Episodes as Deciphered from Palaeo-Glaciation and Geomorphological Signatures." *Proceedings of the Symposium on Snow, Ice and Glaciers. Geological Survey of India, Special Publication* 53: 175–91.

Quigley, Declan. 1994. *The Interpretation of Caste*. Oxford: Oxford University Press.

Radhakrishna, B. P., and S. S. Merh. 1999. *Vedic Sarasvati: Evolutionary History of a Lost River of Northwestern India*. Bangalore: Geological Society of India.

Raghav, K. S., and A. K. Grover. 1991. "Major Sub-Recent Changes in the Upper Reaches of Kantli River Course and Related Environmental Implications, Rajasthan." In *Proceedings Quaternary Landscape of Indian Subcontinent*, 147–52. Baroda: Geology Dept., Maharaj Sahyaji University.

Rai, Alok. 2001. *Hindi Nationalism*. Hyderabad: Orient Longman India.

Raina, Dhruv, and Irfan Habib. 2006. *Domesticating Modern Science: A Social History of Science and Culture in Colonial India*. New Delhi: Tulika.

Raj, Gopal. 2000. *Reach for the Stars: The Evolution of India's Rocket Programme*. New Delhi: Viking.

Raj, Kapil. 2000. "Colonial Encounters and the Forging of New Knowledge and National Identities: Great Britain and India, 1760–1850." *Osiris* 15, no. 1: 119–34.

Rajan, Karai. 2002. *Archaeology: Principles and Methods*. Thanjavur: Manoo Pathippakam.

Rajan, Kaushik Sunder. 2006. *Biocapital: The Constitution of Postgenomic Life*. Durham: Duke University Press Books.

Rajaram, Navaratna Srinivasa. 1993. *Aryan Invasion of India: The Myth and the Truth*. New Delhi: Voice of India.

———. 1995. *The Aryan Invasion Theory and the Subversion of Scholarship*. New Delhi: Voice of India.

Rajaram, Navaratna Srinivasa, and David Frawley. 1997. *The Vedic Aryans and the Origins of Civilization: A Literary and Scientific Perspective*. New Delhi: Voice of India.

Rajawat, A. S., C. V. S. Sastry, and A. Narain. 1999. "Application of Pyramidal Processing on High Resolution IRS-1C Data for Tracing the Migration of the Saraswati River in Parts of the Thar Desert." In *Vedic Sarasvati, Evolutionary History of a Lost River of Northwestern India, Memoir Geological Society of India, Bangalore, No. 42*, edited by B. P. Radhakrishna and S. S. Merh, 259–72. Bangalore: Geological Society of India.

Rajendran, C. P. 2019. "Scientists Part of Studies Supporting Aryan Migration Endorse Party Line Instead." *The Wire,* September 13. Available at https://thewire.in/the-sciences/rakhigarhi-indus-valley-civilisation-aryan-steppe-migration-vasant-shinde, accessed on October 15, 2020.

Raman, K. V. 1991. *Principles and Methods of Archaeology*. Madras: Parthajan Publications.

Raman, Shankar. 2001. *Framing India: The Colonial Imaginary in Early Modern Culture*. Stanford: Stanford University Press.

Ramasamy, S. M. 2005. "Neotectonic Controls on the Migration of Sarasvati River of the Great Indian Desert." In *Remote Sensing in Geomorphology*, edited by S. M. Ramasamy, 59–70. New Delhi: New India Publishing.

Ramasamy, S. M., P. C. Bakliwal, and R. P. Verma. 1991. "Remote Sensing and River Migration in Western India." *International Journal of Remote Sensing* 12, no. 12: 2597–609.

Ramaswamy, Sumathi. 2001. "Remains of the Race: Archaeology. Nationalism, and the Yearning for Civilization in Indus Valley." *The Indian Economic and Social History Review* 38, no. 2: 105–45.

———. 2004. *The Lost Land of Lemuria: Fabulous Geographies, Catastrophic Histories*. Berkeley: University of California Press.

Rao, Anupama. 2009. *The Caste Question: Dalits and the Politics of Modern India*. Berkeley: University of California Press.

Rao, Kotamraju Narayana. 1990. *Mandal Report X-Rayed*. New Delhi: Eastern Books.

Rao, L. S. 2006. "The Harappan Spoked Wheels Rattled Down the Streets of Bhirrana, Dist. Fathehabad, Haryana." *Puratattva* 36: 59–67.

Rao, L. S., N. B. Sahu, Prabash Sahu, Samir Diwan, and U. A. Shastry. 2005. "New Light on the Excavation of Harappan Settlement at Bhirrana." *Puratattva* 35: 60–68.

Rao, L. S., S. B. Sahu, Prabash Sahu, U. A. Shastry, and Samir Diwan. 2004. "Unearthing Harappan Settlement at Bhirrana (2003–04)." *Puratattva* 34: 20–34.

Rao, N. 1994. "Interpreting Silences: Symbol and History in the Case of Ram Janmabhoomi/Babri Masjid." In *Social Construction of the Past: Representation as Power*, edited by G. C. Bond and A. Gilliam, 154–64. London: Routledge.

———. 1999. "Ayodhya and the Ethics of Archaeology." In *Case Studies in Archaeology and World Religions*, edited by T. Insoll, 44–47. Oxford: Archaeopress.

Rao, S. R. 1982. *The Decipherment of the Indus Script*. Bombay: Asia Publishing.

———. 1985. *Lothal*. New Delhi: Archaeological Survey of India.

———. 1993. "The Aryans in Indus Civilization." In *The Aryan Problem: Papers Presented at the Seminar on the Aryan Problem Held at Bangalore in July 1991*, edited by S. B. Deo and Suryanath Kamath, 173–80. Pune: Bharatiya Itihasa Sankalana Samiti, Maharashtra.

Raper, F. V. 1812. "Narrative of a Survey for the Purpose of Discovering the Sources of the Ganges." *Asiatic Researches, or, Transactions of the Society Instituted in Bengal for Inquiring into the History and Antiquities, the Arts, Sciences and Literature of Asia* 11: 446–564.

Rasool, Tabasum. 2017. "Waqf Administration in India." *Journal of Islamic Thought and Civilization (JITC)* 7, no. 1: 1–12.

Rathje, William L., Michael Shanks, and Christopher Witmore, ed. 2013. *Archaeology in the Making: Conversations through a Discipline*. London: Routledge.

Ratnagar, Shereen. 2004. "Archaeology at the Heart of a Political Confrontation: The Case of Ayodhya." *Current Anthropology* 45, no. 2: 239–59.

Raverty, H.G. 1892. "The Mihran of Sind and Its Tributaries: A Geographical and Historical Study." *Journal of the Asiatic Society of Bengal* 61: 155–297.

Ravitchandirane, P. 2007. "Stratigraphy and Structural Context of Arikamedu." *East and West* 57, no. 1/4: 205–33.

Ray, Himanshu Prabha. 2008. *Colonial Archaeology in South Asia: The Legacy of Sir Mortimer Wheeler*. New Delhi: Oxford University Press.

———. 2019. *Archaeology and Buddhism in South Asia*. London: Routledge India.

Reeves, Dache M. 1936. "Aerial Photography and Archaeology." *American Antiquity* 2, no. 2: 102–07.

Reich, David. 2018. *Who We Are and How We Got Here: Ancient DNA and the New Science of the Human Past*. New York: Pantheon.

Reich, David, Kumarasamy Thangaraj, Nick Patterson, Alkes L. Price, and Lalji Singh. 2009. "Reconstructing Indian Population History." *Nature* 461, no. 7263: 489–94.

Renfrew, Colin. 1987. *Archaeology and Language: The Puzzle of Indo-European Origins*. New York: Cambridge University Press.

Reyman, Jonathan E. 1992. *Rediscovering Our Past: Essays on the History of American Archaeology*. Aldershot: Avebury.

Rheinberger, Hans-Jörg. 1997. *Toward a History of Epistemic Things: Synthesizing Proteins in the Test Tube*. Stanford: Stanford University Press.

———. 2005. "A Reply to David Bloor: 'Toward a Sociology of Epistemic Things.'" *Perspectives on Science* 13, no. 3: 406–10.

Rice, Prudence M. 2015. *Pottery Analysis: A Sourcebook*. Chicago: University of Chicago Press.

Rick, John W. 2008. "Context, Construction, and Ritual in the Development of Authority at Chavín de Huántar." In *Chavín: Art, Architecture and Culture*, edited by William J. Conklin and Jeffrey Quilter, 3–34. Los Angeles: Cotsen Institute of Archaeology.

Risley, Herbert. 1969 [1915]. *The People of India*. New Delhi: Oriental Books Reprint Corporation.

Robertshaw, Peter. 1990. *A History of African Archaeology*. London: J. Currey.

Rofel, Lisa. 1999. *Other Modernities: Gendered Yearnings in China After Socialism*. Berkeley: University of California Press.

Rose, Nikolas, and Peter Miller. 1992. "Political Power beyond the State: Problematics of Government." *The British Journal of Sociology* 43, no. 2: 173–205.

Roy, A. B., and S. R. Jakhar. 2001. "Late Quaternary Drainage Disorganisation and Migration and Extinction of the Vedic Saraswati." *Current Science* 81, no. 9: 1188–95.

Roy Burman, B. K. 1992. *Beyond Mandal and after: Backward Classes in Perspective*. New Delhi: Mittal Publications.

Roy, Sita Ram. 2004. "Communal Content in Ayodhya Excavation Report 2002–03." *Social Science Probing* 16, no. 1: 67–74.

Roy, Sourindranath. 1961. *The Story of Indian Archaeology, 1784–1947*. New Delhi: Archaeological Survey of India.

Roychoudhury, Susanta, Sangita Roy, Badal Dey, Madan Chakraborty, Monami Roy, Bidyut Roy, N. Prabhakaran, A. Ramesh, M. V. Usha Rani, H. Vishwanathan, Mitashree Mitra, Samir K. Sil, and Partha P. Majumder. 2000. "Fundamental Genomic Unity of Ethnic India Is Revealed by Analysis of Mitochondrial DNA." *Current Science* 79, no. 9: 1182–92.

Rubiés, Joan-Pau. 2002. *Travel and Ethnology in the Renaissance: South India through European Eyes*. Cambridge: Cambridge University Press.

Rudwick, Martin J. S. 1985. *The Great Devonian Controversy: The Shaping of Scientific Knowledge among Gentlemanly Specialists*. Chicago: University of Chicago Press.

———. 2008. *The Meaning of Fossils: Episodes in the History of Palaeontology.* Chicago: University of Chicago Press.

Ryan, James R. 1998. *Picturing Empire: Photography and the Visualization of the British Empire.* 1st ed. Chicago: University of Chicago Press.

Ryan, Simon. 1996. *The Cartographic Eye: How Explorers Saw Australia.* Cambridge, England, and New York: Cambridge University Press.

Rye, Owen S. 1981. *Pottery Technology: Principles and Reconstruction.* Vol. 4. Washington, DC: Taraxacum.

Sabloff, Jeremy A., and Robert E. Smith. 1969. "The Importance of Both Analytic and Taxonomic Classification in the Type-Variety System." *American Antiquity* 34, no. 3: 278–85.

Sahai, B., A.S. Rajawat, I.M. Bahuguna, A.S. Arya, A.K. Sharma, D.C. Sharma, C.P. Porwal, S.K. Chakravarty, and D.S. Rathore. 1993. "Hydrogeomorphological Mapping of Jaisalmer and Bikaner Districts (Rajasthan) at 1: 50,000 Scale Using Satellite Data." *Journal of Arid Environments* 25, no. 1: 163–72.

Sahlins, Marshall. 1999. "What Is Anthropological Enlightenment? Some Lessons of the Twentieth Century." *Annual Review of Anthropology* 28: i–xxiii.

Salmon, Merrilee H. 1978. "What Can Systems Theory Do for Archaeology?" *American Antiquity* 43, no. 2,: 174–83.

Sankararaman, Sriram, Swapan Mallick, Nick Patterson, and David Reich. 2016. "The Combined Landscape of Denisovan and Neanderthal Ancestry in Present-Day Humans." *Current Biology* 26, no. 9: 1241–47.

Sant, Urmila, T.J. Baidya, N.G. Nikoshey, N.K. Sinha, S. Nayan, J.K. Tiwari, and A. Arif. 2004. "Baror: A New Harappan Site in Ghaggar Valley – A Preliminary Report." *Puratattva* 35: 50–59.

Sarkar, Anindya, Arati Deshpande Mukherjee, M.K. Bera, B. Das, Navin Juyal, P. Morthekai, R.D. Deshpande, V.S. Shinde, and L.S. Rao. 2016. "Oxygen Isotope in Archaeological Bioapatites from India: Implications to Climate Change and Decline of Bronze Age Harappan Civilization." *Scientific Reports* 6, no. 1: 1–9.

Savarkar, Vinayak Damodar. 1923. *Hindutva: Who Is a Hindu?* Bombay: Veer Savarkar Prakashan.

Schiffer, Michael B. 1976. *Behavioral Archeology.* New York: Academic Press.

———. 1987. *Formation Processes of the Archaeological Record.* 1st ed. Albuquerque, NM: University of New Mexico Press.

———. 1988. "The Structure of Archaeological Theory." *American Antiquity* 53, no. 3: 461–85.

Schnapp, Alain. 1996. *The Discovery of the Past: The Origins of Archaeology.* London: British Museum Press.

Schumacher, Ernest F. 1973. *Small Is Beautiful: Economics as If People Mattered.* London: Blond and Briggs.

Scott, David. 1995. "Colonial Governmentality." *Social Text* 43, Autumn: 191–220.

Scott, James. 1998. *Seeing Like a State: How Certain Schemes to Improve the Human Condition Have Failed*. New Haven: Yale University Press.

Secord, James A. 1986. *Controversy in Victorian Geology: The Cambrian-Silurian Dispute*. Princeton, NJ: Princeton University Press.

Sekula, Allan. 1986. "The Body and the Archive." *October* 39, Winter: 3–64.

Sengupta, Indra. 2013. "A Conservation Code for the Colony: John Marshall's Conservation Manual and Monument Preservation between India and Europe." In *"Archaeologizing" Heritage?* edited by M. Falser and M. Juneja, 21–37. Berlin and Heidelberg: Springer.

Shah, A. M., and R. G. Shroff. 1958. "The Vahivanca Barots of Gujarat: A Caste of Genealogists and Mythographers." *The Journal of American Folklore* 71, no. 281: 246–76.

Shanks, Michael. 1992. *Experiencing the Past: On the Character of Archaeology*. London: Routledge.

———. 1997. "Photography and Archaeology." In *The Cultural Life of Images: Visual Representation in Archaeology*, edited by Brian Leigh Molyneaux, 73–107. London: Routledge.

Shanks, Michael, and Christopher Y. Tilley. 1987. *Social Theory and Archaeology*. Cambridge: Polity.

———. 1992. *Re-Constructing Archaeology: Theory and Practice*. London: Routledge.

Shanks, Michael, and Randall H. McGuire. 1996. "The Craft of Archaeology." *American Antiquity* 61, no. 1: 75–88.

Sharma, A. K. 1990. "Animal Bone Remains." In *Excavation at Surkotada 1971–72 and Exploration in Kutch*. Memoirs of the Archaeological Survey of India, No. 87, edited by Jagat Pati Joshi, 372–83. New Delhi: Archaeological Survey of India.

Sharma, Aradhana, and Akhil Gupta. 2006. "Rethinking Theories of the State in an Age of Globalization." In *The Anthropology of the State: A Reader*, edited by A. Sharma and A. Gupta, 1–41. Oxford: Blackwell Publishing.

Sharma, J. R., R. Srinivasan, and S. S. Dhabriya. 1992. 'Studies on Paleo-buried Channels of Kantli River (Western Rajasthan) using IRS-1A Satellite Data.' In International Symposium on Evolution of Deserts, February 11–19, 1992, Abstract Volume, pp. 187–89, Physical Research Laboratory, Ahmedabad.

Sharma, Ram Sharan. 1978. "The Later Vedic Phase and the Painted Grey Ware Culture." *History and Society: Essays in Honour of Professor Niharranjan Ray*, edited by Debiprasad Chattopadhyaya, 131–43. Calcutta: K.P. Bagchi.

———. 1999. *Advent of the Aryans in India*. New Delhi: Manohar.

———. 2001. "The Ayodhya Issue." In *Destruction and Conservation of Cultural Property*, edited by Robert Layton, Peter G. Stone, and Julian Thomas, 127–38. London: Routledge.

Shaw, Julia. 2000. "Ayodhya's Sacred Landscape: Ritual Memory, Politics and Archaeological Fact." *Antiquity* 74, no. 285: 693–700.

Shendge, Malati. 1977. *The Civilized Demons: The Harappans in Rgveda*. New Delhi: Abhinav Publications.

Shepard, Anna Osler. 1956. *Ceramics for the Archaeologist*. Washington DC: Carnegie Institution of Washington.

Shepherd, Nick. 2002. "The Politics of Archaeology in Africa." *Annual Review of Anthropology* 31, no. 1: 189–209.

Shinde, Vasant, Adam Green, Narendra Parmar, and P.D. Sable. 2012. "Rakhigarhi and the Harappan Civilization: Recent Work and New Challenges." *Bulletin of the Deccan College Research Institute* 72/73: 43–53.

Shinde, Vasant, T. Osada, and Manmohan Kumar, ed. 2011. *Excavations at Farmana, Rohtak District, Haryana, India 2006–2008*. Kyoto: Indus Project, Research Institute for Humanity and Nature.

Shinde, Vasant, Yong Jun Kim, Eun Jin Woo, Nilesh Jadhav, Pranjali Waghmare, Yogesh Yadav, Avradeep Munshi, Malavika Chatterjee, Amrithavalli Panyam, and Jong Ha Hong. 2018. "Archaeological and Anthropological Studies on the Harappan Cemetery of Rakhigarhi, India." *PLOS One* 13, no. 2.

Shinde, Vasant, Vagheesh M. Narasimhan, Nadin Rohland, Swapan Mallick, Matthew Mah, Mark Lipson, Nathan Nakatsuka, Nicole Adamski, Nasreen Broomandkhoshbacht, and Matthew Ferry. 2019. "An Ancient Harappan Genome Lacks Ancestry from Steppe Pastoralists or Iranian Farmers." *Cell* 179, no. 3: 729–35.

Simonetti, Cristián. 2013. "Between the Vertical and the Horizontal: Time and Space in Archaeology." *History of the Human Sciences* 26, no. 1: 90–110.

Sinclair, Anthony. 1989. "This Is an Article about Archaeology as Writing in Writing Archaeology." *Archaeological Review from Cambridge* 8, no. 2: 212–33.

Singh, Ajit, and Rajiv Sinha. 2019. "Fluvial Response to Climate Change Inferred from Sediment Cores from the Ghaggar–Hakra Paleochannel in NW Indo–Gangetic Plains." *Palaeogeography, Palaeoclimatology, Palaeoecology* 532: 109247.

Singh, Ajit, Kristina J. Thomsen, Rajiv Sinha, Jan-Pieter Buylaert, Andrew Carter, Darren F. Mark, Philippa J. Mason, Alexander L. Densmore, Andrew S. Murray, and Mayank Jain. 2017. "Counter-Intuitive Influence of Himalayan River Morphodynamics on Indus Civilisation Urban Settlements." *Nature Communications* 8, no. 1: 1–14.

Singh, Bhagwan. 1995. *The Vedic Harappans*. New Delhi: Aditya Prakashan.

Singh, D. P. 2005. "Women Workers in the Brick Kiln Industry in Haryana, India." *Indian Journal of Gender Studies* 12, no. 1: 83–97.

Singh, Shivaji. 1998. "Sindhu and Sarasvati in the Rigveda and Their Archaeological Implications." *Puratattva* 28: 26–38.

Singh, Upinder. 2004. *The Discovery of Ancient India: Early Archaeologists and the Beginnings of Archaeology.* New Delhi: Permanent Black.

———. 2008. *A History of Ancient and Early Medieval India: From the Stone Age to the 12th Century.* New Delhi: Pearson Education India.

Sinopoli, Carla M. 1991. "Approaches to Archaeological Ceramics." In *Approaches to Archaeological Ceramics,* edited by Carla M. Sinopoli, 1–7. Boston: Springer US.

Sivaramakrishnan, Kalyanakrishnan, and Arun Agrawal, ed. 2003. *Regional Modernities: The Cultural Politics of Development in India.* Stanford: Stanford University Press.

Sluyter, Andrew. 1999. "The Making of the Myth in Postcolonial Development: Material-Conceptual Landscape Transformation in Sixteenth-Century Veracruz." *Annals of the Association of American Geographers* 89, no. 3: 377–401.

———. 2001. "Colonialism and Landscape in the Americas: Material/Conceptual Transformations and Continuing Consequences." *Annals of the Association of American Geographers* 91, no. 2: 410–28.

———. 2002. *Colonialism and Landscape: Postcolonial Theory and Applications.* New York: Rowman and Littlefield Publishers, Inc.

Smith, Brian K. 1994. *Classifying the Universe: The Ancient Indian Varna System and the Origins of Caste.* New York: Oxford University Press.

Smith, Linda Tuhiwai. 2012. *Decolonizing Methodologies: Research and Indigenous Peoples.* London: Zed Books.

Smith, Monica L. 2006. "The Archaeology of South Asian Cities." *Journal of Archaeological Research* 14, no. 2: 97–142.

Snelgrove, A. K. 1979. "Migrations of the Indus River, Pakistan, in Response to Plate Tectonic Motions." *Journal of the Geological Society of India* 20, no. 3: 352–403.

Sood, R. K. and B. Sahai. 1983. "Hydrographic Changes in North-Western India." *Man and Environment* 7, nos. 1–2: 166–89.

Spencer, Frank. 1992. "Some Notes on the Attempt to Apply Photography to Anthropometry during the Second Half of the Nineteenth Century." In *Anthropology and Photography, 1860–1920,* edited by Elizabeth Edwards, 99–107. New Haven, London: Yale University Press and Royal Anthropological Institute.

Srikrishna, B. N. 1998. *Report of the Srikrishna Commission Appointed for Inquiry into the Riots at Mumbai during December 1992 and January 1993.* Mumbai: Government of Maharashtra.

Srinivas, M. N. 1987. *The Dominant Caste and Other Essays.* Delhi: Oxford University Press.

Stanislawski, Dan. 1946. "The Origin and Spread of the Grid-Pattern Town." *Geographical Review* 36, no. 1: 105–20.

Star, Susan Leigh, and James R. Griesemer. 1989. "Institutional Ecology, Translations and Boundary Objects: Amateurs and Professionals in Berkeley's Museum of Vertebrate Zoology, 1907–39." *Social Studies of Science* 19, no. 3: 387–420.

Staubwasser, Michael, Frank Sirocko, Pieter M. Grootes, and M. Segl. 2003. "Climate Change at the 4.2 Ka BP Termination of the Indus Valley Civilization and Holocene South Asian Monsoon Variability." *Geophysical Research Letters* 30, no. 8.

Stehr, Nico. 1994. *Knowledge Societies*. London and Thousand Oaks, California: Sage.

Stein, Aurel. 1942. "A Survey of Ancient Sites along the Lost Saraswati River." *Geographical Journal* 99, no. 4: 173–82.

———. 1988 [1943]. "An Archaeological Tour along the Ghaggar-Hakra River, 1940–42." In *An Archaeological Tour along the Ghaggar-Hakra River*, edited by Swaraj Prakash Gupta, 1–98. Meerut: Kusumanjali Indian History Monographs.

Steinmetz, George. 1999. *State/Culture: State-Formation After the Cultural Turn*. Ithaca: Cornell University Press.

Stengers, Isabelle. 2005. "Introductory Notes on an Ecology of Practices." *Cultural Studies Review* 11, no. 1: 183–96.

Stoltman, James B. 2001. "The Role of Petrography in the Study of Archaeological Ceramics." In *Earth Sciences and Archaeology*, edited by Paul Goldberg, Vance T. Holliday, and C. Reid Ferring, 297–326. Boston: Springer US.

Strathern, Marilyn. 1999. *Property, Substance, and Effect: Anthropological Essays on Persons and Things*. New Brunswick, NJ: Athlone Press.

Supreme Court. 2019. "Supreme Court Ayodhya Judgement." Available at https://www.sci.gov.in/pdf/JUD_2.pdf, accessed on October 31, 2020.

Talageri, Shrikant. 1993. *Aryan Invasion Theory and Indian Nationalism*. New Delhi: Aditya Prakashan.

———. 2000. *The Rigveda: A Historical Analysis*. New Delhi: Aditya Prakashan.

Tanner, James Mourilyan. 1981. *A History of the Study of Human Growth*. Cambridge, UK, and New York: Cambridge University Press.

Tassi, Francesca, Stefania Vai, Silvia Ghirotto, Martina Lari, Alessandra Modi, Elena Pilli, Andrea Brunelli, Roberta Rosa Susca, Alicja Budnik, and Damian Labuda. 2017. "Genome Diversity in the Neolithic Globular Amphorae Culture and the Spread of Indo-European Languages." *Proceedings of the Royal Society B: Biological Sciences* 284, no. 1867: 20171540.

Taussig, Michael T. 1987. *Shamanism, Colonialism, and the Wild Man: A Study in Terror and Healing*. Chicago: University of Chicago Press.

———. 1997. *The Magic of the State*. New York: Routledge.

Taylor, Philip Meadows. 1929. *Megalithic Tombs and Other Ancient Remains in the Deccan*. Hyderabad: State Archaeological Department.

Thakran, R. C. 2000. "Implications of Partition on Protohistoric Investigations in the Ghaggar-Ganga Basins." *Social Scientist* 28, no. 1: 42–67.

Thangaraj, Kumarasamy, Gyaneshwer Chaubey, Vijay Kumar Singh, Ayyasamy Vanniarajan, Ismail Thanseem, Alla G. Reddy, and Lalji Singh. 2006. "In Situ Origin of Deep Rooting Lineages of Mitochondrial Macrohaplogroup 'M' in India." *BMC Genomics* 7, no. 1: 1–6.

Thapar, Bal Krishen. 1957. "Maski 1954: A Chalcolithic Site of the Southern Deccan." *Ancient India* 13: 4–142.

———. 1967. "Prakash 1955: A Chalcolithic Site in the Tapti Valley." *Ancient India* 20–21, no. 21: 5–167.

———. 1969. "The Pre-Harappan Pottery of Kalibangan: An Appraisal of Its Inter-Relationship." In *Potteries in Ancient India*, edited by B. P. Sinha, 251–56. Patna: Department of Ancient Indian History and Archaeology, Patna University.

———. 1970. "The Aryans: The Reappraisal of the Problem." In *India's Contributions to World Thought and Culture*, edited by Lokesh Chandra, 147–64. Madras: Vivekananda Memorial Committee.

———. 1975. "Kalibangan: A Harappan Metropolis beyond the Indus Valley." *Expedition* 17, no. 2: 19.

Thapar, Romila. 1984. *From Lineage to State: Social Formations in the Mid-First Millennium B.C. in the Ganga Valley*. New Delhi: Oxford University Press.

———. 1996. *Time as a Metaphor of History: Early India*. New Delhi: Oxford University Press.

———. 2001. "The Theory of Aryan Race and India: History and Politics." In *Cultural Pasts: Essays in Early Indian History*, edited by Romila Thapar, 1108–40. New Delhi: Oxford University Press.

Thomas, David Hurst. 2000. *The Skull Wars: Kennewick Man, Archaeology, and the Battle for Native American Identity*. 1st ed. New York: Basic Books.

Thomas, Edward. 1883. "The Rivers of the Vedas, and the Way the Aryans Entered India." *Journal of the Royal Asiatic Society of Great Britain and Ireland* New Series 15, no. 4: 357–86.

Thompson, Edward P. 1967. "Time, Work-Discipline, and Industrial Capitalism." *Past and Present* no. 38: 56–97.

Tierney, Patrick. 2002. *Darkness in El Dorado*. New York: W. W. Norton and Company.

Tilley, Christopher Y. 1989. "Excavation as Theatre." *Antiquity* 63, no. 239: 275–80.

———. 1993. *Interpretative Archaeology*. London: Berg.

Tod, James. 1832. *Annales and Antiquities of Rajasthan, Or the Central and Western Rajpoot States of Indian*. London: Smith, Elder, and Co.

Trautmann, Thomas R. 1997. *Aryans and British India*. Berkeley: University of California Press.

———. 2008. *The Aryan Debate*. New York: Oxford University Press.

Trautmann, Thomas R., and C. M. Sinopoli. 2002. "In the Beginning There Was the Word: Excavating the Relations between History and Archaeology in South Asia." *Journal of the Economic and Social History of the Orient* 45, no. 4: 492–523.

Travers, Robert. 2008. *Ideology and Empire in Eighteenth-Century India: The British in Bengal*. Cambridge: Cambridge University Press.

Trigger, Bruce G. 1981. "Anglo-American Archaeology." *World Archaeology* 13, no. 2 (Regional Traditions of Archaeological Research I): 138–55.

————. 1984. "Alternative Archaeologies: Nationalist, Colonialist, Imperialist." *Man* 19, no. 3: 355–70.

————. 1989. *A History of Archaeological Thought*. Cambridge: Cambridge University Press.

Tripathi, Alok. 2007. *The Ancient Monuments and Archaeological Sites and Remains Act, 1958*. New Delhi: Universal Law Publishing.

Tripathi, J. K., B. Bock, V. Rajamani, and A. Eisenhauer. 2004. "Is River Ghaggar, Saraswati? Geochemical Constraints." *Current Science* 87, no. 8: 1141–45.

Trivedi, Mudit. 2018. "On Taking from Others: History and Sensibility in Archaeologists' Arguments for Treasure Trove Legislations." *Public Archaeology* 17, nos. 2–3: 110–36.

Trivedi, P. K. 2009. *Excavations at Tarkhanewala-Dera and Chak 86 (2003–2004)*. Memoirs of the Archaeological Survey of India; No. 99. New Delhi: Director General, Archaeological Survey of India.

Trivedi, P. K., and J. K. Patnaik. 2004. "Tarkhanewala Dera and Chak 86 (2003–04)." *Puratattva* 34: 30–34.

Twitchell, James B. 1983. *Romantic Horizons: Aspects of the Sublime in English Poetry and Painting, 1770–1850*. Columbia: University of Missouri Press.

Ucko, Peter J. 1987. *Academic Freedom and Apartheid: The Story of the World Archaeological Congress*. London: Duckworth.

————. 1995. *Theory in Archaeology: A World Perspective*. London: Routledge.

Valdiya, K. S. 2002. *Saraswati: The River That Disappeared*. New Delhi: Orient Longman.

Van Pool, Christine S, and Todd L. Van Pool. 1999. "The Scientific Nature of Postprocessualism." *American Antiquity* 64, no. 1: 33–53.

Varghese, Rachel A. 2018. "'Order'-Ing Excavations: Constitution of Archaeology as Legal Evidence in the Ayodhya Case." *Public Archaeology* 17, nos 2–3: 89–109.

Varma, Supriya, and Jaya Menon. 2010. "Was There a Temple under the Babri Masjid? Reading the Archaeological 'Evidence.'" *Economic and Political Weekly* 45, no. 50: 61–72.

Vats, Madho Sarup. 1925. "Unpublished Votive Inscriptions in the Caitya Cave at Karle." *Epigraphia Indica* 18: 325–29.

————. 1940. *Excavations at Harappa*. Vol. 1–2. Delhi: Manager of Publications.

————. 1951. "Notes." *Ancient India* 7: 1–2.

Veeramah, Krishna R. 2018. "The Importance of Fine-Scale Studies for Integrating Paleogenomics and Archaeology." *Current Opinion in Genetics and Development* 53: 83–89.

Vishnu Bhat v. The Union of India on April 3, 2014, Central Administrative Tribunal – Delhi.

Visvanathan, Shiv. 1985. *Organizing for Science: The Making of an Industrial Research Laboratory*. Delhi and New York: Oxford University Press.

———. 1997. *A Carnival for Science: Essays on Science, Technology and Development.* Delhi and New York: Oxford University Press.

Vitelli, Kare, and Chip Colwell-Chanthaphonh. 2006. *Archaeological Ethics.* Lanham, MD: Altamira Press.

Wald, E. 2014. *Vice in the Barracks: Medicine, the Military and the Making of Colonial India, 1780–1868.* London: Palgrave Macmillan.

Walker, Mark, and Dean J. Saitta. 2002. "Teaching the Craft of Archaeology: Theory, Practice, and the Field School." *International Journal of Historical Archaeology* 6, no. 3: 199–207.

Walters, William, and Jens Henrik Haahr. 2005. "Governmentality and Political Studies." *European Political Science* 4, no. 3: 288–300.

Warren, John. 1812a. "An Account of Experiments Made at the Observatory near Fort St. George, for Determining the Length of the Simple Pendulum Beating Seconds of Time at That Place, and c." *Asiatic Researches, or, Transactions of the Society Instituted in Bengal for Inquiring into the History and Antiquities, the Arts, Sciences and Literature of Asia* 11: 294–308.

———. 1812b. "An Account of the Petrifactions near the Village of Treevikera in the Carnatic." *Asiatic Researches, or, Transactions of the Society Instituted in Bengal for Inquiring into the History and Antiquities, the Arts, Sciences and Literature of Asia* 11: 1–10.

Watson, Patty Jo. 1979. *Archaeological Ethnography in Western Iran.* Tuczon: University of Arizona Press for the Wennergren Foundation for Anthropological Research.

———. 2009. "Archaeology and Anthropology: A Personal Overview of the Past Half-Century." *Annual Review of Anthropology* 38, no. 1: 1–15.

Watson, Patty Jo, Steven A. LeBlanc, and Charles L. Redman. 1971. *Explanation in Archeology; an Explicitly Scientific Approach.* New York: Columbia University Press.

Webster, Frank. 2006. *Theories of the Information Society.* London: Routledge.

Wheeler, Robert Eric Mortimer. 1927. "History by Excavation." *Journal of the Royal Society of Arts* 75, no. 3894: 814–34.

———. 1943. *Maiden Castle, Dorset.* Oxford: Society of Antiquaries of London.

———. 1946a. "Notes." *Ancient India* 1: 1–3.

———. 1946b. "Notes." *Ancient India* 2: 1–3.

———. 1947a. "Brahmagiri and Chandravalli 1947: Megalithic and Other Cultures in the Chitaldrug District, Mysore State." *Ancient India* 4: 180–310.

———. 1947b. "Harappa 1946: The Defense and Cemetery R37." *Ancient India* 3: 58–130.

———. 1947c. "Technical Section: The Recording of Archaeological Strata." *Ancient India* 3: 143–50.

———. 1948. "Technical Section: Further Notes on Digging and Recording." *Ancient India* 4: 311–21.

———. 1949. "Archaeological Fieldwork in India: Planning Ahead." *Ancient India* 9: 4–11.

———. 1950. *Five Thousand Years of Pakistan; an Archaeological Outline.* London: C. Johnson.

———. 1953. *The Indus Civilization.* Cambridge: Cambridge University Press.

———. 1954. *Archaeology from the Earth.* Baltimore: Penguin Books.

———. 1956. *Still Digging.* New York: E. P. Dutton & Co.

———. 1959. *Early India and Pakistan: To Ashoka.* New York: Frederick A. Praeger.

———. 1962. *Charsada: A Metropolis of the North-West Frontier.* Oxford: Oxford University Press.

———. 1966. *Civilizations of the Indus Valley and Beyond.* New York: McGraw-Hill.

———. 1968. *The Indus Civilization: Supplementary Volume to the Cambridge History of India.* 3rd ed. Cambridge: University Press.

———. 1976. *My Archaeological Mission to India and Pakistan.* London: Thames and Hudson.

Wheeler, Robert Eric Mortimer, Amalananda Ghosh, and Krishna Deva. 1946. "Arikamedu." *Ancient India* 2: 58–130.

Wheeler, Robert Eric Mortimer, and Tessa Verney Wheeler. 1936. *Verulamium, a Belgic and Two Roman Cities.* London: Society of Antiquaries of London.

Wilhelmy, Herbert. 1999. "The Ancient River Valley on the Eastern Border of the Indus Plain and the Sarasvati Problem." In *Vedic Sarasvati, Evolutionary History of a Lost River of Northwestern India, Memoir of the Geological Society of India, Bangalore, No. 42,* edited by B. P. Radhakrishna and S. S. Merh, 95–111. Bangalore: Geological Society of India.

Willey, Gordon R., and Jeremy A. Sabloff. 1993. *A History of American Archaeology.* New York: W. H. Freeman & Co.

Witmore, Christopher L. 2007. "Symmetrical Archaeology: Excerpts of a Manifesto." *World Archaeology* 39, no. 4: 546–62.

Witmore, Christopher, and Michael Shanks. 2013. "Archaeology: An Ecology of Practices." In *Archaeology in the Making: Conversations through a Discipline,* edited by William L. Rathje, Michael Shanks, and Christopher Witmore, 380–98. London: Routledge.

Witzel, Michael. 1987. "On the Localization of Vedic Texts and Schools (Materials on Vedic Śakhas, 7)." In *India and the Ancient World: History, Trade, and Culture before AD 650,* edited by Gilbert Pollet, 173–213. Leuven: Departement Oriëntalistiek.

———. 1995. "Early Sanskritization. Origins and Development of the Kuru State." *Electronic Journal of Vedic Studies* 1, no. 4: 1–26.

———. 1997. "The Development of the Vedic Canon and Its Schools: The Social and Political Milieu (Materials on Vedic Śakhas, 8)." In *Inside the Texts, beyond the Texts: New Approaches to the Study of the Vedas*, edited by Michael Witzel, 257–345. Cambridge: Harvard Oriental Series, Opera Minora 2.

————. 1999. "Substrate Languages in Old Indo-Aryan (Rigvedic, Middle and Late Vedic)." *Electronic Journal of Vedic Studies* 5, no. 1: 1–67.

————. 2001. "Autochthonous Aryans? The Evidence from Old Indian and Iranian Texts." *Electronic Journal of Vedic Studies* 7, no. 3: 1–93.

Woo, Eun Jin, Pranjali Waghmare, Yongjun Kim, Nilesh Jadhav, Go-Un Jung, Won Joon Lee, Yogesh Yadav, Avradeep Munshi, Malavika Chatterjee, and Amrithavalli Panyam. 2018. "Assessing the Physical and Pathological Traits of Human Skeletal Remains from Cemetery Localities at the Rakhigarhi Site of the Harappan Civilization." *Anthropological Science* 126, no. 2: 111–20.

Woolley, Leonard. 1930. *Digging Up the Past*. London: Penguin Books.

————. 1993 [1939]. "A Report on the Work of the Archaeological Survey of India." *Harappan Studies* 1: 17–56.

Wright, Rita P. 2009. *The Ancient Indus: Urbanism, Economy, and Society*. New York: Cambridge University Press.

Wylie, Alison. 1985. "The Reaction against Analogy." In *Advances in Archaeological Method and Theory*, edited by Michael B. Schiffer, 63–111. San Diego: Academic Press.

————. 2002. *Thinking from Things: Essays in the Philosophy of Archaeology*. Berkeley: University of California Press.

Yang, Melinda A, Xuechun Fan, Bo Sun, Chungyu Chen, Jianfeng Lang, Ying-Chin Ko, Cheng-hwa Tsang, Hunglin Chiu, Tianyi Wang, and Qingchuan Bao. 2020. "Ancient DNA Indicates Human Population Shifts and Admixture in Northern and Southern China." *Science* 369, no. 6501: 282–88.

Yarrow, Thomas. 2003. "Artefactual Persons: The Relational Capacities of Persons and Things in the Practice of Excavation." *Norwegian Archaeological Review* 36, no. 1: 65–73.

Yashpal, B. S., R. K. Sood, and D. P. Agarwal. 1980. "Remote Sensing of the 'Lost' Saraswati River." *Proceedings of the Indian Academy of Sciences (Earth and Planet Science)* 89, no. 3: 317–31.

Zide, Arlene R. K. 1970. "A Brief Survey of Work to Date on the Indus Script." *Journal of Tamil Studies* 2, no. 1: 1–12.

Zimmerman, Larry J. 2003. *Presenting the Past*. Vol. 7. Lanham, MD: Rowman Altamira.

————. 2006. "Liberating Archaeology, Liberation Archaeologies, and WAC." *Archaeologies* 2, no. 1: 85–95.

Zvelebil, Kamil V. 1985. "Recent Attempts at the Decipherment of the Indus Script." In *Indus to Mekong Delta: Explorations in Epigraphy*, edited by Nororu Karashima, 151–88. Madras: New Era Publications.

Index

additional director general (ADG), 17, 72, 75, 77, 98n6, 102

Agarwal, Sudhir, 232, 235–36, 252n2, 255n16, n19

Ahichchhatra, 28n21, 52

Ahmedabad, 61n5, 189–90, 203n12, 217

Allahabad High Court, 19, 28n18, 229–30, 232, 255n19

Ambedkar, B. R., 101n29

ancient DNA (aDNA), 49–50

Ancient India (journal), 52, 132, 137, 143, 151n6

Ancient Monuments and Archaeological Sites and Remains Act, 116–17, 125n10, 240

anthropological discourse, 4

Anthropological Survey of India (ASI), 1–4, 9–10, 12–25, 25n1, 26n10, 28n18, n20, 29n24–n26, 29n30, 30n32, n34, 31n41, n43, n45, 32n47, 33–34, 40, 42–45, 50, 52, 54–60, 61n5, 66n42, 68n49, n50, 69n54, 70–97, 98n5, n7, 99n8, n9, n14, n16, 100n19, n20, n23, n24, 102–24, 124n1, n2, 125n4, n5, n9, n10, 126n14, 127n20, 129–42, 143, 145, 148–49, 150n2, n3, n5, 151n8, 151n10, n11, n13, 153–58, 160–61, 163, 170–75, 177, 177n11, 178, 179–94, 196–200, 202n8, 203n12, n14, 204n16, n17, 207–08, 210–13, 216, 218, 220–21, 224–25, 227–52,

252n3, 253n7, n8, 254n9–n11, 254n15, 255n19, n20, 256n22, n23, 256n26, 257n27, n28, n31, 258n33, n34, 259–65, 266n1

anthropometric, 36, 219–20

antiquarian, 17, 26n10, 51, 104–05, 122, 134, 141, 152n16, 161, 224

antiquity, 6, 14, 17, 20, 64n29, 74, 79, 123, 137, 141, 151n10, 153, 161, 163, 165–66, 168, 180–83, 186–87, 192–93, 198–200, 203n15, 204n16, 207, 209–10, 223, 230, 238, 244, 247–48, 252, 254n12

antiquity class, 180, 182–83, 192

archaeogenetics, 48–51, 54

archaeological artifacts, 129, 140, 167, 181, 183, 201n4, 204n17

archaeological epistemology, 9

archaeological evidence, 10, 36, 44, 54, 141, 154, 156–57, 181, 198, 215, 235, 259

archaeological features, 165

archaeological field, 7–8, 83, 104–05, 129, 228, 233

archaeological knowledge, 1, 3, 9, 20, 25n2, 50, 79, 97, 105, 129, 131, 221, 224, 263

archaeological methods, 7–8, 26n6, 104, 134, 150n2, 165, 182, 213

archaeological photography, 133, 211–12, 213, 215–17

archaeological project, 9, 95, 105, 111–12, 115, 134, 200n1, 201n4, 211, 221–22, 224–25, 247 archaeological site, 1–3, 7, 9–11, 16–17, 20, 22, 31*n*42, 34, 37, 43, 56–61, 80, 83–84, 95–97, 103–04, 116, 119, 121, 124, 129–30, 136–37, 139–40, 142–43, 145, 150*n*2, 156–57, 161, 163, 170, 184, 186, 188, 190, 193, 211, 224, 228, 235, 249, 259, 265

Archaeology from the Earth, 80, 143, 160

Architecture of the camp, 109–11

Arikamedu, 16, 138, 144, 161–63, 177*n*6, 202*n*10

artifacts, 2–4, 9–10, 16, 20, 31*n*41, 43, 121–23, 127*n*17, 129–30, 139–40, 149, 156, 158, 161, 163–65, 167, 171, 174, 177, 179–94, 197–200, 201*n*4, 204*n*17, 207, 209–10, 230–31, 234, 239–42, 247–48, 252, 253*n*9, 262

artifact typologies, 159–60

artifactual, 193, 200

Aryans/Aryan race, 14, 34–38, 41–43, 48, 51–54, 56, 58, 62*n*9, 63*n*15, 66*n*39, *n*41, *n*43, 67*n*44, 93–94, 262

asli, 9, 76, 105, 153, 208, 219, 250

assistant archaeologist (AA), 8–9, 25, 60, 70–73, 75–77, 79–80, 84–91, 93–94, 98*n*3, *n*7, 100*n*23, 101*n*26, 116, 121–22, 128–29, 137, 140, 155–57, 172–75, 178, 180–84, 186–87, 189–93, 195–96, 198–200, 205–08, 210–11, 213, 218, 228–34, 237–38, 241–42, 244, 246–50, 253*n*6

Ati-Shudras, 93–94

Ayodhya, 19, 22, 35, 53, 83, 100*n*24, 203*n*12, 227–31, 233, 236, 240, 246, 252*n*1, 254*n*14, 255*n*15, 256*n*25, 259, 262

Ayodhya excavation report, 231–32, 234, 246

B. B. Lal Review Committee/Lal Committee, 18, 72–73, 77, 87, 90, 240, 243, 245

Babri Masjid, 53, 99*n*11, 227, 234–36, 259

babugiri, 227, 243, 245

*babu*s, 71, 245

balks, 70, 119, 130, 135, 139, 145, 147–48, 154–56, 170, 212–13

Banawali, 33, 45, 54, 56, 61*n*1, 62*n*5, 68*n*48, 256*n*25

Banerji, Rakhaldas, 14, 29*n*27, 43

barbed-wire, 109–10, 121, 125*n*5

Baror, 22, 33, 56, 58, 60, 70, 82, 86, 88–89, 91, 95, 109, 112, 114, 117, 120–21, 125*n*5, *n*6, 130, 133, 137, 139–40, 142, 152*n*14, 175, 177*n*9, 178, 180, 186–87, 191, 197, 211, 226*n*5, *n*6, 232, 237, 245–46, 251, 257*n*30

Basu, Nilotpal, 19, 25*n*1, 31*n*46, 55, 57, 241, 245–46

bhagwa, 56, 233, 254*n*13

Bhagwanpura, 45, 54, 130

Bharatiya Jana Sangh, 53, 225*n*3

Bharatiya Janata Party (BJP), 53, 56–57, 69*n*54, 82, 206, 225*n*2, *n*3, 233, 266*n*1

Bharatiyata, 260

Bhatinda Line, 87–88

Bhirrana, 22, 33–34, 56, 58–60, 61*n*3, *n*4, 77, 95, 109, 113–14, 117, 120, 130, 139, 142, 152*n*14, 157, 159, 178, 182, 185, 194–96, 202*n*9, *n*11, 212, 214 226*n*5, *n*6, 231, 248, 250–51, 257*n*30

Bhubaneshwar Ex. Br., 58, 60

Bhuj, 119, 122–23, 127*n*22, 189, 206

Bisht, R. S. (Dr. Bisht), 38, 54, 56–59, 61*n*1, 63*n*12, 64*n*20, 65*n*33, 69*n*56, *n*58, 79, 81–84, 96–97, 100*n*24, 102, 123–24, 130, 140,

143, 147, 152*n*14–16, 177*n*9, 183, 188–90, 201*n*2, 202*n*6, *n*9, 226*n*5, *n*10, 233, 238, 242, 256*n*22, *n*25, 260, 262

bone-expert, 189–90

bones, 54, 129, 135, 181–82, 184–85, 187, 189–91, 194, 196, 204, 224, 228, 230, 254*n*9, *n*12

boonga, 112–13, 153, 244

border, 9, 33, 70, 110, 125*n*6, 208

boundary object, 47–48, 53

Brahmagiri, 16, 134, 138, 161, 177*n*5

Brahmin, 1, 71, 98*n*3, 118–119, 127*n*21

British, 1, 12, 20, 39, 43, 61, 64*n*28, 78, 108, 131, 133, 135, 162, 164

Buddhist, 14, 16, 20, 28*n*17, *n*23, 29*n*24, *n*27, 30*n*30, 52, 81, 141, 151*n*11, 161, 204*n*16, 232, 238, 251, 256*n*26, 262

bureaucracy, 1–4, 13, 15, 17–18, 20, 24–25, 29*n*29, 74, 83–84, 98*n*3, 103, 106–09, 111, 114, 131–33, 135, 146, 191, 224, 226*n*7, 231–32, 236, 244, 247, 261, 265

bureaucratic apparatus, 12, 74, 116–17, 160

bureaucrat-archaeologist, 3, 73, 97, 99*n*13, 148, 208, 236, 244, 249

bureaucratic archaeology, 2–3, 5, 7–12, 20, 24, 78, 105, 110, 131, 138, 145, 261, 263–64

bureaucratic authority, 173

bureaucratic capital, 252

bureaucratic community, 89

bureaucratic compulsion, 83

bureaucratic culture, 88

bureaucratic determinism, 229

bureaucratic ecology, 2, 80, 248

bureaucratic efficacy, 148

bureaucratic governmentality, 23

bureaucratic hierarchy, 81, 93, 97–98, 111–12, 158, 262

bureaucratic iconography, 115

bureaucratic ideology, 107

bureaucratic institutions, 21

bureaucratic intervention, 104

bureaucratic knowledge-production mechanism, 80

bureaucratic ontology, 246

bureaucratic organizations, 76

bureaucratic politics, 101*n*27

bureaucratic practice, 124

bureaucratic project, 95

bureaucratic rationality, 3, 146, 198, 261

bureaucratic regime, 116

bureaucratic science, 5

bureaucratic state, 95, 106, 109

bureaucratic structure, 54, 72, 74–75, 82, 90

bureaucratic work, 243, 260

burials, 18, 34, 50, 59, 120–21, 128, 200

campsite, 1, 22, 33, 79, 101*n*30, 102–03, 106–08, 110–11, 113–14, 116, 128, 252

cantonments, 107–08, 114

Carbon-14/radiocarbon, 34, 47, 60, 61*n*4, *n*5, 62*n*6

carnelian beads, 122, 153, 155, 177*n*1, 185, 187, 247

Cartesian, 13, 130–31, 143, 145–49, 152*n*18, 167

Cartesian perspectivalism, 147–48

cartographer, 14, 41, 67

cartographic, 39, 41–42, 145, 147, 152*n*17, 159, 164–65, 167, 257*n*29

cartographic ontology, 142–50

cartographical, 40, 142–43, 146, 148, 161, 165–66

Cemetery "H", 36, 38, 52

Central Advisory Board of Archaeology (CABA), 78, 138, 152*n*13, 239, 246, 256*n*23

Central Antiquity Collection (CAC), 20, 32*n*48, 198–99, 203*n*15

Central Bureau of Investigation (CBI), 22–23, 85, 249–51, 258*n*34
ceramics, 55, 60, 113, 122–23, 162–63, 166, 181–82, 188–89, 193–200, 202*n*11, 204*n*16, *n*18, 207, 209, 228, 230, 247
chain of command, 75, 134, 193
chain of credibility, 186, 191–93
Chak 86, 22, 56, 58, 60, 82, 117, 257*n*30
Chalcolithic, 38, 139, 141, 177*n*8
Chanhudaro, 63*n*19
Charsada, 139, 224
Chatterjee, Gauri, 27*n*13, 47, 253*n*7, 254*n*15
chief minister, 126*n*14, 205–06, 210
Childe, V. Gordon, 36, 63*n*16, 137
chowkidar (watchmen), 94, 96, 101*n*30, 109–10, 115, 119, 128, 190
chronological, 7, 13, 30*n*30, 139, 160–62, 164, 166, 169, 192, 194, 207
chronology, 26*n*10, 34, 43, 47, 63*n*15, 135, 163, 170, 177*n*5
circle, 14–17, 29*n*25, 31*n*36, 44, 62*n*5, 70–72, 83–85, 88, 117, 122, 128, 143, 176, 199, 205–06, 210, 225*n*2, 237, 246, 250–51, 254*n*14, 257*n*31
citadel, 1, 59–60, 128, 140–41, 153, 155, 168, 176, 187, 190, 194, 207, 209, 215, 217–18, 238
civilizing mission, 27*n*16, 35, 43, 143
colonial, 2, 4, 7, 11, 13–16, 20, 24, 26*n*10, 27*n*16, 28*n*19, 29*n*27, *n*29, *n*30, 30*n*31, *n*34, 36, 38–43, 45, 64*n*23, *n*27, 65*n*31, 71, 74–75, 97, 99*n*10, 104–08, 110–11, 114, 116, 121, 125*n*10, 126*n*12, 127*n*22, 129–36, 143–46, 148, 161–62, 218–25, 260–63, 265
colonial archaeological project, 9, 95, 105, 111–12, 115, 211, 222, 224–25, 247

colonial genealogy, 1, 84, 219, 261, 265
colonial India, 2, 13, 30*n*31, 39–40, 98*n*3, 136, 220
colonial project, 42, 143, 145, 221, 225
colonialism, 7, 35, 146
colonial state, 1–3, 11, 27*n*16, 28*n*20, 91, 97, 117, 146, 262, 265, 266*n*1
colony/colonies, 1–2, 12–13, 27*n*10, *n*13, 28*n*16, 30*n*30, 36, 39–41, 43, 105–06, 130, 162–63, 179, 263–64
commonsensical, 185, 215–16
Comptroller and Auditor General of India (CAG), 18, 20–21, 24, 31*n*44, 32*n*47, 62*n*5, 74, 199, 204*n*16, 239, 243, 245, 251, 256–57*n*27, *n*28, *n*31
conservation, 2, 14–15, 17, 20–21, 31*n*39, *n*41, 32*n*47, 55, 59, 68*n*51, 72, 75, 78, 80, 100*n*19, 135, 190, 250–51
control pit, 157
coolie, 148, 152*n*20, 223, 265
corruption, 12, 23, 85, 88–89, 101*n*27, 109, 228, 237, 239, 247–52, 257*n*32, 261
cryptography, 162, 165–66
cultural, 2–7, 10–12, 22–23, 30*n*35, 31*n*37, 34, 39–40, 50, 52, 56, 59–60, 62*n*11, 69*n*52, 95, 98, 105, 129, 138–41, 159, 165–66, 170, 178, 193–94, 200, 222, 233, 238–40, 247, 264
culture-history, 5, 134, 159, 193, 200, 237, 260
Cunningham, Alexander, 13–15, 28*n*17, *n*21, *n*22, *n*23, 29*n*24, *n*27, 30*n*30, 42–43, 52, 65*n*34, 66*n*40, 84, 161

dahari, 81, 89
daily life, 112, 115–16, 158

daily practice, 58, 72, 102, 112, 124, 156, 164, 175, 182, 230, 262, 264–65

daily wage, 81, 87–89, 94–96, 103, 118–19, 175, 190, 198

Dalit, 1, 33, 93, 95, 101*n*29, 123, 126*n*12, 190

dasyu, 94, 101*n*28

Deccan College, 138, 150*n*2, 180, 203*n*12, *n*13, 246

dehati, 88, 107, 148, 184, 208, 218, 225, 265

Delhi Excavation Branch (Ex. Br), 58, 61, 81, 85, 137

Department of Science and Technology, 19–20

deputy superintending archaeologist (Dy. SA), 17, 25, 70–73, 75, 80, 84–86, 93, 233, 245, 249–50, 253*n*6, 257*n*31

Dholavira, 8–9, 22–23, 33, 54, 56, 58–59, 62*n*5, 67*n*43, 69*n*57, 75, 79–81, 83-84, 89, 91–92, 94, 96–97, 100*n*24, 102–03, 107, 110, 112–15, 117–20, 122–24, 125*n*6, 126*n*14, 128, 130, 138–41, 143, 147, 150*n*1, 151*n*14, *n*16, 153, 155–56, 159, 159, 168–69, 174, 176, 177*n*1, *n*9, 178, 182–83, 187–91, 193–95, 197–200, 201*n*2, 202*n*6, *n*9, 205–08, 210–12, 215, 217–20, 226*n*5, *n*10, 227–29, 233, 236, 238, 242–44, 247–48, 251, 252*n*3, 262

dhoti, 128, 218, 226*n*8–*n*10

diagnostic ceramic/diagnostic pottery, 198–200, 204*n*18

diagram, 164–65, 167, 179, 222–24, 232, 240

Dikshit, K. N., 60, 61*n*4, 127, 137, 150*n*5, 151*n*12, 152*n*20, 256*n*25

director, 1, 8–10, 17, 33, 59, 72, 76, 78–79, 81–85, 89, 100*n*24, 102–03, 112, 114–16, 119, 123, 124*n*1, 128–29, 148, 151*n*10, 153, 156, 168–69, 174–76, 178, 180, 183, 185–86, 192, 197, 199, 205–07, 209–10, 214, 231, 237–39, 243–44, 246, 248, 250, 253*n*6, 254*n*14, 255*n*15, 258*n*34

director general (DG), 3, 14–15, 17, 22, 24–25, 29*n*24, *n*25, 30*n*36, 42, 52, 55–56, 59, 68*n*49, 72, 74–79, 81–82, 84–85, 91, 96, 98*n*6, 99*n*11, 102, 124*n*1, 126*n*11, 127*n*20, 131, 133, 135, 137, 150*n*5, 151*n*8, *n*11, *n*13, 161, 207, 210, 230–31, 237–38, 240, 243–44, 248, 252*n*1, 253*n*7, 254*n*14, *n*15, 256*n*26

Director of Excavation and Exploration, 81, 102

disciplinarian, 2, 5–6, 8–9, 11, 15, 18, 26*n*10, 41, 112, 115–16, 130–31, 143–46, 148, 160, 165, 167, 225, 262–63

disciplinarian discourse, 2, 41, 225, 263

discovery, 1, 14, 29*n*27, 30*n*30, 33–34, 36, 42–45, 61*n*2, 62*n*10, 64*n*29, 65*n*31, *n*34, 67*n*43, 80, 86, 104–05, 121–24, 135, 137, 161–62, 164, 180–81, 184–93, 202*n*5, 205, 210, 217

disenchantment, 79, 83, 249

draughtsman, 34, 71, 77, 79, 88, 142, 175–76, 179, 227, 248, 253*n*6

Dravidian, 37, 63*n*18

early Harappan, 34, 46, 59–60, 61*n*4, 63*n*15, 168, 171, 191–92, 194, 202*n*7, *n*8, 237

East India Company, 12, 40

ecology of practices, 8, 97

Empire, 1, 14, 105, 111, 160, 163

empirical facts, 2, 45, 53, 217

Employment News, 91

Enlightenment, 11, 39–40, 43, 166, 221, 223

epistemic, 48, 53, 80, 83, 104–06, 136, 144, 149, 152*n*18, 158, 201*n*3, 218, 233, 260, 263

epistemic agency, 186

epistemic artifact, 171, 177, 183, 191

epistemic community, 47

epistemic cultures, 11

epistemic entity, 65*n*36

epistemic epiphany, 218

epistemic evidence, 216

epistemic labour, 186

epistemic leitmotiv, 16

epistemic marker, 212–17, 220–21, 223–25

epistemic materiality, 146, 148

epistemic narrative, 233

epistemic murk, 35, 145

epistemic practice, 177

epistemic spatiality, 9, 149, 177

epistemic square, 145

epistemic things, 183

epistemic traditions, 263

epistemic universe, 146, 148, 248

epistemic valence, 53, 124

epistemic vibrations, 260

epistemological clutter, 211

epistemological data, 49

epistemology, 2, 4, 8–9, 39–41, 98, 145, 172, 208, 252, 263

estimates committee, 18

ethnic marker, 217–25

ethnography, 2, 4–13, 16, 18, 20–25, 30*n*34, 33, 35, 52, 54, 58–61, 74, 94, 96–97, 98*n*6, 101*n*27, 118, 131, 140, 145, 149, 150*n*2, 154, 175, 184, 187, 197–98, 200*n*1, *n*4, 208, 211, 225*n*1, 237, 239–40, 243, 247, 250–51, 260

evidence, 2–3, 7, 10, 14, 23–24, 35–36, 40–41, 44, 46, 49–52, 54, 62*n*8, *n*10, 63*n*11, *n*14, *n*17, 64*n*22, 66*n*41, 67*n*44, *n*46, 74, 89, 100*n*18, 131, 141, 144, 153–54, 156–57, 164–65, 168, 170, 177, 179, 181, 187, 192–93, 198, 204*n*16, 210, 213, 215–16, 219, 231, 235–36, 238–39, 255*n*17, 259, 261, 264

Excavation Branch (Ex. Br.), 17, 33, 58, 60–61, 71–72, 79–86, 88, 90, 99*n*15, 117, 120, 124*n*1, 128, 137, 142, 157, 213, 230, 232, 238, 244, 248, 250–51

excavation reports, 21, 52, 140, 145, 197, 229, 231–33, 236–49, 256*n*22, 257*n*27, 259

excavation season, 22, 81, 118, 124*n*1, 183, 189, 195

excavation site, 9, 21–23, 33, 58, 75, 77, 80, 83–84, 86, 92, 97, 101*n*30, 103, 106, 109, 116–21, 124, 125*n*4, 128–30, 140, 146, 148–49, 154, 158–59, 170, 175, 178, 180, 182–84, 186, 188–89, 194, 196, 198–200, 208, 210–13, 217, 231, 246, 260, 264

experiment, 5, 10, 27*n*11, 40, 167

factory time, 115, 265

facts, 2, 13, 25, 35, 37, 40, 45, 53–54, 57, 66*n*43, 67*n*47, 77–78, 85, 130, 132, 136, 165, 167, 177, 181, 193, 210, 216–17, 219, 234, 241, 244, 246–47, 252*n*1, *n*2, 261–64

faunal remains, 67*n*44, 181–82, 195, 197, 202*n*6

fetish, 3, 28*n*23, 146–47, 161, 183, 211, 251, 263

field, 8, 11, 16, 21, 23, 27*n*12, 28*n*17, 33–35, 39–41, 52, 54, 62*n*10, 69*n*56, 71, 76, 80–81, 83, 85–86, 89–90, 100, 102, 104–07, 111, 114, 116, 133–35, 142–45,

149, 151*n*10, 160, 164, 180–81, 186–87, 191, 197, 216, 225, 230, 232, 234, 244–45, 254*n*12

fieldwork, 7–8, 18, 20, 24, 55, 72, 74, 80, 91, 103–05, 109, 114, 125*n*7, 126*n*12, 129, 131–34, 150*n*2, 180, 227–28, 233, 241, 248, 251, 258*n*35, 260, 265

fortification, 1, 44, 59–61, 128, 135, 139–41, 156, 178, 187–88, 207, 210, 212, 214, 217–19, 237

Gadhvi, Shambhudan, 122–23, 127*n*21

Ganga, 31*n*37, 38, 64*n*22

genetics, 35, 48

geographic, 13, 28*n*23, 36, 39, 41, 43, 45, 51, 53, 81, 85, 107, 148, 152*n*19, 260, 263

Geological Survey of India, 28*n*20, 29*n*28, 31*n*45, 45, 75, 87, 99*n*9, 203*n*12

geology, 13, 27*n*12, 35, 42, 45–48, 104, 135, 167, 203*n*13

geometric, 39, 130, 146–47, 149

Ghaggar, 31*n*37, 42, 57, 59, 67*n*48

Ghaggar–Hakra, 37, 44–47, 53–54, 56, 58, 65*n*33

gherao (picketing), 91

Ghosh, Amalananda/A. K Ghosh, 15–16, 31*n*37, 45, 60, 65*n*33, 69*n*59, 89, 105, 117, 120, 126*n*12, 127*n*18, 133–34, 137–38, 151*n*8, 161, 163, 170, 202*n*10, 216, 256*n*22

godhuli, 129

Government of India, 15, 69*n*56, 73–75, 77, 100*n*18, 119–20, 240

governmentality, 11–12, 20, 27–28*n*16, 39–40, 148, 264

gridded, 139, 146–47, 149, 170, 175, 181

Gujarat, 22, 29*n*28, 32*n*51, 33, 37, 44–45, 55, 58, 67*n*43, *n*48,

83–84, 96, 117–19, 122, 126*n*14, 127*n*21, 205–07, 225*n*1, 226*n*4, 244

Gupta, Swaraj Prakash/S. P. Gupta, 53, 56–57, 61, 63*n*12, 64*n*20, 65*n*33, 68*n*49, 69*n*54, 233, 235, 255*n*17

Hakra ware, 191, 198, 202*n*7

Hansi, 1, 22, 56, 58, 61, 69*n*55, 95, 109, 130, 137, 156, 173, 184, 194–95, 209, 241, 249, 257*n*30

Harappa/Harappans, 14, 16, 20, 29*n*27, 31*n*37, *n*38, 34–38, 44, 46–53, 56, 58–60, 61*n*4, 62*n*10, 63*n*12, *n*15–*n*19, 64*n*21, 65*n*32, *n*34, 66*n*41, 67*n*44, 68*n*48, 69*n*58, 70, 76, 81, 114, 128, 134, 137–42, 146, 155–56, 161, 168, 171, 177*n*1, *n*4, 182–83, 185, 187, 189, 191–94, 197, 201*n*2, 202*n*7, *n*8, 212, 219, 224, 237, 247

Harappan civilization, 14, 34–36, 42–45, 47, 50–51, 56, 65*n*31, 67*n*43, 72, 122, 150*n*1, 151*n*11, 153, 160, 262

Harappan script, 59

Harappan site, 9, 14, 16, 23, 29*n*27, 33–34, 44–45, 53–54, 58, 60–61, 61*n*1, 67*n*43, 81–82, 103, 110, 112, 124, 129–30, 138, 154, 163, 171, 181, 186–87, 194, 213, 218, 238, 241, 250, 258*n*34

hardkana, 93

Hargreaves, Harold, 137, 219

Haryana, 1, 22, 33, 37, 42, 46, 50, 55, 58–59, 61, 67*n*48, 83, 88, 117, 251, 256*n*25, 258*n*34

Hastinapur, 52, 66*n*41, 138, 202*n*10

headquarters, 17, 22, 24, 31*n*36, 59, 72, 74–79, 82, 119, 122, 127*n*22, 128, 187, 230

heritage, 1–3, 6, 15–17, 19–21, 30*n*31, *n*35, 31*n*42, 44, 48, 76, 80–81,

97, 100*n*19, 125*n*10, 133, 141, 206, 213, 221, 233, 236, 241, 246, 251, 262, 266*n*1

hierarchy, 4, 9, 24–25, 70–74, 78, 80–81, 83–84, 86, 88–89, 93–97, 102, 107, 111–16, 158, 174–75, 178, 184, 192, 203*n*14, 239, 261–62, 265

High Court, 19, 28*n*18, 86, 203*n*12, 227, 229–35, 255*n*19, 259

Hindi, 1, 23, 64*n*21, 92–93, 95, 101*n*30, 103, 109, 115, 129, 172, 207, 216–17, 255*n*19, 257*n*32

Hindu, 14, 20, 35, 38, 48, 51–52, 56–57, 66*n*39, 69*n*54, 102, 104, 120, 225*n*1, *n*3, 228–30, 232–33, 235, 259–60

Hindutva, 35–36, 51–56, 62*n*9, 66*n*39, *n*42, 67*n*47, 69*n*54, 233, 235, 255*n*17, 261–62

horizontal excavation, 130, 136–41, 150*n*2, 156, 252

human figures, 216, 221

hydrological, 39, 41–42, 44–48, 53, 55–56

ideological, 2–4, 7, 9, 11–14, 16, 27*n*10, 29*n*30, 33, 39–40, 51, 53–54, 56, 58, 93, 97–98, 103, 105, 107, 115–16, 134, 147–48, 161, 163, 224–25, 261, 263–65

ideology, 2, 4, 13, 43, 52, 64*n*23, 69*n*54, 107, 115, 124*n*3, 134, 151*n*9, 162, 265

imperialism, 7, 35

Indian Administrative Service (IAS), 73, 76–77, 79, 99*n*10, *n*11

Indian Archaeology: A Review (IAR), 31*n*43, 33–34, 53, 58, 60, 61*n*1, 69*n*55, 122–23, 127*n*18, 140, 145, 147, 152*n*14, *n*15, 177*n*9, 191, 224, 226*n*5, *n*6, *n*10, 240–41, 257*n*27

indigenous, 6, 26*n*3, 32*n*51, 35–37, 51, 54, 163

Indo-Aryan invasion, 48

Indo-European, 35

Indo-European Aryans, 36

Indo-European languages, 37, 49, 51

Indo-European linguistics, 35–36

Indo-Gangetic civilization, 160

Indological, 13–14, 26*n*10, 37, 40, 42–43, 63*n*14, 136

Indology, 38–42

Indus, 35, 37, 42, 44, 53, 64*n*22

Indus civilization, 29*n*27, 34, 37, 53, 64*n*21, 70, 137, 146, 160

Indus seal, 122–23, 151*n*10, 182

inscription field, 39–41

Institute of Archaeology, 34, 51–53, 61*n*5, 72, 81, 83, 86–87, 89–91, 100*n*24, 100*n*25, 116, 127*n*20, 131, 142, 155, 172, 180–81, 184, 192, 203*n*12, *n*14, 241, 250

Institutional apparatus, 2, 12, 15, 35, 39

Iron Age, 61, 68, 135, 177*n*4

Jagmohan, 55–57, 69*n*53, 82, 91, 126*n*14, 233

joint director general (Jt DG), 17, 25, 30*n*36, 55, 59, 72, 75, 77, 82, 84, 96, 98*n*6, 252*n*1, 253*n*7, 254*n*14

Jones, William, 6–7, 13, 28*n*18, 30*n*30, 36, 39–40, 52, 131, 152*n*17, 157, 217, 239

Joshi, Jagat Pati/Joshi, J. P., 54, 58, 68*n*49, 69*n*54, 117, 122–24, 127*n*18, *n*20, 130, 141, 177*n*4, 202*n*9, 235

Joshi, M. C., 68*n*49, 69*n*54, 99*n*11, 256*n*26

Juni Kuran, 22, 56, 58, 82, 102, 113, 115, 117, 125*n*4, *n*6, 177*n*9, 226*n*5, 251, 257*n*30 *kaam*, 76, 93, 96, 121–22, 142, 175, 184, 187, 189, 196, 199, 227, 232, 260

Kalibangan, 16, 45, 47, 54, 56, 60, 65*n*32, 67*n*43, *n*45, 68*n*48, 72, 81, 84, 118, 130, 133, 138, 175, 190, 241, 243, 247–48, 252*n*3

Kesariya, 254*n*13

khadi, 115, 123, 226*n*9

knife, 77, 153, 168–69, 171–75, 178, 188, 192–93, 211, 214

knowledge production, 2–3, 8, 10–11, 13, 20, 35, 64*n*23, 65*n*31, 80, 95, 104–06, 129–30, 135, 140, 144, 155, 158, 167, 179, 182, 201*n*3, 217, 221–22, 224–25, 233, 247, 262–64

Kot Diji, 34, 45, 68*n*48

Kshatriya, 71, 127*n*21

Kuhnian, 5

Kutch/Rann of Kutch, 37, 46, 58, 75, 112, 119, 122, 127*n*22, 130, 206, 226*n*4, 229

Kutchi, 217–18, 228

labels, 9, 32*n*50, 146, 176–77, 180–83, 185–86, 193–96, 209–10, 215, 247, 252

laboratory, 10–11, 27*n*14, 40, 61*n*5, 104, 130, 134, 146, 156, 167, 201*n*4

laborers, 22–23, 70, 75, 79, 83–84, 88, 91–98, 101*n*30, 103, 109, 113, 115–16, 118, 121, 123, 128–29, 140, 142, 144, 148, 151*n*12, 152*n*20, 153–54, 158, 172, 175–76, 178, 180, 184–93, 195–96, 198, 201*n*4, 205, 209–11, 213–14, 217–19, 221, 224, 229–31, 265

Lal, Braj Basi/B. B. Lal, 18, 30*n*35, 31*n*37, 52–54, 56, 63*n*12, 64*n*20, 67*n*45, 72–74, 77–79,

87, 89–90, 101*n*26, 130, 133, 138, 151*n*8, 175, 177*n*3, *n*10, 190, 202*n*10, 233, 235, 240–43, 245, 247–48, 256*n*25

landscape, 9, 39, 41, 56, 95, 103–06, 109–10, 116, 120–21, 124, 126*n*17, 129–30, 138–39, 142–43, 145–49, 154, 157–58, 167, 170, 184, 186, 194, 202*n*8, 206, 223–24, 228, 247, 257*n*29, 265

large-scale excavation, 16, 56, 81, 89, 123, 130, 136–41, 150*n*2, 237, 240, 242, 246, 250–52, 256*n*25

Latour, Bruno, 10–11, 32*n*50, 40

license, 3, 21, 50, 138, 151*n*13, 239–40, 249, 257*n*31

linguistics, 13, 35–37, 39–40, 48, 51, 62*n*11, 63*n*13, 202*n*5

Lothal, 16, 45, 54, 67*n*43, *n*46, 81, 84, 130, 252*n*3, 256*n*26

lower division clerk (LDC), 25, 81, 92, 253*n*6

Lower Town, 59–60, 128, 147, 178, 187, 212

Mackay, Ernst, 137, 151*n*10, 182

Mahabharata, 38, 52–53, 68*n*48

Mahajan, Pramod, 206, 225*n*2

man-management, 80, 97, 134

Mandal Commission report, 71

Mani, B. R., 99*n*13, 100*n*24, 229, 231–35, 255*n*18, 260, 262

Manjhi, Hari, 229, 231–35, 255*n*18, 262

Manusmriti, 49, 71, 98*n*1

mapping, 13, 29*n*24, 31*n*45, 39, 42, 66*n*38, 135, 141–42, 152*n*17, 160–61, 201*n*1

Marshall, John, 14–15, 29*n*26, *n*27, 42–44, 64*n*29, 65*n*31, 131, 133, 137, 139, 151*n*10, *n*11, *n*12, 152*n*20, 182

Masjid, 232

Maski, 106, 138

material culture, 2–3, 7–10, 14, 20, 30n31, 36, 38, 43–44, 51–53, 56, 61n4, 65n32, 74, 105–06, 140–41, 143, 156–57, 163–64, 170, 177, 179, 181, 183, 191, 194, 200, 202n4, n7, 210, 213, 231, 234, 240, 252n2

materiality, 1, 9, 105, 110–11, 146, 148, 170, 215

materialized epistemic space, 152n18

Mature Harappan, 47, 50, 59–60, 61n4, 63n15, 130, 139, 153, 155, 168, 194, 212

Meadow, Richard H., 29n28, 67n44, 190, 202n6

measurement, 34, 153, 165, 167, 180–82, 185, 195, 247, 254n9

medieval, 1, 14, 42, 61, 68n48, 78, 81, 127n21, n22, 166, 194, 198, 228, 230, 252, 262

Mediterranean, 137, 163

Mesopotamia, 15, 43–44, 139, 160

meta-narratives, 7–8, 162–63, 259

meta-theoretical, 7–8, 263

micro-politics, xvii

micro-practices, 7, 10, 154, 171, 179, 192

micro-processes, 7, 9, 141

Middle Town, 59, 128, 168, 182, 188, 207, 210, 228, 238

military, 12–14, 39–40, 64n28, 75, 84, 106–08, 110–11, 115, 125n7, 134, 145–46, 164–67, 178, 265

Ministry of Tourism and Culture, 56

Mirdha Committee, 18–19, 32n47, 90, 243

mitochondrial DNA (mtDNA), 48–49

modernity, 4, 25n3, 27n16, 39–40, 65n31, 146–47, 264

Modi, Narendra, 126n14, 206–07, 225n1

Mohenjo-Daro, 14, 16, 29n27, 37, 43–44, 63n17, n19, 68n49, 130, 137, 139, 141, 146, 150n1, 151n10–n12, 152n20, 224

Moily Committee, 18

monumental, 1–2, 9, 30n30, 37, 44, 59, 94, 128, 132, 137, 139–41, 156, 201n1, 207, 213, 217–18, 224, 235, 240, 242, 256n26, 259, 264

monuments, 6, 14, 17, 20, 31n41, n42, 55, 66n40, 69n53, 85, 100n19, 117, 120, 132, 141, 161, 199, 223–24, 241, 246

mosque, 18, 229, 235–36, 259

Moulik, Achala, 99n11

mound, 1, 9, 23, 33–34, 60–61, 61n3, 63n19, 70, 80, 91, 117, 120–22, 130, 137, 139, 141–42, 151n12, 156, 178, 186–87, 191–92, 217, 222

mud brick, 34, 70, 139–40, 171, 191–92, 214

Mughal, Rafique, 45, 65n33

Mughals, 61, 98n3, 259

museum, 17, 20, 32n47, 33, 51, 74–75, 78, 84, 116–18, 120, 122–23, 127n22, 130, 132, 135, 151n6, 164, 182–83, 204n16, 207, 218–20, 224

Muslims, 1, 33–34, 59, 81, 95, 98n7, 120–21, 225n1, 230–33

muster-roll call, 91–92

myths, 35, 94

Nadistuti-sukta hymn, 41, 45

Nagpur Excavation Branch (Ex. Br.), 33, 58, 81–82, 157, 213

narrative of the past, 51

Nath, Amarendra, 38, 50, 54, 65n33, 100n24, 130, 152n14, 177n9, 202n9, 244, 250, 258n33, n34, 260

nation, 1, 6–7, 11–12, 35, 43, 51–52, 75–
    76, 105–06, 111, 116, 119–21,
    152, 205–06, 208, 227, 260
National Democratic Alliance (NDA),
    57, 82
nationalism, 6–7, 51–52, 66*n*43,
    260–62
nationalistic, 3, 51, 262, 264
native, 27*n*16, 29*n*27, 51, 108, 136,
    143, 145, 148, 162–63, 200*n*1,
    208, 219–24, 265
necropolis, 50, 138
New Archaeology, 5–6, 80, 121
nineteenth century, 3, 5, 14, 30*n*33,
    39–42, 44, 51, 64*n*23, 71,
    101*n*29, 124, 129, 134, 149,
    165, 212, 219, 223, 235
Niti Aayog, 14, 18, 24, 31*n*42, 74,
    100*n*20, 100*n*25, 266*n*1

office, 22, 54, 56, 71–72, 74–75, 81,
    84–85, 88, 91, 99*n*9, 106, 108,
    111, 114, 116, 118–19, 126*n*11,
    133, 136, 142, 213, 228, 230,
    237–38, 243–45, 248
officer cadre, 73, 86
officers, 22–23, 29*n*25, 71–77, 79–80,
    84–86, 88, 91, 94–95, 98*n*4,
    106, 108, 112–13, 122, 124*n*1,
    126*n*11, 131, 135, 148, 151*n*10,
    164, 175, 189–90, 192–93,
    207–08, 210, 230, 238, 245,
    248–50, 257*n*28, *n*31, 265
ontology/ontological, 3–4, 8–10, 24,
    116, 131, 142–50, 153–59, 172,
    183, 246–47, 260, 264
open-area excavation, 136, 140
oppressive/oppression, 4, 28*n*16, 74, 93,
    111, 158, 225, 261, 264–65
optically stimulated luminescence
    (OSL), 47
organization, 1–3, 11, 13, 15–16,
    18–22, 24, 26*n*10, 28*n*20, 30*n*30,

31*n*45, 35, 44, 57–58, 69*n*54,
    72–73, 75–80, 87, 89, 97, 103,
    116–17, 120, 136–39, 145–47,
    151*n*9, 158, 178–79, 187, 194,
    227, 229, 235, 241, 247, 260,
    265
orientalist, 40, 161
Other Backward Classes (OBC), 71,
    98*n*7, 100*n*18
Out of India theory, 36, 38, 51

Painted Grey Ware (PGW)
paisa banaana, 85
Pakistan, 9, 16, 33–34, 37, 44–46, 50,
    65*n*33, *n*34, 67*n*48, 70, 110, 114,
    125*n*6, 141, 206, 208, 226*n*4
paleo-channel, 37, 44–47
Paleo-climatic research, 46
panopticon, 146
partition of South Asia, 16, 35, 44–45,
    59, 65*n*34, 120, 132, 229
past, 1–9, 14, 19, 27*n*10, 30*n*30, 35, 43,
    49–51, 53, 58, 61*n*3, 74, 76, 88,
    104–05, 119, 129–31, 136, 138,
    156, 160–77, 190, 216, 219, 221,
    223–25, 238, 242, 252, 252*n*2,
    259–64, 266*n*1
Patel, Ajita K., 190, 202*n*6
Patna Excavation Branch (Ex. Br.), 58,
    60, 85, 120, 142
pending excavations, 257*n*27
Petrie, Flinders, 46, 83, 97, 105, 124*n*2,
    139, 150*n*1, 151*n*10, 165–66,
    213, 263
photographer, 80, 88, 115, 133, 176–
    77, 179, 211–20, 233, 236–37,
    242, 253*n*6
photography, 88–89, 133, 141, 153,
    209–25, 234, 253*n*9
Pitt Rivers, 134–35, 164–67
political, 3, 5, 7, 9, 12, 25*n*2, 28*n*16,
    29*n*30, 32*n*51, 35, 38, 43, 53–54,
    56–58, 63*n*17, 65*n*32, 66*n*37,

*n*43, 81, 98*n*3, 105, 118, 122, 125*n*9, 132, 206–07, 225*n*3, 226*n*9, 229, 250–51, 255*n*19, 260, 264–65
polymerase chain reaction (PCR), 49
postcolonial, 5, 8–9, 11, 24, 28*n*20, 35, 52, 94, 108, 110, 115–17, 125*n*10, 131–32, 138–39, 158, 178, 208, 229, 230–31, 234, 242, 246, 248, 260–62, 264
postcolonial ASI, 12–21, 44, 72, 133
postcolonial bureaucracy, 1–2, 4, 9, 12, 18, 98*n*3, 148, 225, 236, 261–62, 264
postcolonial ecology, 2, 261
postcolonial geological science, 253
postcolonial geology, 45–48
postcolonial metropole, 106
postcolonial polity, 4
postcolonial science, 4, 11, 45, 236, 260
postcolonial state, 2–3, 11, 91, 97, 117, 146, 262, 265, 266*n*1
postcolony, 1–2, 106, 263–264
post-processual, 3, 7–8, 26*n*7, *n*8, 90, 129, 262–264
potshard, 184–87, 189, 193–96, 198–200, 201*n*4, 228, 231
pottery, 82, 129, 137, 162–63, 166, 177*n*4, 181–82, 193, 247, 252, 254*n*9
pottery-dump, 200
pottery yard, 188–89, 193–200, 202*n*10
Prime Minister, 18, 66*n*41, 78, 225*n*1, 239, 259
processual, 3, 5, 7–8, 26*n*5, *n*8, 90, 129, 262–64
promotions, 71–74, 77, 86–87
proto-historic, 20, 228
Public Works Department (PWD), 80, 99*n*14, 238
Purana Quilla, 32*n*48
Puranic, 38–39, 41, 51
Purusha Sukta, 70–71, 93

quadrant number, 140, 142, 194–95, 198
quadrants, 119, 121, 128, 140, 142, 147, 149, 152*n*16, 156–58, 168, 172, 176, 180–82, 184, 188, 191–92, 194–95, 198–200, 210, 213, 237

Rajasthan, 22, 33, 37, 42, 46, 55, 58, 60, 67*n*48, 70, 83–84, 88, 117, 187
Rajput, 1, 61, 65*n*32
Rajya Sabha, 19, 206
Rakhigarhi, 22–23, 50–51, 54, 56, 68*n*48, 84, 130, 138, 150*n*1, 152*n*14, 177*n*9, 187, 202*n*9, 242, 244, 250–51, 258*n*33, *n*34
Ram Janmabhoomi, 53, 57, 227
Rama, 35, 236–37
Ramayana, 53, 236
Rangpur, 16, 44
Rashtriya Swayamsevak Sangh (RSS), 53, 56–57, 66*n*43, 69*n*54, 232, 235
Reddy, Jaipal, 57
Reich, David, 48–50, 66*n*37
religion, 35, 66*n*39, 95, 181
religiosity, 38, 102, 104
representations, 10–12, 39–40, 54, 101*n*29, 111, 114, 141–44, 146, 148, 165–67, 170, 177, 183, 200, 210–13, 215–19, 221–25, 230–31, 239
reservoirs, 59, 128, 140, 147, 168, 207, 217, 238
Review committee, 18, 240
Rig Veda, 34, 38, 41, 46, 63*n*14, 64*n*22, *n*26, 70–71
ritual, 67*n*46, 70, 91–92, 102, 124*n*1, 128–29, 176, 178, 182–83, 201*n*1, 208
Roman, 115, 131, 135, 161–63, 167
Roman Arrentine ware, 163, 177*n*7
Ropar, 67, 81, 243

Sahni, Daya Ram, 14, 29*n*27, 65*n*34
Sangh Parivar, 53
Sanskrit, 13, 30*n*30, 37–38, 40, 42–43, 51, 53–54, 67, 71, 100*n*18, 101*n*26, 102–03, 115, 157
Saraswati, 34, 37–48, 53–57, 59, 64*n*22, 67*n*43, 67*n*47, 69*n*52, 238, 262
Saraswati Heritage Project (SHP), 33, 38, 54–58, 61, 81–83, 102, 117, 126*n*13, 141, 203*n*13, 233, 237, 251, 256*n*22, 262
sarkari, 109, 114, 178, 227, 231, 243, 260–61
sarkari Hindi, 115
Saurashtra, 37, 45, 82
scale, 16, 56, 63*n*17, 81, 85, 87, 89, 100*n*20, 123, 130, 136–42, 149, 150*n*2, 151*n*9, 215–21, 237, 240, 242, 246, 250–52, 256*n*25
Scheduled Castes and the Scheduled Tribes, 71
science, 2–8, 10–11, 17, 19–20, 27*n*13, *n*14, 31*n*41, 35, 39, 43, 45, 47–49, 52, 76, 80, 105, 135–36, 146, 154, 164–66, 170–72, 177, 179–81, 219–20, 227, 236, 260–64
scientific knowledge, 3, 10, 40, 105, 129–30, 135, 146, 165–66, 216, 221–22
scientific laboratory, 130, 134, 145
scientific method, 3, 5, 11, 98, 104, 193, 252*n*2, 264
script, 35, 54, 59, 62*n*11, 67*n*43, 115, 157
section, 80, 84, 93, 112, 135, 138–39, 143, 145, 152*n*13, 157, 167–77, 179, 188, 191–93, 209–11, 214, 222–23, 229, 234–35, 244, 248, 255*n*18
section-cutters, 93, 168, 175, 191, 214
Sengupta, Gautam, 14, 78–79
Shinde, Vasant, 50–51, 54, 99*n*13, 138
Shiv Sena, xxii*n*2

signboard, 59, 109
site director, 33, 123, 156, 174–75, 178, 180, 185–86, 192, 197, 205–07, 209, 237–38, 246, 256*n*25
site tour, 1, 34, 93, 206–08
site visit, 147, 207–09
social, 2, 4–5, 10–12, 22, 32*n*51, 35, 37–38, 44, 48, 62*n*9, 90, 95–98, 103, 105–07, 111, 116, 118, 124*n*2, 146, 178, 182, 184, 223, 250, 262, 264
Sringaverpur, 138
staff, 8–9, 22–23, 30*n*36, 68*n*50, *n*51, 71, 73–75, 80–86, 88–89, 93–96, 102–03, 106, 112, 115, 125*n*4, 128, 132–33, 135, 160, 172, 177, 179–80, 182, 186, 195, 205, 208, 211, 227, 230, 236, 238, 244, 246, 250, 253*n*7
Staff Memorandum, 80, 160, 238
Staff Selection Commission (SSC), 72, 87, 100*n*22
state, 1–3, 5–7, 11–12, 15, 17–18, 20–21, 24, 27*n*16, 28*n*20, 29*n*28, 31*n*39, *n*42, *n*43, *n*45, 33, 35, 45, 52, 56, 65*n*32, 73, 75, 77, 79, 85, 90–91, 95–97, 103, 106–07, 109–11, 116–17, 122–23, 126*n*12, 127*n*22, 131, 132–33, 137, 151*n*9, 153, 160, 199, 203*n*14, 205–08, 223, 234, 243–44, 246, 256*n*23, 260, 262, 264–65, 266*n*1
statist, 4, 12, 18, 35, 38, 74, 102, 106, 109–10, 115, 120, 264
statist actors, 3, 208
statist apparatus, 1, 23
statist architecture, 111
statist authority, 3, 25*n*2, 240, 265
statist bureaucracy, 24, 116, 2602
statist hegemony, 261
statist institution, 240, 260
statist machinery, 3, 54, 108

statist power, 224
Stein, Aurel, 43–45, 65*n*33, *n*34, 69*n*59, 198, 204*n*16
stratigraphical layers, 139, 200, 214–15
stratigraphical section, 167–68, 171–72, 223
stratigraphy, 23, 77, 93, 131, 134–35, 139, 144–45, 156–57, 159–64, 166–77, 179–80, 192–93, 200, 210, 214–15, 222–24, 234, 239, 241, 247, 249, 255*n*15, 256
structural feature, 70, 140–41, 164, 184, 240
structures, 2, 4, 10–12, 15, 17, 21, 27*n*10, 29*n*30, 31*n*42, 34, 36, 47, 54–55, 59–61, 66*n*38, 72–75, 80, 82–83, 90, 97, 105, 108, 111–14, 116–17, 121, 135, 141, 155, 158, 168, 174, 179–81, 187–88, 191–93, 200, 210, 213–14, 216–17, 230, 235, 237, 241, 259, 262, 264
subaltern, 27*n*13, 84, 95, 108, 123, 125*n*9, 158, 175, 178, 221–25, 265
subject preparation, 209–12, 217
superintending archaeologist (SA), 17, 25, 31*n*36, 33–34, 56, 58, 70–73, 75, 79–80, 82–86, 88–89, 93, 98*n*5, 100, 117, 124*n*1, 133, 137, 171, 174, 184, 192, 205–06, 211–12, 231, 233, 237–38, 245–46, 249–51, 253*n*6, 254*n*14, 257*n*31
Supreme Court, 99*n*18, 150*n*4, 235, 259
Surkotada, 16, 45, 54, 67*n*44, 81, 84, 122, 127*n*20, 130, 141, 191, 202*n*9
Survey of India, 13, 19, 28*n*20, 31*n*45, *n*46, 75, 99*n*9
survey-map, 142–43, 145
surveyors, 14–15, 29*n*24, 41, 71, 80, 88, 127*n*18, 142, 177, 231, 253*n*6

Sutlej, 42, 46–47, 64*n*22
system, 11–12, 15, 28*n*17, 34, 40, 42, 47, 59, 71, 79, 84, 90, 94, 98*n*2, 105, 134, 140, 142–43, 149, 152*n*16, 159, 178, 183, 202*n*5, 224–25, 227, 243–44, 246, 251

tacit skills, 11, 188, 191
Tarkhanewala Dera, 22, 56, 58, 60, 82, 117, 257*n*30
Taxila, 16, 28*n*21, 134, 137–39, 161
Taxila field school, 180
Taxila School of Archaeology, 15, 52, 133, 134
taxonomic, 164–66
technical section, 135, 143
technical staff, 30*n*36, 71, 75, 80–81, 84, 86, 88, 133, 172, 177, 179–80, 182, 186, 195, 205, 227, 230, 236
technology, 4, 10, 19, 27*n*14, 49, 130–31, 134, 145–46, 177*n*1, 201*n*1, 213
temple, 14, 17–18, 53, 229, 232, 234–36, 259
temporality, 29*n*30, 115, 121, 159–61, 163–64, 170, 172, 177, 230
tents, 23, 77–78, 89, 103, 109–10, 112–15, 178, 182, 198, 206, 229–30, 237, 247–48, 250, 252
terrestrial, 13, 34, 56, 64*n*22, 104–05
territoriality, 9, 106, 265
territory, 12–13, 16, 39–40, 65*n*31, 81, 105, 120, 130, 145, 147–48, 265
Tewari, Rakesh, 78
Thapar, B. K., 36–38, 79, 106, 127*n*18, 133, 138, 151*n*8, 156, 161, 190, 192, 235, 256*n*26
Thar Desert, 45–47
theory, 1, 5–8, 11–12, 36–38, 43, 48, 51, 54, 66*n*39, 67*n*43, 70, 98*n*3, 104–05, 129, 134, 151*n*7, 204*n*18, 249, 260, 262–63

theory of practice, 2–3, 11, 134, 210, 263

three-dimensional, 130, 145, 157–59, 165–67, 180, 182, 185, 194, 201*n*1

trench, 1–2, 9–10, 21, 33–34, 61, 70–71, 77, 90, 92–95, 119, 121, 128, 130, 135, 137–40, 142, 147, 149, 154–60, 164, 167–72, 174–89, 191–95, 199, 201*n*4, 202*n*8, 209–15, 217, 221, 228–30, 232, 237, 244, 248, 252, 253*n*5, *n*9, 255*n*15, 262

trench number, 140, 149, 153, 198, 247

two-dimensional, 143, 145, 158, 194, 223, 257*n*29

typologies, 5, 159–60, 164–66, 192, 200

Union Public Service Commission (UPSC), 72, 87, 99*n*18, 100*n*21

United Progressive Alliance (UPA), 57

upper division clerk (UDC), 25, 81

Vadodara Circle, 62, 199, 205–06, 210

Vadodara Excavation Branch (Ex. Br.), 58–59, 80–83

Vats, Madho Sarup, 14, 16, 137, 151*n*11, 182

Vedas, 34

Vedic Aryan, 37, 41, 51, 53, 56, 93

Vedic Harappans, 34, 36–37, 54, 56, 58, 63*n*12, 67*n*44

vertical excavation, 138–39

visionary object, 53, 65*n*36

Wakf Act, 1955, 120

Wakf Board, 120–21

Wheeler Method, 130–31, 140, 145, 148–49, 150*n*2–5, 151*n*7, *n*8, 152*n*16, 167, 222

Wheeler, Mortimer, 15–18, 26*n*10, 30*n*30, *n*34, 36–37, 44, 52, 63*n*16, *n*17, 77, 79–80, 83–84, 86, 89, 97, 99*n*15, 105, 112, 124*n*2, 130–40, 143–47, 154, 156–67, 170–72, 175–76, 177*n*5, *n*6, 178, 180, 202*n*10, 211, 216–17, 220–21, 223–24, 238–39, 242–43, 256*n*22, 261, 263

Wheelerian archaeology, 134, 170, 261

Wheelerian balks, 194, 212–13

Wheelerian genealogy, 216

Wheelerian Grid, 70, 129–36, 139–40, 142–50, 150*n*2, *n*3, 152*n*18, 154–55, 157–58

Wheelerian square, 158

Wheeler's stratigraphy method, 179

wild, 102–103, 107, 114, 116, 143, 145, 148

Woolley, Leonard, 15, 18, 97, 104–05, 124*n*2, 131–32, 139, 150*n*5, 160, 242, 263

World Archaeological Congress/WAC 3, 6, 77

Worsaae, J. A., 129

Yamuna, 38, 42, 46–47, 64*n*22